Match-Fixing in International Sports

M.R. Haberfeld • Dale Sheehan

Editors

Match-Fixing in International Sports

Existing Processes, Law Enforcement, and Prevention Strategies

 Springer

Editors
M.R. Haberfeld
City University of New York
John Jay College of Criminal Justice
New York, NY, USA

Dale Sheehan
Interpol Secretariat General
Lyon, France

ISBN 978-3-319-02581-0 (hardcover)   ISBN 978-3-319-02582-7 (eBook)
ISBN 978-3-319-09926-2 (softcover)
DOI 10.1007/978-3-319-02582-7
Springer Cham Heidelberg New York Dordrecht London

Library of Congress Control Number: 2013953872

Printed on acid-free paper

Springer is part of Springer Science+Business Media (www.springer.com)

To my father, Colonel (retired) Michael Sadykiewicz, who always contributes to my academic growth and publications, and to my daughters, Nellie and Mia, who are behind my never-ending drive.

M.R. Haberfeld

To Carol, Curtis and Christopher, who have always been my inspiration, and to my grandfather, Asa Fred Cloutier, who shared with me his passion for literature.

Dale L. Sheehan

Foreword

Terrorism, crimes against children, sex trafficking, drug trafficking, illegal firearms, piracy, counterfeiting and illicit goods – these are some of the many serious crime areas that INTERPOL and its 190 member countries combat every day.

Amidst our untiring work against this parade of criminal activity comes the book you are reading, and with this book come two questions.

First, why does match-fixing even make it onto INTERPOL's radar in the first place? Next to terrorism, drugs, human trafficking, and the like, the illegal tampering with sporting events does not seem like a huge problem.

Second, why is INTERPOL supporting the production of a book of academic contributions to the problem of match-fixing?

These questions find their answers when we look to INTERPOL's vision, its mission, and the strategic priorities it has established to actualize that mission.

"Connecting police for a safer world" is INTERPOL's vision. We envision a world where the safety of the population is protected because law enforcement everywhere can use INTERPOL to "securely communicate, share and access vital police information." We envision a world where INTERPOL constantly provides and promotes "innovative and cutting-edge solutions to global challenges in policing and security," while respecting the national sovereignty of our member countries and the human rights of individuals.

INTERPOL's role in actualizing this vision is its mission: "Preventing and fighting crime through enhanced international police cooperation." A crucial part of that mission is capacity building: Fostering "continuous improvement in the capacity of police to prevent and fight crime and the development of knowledge and skills necessary for effective international policing."

It is in this context – of capacity building to better empower police worldwide to fight crime – that INTERPOL has come to tackle the issue of match-fixing. In recent years, match-fixing has become a global problem which undermines the underpinnings of our society and corrupts our youth. It permits organised crime the opportunity to spread worldwide its illegal and violent activities which include murder, extortion and assault and which cause tax revenue and other losses of billions of dollars every year. Match-fixing is no longer a molehill, if it ever was. It is a mountain of its own.

To combat match-fixing, we have to understand it. A significant aim in crime fighting is "target shrinking," the reduction of criminal opportunities and the increase of costs to criminals if they take advantage of these opportunities. Constantly improving our understanding of how match-fixing works – from the motivations and calculations at the highest rungs of the shadowy transnational organised crime groups to the thought processes that lead a young player to succumb to corruption – is essential if we are to address it effectively.

One way to shrink the target is to raise the cost of match-fixing by enhancing and coordinating law enforcement activities worldwide so that police worldwide can keep up with organised crime syndicates and bring them to justice. If criminals are more likely to get caught and face stiff punishment for match-fixing, they will be less attracted to sports.

Another way to shrink the target is through education and prevention. In 2011, we entered into a historic 10-year agreement with FIFA, the world's leading international football organisation, for the purpose of furthering education and training to combat match-fixing and illegal betting.

Since that historic agreement, we have been working to deepen our understanding of the problem match-fixing presents. Our goal is to create educational curricula tailored to the most at-risk groups in football so that we can inoculate as many players, coaches, team officials and referees as possible against the treat and temptations of corruption.

To further our goals both in law enforcement and in preventative education, we must use society's academic resources to our advantage. In doing so, we can deepen our understanding of match-fixing, keep up with changing developments and adapt our policing efforts accordingly, and develop an effective educational programme to protect our youth, our sports and our society from corruption.

The contributions in the book you are holding are the first fruits of this research. The data is sometimes shocking and always eye-opening. The analyses will help us continue to engage this problem most effectively and bring about through our collective efforts our vision of connecting police for a safer world.

Secretary General, INTERPOL   Ronald K. Noble

Preface

Match Manipulation by Organised Crime Groups

The suspense, the uncertainty, the endeavour, the adrenaline and, ultimately, the prize are what football is all about. Spectators are attracted by its dynamics and tactical changes together with the effort put in by the teams and the risks they take and, above all, by not knowing who is going to win as the game draws to a close. In many parts of the world, football evokes great passion and plays an important role in the life of fans, communities and even nations, making it the most popular sport in the world.

Football is the ultimate team sport. Although it calls for individual physical strength and technical skills, it is equally important that players always respect, support and encourage their teammates in order to reproduce the tactics on the pitch. In cup matches, the underdogs sometimes beat the supposedly superior team because they are driven by a higher team spirit or passion. Despite the best preparations, we have all witnessed individual mistakes, even from top-quality players who have been guilty of poor ball control, missing the goal or defending poorly. In the heat of the moment, with the heart thumping and the rush of adrenaline, we naturally believe that the error was not intentional and that everyone on the pitch wants to win the game. But is this really the case?

There is a tendency to ignore what does not affect us. Match manipulation is not a new problem, but it is on the rise. In recent years, football has been under sustained attack worldwide from organised crime, with criminal groups infiltrating clubs and football associations in order to entice players, referees and officials into manipulating the course of a football match – determining in advance the result or the dynamics of a game. Referees and players are tempting targets for match-fixers because their decisions can significantly alter a game's outcome. The profits made on fixed games are so vast, in particular on the Asian betting market, that organised crime recently switched from drug trafficking to match-fixing (as stated by a match-fixer to the Director of FIFA Security). The risks of being prosecuted are very low due to lack of evidence or legal loopholes. Thanks to the Internet and the ability to bet on every possible outcome, the chances of making a massive financial profit are very high compared to the likelihood of getting caught, making the business of match manipulation irresistibly attractive to international organised crime. Organised crime could potentially target hundreds of national football leagues (offered on the betting market), cup matches, international competitions and friendlies for possible match manipulation, and every country is vulnerable, regardless of its record on corruption. The infiltration of football is taking place in all regions of the world and at all levels of football. Match manipulation damages players, fans and the sport, and the integrity of the latter is ruined if the outcome of the game is known in advance. The reports of match manipulation scandals are clear: Even big clubs, rich clubs, top players and huge tournaments are not above suspicion. In the first 5 months of 2013 alone, FIFA imposed sanctions on more than 200 individuals from the football community due to their involvement in match manipulation. Disgraced players and referees, disillusioned fans, a loss of credibility and no real deterrent to such criminal actions: What can be done to counteract organised crime?

Manipulating matches is a perfect opportunity for organised crime. The major motivations behind match manipulation are financial gain, money laundering and future team advantage. As well as constituting a huge threat to football, the phenomenon of match manipulation has a huge impact at social, economic, political and cultural levels. The football community has clearly not been prepared for such a substantial challenge. Every weakness in governance continues to be brutally exploited. Money attracts organised crime, and football organisations provide an excellent opportunity. Some football organisations are structurally unsound, financially unstable or lack awareness and, therefore, do not question an individual's intentions or identity. They are also a cultural and international melting pot and have fewer controls and codes in place than other sectors. Players and referees are often young and in the public spotlight, lacking experience and dreaming of overnight success. This creates vulnerability. Furthermore, it is very difficult to obtain significant forensic evidence. Did the player miss the ball intentionally? Did he deliberately miss the penalty? Did the referee deliberately favour a certain team? Through monitoring, it is possible to detect match manipulation by tracking irregular betting patterns and liquidity changes in the betting market, sometimes before the match but mainly live. Unfortunately, monitoring alone does not provide sufficient evidence. In addition, its effectiveness is limited, mostly because it is unclear what is going on in the illegal betting market. In addition, data protection issues and the cost of setting up and maintaining detection and monitoring mechanisms need to be looked into further. Football's capacity to sanction wrongdoing on the pitch depends greatly on hard facts, such as written statements by the individuals involved, photographs and video evidence. The FIFA Disciplinary Committee and FIFA Ethics Committee may pronounce the sanctions described in the FIFA Statutes, the FIFA Code of Ethics and the FIFA Disciplinary Code on officials, players and match and players' agents. This procedure functions well enough for red cards or banning players, but it cannot prove corruption, match manipulation or betting fraud. Another problem is that individuals are not willing to confess unless there is clear evidence against them, as they fear persecution, substantial threats by organised crime or the end of their career. Moreover, the sharing of information with police authorities is very difficult due to data protection laws.

Nevertheless, every effort must be made to eradicate the problem of match manipulation and corruption in order to safeguard the credibility and integrity of the game, maintain safety and confidence in the betting market and combat international organised crime. Match manipulation should be a priority for all stakeholders, and a concerted effort must be made on a global scale to fight it. The problem of corruption and match manipulation has to be tackled in a proactive way in order to achieve long-term results. There are five main areas involved in combating match manipulation: prevention (awareness raising, education and revision of codes), detection (monitoring), intelligence gathering, investigation (fact finding) and sanctions. The integrity of football has come to the fore and is the focus of FIFA's fight against the threat of match manipulation. FIFA's objective is to safeguard without compromise fairness in football as well as the physical and moral integrity of sportsmen and women. FIFA has adopted a zero-tolerance approach towards match manipulation and started to take significant steps towards ensuring the integrity of football worldwide as early as 2005. FIFA's subsidiary Early Warning System (EWS) was founded with the aim of monitoring FIFA competitions, identifying any irregular activity on the sports betting market and exposing potential manipulation attempts. The principal area of analysis is the betting market/betting providers"? and detection is still generally on a reactive basis as it is mainly based on live betting. EWS currently monitors 1,500 matches per year, including all FIFA competitions and qualifying matches, selected international friendly matches and selected matches (proactive monitoring) on request for individual national football leagues. A range of educational, prevention and detection measures have also been developed through the funding of a 10-year partnership with INTERPOL in the form of a corruption prevention training programme. In addition, FIFA offers a confidential reporting system to the football community and general public.

The FIFA integrity initiative embraces all 209 member associations and focuses on various aspects, such as the five main areas mentioned above (prevention, detection, intelligence gathering, investigation and sanctions) and the creation of a FIFA integrity team, who will analyse and assist member associations and confederations on request and establish basic structures and processes for fighting match manipulation. This integrated approach will cover legal and disciplinary, security, betting monitoring, and fraud detection and prevention matters and involve the reviewing of policies and procedures, conducting analyses of threats and vulnerability and assessing the effectiveness of regulations and applicable laws against match manipulation at the national and/or confederation level. The FIFA integrity team is very much committed to exchanging good practices and networking to prevent the manipulation of matches. The awareness and understanding of corruption in football must be enhanced and promoted. Prevention, detection, good governance, exchange of best practices and coordination play a key role in the fight against match manipulation. Through targeted training, education and awareness-raising programmes for football confederations, associations, officials and players, knowledge can be improved, guidance provided, cooperation among the football community and law enforcement ensured and resources in the fight against match manipulation strengthened at regional, national and international levels. Together with INTERPOL, the FIFA integrity team is identifying those countries where action is most needed. The primary objective of the FIFA-INTERPOL integrity initiative is raising awareness and education (e.g. the modus operandi of organised crime) in order to alert all relevant stakeholders about the danger represented by match manipulation for the integrity of football. It is essential to explain the basics of match manipulation, how to recognise it, how to avoid it and report suspicious cases. Everyone must realise the extent to which the threat of match manipulation affects careers and the financing of football. The second aim is to create a global network of contact persons to improve cooperation among the different stakeholders. The FIFA PERFORMANCE Programme has recently integrated integrity as a key theme. It is the fruit of several decades worth of experience and careful consideration within FIFA on the subject of football development at the global level and has been developed to allow FIFA's member associations to reach their maximum potential both on and off the pitch. Since those involved in organised crime attempt to corrupt parties who are able to influence the course of a match and the global experience is that referees and assistant referees are the primary target of match-fixers, it is essential that all referees and assistant referees are clearly and unequivocally aware of the threat. FIFA international referees, assistant referees, futsal referees and beach soccer referees are not only offered a FIFA-INTERPOL awareness-raising programme, they are also requested by FIFA to commit to protecting the game's integrity by signing and returning the FIFA integrity declaration form.

It is also essential that appropriate rules are in place that ensure transparency, that the decisions taken benefit the sport and that anyone who does not play by the rules is sanctioned. Football associations and law enforcement agencies must have a clear and robust regulatory framework and the right codes to work with. FIFA codices and regulations (disciplinary, ethics, conduct, stadium safety and security), such as the regulations governing international matches, have been revised to provide minimum guidelines for member associations. FIFA's interdisciplinary team (FIFA Security/Legal and EWS) involved with the integrity initiative is also launching studies to explore relevant issues in the fight against the manipulation of matches by performing on-site assessments to define processes and structures for a concrete action plan. FIFA security officers active in stadiums during competitions focus not only on safety and security aspects but also on integrity matters. Assistance, collaborative work and investigation to promote effective prevention, disruption and deterrence are the main objective, although FIFA is clearly bound by its own regulations (for FIFA competitions and qualifying matches, such as the FIFA Disciplinary Code and the FIFA Code of Ethics). As the football community is not in a position to create an investigatory police body, it must be able to fully ensure the protection of the game. A comprehensive and holistic approach needs to be established. To fight the manipulation of matches, the various stakeholders must act in unison and facilitate a common understanding of the problem by identifying recommendations for the fight against match manipulation and the acts that should be punishable under the relevant law. Every country should have adequate legal tools with which to combat match manipulation. Fraud law is not the proper solution: A specific law relating to sport manipulation should be established. Legislative loopholes have to be closed. The obstacles between investigating and prosecuting international cases of match manipulation also appear to be mainly of an operational nature. As police forces have competing priorities, match manipulation does not receive the attention it deserves. The football community clearly needs the full support of the relevant stakeholders in order to safeguard the integrity of its competitions. Strong international support is vital to tackle match manipulation. The FIFA integrity team is striving to identify recruiters and structures in order to improve the exchange of information and cooperation and to gather information not only from confederations/member associations, law enforcement agencies, other informants/sources and its own investigations, but also from the recently introduced confidential reporting system (general public) and Integrity Hotline (football community). Efforts need to be constantly intensified and expanded. It is also imperative that the cooperation with law enforcement agencies takes place on a global level and that individuals coming forward with valuable information are protected. Witnesses who report match-fixing schemes by organised crime syndicates are living in fear in many countries. Everyone should reject a corrupt offer but, more importantly, be able to report it without fear of the consequences.

The match-fixing scandals that are undoubtedly occurring should no longer go undetected. Effective, dissuasive sanctions are in place to deter such acts. Measures must be implemented to strengthen football organisational structures and to promote transparency at all levels and ensure sound financial management by associations, clubs and federations, including ensuring that players are paid on time in order to prevent their becoming susceptible to unscrupulous offers. Binding guidelines for the investigation of suspicious cases and containing clear responsibilities should be set up at national and international levels. Mutual support between the football family and other relevant stakeholders and the strengthening of judicial cooperation mechanisms are needed in order to effectively protect the integrity of football against match manipulation.

Football's strength comes from its integrity.

FIFA, Zurich, Switzerland   Ralf Mutschke

Acknowledgements

Our acknowledgement for this book goes, first, to Katherine Chabalko who provided, as usual, the much needed support and conceptual recognition of the importance of the topics discussed by our contributors; to Welmoed Spahr, who is always willing to approve publications of many innovative ideas; and, finally, to all the other employees of the Springer Publishing House, who continue to exemplify the best of the publishing world.

Second, our profound gratitude is extended to the INTERPOL employees and consultants, starting with Michaela Ragg, whose dedication to the projects related to fight against match-fixing is unparalleled, and to Ellen White, Julie Norris, David Graham, Daniela Giuffre, Jenny Prasertdee, Dinis Adriao, Innika La Fontaine, Angela Lopez and Patricia Marcelino. Without your dedication to the cause, we would not have been able to complete this book – our wholehearted gratitude is extended to all of you.

New York, USA   M.R. Haberfeld
Lyon, France   Dale Sheehan

Contents

Part I
Corruption in Sport: Match Fixing – Definitional and Operational Issues

Introduction: Match Fixing as a Modality of Sports Related Crimes (SRC)

M.R. Haberfeld and John Abbott

Abstract It is always harder to follow up after theoretical threads that bind together chapters of an edited manuscript, as opposed to a sole or co-authored volume. This introductory chapter provides an overview of the structure of this book, together with some operational definitions and the reasons behind ideas presented in various chapters. Since our book is divided into three parts, the introductory chapter provides readers with some conceptual scaffolding behind subsequent chapters and the rationale behind grouping certain concepts in the respective segments of this volume.

Although the reader will encounter some redundancy in the case studies and approaches depicted by various authors the importance of this book is to incorporate the various perspectives on the problem that are yet to be conceptually clearly defined and this can be done through an amalgamation of a variety of scholarly perspectives. The main purpose of this book is to start an academic awareness and discussion about operationalization of Sports Related Crimes (SRC) (Haberfeld 2012), in order to facilitate an effective Criminal Justice response worldwide.

The book is divided into three main themes: Definitional Issues, Current Situation and Response for the Future.

Each part/theme overviews the problems inherent in the adequate response to the growing phenomenon of match fixing by highlighting the obstacles, impediments and possible solutions.

M.R. Haberfeld (✉)
John Jay College of Criminal Justice, 899 Tenth Avenue, New York, NY 10019, USA
e-mail: mhaberfeld@jjay.cuny.edu

J. Abbott
INTERPOL, INTERPOL General Secretariat, c/o Integrity in Sport Unit,
200 Quai Charles De Gaulle, 69006 Lyon, France
e-mail: c.m.a@tesco.net

M.R. Haberfeld and D. Sheehan (eds.), *Match-Fixing in International Sports:*
Existing Processes, Law Enforcement, and Prevention Strategies,
DOI 10.1007/978-3-319-02582-7_1, © Springer International Publishing Switzerland 2013

The global nature of this threat is highlighted by the number of countries featured as case studies in the book, which represent only a fraction of what appears to be a much larger and broader criminal menace.

The following overview of the book s' chapters provides for a broad overview of the issues and dilemmas that are presented by the respective authors and allows the reader to identify the running themes of this project, as they evolve towards the final chapter where the major hurdles, obstacles and quandaries are summarized and paired with some implementable solutions.

Part I: Definitional Hurdles

Chapter 2: Match Fixing in Western Europe

Feltes opens his chapter posing a question: is Football at Risk? His response is based on the assertion that football is indeed at risk as not only in Asia but also in Germany, match fixing has become a real problem that causes high financial losses for associations, players, bet providers and individual players.

Through an analysis of the most interesting cases of match fixing in Germany, Feltes outlines a number of solution statements to cope with match fixing in the future. His proposed 12 remedies range from developing a better and more comprehensive cooperation between all the stakeholders involved, like law enforcement agencies, sports federations and bookmakers, through restructuring of the monitoring mechanisms to unification and standardization of the worldwide legal response.

The author concludes his chapter by labeling betting fraud as an organized crime activity, against which we need to unite in the fight against trivialization and lack of awareness. According to Feltes, this forceful response can only be achieved through a professional management of football associations with independent people from "outside" and not, the currently in place, "old-boys-network" structures, where positions are filled with those, who served (in the real meaning of the word) and behaved properly (in the view of the officials in charge) over years.

Chapter 3: Reflections from Uganda

In contrast to the situation in Western Europe, as depicted by Feltes, Mukasa examines the situation in Uganda that illustrates the insidious threat of sports betting and corruption with all its attendant manifestations. The author seeks to examine how national laws have sought to, or have failed to, regulate sports betting and gaming; how far have sports bodies been ready to handle this problem? He poses a number of questions regarding the nature of the problem ranging from socio-economic factors, the impact of globalization, liberalization of trade markets, the information age and consumerism to peoples cultural predispositions and dispositions. Based on an in-depth analysis of the factors, the author identifies a comprehensive list of 13 containment, prevention and eradication mechanisms.

The proposed solutions touch upon, among other ideas, the need to strengthen the regulatory framework, through formation of Steering, Monitoring and Action committees, to international law enforcement cooperation on a local and federal level. Finally, Mukasa emphasizes the active role INTERPOL, FIFA and the Academe should play in creating and facilitating a real change.

Chapter 4: It's Not Just Cricket in India

From Africa to India, where Qureshi and Verma introduce the reader to the game of cricket, that has been tarnished by betting and fixing match outcomes through corrupt practices. From the star players to club officials, plenty of evidence about major matches, even during the World Cup, points to games being seriously compromised. In addition to the in person attempts to corrupt the games, the spread of illegal betting in cricket has expanded with the advent of technology, when(where?) the Internet spread has facilitated growth of illegal gambling.

Although this chapter focuses on the betting phenomenon and some major incidents associated with growing corruption in cricket, the processes involved are either identical or very similar to the ones found in soccer related match fixing violations. Hence, the policy responses of major cricket playing nations that are overviewed in this chapter, along with suggestions for strategies to be adopted to curb corruption in cricket can easily be adopted by countries that struggle with match fixing in soccer or any other sports related corruption. Learning from best practices adopted by other nations to target corrupted behaviors in various sports related disciplines can provide a baseline template that can be customized to other corrupted sports environments.

Chapter 5: Case Studies from Greece and Ireland

From India back to Europe, where the main contribution of the chapter written by Petropoulos and Maguire is to provide an overview of the current status of soccer match-fixing cases and allegations of such inappropriateness in Greece and Ireland, albeit based on the scarcity of academic attention devoted to the problem. While there is a considerable body of literature about the "usual suspect countries" like Germany, Italy, the Netherlands, there is a dire need to assess the gravity of the situation in other countries that struggle, albeit in a more covert manner, with the same corrupted phenomenon. Highlighting the experiences of countries that are currently under the radar of the academics and popular media outlets will showcase the gravity and the widespread nature of match fixing.

Given that no empirical research has been conducted on this issue so far, the chapter focuses on the historical background of Greek and Irish football and the cases that have been investigated to date by the football associations, law-enforcement and judicial authorities. This overview is primarily based on a content analysis of cases publicized by the media. In addition, the authors evaluate the effectiveness of the available legislative and administrative tools to combat match-fixing.

Based on some insights into the cultural and societal impediments a number of avenues which could be explored by the Greek and Irish authorities to combat match-fixing more effectively are suggested, including reform of governance mechanisms, as well as accountability and organizational structures.

Chapter 6: Match Rigging in Italian Professional Soccer

In Chap. 6, Boeri and Severgnini introduce the reader to the situation in Italian pro-fessional soccer, from the perspective of an economic lance. The scandals investi-gated by the Italian police were connected with two of the largest match fixing scandals in Europe involving criminal organizations, soccer players, team manag-ers, and referees. These investigations, also known as *Calciopoli* and *Scommessopoli*, offer unique case studies to understand the mechanisms behind match fixing in pro-fessional football.

In their chapter, the authors analyze the information collected from the investiga-tions to evaluate the economic determinants of corruption in sports. Boeri and Severgnini attempt to explain the differences of the cases reported by the police using some previously unused tools, more specifically the decision trees, provided by economic theory. Based on this economic approach to the match fixing phenom-enon the authors provide some suggestions as to how to detect and prevent future occurrences of match rigging.

A similar, economic theory approach will be further introduced by Forrest, in Chap. 10, while dealing with the problem of match fixing from the perspective of a broader, contemporary, response.

Approaching match fixing as an economic problem adds another dimension to the definitional/operational quandary and thus, by default adds another hurdle to the effective response quandary.

Chapter 7: The Russian Case

In the final chapter of Part I of the book, that was devoted, primarily, to the defini-tional and operational issues related to match-fixing, Cheloukhine discusses the complexity of the situation in Russia where for years soccer championships were accompanied by continuous accusations of the total sale of matches and the bribing of soccer officials, and a dysfunctional legislation which does not allow for an effective response.

Russia seems to represent yet another country where soccer officials diligently delegate the responsibility for investigating fixed games to law enforcement agencies which, in turn, do not want to interfere since, historically, such investigations were plagued by lack of evidence against the perpetrators and reluctant victims. In addition, the legislation of the Russian Federation in this area is far from perfect: the only legal article in the Criminal Code of the RF is Article 184 of the Criminal Code, which allows for punishing of the participants and organizers of "the fixed matches." This Article focuses on the case of transferring money in exchange for desired results and it is quite clear that the legislation considerably lags behind the real life different forms of misconduct.

The future, according to the author, appears to offer little change despite a proposed Bill "Combating Match Fixing" introduced on November 6, 2012 which provides for some Amendments to the Federal Law on Physical Culture and Sport, Taxation and Criminal Laws. As history of such and similar legislations in Russia teaches us, that most of the attempts to remedy the situation remain on paper, and the implementation becomes rather problematic.

Part II. Contemporary Responses

Chapter 8: Safeguarding Sports Integrity: The Australian Perspective

In the first chapter dealing with the contemporary response to match fixing, the authors, very appropriately, place the need for safeguarding the integrity of international sports as the dominant and urgent theme of their chapter. Misra, Anderson and Sunders, point to the undeniable fact that Sports bodies, associations, clubs, national teams, sports officials and law enforcement agencies today are facing a growing variety of threats and challenges ranging from match-fixing to corruption, illegal betting and use of performance and image enhancing drugs in sport.

Their chapter overviews an Australian perspective on the nature of integrity threats that various sporting codes in Australia are facing and measures that can help deal with them. The authors analyze a number of match-fixing cases in National Rugby league, A-League Football and cricket in Australia and identify different variants of sports corruption and vulnerabilities of professional sports to transnational and organized crime. The authors focus their attention on how sports corruption, from being a blind spot of the law enforcement agencies in Australia until some years ago, has become one of their top priorities, yielding encouraging outcomes on various counts.

Despite the fact that this chapter overviews a variety of measures undertaken by the Commonwealth and state institutions, sports bodies and federations, clubs and national associations, and the law enforcement agencies to curb match-fixing, corruption and drug use, in Australia, the recommendations proposed by the authors could be relevant and valid for other countries struggling with similar hurdles.

Chapter 9: Factors Favouring Betting Related Cheating in Sports

Rebeggiani and Rebeggiani open their discussion about match fixing by posing a question regarding the nature and specificity of the factors that contribute to cheating in the sports arena. The authors approach the match fixing phenomenon from an economic point of view, focusing on the threats to the integrity of sports. Such threats put in jeopardy the whole commercialization of sports related activities. This chapter analyses the incentives for cheating connected to traditional and new betting types in the sports betting sector and the way they might affect the behaviour of sportsmen, coaches, and officials.

Rebegianni and Rebeggiani develop and introduce a simple theoretical model and derive from it some political implications which they recommend, among others, for the ongoing reform of the German sports betting market. A host of policy recommendations range from the governmental involvement, through educational programs to appointment of referees.

It is the authors hope that these recommendations will contribute to an effective prevention of scandals like those unveiled in European football in recent years. Their approach compliments nicely the concepts launched by Boeri and Severgnini as well as the ideas introduced by Forrest in the following chapter.

Chapter 10: Match Fixing: An Economics Perspective

Following the economic theory approaches to match fixing, as introduced in Chaps. 6 and 9, Forrest posits that match fixing to serve betting interests is certainly as old as organized sport itself, for example it is believed to have been common in the case of eighteenth century professional cricket in England , and more recently, in the twentieth century, the history of sport events was filled with high-profile scandals, including fixes in the baseball World Series of 1919 and in the South Africa – England cricket series in 1990.

Hence, claims the author, match fixing is nothing new but, on the other hand, reports of fixing appear to have become much more frequent in the twenty-first century and the sheer number of proven instances points to a steep increase in incidence over the last decade. Forrest points to the rather alarming fact that in 2013, Europol named nearly 300 matches between teams which, it alleged, to have been the subject of fixing; and criminal trials of players and officials took place in countries such as Italy, Hungary, South Korea and China.

The author discusses the problem of match fixing within the context of an economics model and, based on its nature, urges us to recognize the fact that education in itself, is rather unlikely to eradicate the supply and demand, as the expected returns will outweigh the expected costs. Protecting sports integrity, argues Forrest, will require additional measures, which may be harder than education for sports to accept because they may be more costly to implement or involve trade-offs between reducing corruption and other commercial goals. Legislation may provide one partially adequate solution but the author also identifies a host of other mechanisms that can potentially make a difference, even if at first just a marginal one.

Chapter 11: Compliance Mechanisms as Possible Tools of Prevention

Following an overview of an economic perspective to match fixing, Jones introduces a number of initiatives that have been engaged by sports organizations as a means of providing governance in the area of preventing sports corruption. According to the author these initiatives, which mirror similar responses found in the corporate world, represent compliance initiatives that are usually part of a more comprehensive governance scheme that includes these internal initiatives and external oversight.

The author analyzes various compliance initiatives by exploring limitations, and exposing their weaknesses as well as the absent angles. In addition, Jones examines sport activities as a concept of an organization, within the context of the core principles of organizational governance, good governance and sports organization governance. In an effort to establish some form of critical oversight and accountability, this chapter goes further to explore the use of accreditation (and certification) and licensing, as tools to reinforce existing compliance initiatives and form part of a more comprehensive governance strategy in efforts to help prevent match-fixing.

Chapter 12: Prevention of Match Fixing in Brazil

From the conceptual approach introduced by Jones in the previous chapter, to a case study depicted in this chapter considering the situation of Match Fixing in Brazil, Godinho and Barbosa consider the development of an academic agenda about Match Fixing, while analyzing the Criminal Justice institutional structure and its capacity to fight and prevent, within the context of the current Justice System and institutions that are charged with ensuring justice in sports.

The authors focus on the role that the academe can, and should, play in assisting with the proposals of policy recommendations and adequate means to fight the phenomenon of Match Fixing and also be in the forefront of creating a public agenda on the theme. Godhino and Barbosa claim that one of the important constraints to the existence of adequate reactions to Match Fixing events is the low priority of this offense for the justice system as law enforcement institutions in Brazil have no history of intervention in this area and, consequently, there is an absence of economic and political resources specially directed to fight theses violations. The emphasis on creating a sports integrity culture is the main theme of this chapter that charges the academe with the responsibility to expose the nature and seriousness of the problem and create a strong enough awareness that will, in turn, generate real changes in the Brazilian Criminal Justice System.

Chapter 13: A Game Theory Approach to Match Fixing

To conclude the contemporary responses part, Hakeem takes the reader from the previously discussed case study of the Brazilian approach to a more conceptual game theory related approach to match fixing.

The author approaches Sports-related crime as a variant of white-collar crime, and more specifically, refers to match fixing as a modern day version of what used to be part of a broader category of work related criminality. Hakeem's chapter uses the Game Theory approach to analyze the problem of sports-related crime. Game theory is applied to gain insight regarding the conflict between thoughtful and deceitful adversaries and is employed to analyze the interactions between law enforcement and defendants who commit sports-related crimes.

The author uses the concept of "The Prisoner's Dilemma" to gain further insight into the dynamics that ensue amongst the various players – law enforcement, prosecutors, and players. After examining the levels of sports-related crime, formulating a cognitive valence map along with its approximations, and estimating its legal parameters and implications, Hakeem proposes a number of preventive legal strategies.

The chapter concludes by highlighting the crucial need for more data at a global level that could assist researchers, law enforcement, and academics to get a better insight into the match fixing problem, while proposing a creation of a Global Database on Sports-Related Crime. This approach provides a perfect transition into the last part of this volume, about the best practices to be employed in the future in a fight against Sports Related Crimes.

Part III. The Future

Chapter 14: INTERPOL's Match Fixing Response Template

As for the future... Abbott and Sheehan overview the history of INTERPOL's engagement in tackling corruption in sports that, so far, lead the way for an effective and effort rich response. This involvement included coordination of operations in several countries to crack down on illegal gambling dens, supporting the security and safety of major sporting events and bringing together law enforcement investigators engaged in tackling match fixing to share information and good practice, and assist each other in their investigations.

These efforts took a new shape in May 2011, when INTERPOL embarked on a new venture with FIFA under the headline 'the INTERPOL – FIFA Anti Corruption Initiative'. Based on this agreement, INTERPOL committed itself to providing football related anti-corruption training, education and prevention programs in order to better tackle the problem of corruption in football, especially corruption linked to match fixing and irregular and illegal betting.

The chapter highlights case studies (some of which were also tackled by other authors in this volume) and a range of initiatives that led to a more effective grasp on the complex variety of criminal activities encompassing football related crimes.

The three –prong approach, composed of Training, Education and Prevention "pillars", represents a holistic, INTERPOL – FIFA initiative that seeks to increase awareness among all stakeholders with a responsibility to protect football from the dangers of match fixing and to urge them to put in place a series of measures and mechanisms designed to mitigate criminal opportunities.

Chapter 15: The Role of the Academe in Sports Integrity

Following the law enforcement response, two of this volume's contributors ponder the role of the Academe in creating, maintaining and enhancing sports integrity. Segal, in her chapter, discusses the ideas of creating and shaping academic courses that will focus on moral reasoning and afford students with the skills necessary to navigate the situational pressures present in the world of sports.

The importance of targeting the individual decision maker is highlighted within the context of conventional morality, the individual understanding of the good of the larger society and the importance of critical advancement over the selfish personal perspective, especially given one's group pressure to conform.

Since research points to college-age individuals as the most likely cohort to resist the pressures of bribe taking and the ability to see the larger picture of the damage caused by this type of corruption, creation of sports integrity related courses presents a very attractive solution to targeting some vulnerable populations.

Chapter 16: The Role of the Academe in Match Fixing

Vodde, in similar vein to Segal, discusses the historical evolution of the role of academe in modern society emphasizing its role in development of individuals, fostering or knowledge, understanding, critical thinking and engagement in civic and public service.

Given its focus on research, training and education, and providing public service to the greater community, Vodde proposes a new role for the academe within the context of the match fixing problem. His proposed solutions include research and data analyses into identifying the scope and breadth of the problem, collaborative partnership with the various stakeholders in developing strategies and tactics to mitigate and marginalize match-fixing and related corruption, serving as a conduit and venue for bringing together the various stakeholders who possess the power and influence to address the problem of match-fixing. Furthermore, he argues, the academe should provide qualified experts and subject specific training and education to players, coaches, referees, team owners, sponsors, fans and spectators, legitimate betting organizations, legislators, police and law enforcement, the media, and the general public.

Chapter 17: Catching Cheaters: Successful Police Operation

To finalize the effective response loop, from law enforcement proposed solutions on an international level, through the academic approach and back to the law enforcement, but this time local response, the authors, in their chapter about "catching cheaters", provide a successful template for police operation based on a Turkish case study.

Following the success of their case study, Demir and Karademir introduce some policy implications based on outreach to the millions of the soccer fans while engaging the movie industry, in an unorthodox way, in order to raise awareness and trigger a grassroots resistance against corruption in football.

The idea is based on the notion that education of certain identifiable targets such as players, coaches or club managers is quite feasible. Such educational efforts can be accomplished through the mobilization of the official entities like FIFA, INTERPOL, or other local governmental authorities.

However, education of billions of unidentified targets all over the world, such as fans and supporters, may not be as practicable through more conventional means as it applies to the former groups. Since society cannot afford to disregard the importance of raising awareness about the problem within the football fans' world, the authors propose some unorthodox and unconventional means of indirect education should be considered to reach out to these masses and ensure their involvement and inputs into the fight against match fixing.

Chapter 18: Way Forward: Law Enforcement – Academic Paradigm

In the final chapter of this volume Haberfeld and Abbott recapture the November 2012 conference in Singapore, sponsored by the INTERPOL, which brought together international experts from the academe to discuss issues surrounding match-fixing and how to combat corruption in football through channels of education.

The final chapter provides a broad-spectrum framework of concepts that were identified by the participants to be introduced, further discussed, vetted and/or implemented in the future. Furthermore, some additional suggestions are presented about the possibility of engaging INTERPOL in a future collaboration between the academic and practitioners worlds, bringing together a blend of ideas in the field of legislation, law enforcement and academic response. Each of these entities should, and can, influence each other in terms of what needs to be done, when and how, in order to achieve an implementable and effective solution to the fight against Sports Related Crimes.

Reference

Haberfeld, M.R. (2012) field notes, Match Fixing Conference, Singapore.

Match Fixing in Western Europe

Thomas Feltes

Abstract Not only in Asia but also in Germany Match Fixing has become a real problem that causes high financial losses for associations, players, bet providers and individual players.

The following chapter points out to the most interesting cases of Match Fixing in Germany and develops solution statements to cope with Match Fixing in the future.

Football at Risk?

Is football at risk through match fixing? And if so, why should we protect those gamblers and wagerer? These two questions shall guide us through the following article, showing that we do in fact have a problem with match fixing, and not only in Asia, and that the integrity of football is at risk, as the FIFA Director of Security, Ralf Mutschke (2012), pointed out: "The values of fair play, respect, discipline and honesty are under threat. ... If we look at those perpetrating it, we're definitely talking about criminals – you might even say organized criminality". Match fixing is indeed a serious problem in Europe: It is, in the words of Emine Bozkur (2012), Member of European Parliament, "a form of crime with high revenues and excessively low sentences and detection rates, and thus used as a tool by criminal organizations to make and launder money from criminal activities such as human and drug trafficking". And finally, to quote Ronald K. Noble (2012), INTERPOL Secretary General, who reported about the four SOGA operations during the meeting in Singapore: "As a result of transnational organized crime's global reach, of the huge profits associated with illegal gambling, of the vulnerability of players and of the

T. Feltes (✉)
Criminal Policy and Police Science, Ruhr-University Bochum,
Universitätsstraße 150 GC 5/144, 44801 Bochum, Germany
e-mail: Thomas.Feltes@rub.de

M.R. Haberfeld and D. Sheehan (eds.), *Match-Fixing in International Sports:*
Existing Processes, Law Enforcement, and Prevention Strategies,
DOI 10.1007/978-3-319-02582-7_2, © Springer International Publishing Switzerland 2013

internet, which has made gambling on matches anywhere in the world extremely easy and accessible, we are seeing more and more cases of match fixing and suspicious results". The background of Noble's statement is the fact, that nearly 300 people have been arrested in police operations ahead of and throughout the EURO 2012 championships, targeting illegal soccer gambling networks across Asia. Law enforcement officers carried out more than 200 raids on illegal gambling dens, estimated to have handled around USD 85 million worth of bets. Operation SOGA IV – short for soccer gambling – was the fourth action of its and the operation has "underlined the results which can be achieved through national and international police cooperation in breaking up illegal gambling dens and the criminal networks behind them" (Yau 2012). In total, the combined four SOGA operations have resulted in more than 7,000 arrests, the closure of illegal gambling dens which handled more than USD 2 billion worth of bets and the seizure of nearly USD 27 million in cash. Illegal betting which drives match-fixing encompasses a market that is said to be in the range of hundreds of billions of Euros per year – the revenue of a company like Coca-Cola. And to quote Mr. Noble (2013) a last time: "Criminal organizations benefit from match-fixing both in the profits it promises and in its ability to launder their ill-gotten gains from other criminal activities. Match-fixing is clearly a many-headed dragon that we must slay with a coordinated national and international effort".

Corruption and the manipulation of sport results jeopardize not only the ethical value and structures of sport; once the sport is ethically devaluated and the trust into sports is lost, the sources of finance will collapse. And there will be more rigged matches in future if we close our eyes. Eventually the credibility of results will be called into question and finally the entire credibility of sport will vanish. It should be in the very own interest of the clubs, originations and associations to fight match fixing by all possible means.

Another aspect should not be forgotten: Many of those, who bet, are pathological or problem gamblers. The number of "problem gamblers" or "addicted gamblers"[1] in Germany is estimated at about 300,000, and the social costs of gambling in Germany are calculated at about USD 60 billion per year – to be paid by tax payers. On the other side, organized crime is using gambling and betting to earn money, which is not traceable and can be used in the world-wide market of illegal (and semi-legal) drugs, weapons, and smuggling of human beings.

This chapter analyses the history of match fixing cases in Germany between 1970 and 2011, showing different backgrounds, reasons and consequences. Special focus is given to the case of Ante Sapina (*"Don Ante"*), in which in November 2009, after a year of telephone tapping, 50 people were arrested and charged with corrupting over 320 football matches in 10 European countries. The leader of the gang was

---

[1]Pathological gambling is associated with both social and family costs. For the new DSM 5.0, pathological gambling is being considered as an Addictive Disorder. This reflects the increasing and consistent evidence that some behaviors, such as gambling, activate the brain reward system with effects similar to those of drugs of abuse and that gambling disorder symptoms resemble substance use disorders to a certain extent, see http://www.psychiatry.org/practice/dsm/dsm5.

sentenced in 2011. He placed bets of about €1 million per month on 30 matches, and sought to corrupt on average one match per week. Co-offenders were also on trial, and the case is still going on, due to appeals. It is argued, that we do have to think about match fixing in Germany, although the "point of origin" or the "sales point" of these activities are located not in Europe, but mainly in Asia. Although most Germans would argue, that there might be corruption in Germany[2] – but not in the German soccer leagues – no matter whether they are ordinary citizens, police officers or lawyers, as often, reality is different. The article refers to a most recent study by KEA (2012), which illustrates how match-fixing is covered in national criminal law in Europe. Finally, criminological and forensic evidence is presented, showing that investigating such activities is very difficult and time consuming due to clandestine structures, very well (illegally and legally) connected actors. Germany might be seen as a "safe haven" for internationally organized, but locally networked groups. Consequences for law enforcement on national, trans- and international level are discussed and recommendations given for the training of law enforcement officers, club representatives and referees, and for the re-structuring of investigation bodies.

Germany: Safe Haven?

Germany, famed for the quality of its products rather than the largesse of its bribes, has been rocked by corruption scandals some years ago: Siemens was embroiled in the largest bribery case in the history of Germany but other well-known German companies were accused although: Volkswagen, DaimlerChrysler, Deutsche Bank, Infineon, Deutsche Bahn, GM/Opel, and Ratiopharm. However, nearly all these scandals had their point of origin in foreign countries, not in Germany, and – even more important – they had to do with legal enterprises. So why worry about corruption and match fixing in German Football? Germany was listed on rank 10 of "*the ten most corrupt football leagues ever*". Spurling (2013), the author of the article about "*bent leagues in the world and the hookers, murderers and extortionists who populate them*", ranks Germany just behind Italy (No. 8) and Columbia (No. 9). But the example used by the authors is an outdated one from the late 1970ies in the (former) GDR.[3]

So why worry? There are good reasons: First, illegal betting on football is everywhere in the world, no country is immune to it, because it is about money – to earn money and to launder money. Second, there is a huge demand for betting in Europe, and not only in Asia, where betting and gambling is deeply ingrained in the culture

---

[2]German is listed on rank 14 in the Corruption Perceptions Index by Transparency International http://cpi.transparency.org/cpi2011/results/ (Aug. 22, 2012).

[3]In 1978, Stasi chief Erich Mielke announced at a meeting that it was time Dynamo Berlin began to win trophies in East Germany's Oberliga. Referees were nobbled, as the Stasi had final say over which officials went on the list for coveted UEFA and FIFA matches.

and is an accepted form of social intercourse. It is said in China that "a little gambling is good for the health, but too much can drive you mad".[4] *"There are matches played by Scottish teenagers watched by about 20 people and three dogs. But in the crowd will be one or two Chinese – like Zing and Xi – who relay information back to the vast illegal gambling markets of Beijing, Bangkok or Batam"*(Hill 2008b). In the multi-billion pound sports betting market, only 30–40 % is in the legal market, the rest is in the, mostly illegal, Asian gambling markets.

It is all about money: In 2012, the 36 clubs of the German Soccer League (DFL, 1. and 2. Bundesliga) had yearly turnovers of more than € 2 billion, one more reason to think about corruption and manipulation. The German soccer league attracts more visitors than elsewhere – 44,000 in average per match (in Dortmund even more than 80,000).

The *5th World Sport Ministers Conference* (MINEPS V in Berlin [Germany]) in May 2013 addressed the fight against match fixing as a key topic, and together with illegal betting, as well as doping and corruption in sport it is mentioned in the final "Declaration of Berlin".[5] In this declaration, the Ministers pointed out that the Sport Movement alone cannot successfully prevent and fight doping in sport and the manipulation of sport competitions, particularly when corruption and transnational organized crime are involved. They also saw the integrity of sport threatened by doping in sport, the manipulation of sport competitions and corrupt practices at local, national, regional and international levels. For the Ministers, the manipulation of sport competitions combined with betting offers large scale business opportunities and potential revenues for transnational organized crime and so they expressed their concern, that the rapid growth of unregulated sport betting, especially through the Internet, and by insufficiently regulated betting markets attracts transnational organized crime.

The ministers also called at UNESCO Member States to commit to giving due importance and funding for investigations of criminal activities taking place in the field of sport and to ensure adequate operational capacity to fight the manipulation of sport competitions in law enforcement and juridical authorities. The states should consider the introduction of criminal sanctions which would act as a deterrent against the manipulation of sport competitions, and against doping in sport and develop national and international cooperation between the law enforcement authorities and betting regulators in the fight against manipulation of sport competitions (e.g. mutual legal assistance, joint task forces), involving the Sport Movement and the betting operators. They also should explore the feasibility of creating a public prosecutor's office specialized in sport-related crimes.

---

[4]http://www.betsir.com/gambling-asian-culture.html the Chinese culture is uniquely steeped in gambling, with its history including the oldest recorded accounts of gambling worldwide more than 3,000 years ago. In modern China, social gambling is a common and accepted form of entertainment and celebration. See also Godot (2013), Loo et al. (2008) and Raylu and Oei (2004).
[5]http://www.mineps2013.de/fileadmin/Dokumente/pdf/MINEPS%20V%20-%20%20 Declaration%20of%20Berlin%20%28Original%20English%20Final%29.pdf.

The Ministers also called at the Sport Movement to Establish or reinforce transparent, democratic decision-making structures to enhance integrity, accountability, equal treatment and sustainability. In the view of MINEPS V, the following prevention measures against the manipulation of sport competitions must be implemented:

- Comprehensive education programs, in particular face-to-face-training targeted at athletes and also involving their close entourage, sport agents, coaches, referees, representatives of the associations/clubs and the sport federations;
- Appointment of ombudsmen, respected by the relevant target groups, as well as integrity officers at the national and international levels;
- Enforceable Codes of Conduct, committed to fair play and ethical standards
- Amnesty or incentive measures for persons helping to achieve legal action or prosecution;
- Adequate systems for encouraging and protecting whistle-blowers, and for managing suspicious information so as to grant priority to prevention;
- Strict policies for referee announcement timeframes and referee-athlete interactions prior to competitions;
- Integrity agreements with legal betting operators that outline details on the provision of betting services and information sharing protocols, in accordance with national and international law.

The conference also asked to adopt binding good governance rules, which include measures to strengthen democratic structures and transparency at the level of federations and associations/clubs. Individual actors, including sponsors and investors, must not use their influence to undermine the integrity of sport and reliable and sound management of financial affairs (including salary payment according to work contract provisions).

Accusations of corruption at the sport's governing body are nothing new but things heated up in July 2012 when a Swiss prosecutor released legal documents which said former FIFA president and IOC member Joao Havelange and former FIFA executive committee member Ricardo Teixeira took multi-million bribes on World Cup deals in the 1990s from the now defunct sports marketing body ISL (Pfanner 2011). Current FIFA president Blatter, also an IOC member, has denied any knowledge of the bribes, but evidence has been provided by Thomas Kistner (2012) in his book "FIFA Mafia". Several prominent members of the German Football Association (DFB) and the German Soccer League (DFL), including both Presidents Wolfgang Niersbach and Reinhard Rauball have called for Blatter to step down. Blatter denied all accusations of corruption and instead suggested that Germany had used bribery to secure the 2006 World Cup.

In addition to the initiatives adopted by betting operators and sport organizations, EU Member States and European organizations have shown their commitment to fight against match-fixing. 2011/12, the Council of Europe adopted the Recommendation on promotion of the integrity of sport against manipulation of results, the EU Council the Conclusions on combating match-fixing, and the European Parliament the Resolution on the European Dimension of Sport.

A study by KEA (2012) illustrates how corruption in sport, specifically match-fixing, is covered in national criminal law. A survey with national ministries in the 27 Member States, sporting organizations and betting operators was carried out. The study shows, that the European legal landscape is not uniform; whilst some countries focus on general offences of corruption or fraud, others have implemented specific sport offences to cope with match-fixing -contained either in their criminal codes (Bulgaria, Spain), sports laws (Cyprus, Poland, Greece) or special criminal laws (Italy, Malta, Portugal). In the UK, betting related match-fixing episodes are punished under the offence of cheating at gambling. Overall, these provisions differ greatly as regards the act to be criminalized as well as the scope, objective and subjective elements of the offences or the relevant sanctions.

Legal Problems

In the context of legal requirements to prosecute match fixing, a lawyer must ask what the object of "legal protection" (Rechtsgut) is or might be. Who exactly is the aggrieved party, what is the loss/damage/harm and how should be it calculated, when must the fraud activity take place (e.g. no fraud, when the bet is done before the manipulation), and whether the manipulative activity was objectively able to influence the chance to win, etc. If we cannot answer these questions from national our legal point of view, we will get in trouble with law enforcement – as the recent case in Germany has shown. A relevant corpus of jurisprudence and scholarly publications around the issue of criminal law and match-fixing exist in Germany, where several court decisions have applied the crime of fraud to betting related match-fixing events. Nevertheless, the situation is not satisfying. Fraud in Germany is punishable under section 263 of the German Criminal Code (Strafgesetzbuch, StGB). Section 263[6] punishes anyone with the intention of obtaining for himself or a third person an unlawful material benefit – who damages the property of another by causing or maintaining an error or by distorting or suppressing true facts – with up to 5 years imprisonment or a fine. In particularly serious cases the penalty is a prison sentence to 10 years. Sect. 263 StGB defines fraud as the real intention of an individual to obtain for himself or a third person unlawful material benefit and damage to the assets of another – for example, of the betting operator and the bettors (Fritzweiler 2007, p. 711).

The key element of the crime of fraud is therefore patrimonial damage. In the so called "Hoyzer case", the court developed a specific category of detriment, the "Quotenschaden", which can be translated as a 'detriment caused by a shift of odds'

---

[6](1) Whoever, with the intent of obtaining for himself or a third person an unlawful material benefit, damages the assets of another, by provoking or affirming a mistake by pretending that false facts exist or by distorting or suppressing true facts, shall be punished with imprisonment for not more than 5 years or a fine. (2) An attempt shall be punishable.

(Rotsch 2009) and relates specifically to financial loss in sports betting. It is calculated as follows: Damage = (real payment *minus* real input) *minus* (hypothetical payment *minus* hypothetical input). *Example:* real payment 100,000.- minus real input 10,000.-=90,000.- minus hypothetical payment 20,000.- minus hypothetical input 10,000.- = damage/loss of 80,000.-.

In similarity with the "Sapina case", it is necessary to consider whether there is damage to betting operators, regardless of whether manipulations have led to a defeat during the competition. What might matter is that the betting operators would not have concluded a betting contract if they knew that intentional manipulation would take place. It needs to be was proven that the perpetrator misled the betting organizers and the referee and players were both considered to be implicated in the offence and to have committed the fraud as part of a gang. What matters is that the betting operators would not have concluded a betting contract if they knew that intentional manipulation would take place. In both cases it was proven that the perpetrator misled the betting organizers and the referee and players were both considered to be implicated in the offence and to have committed the fraud as part of a gang.

First Case: The Bundesliga-Scandal (1970–1971)

The Bundesliga-Scandal was the first major case in Germany where the offence of fraud was considered in relation to the manipulation of sport results. This occurred in the 1970–1971 season during a series of matches which were fixed to avoid relegation. The German Football Association (DFB) sanctioned 52 players, two coaches, six managers and the Bielefeld and Offenbach clubs. The case went to the Federal Court but all the accused were acquitted because it was considered that there was no financial loss to the detriment of the federation and financial loss was a necessary element for implementing charges of fraud. One commentator argued that the only offense for which they could have been prosecuted was perjury (sect. 154 StGB), for denying their involvement in the manipulation (Fritzweiler 2007, p. 715).

Second Case: Robert Hoyzer (2000)

The second match-fixing case in Germany occurred in 2000. This was a betting related case involving Robert Hoyzer a German national-league referee, and Ante Sapina, who was linked to betting mafia. The ring reportedly placed enormous bets with Asian bookmakers and Turkish international players were said to be involved in the fraud. The accused were primarily Kosovans, and Sapina was convicted of fraud in 2005 and sentenced to 35 months in prison for fixing or attempting to fix 23 games by paying Hoyzer to rig matches Sapina and his brothers bet on. Sapina's brothers were given suspended sentences. Hoyzer was convicted of fraud and sentenced to 29 months in prison.[7] At a later date, the Federal Appeals Court rejected the prosecution's request to overturn Hoyzer's convictions. Their main argument was based on the lack of a legal infrastructure for prosecuting match-fixing. The Federal Supreme Court (Bundesgerichtshof, BGH) ruled, on 15 December 2006 that fraud had taken place[8] and refused to reduce the penalties fixed by the district court of Berlin due to the financial loss suffered by the Federation and the loss of public confidence in the fairness of the sport. The German Football Federation (DFB) introduced a lawsuit against Hoyzer requesting eight million Euros compensation for the damage caused to the whole of German football (Transparency International 2008). Hoyzer described the process in his own words: "It was an ongoing process that I wasn't aware of any more in the end. It affected me in a way that I stopped noticing things going on around me. I only hung out at this cafe, at some point it was like my second living room. I was around all the time. I was there 8 days out of the week and was treated by them like a very special person" (Hill 2008a, p. 166).

Third Case: Lim Bee Wah (2007)

Section 263 StGB was also applied in another betting case which ended with prison sentences for a Malay-Chinese national and a player (KEA 2012, p. 30). Following the contestation of the sentence dating from August 31, 2007, the Landgericht Frankfurt/Main (District tribunal) sentenced a player to pay a fine.[9] Investigations began after a tip-off from a second division African player who said he had been approached to throw games. Lim was under surveillance for only 2 weeks, but during that time he attempted to fix 10 games. He is said to have won more than 2.3 million Euros in one match. The German court released him in the middle of the trial on € 30,000 bail. As part of the deal, they gave him back casino chips worth € 150,000. He went to the casino, cashed in the chips, paid his lawyer and has not been seen since. He was sentenced in absentia to 2 years and 5 months in jail (Hill 2008b). What happened? There is no suspicion that the German police, prosecutors or judges were corrupt. Rather, they were, as Hill (2008a, p. 187) put it, "purely and simply ignorant. ... they did not know what they did not know". And what did the German Football Association? A police officer, quoted by Hill (2008a, p. 186), said: "No one wants to know about this case. Everyone wants to believe in a clean game. So the German Football Association does not want to talk about this case". They wanted to keep the bad publicity away or at least to go away as soon as possible. Is this also the reason why the German Football League (DFL) provided material on corruption and match fixing to the clubs, referees and players in 2013 without any

---

[7]LG Berlin (512) 68 Js 451/05 Kls (42/05) and (512) 68 Js 451/05 Kls (25/05).
[8]BGH 5 StR 181/06.
[9]LG Frankfurt/Main, judgment from 4 February 2009, 2 StR 165/08.

PR-support? They wanted to show (whomsoever), that they had done something in this respect, but they do not want the public to know that – to avoid bad publicity and the rumor, that it might be necessary to undertake such activities. In fact, it is necessary, in Germany like elsewhere in Europe at a time, the Bochum police special investigators look (in the summer of 2013) at some dozens of matches in Germany which are under suspicion for being fixed. The chief investigator, Friedhelm Althans, asked politicians in connection with the MINEPS V conference in Mai 2013 in Berlin for better laws to make their investigation easier. He also noted that worldwide cooperation between police is necessary and that besides the organized crime actors, operating from Singapore, the biggest threat for the integrity of football are syndicates in China and Russia (Anonymus 2013a). Both countries are not on the list of those 30 plus countries, who were involved in the investigations by the task force "Flankengott" (cross god), which have been started with the "Sapina Case" in 2009 (see below). At the same time (in June 2013), the Austrian Police task force "Matchfixing" announced, that they are investigation against 15 potential cases in Austria over the last 3 years, two "well known" football activists included (Anonymus 2013b). As in Germany, the officials from the Austrian Football Association see "no substantive evidence" to start their own investigations (Anonymus 2013c).

Fourth Case: René Schnitzler (2011)

In January 2011 the German magazine Stern reported that a former striker at FC St. Pauli of Hamburg, René Schnitzler, had received more than € 100,000 from gamblers. St. Pauli said in a statement that it was aware that Schnitzler, during his time with the club, had suffered from "private, particularly financial, problems." Schnitzler, in an interview with Stern, had described himself as a betting addict. The club said it had not come across any signs of match-fixing, but said it was cooperating with the investigators. Later he published a book on his case and how things developed (Schnitzler 2011).

Fifth Case: Ante Sapina ("Don Ante") (2011–2013)

One of the main actors in the most recent corruption case in Germany, dealt by the Bochum Criminal Court since 2011, is *Ante Sapina*. To *Sapina*, called *"Don Ante"*, a Berlin-based gambler, a five-star rating denoted a match in which he had bribed several players or even the referee to rig the outcome. He told the court in Bochum that he had sometimes staked hundreds of thousands of Euros on games like these in what officials call the biggest match-fixing scandal in the history of European soccer.

The case involves at least 32 matches in Germany and 200 in the continent, including three matches of the Champions League. Three of the men implicated, described by the prosecutor as 'enemies of sport' where sentenced in April 2011 by the Bochum District Court for to up to 3 years and 11 months in prison for trying to fix matches and bribe players.[10] It is the outcome of a vast inquiry which began – by accident – at the end of 2008. At the time, the police were investigating a prostitution and narcotics ring run by a transnational criminal organization based in Bochum (Germany). But the investigators discovered that the criminals were also running a vast network instigating corruption in sport and rigging bets to launder the fruits of their activities. On 19 November 2009, after a year of telephone tapping, 50 people were arrested and charged with corrupting over 320 football matches in 10 European countries. International and European Cup games were included in the investigation (Boniface et al. 2012).

In both the Hoyzer and Bochum cases the Court took into account the collaboration of the accused with the justice system to reduce the penalties. It is worth noting that all the cases which resulted in convictions were related to betting. A loose confederation of corrupt gamblers, centered in Germany but with links across Europe and Asia, is suspected of manipulating hundreds of matches, including World Cup qualifiers, UEFA Europa League encounters and even youth league games. Since the arrest of *Sapina* and several alleged co-conspirators in November 2009, the investigation has prompted additional arrests in Germany, Switzerland, Turkey and other countries. Dozens of players have been implicated; and UEFA, the governing body of European soccer, has suspended two referees for life.

While prosecutors have described Sapina as a ringleader of a German-based conspiracy, Hill (2010) said he and the men who had been charged in the case were merely the "jetsam and the flotsam of a huge tide in global gambling". In his view, the presence of vast amounts of money in illegal Asian betting pools, with gamblers eager to bet on any match, no matter how trivial, had made the European game increasingly susceptible to scandal. There is a "globalization of the gambling business". Ante Sapina had placed most of his bets in Asian gambling markets because legitimate bookmakers in Europe generally have restrictions on the size of wagers. "In the normal markets it is just not possible to make the kind of money you can win in Asia," he said (Pfanner 2011). While Sapina described himself as a habitual gambler since childhood, he brought forensic discipline to his operations, developing the star system to assess the effectiveness of a potential fix.

Match Fixing Is Organized Crime

For the German BKA, "Organized Crime" is the planned commission of criminal offences determined by the pursuit of profit and power which, individually or as a whole, are of considerable importance and involve more than two persons, each

---

[10]LG Bochum 12 KLs 35 Js 141/10 – 16/11.

with his/her own assigned tasks, who collaborate for a prolonged or indefinite period of time by using commercial or business-like structures, by using force or other means of intimidation or by exerting influence on politics, the media, public administration, judicial authorities or the business sector. Whereas the first elements of this definition without any doubt apply for the most recent match fixing cases, the last element (influence on politics, the media, public administration, judicial authorities or the business sector) might be doubted (BKA 2013).

The UK-Government's Organized Crime Strategy defines organized crime as "individuals, normally working with others, with the capability to commit serious crime on a continuing basis, which includes elements of planning, control and coordination, and benefits those involved. ... Successful organised crime groups often consist of a durable core of key individuals. ... Collaboration is reinforced by shared experiences (such as prison), or recommendation from trusted individuals. Others are bonded by family or ethnic ties" (SOCA 2013). Bearing this in mind, and looking at what we know from the worldwide structure of match fixing activities, the "durable core of key individuals" is still not known – and perhaps will never be known due to their very clandestine structure and violent habits.

The most recent Organized Crime Situation Report for the Federal Republic of Germany by the BKA is not mentioning gambling or match fixing at all. The list of the crimes includes different crimes and areas, but at least some of the regional LKA have information on relations between parts of the well-known organized crime groups and gambling or betting (e.g. in context with legal gambling machines). Germany might be seen as a "safe haven" for internationally organized, but locally networked groups. We know that from the Italian Mafia: The mafia is expanding its influence on the economy and politics in Germany, as the BKA in a recent report has shown. Nearly 250 members of the Italian Mafia are living in Germany (BKA 2011).

In 2012, an EU-parliament special committee pointed out, that "criminal organizations ... are increasingly using online sports betting as a tool for making and laundering money around the globe. Since websites providing sports betting can be located anywhere in the world, criminals shop for countries where there is the least oversight and control from public authorities for their criminal operations. ... the recent development of online sports betting has proved to be a massive threat to the integrity of sport. Additionally sports fraud is extremely interesting for organized crime due to its relatively high revenues and low sentences" (Bozkurt 2012) Criminal organizations have – in the view of this committee, "deeply penetrated the football establishment". Strong ties exist between the football establishment and criminal organizations especially in Eastern Europe and the Balkans. In countries such as Russia, Ukraine, Bulgaria and Serbia criminals have infiltrated in the clubs and federations and are operating from within, while using the clubs as covers for a multitude of criminal activities. And "Organized crime in sport" was the name of a hearing which has been organized on September 19, and 20, 2012 in the European Parliament by the Special Committee on organized crime, corruption and money laundering (Fajon and Bozkurt 2012).

Criminological Background and Forensic Evidence

Investigations in the field of match fixing are very difficult and time consuming due to clandestine structures, very well (illegally and legally) connected actors, different legal structures, different law enforcement cultures, language problems (e.g. in the Lim-Bee-Wah-case, the investigators did not know what language Lim spoke (it was Kookien or Hakka) (Hill 2008a, p. 186). Furthermore, the cooperation within Europe with now 27 states is difficult and lengthy: During one fixed match more than 50 persons in 10 states have been involved in different criminal activities. A coordination of all law enforcement activities in these 10 states within due time is just impossible. The different criminal liability for match fixing and betting with e.g. different acceptance of benefit, granting of an undue advantage, betting fraud, organized economic crime, and the formation of a criminal association – all these illegal activities have different regulations in different countries. And finally, it is extremely difficult to get the evidences for the bets, especially in Asia.

Ante Sapina was born in 1976 born in Raško Polje (Croatia) and raised in Duisburg, Germany, as the youngest of three sons. His father died 1988, and the family moved to Berlin. Ante is good in mathematics in school, and with 14 years he sent money to Ireland for sports betting (30 German Marks in each envelope). In 1999 he won € 76,000 at a betting machine in Berlin, invested directly 50,000 in the German Bundesliga Champion and won 100,00. Later he called this his "break-through". He studied business economics at a university, but found his profession in bets. When he got in trouble with private bookies – he is too good for them – he got limits, some sports are blocked for him, so he went to the state-run Oddset, with the "worst odds in Europe" (Sapina). As a consequence, he moves to the Asian market with better options. In 2004 he met the referee Hoyzer at Cafe King in Berlin, owned by his brother Milan. Sapina and Hoyzer get friends and agree on match fixing. Sapina is said to loves football, he also met Messi during 2006 championship. In August 2004 Sapina won € 751,365 (match fixed by Hoyzer). Hoyzer and Sapina were sentenced, Sapina got 2 years and 11 months in prison, but he was released on probation after half time (which is very seldom in Germany). Sapina stays in the milieu, bets again, and fixes matches. He is diagnosed as pathological gambler, and he lost his Porsche to the public prosecutor during the investigations. The car had the license plate "B-OG"for "Bog", the Croatian word for god. Sapina is a catholic, goes to church whenever possible. People describe Sapina as a very bright boy, good in mathematics. He started gambling with small bets (as all gambling addicts). As a young boy, he was looking for challenges. With bigger bets and (financial and societal) success, he got addicted (pathological gambling). The cultural and business environment of Cafe King fascinated him, and his private, personal success and appreciation by others influenced him, so that he was looking for higher aims, which he found at the Asian betting market. This is when he got in contact with and appreciation by Organized Crime representatives. It is still unclear whether Sapina approached these people or vice versa, but it would make sense for OC representatives to use somebody like Sapina for their business. Finally, Sapina was caught by the police by coincidence. They were not looking after him or investigating his activities, but they were phone tapping another person, and found him like a "chance find". Overall, Sapina is not a typical member of organized crime structures, and perhaps this is the reason, why he got caught and sentenced.

But what were the reasons for his success? Sapina was and still is smart, polite, and trustful. He is able to "read" people, to find their very personal chinks or weak points. He knows how to deal with characters like Hoyzer on the one side and organized crime activists on the other side. The fact, that he was released after half sentence in 2006 shows, that he was able to convince the prison authorities and the courts that he is rehabilitated – because a release after half sentence is legally possible, but very rare in Germany (even release after two third is nowadays seldom). And the same happened when he was released from pre-trial custody in 2011 because he was "cooperative".

Consequences and Recommendations

Match Fixing causes high financial losses for associations, players, bet providers and individual players. Clubs may end up with high debts after relegation or elimination of international competitions. The results can be job cuts on sides of professional players and coach, club can go insolvent. But as citizens are losing trust in sports, as also athletes and functionaries, the fascination of matches and sporting events will disappear, and with that the possibility for clubs, players, and media, PR-companies, and sponsors, to earn money. The money draws back from sports, which is shaken to the very foundations and suffer considerable image damage.

Monitoring systems are (at least at the moment) not effective because they deliver no facts or data, which can be used in investigations and trials. They have no evidentiary value, and they are suggested to be monitored by those criminal networks, or even tactically used by such networks for their own bets. Monitoring systems are a net with very large mesh, because Asian fixers do not bet with Betfair or English betting companies.

So one solution could be to intensify training and education, as the German Soccer League (DFL) is recently trying to do. The target groups for education should be law enforcement officers, athletes, club representatives, managers, referees. The program and the documents should be specially tailored and should include the risk of gambling addiction. Examples from other sports may be used, like from the U.S. National Collegiate Athletic Association. They have a former Mafia capo lecture their players about how the mob really works. We need more education or training for players on how to avoid criminals or the dangers of dealing with them. Players get educated how to deal with the media – but not with the Mafia.

Bearing this in mind, the following recommendations can be made:

1. Better cooperation between all stakeholders (law enforcement, sports federations, bookmakers/bookies, etc.).
2. Exchange of Information between law enforcement agencies in different countries, both on the formal and informal level.

3. Better knowledge about worldwide acting betting cartels and organised crime networks and structures.
4. Monitoring systems must be re-structured and an independent body must overview and evaluate their work; early detection is crucial; uniform procedure for handling suspicious cases.
5. Investigations by using all tools incl. undercover agents on all levels and on all potential actors.
6. Ombudsmen or independent commissions, where people can anonymously report suspicious activities or observations.
7. Unification (in Europe and worldwide) of laws, law enforcement activities, court decisions, data bases.
8. Standards for legal and administrative cooperation.
9. Cooperation with sports federations (UEFA, national organizations, not only football); they should inform police about suspicious matches.
10. Licensing of bookmakers should be combined with agreement to provide information about suspicious matches, persons, and clubs.
11. Regulatory authorities should agree on standards to supervise and control the betting market and bookmakers (the problem in Germany: No nation-wide agency is possible like in France, Italy or UK due to the federal system and urban, communal regulatory agencies in cities.
12. Integrity delegates in sports federations and betting providers/bookmakers for cooperation with law enforcement agencies.

In the same direction goes the Position Paper of the Federal Ministry of Interior in Germany for the 2013 World Sports Ministers Conference in Berlin.[11] It asked for effective good governance policies and ethics codes help strengthen the autonomy of sport in relation to state authority, create a relationship based on trust and mutual respect and strengthen the integrity of sport. For the fight against corruption to be successful an organizational culture based on integrity, fairness, transparency and equal treatment is needed. Democratic structures within the football associations are necessary with transparent, reliable and sound management of financial affairs. Individual actors including sponsors and investors must not have too much influence on the clubs and associations and a code of conduct committed to fair play and ethical standards must be installed. The clubs together with the football association should agree on rules for managing conflicts of interest, preventive measures, warning, advice and reporting points, and effective control mechanisms. As betting fraud is organized crime, we need to unite in the fight against trivialization and lack of awareness. Only really professional management of football associations with independent people from "outside" can guarantee that, not the "old-boys-network"-structures, where positions are filled with those, who served (in the really meaning of the word) and behaved properly (in the view of the officials in charge) over years. The public awareness and acceptability of investigations must be increased, misleading information by

---

[11]http://www.mineps2013.de/fileadmin/Dokumente/pdf/MINEPS%20V_Media%20E%20Kit_eng.pdf.

media and associations must be contradicted. Finally, national regulatory authorities should be established, and the supranational cooperation between betting-companies, regulatory authorities, sport associations and law enforcement agencies need to be increased. Specified, independent units within soccer associations like UEFA, DFL, DFB and security departments must protect and police the game. Football needs to be taken away from so called "honorary officials" who's only qualification besides to rake in money is that they have none.

References

Anonymus (2013a). Bochumer Chefermittler fordert härtere Gesetze gegen Wettbetrug [Online Document] URL http://www.finanznachrichten.de/nachrichten-2013-05/26937860-bochumer-chefermittler-fordert-haertere-gesetze-gegen-wettbetrug-003.htm (16.07.2013).

Anonymus (2013b). Fußball-Wettbetrug mit "bekannten Namen" [Online Document] URL http://wirtschaftsblatt.at/home/life/1421746/FussballWettbetrug-mit-bekannten-Namen?_vl_backlink=/home/index.do (16.07.2013).

Anonymus (2013c). Wettbetrug in Österreich Anklagen stehen bevor [Online Document] URL http://diepresse.com/home/sport/fussball/national/1421801/Wettbetrug-in-Oesterreich-Anklagen-stehen-bevor (16.07.2013).

BKA (2013). Orginased Crime [Online Document] URL http://www.bka.de/nn_194550/EN/SubjectsAZ/OrganisedCrime/organisedCrime__node.html?__nnn=true (16.07.2013).

BKA (2011). Organisierte Kriminalität. Bundeslagebild 2011 [Online Document] URL http://www.bka.de/nn_193314/SharedDocs/Downloads/DE/Publikationen/Jahresberichte UndLagebilder/OrganisierteKriminalitaet/organisierteKriminalitaetBundeslagebild2011,temp lateId=raw,property=publicationFile.pdf/organisierteKriminalitaetBundeslagebild2011.pdf (16.07.2013).

Boniface, P. et al. (2012). Sports betting and corruption: How to preserve the integrity of sport [Online Document] URL http://www.sportaccord.com/multimedia/docs/2012/02/2012_-_IRIS_-_Etude_Paris_sportifs_et_corruption_-_ENG.pdf (16.07.2013).

Bozkurt, E. (2012). Match fixing and fraud in sport: putting the pieces together [Online Document] URL http://static.euractiv.com/sites/all/euractiv/files/17Sep%20Crim%20Bozkurt%20fv.pdf (16.07.2013).

Fajon, T./Bozkurt, E. (2012). Organized crime and sport: Euro-deputies fight against match fixing Online Resource URL http://www.youtube.com/watch?v=CwsZ94U9N60 (16.07.2013).

Fritzweiler, J. (2007). Praxishandbuch Sportrecht. C.H. Beck: München.

Godot, D. (2013). Cultural Factors in Problem Gambling among the Chinese [Online Document] URL http://davidgodot.com/cultural-factors-in-problem-gambling-among-the-chinese/ (16.07.2013).

Hill, D. (2010). The Fix. McClelland & Stewart: Toronto.

Hill, D. (2008a). Soccer and Organized Crime. McClelland & Stewart:Toronto.

Hill, D. (2008b). Match-fixing: European football's dark and dangerous side [Online Document] URL http://www.telegraph.co.uk/sport/football/competitions/premier-league/3224065/Match-fixing-Premier-League-footballs-dark-and-dangerous-side-Football.html (16.07.2013).

KEA. (2012) Match-fixing in sport. A mapping of criminal law provisions in EU 27 [Online Document] URL http://ec.europa.eu/sport/news/documents/study-sports-fraud-final-version_en.pdf (16.07.2013).

Thomas Kistner (2012). FIFA Mafia. Die schmutzigen Geschäfte mit dem Weltfußball. Droemer: München.

Loo, J.M.Y., Raylu, N., & Oei, T.P.S. (2008). Gambling among the Chinese: A comprehensive review. Clinical Psychology Review, 28, 1152–1166.

Mutschke, R. (2012). Match-fixing must be combated [Online Document] URL http://www.fifa.com/aboutfifa/organisation/administration/news/newsid=1593037/index.html (16.07.2013).

Noble, R. K. (2013). Valcke: We must battle match-fixing together [Online Document] URL http://www.fifa.com/aboutfifa/organisation/footballgovernance/news/newsid=1987215/index.html (16.07.2013).

Noble, R. K. (2012). No quick fix to fighting sports corruption, INTERPOL chief tells FIFA Congress [Online Document] URL http://www.interpol.int/News-and-media/News-media-releases/2012/PR044 (16.07.2013).

Pfanner, E. (2011). Corruption Eroding Level Playing Fields of Europe [Online Document] URL http://www.nytimes.com/2011/01/07/sports/soccer/07iht-match07.html?pagewanted=all (16.07.2013).

Raylu, N. & Oei, T.P. (2004). Role of culture in gambling and problem gambling. Clinical Psychology Review, 23, 1087–1114.

Rotsch, T. (2009). Concerning the hypertrophy of law. Zeitschrift für Internationale Strafrechtsdogmatik, 3, 89–96.

Schnitzler, R. (2011). Zocker Liga. Gütersloh.

SOCA (2013). Organised crime groups [Online Document] URL http://www.soca.gov.uk/threats/organised-crime-groups (16.07.2013).

Spurling, J. (2013). Drugs, Mafia And Murder: The Ten Most Corrupt Football Leagues Ever [Online Document] URL http://www.sabotagetimes.com/football-sport/10-most-corrupt-football-leagues-ever/ (16.07.2013).

Yau, C. (2012). Arrests across Asia in INTERPOL-led operation targeting illegal soccer gambling networks [Online Document] URL http://www.interpol.int/en/Internet/News-and-media/News-media-releases/2012/N20120718 (16.07.2013).

Impact of Sports Betting and Corruption: Reflections from Uganda

Mulema Mukasa Richard

Abstract This chapter focuses on Uganda as one country with the insidious threat of sports betting and corruption with all its attendant manifestations. It seeks to examine how the national laws have sought to, or have failed to, regulate sports betting and gaming; how far have the sports bodies been ready to handle this affliction? Have the socio-economic factors contributed to this nascent problem? How has the impact of globalization, liberalization of trade markets, information age and consumerism been? How have the people's cultural dispositions been conducive to this malaise? Finally, some recommendations for the future are presented in the conclusion section.

Introduction

In 2003, Uganda's top tier football league, The Super League, ended with about 70 % of the games bearing the makings and trappings of match-fixing and corruption. It was presided over by centre match officials who were contemptuously given the moniker "Arrow Boys" and thus the country recorded its abysmal football league scandal and the lowest point the game sank.[1] The aspects of match-fixing and corruption had been in existence before this debacle and are, by no means, extinguished to date.

The incidence of sports betting and corruption has been adequately highlighted in the Western world and the major emerging economic regions but rarely is this illuminated in what are considered to be backwaters of sport in which Uganda falls.

---

[1] http://www.observer.ug/index-php?option=com-content&view=article&id=4316%3Ahb-ziwa-22-1win over-akol-

M.M. Richard (✉)
M/s Kigozi Ssempala Mukasa Obonyo (KSMO) Advocates,
Crested Towers, 5th Floor, Short Tower, 17 Hannington Road, 23064, Kampala, Uganda
e-mail: ksmo@ksmo.biz; mulema@ksmo.biz; www.ksmo.biz

M.R. Haberfeld and D. Sheehan (eds.), *Match-Fixing in International Sports:*
Existing Processes, Law Enforcement, and Prevention Strategies,
DOI 10.1007/978-3-319-02582-7_3, © Springer International Publishing Switzerland 2013

This is notwithstanding that the same levels of sporting integrity and uniformity of application of sporting rules are required of the sports governing bodies, the players, athletes/participants, the sovereign Governments, the referees/match officials, fans, technical persons in these developing countries as those in the Western world or developed world. In the developing world, especially the often impressionable yet passionate youths, have been engulfed in the global problem.

This chapter is not a be-all-end-all study and discussion of sports betting and corruption in Uganda but there is a sincere belief and hope that it has considerably dealt with the impact. Henceforth, the stakeholders in Uganda, the bigger African region and wider international players, will take the necessary attention and devise measures to check the myriad negative ramifications of sports betting.

Background

> Because of our close cooperation in the past, when corruption allegations surfaced and became a major concern undermining the integrity of football, FIFA and INTERPOL were able to put in place a robust and sustainable anti-corruption training in football programme. It was apparent to FIFA and INTERPOL's leadership that if we acted quickly and forcefully, we could reassure football players, supporters and the public that this serious problem would be dealt with in a comprehensive and continuing manner. What was most concerning, from a law enforcement point of view, were the links between match – fixing, illegal betting and transnational organized crime on a global scale. As a result of the huge profit associated with illegal gambling, of the vulnerability of players and of the ease with which matches of all levels are accessible for betting on via the internet, corrupting matches or their outcomes has become an activity of interest to transnational organized crime groups.
> Ronald K. Noble, Secretary General of INTERPOL, 25th May, 2012.[2]

The birth of the Integrity in Sport Program by INTERPOL in collaboration with FIFA in 2011 is a monumental and far reaching initiative that will undoubtedly curb the problems appertaining to match-fixing and corruption in football. They will help the developing world, given the global outreach and presence of INTERPOL in every sovereign state, which is synonymous with that of FIFA through affiliate national federations, and perhaps other international sports bodies like the IOC, ITF, ICC, IAAF and FIBA among others.

If such networks are created and harnessed overtime, then the transnational criminal activities and organized groups can be checked, and the integrity of the different sports disciplines kept intact. It will then be left to the national and international sports bodies to continue to fight internally, the mundane and oft-occurring incidences of match-fixing and corruption through their Ethics and Integrity Committees, Disciplinary bodies, Security Committees, Independent Governance Committees, etc.

Sports betting creates a great opportunity to many persons with criminal intentions to realize their intentions especially money launderers, drug and narcotics

---

[2] Address by INTERPOL Secretary General at the 62nd FIFA Congress, 25th May, 2012, Budapest, Hungary, www.interpol.com/News-and-media/Speeches

traffickers, tax fraudsters, speculators over international currencies, corrupted business people and criminal gangs. The organization of sports, both at national and international levels, is hardly adept and sufficiently galvanized to face up to the challenges of these powerful and sophisticated global networks.

The interest of INTERPOL therefore in the tackling of this global problem, with its experience and cooperation engendered by sovereign states is a good shot in the arm for the benefit of international and national sports bodies. INTERPOL, hitherto a lone ranger, in the campaign to crack down sports betting related crime over international borders, has over the last 1 year period, been joined by natural partners whose foremost obligation is to promote and protect the integrity of the sport.

INTERPOL, in doing this has devised a strategy of creating and executing this global programme, with the objective of improving awareness and the understanding of the phenomenon by the actors involved, the strategies used by its perpetrators and the methods to detect and counteract them.[3] They attempt to tackle three areas in execution of this program; Training, Education and Prevention. This Global Academic Experts Meeting/Conference was geared towards the first two but also indirectly aiding the other.

Uganda, as a case study, succinctly represents a developing country that through globalization and consumerism, is fast taking in the manifestations, both positive and negative, of sports betting. The spectre and practice, is not any different from any Sub-Saharan African country and unfortunately, not much focus of the INTERPOL Integrity in Sport Program has been directed to this continent.

In carrying out research for this chapter, the author has interviewed many stakeholders in different sports in Uganda; the Government bodies charged with national regulation generally, Governmental sports authorities, Sports Associations/Federations, Club owners and officials, Match officials, Referees, Sports Fans Associations, League Managers/Officials, Coaches/Managers, Players' Association officials, Sports Betting Owners and officials, Punters and others. The input from these interviews will be presented henceforth.

The final part of the chapter represents an attempt to provide for some recommendations and solutions. What can be done as a national legislative and regulatory mechanism and the need to engender and foster probity in sports governing bodies and game-related investments, will be discussed.

Organisation of Sports in Uganda

The organization of sports in Uganda derives from the socio-economic, cultural and political governance of the country but much focus should be placed on the socio-economic angle.

---

[3] INTERPOL Integrity In sport Fact Sheet: www.interpol.com

The Socio-economic Set-Up

Uganda is a sovereign country that lies in East Africa which is part of a bigger region popularly known as Sub-Saharan Africa by the Bretton Woods Institutions. According to the World Bank's latest statistics of 2011, it has a population of 34.51 Million people with a GDP of US. $16.81 billion and is described as a low-income level developing country.[4]

The country runs a liberalized economy with a splattering of a few multi-national and private companies but the economy largely depends on the subsistence agricultural economy with coffee, cotton, tea being some of the major foreign-exchange earners. Others are tourism and fisheries. The prospects are raised by the recent discovery of extractable and commercial oil.

It has one of the fastest growing populations while ironically having one of the highest infant and maternal mortality rates in the world. "Uganda remains a very poor country and far from the middle income status it aspires to achieve in one generation. There are concerns about uneven progress, with inequality increasing while there are distinct geographical patterns of unequal outcomes in health and education, and uneven access to basic social services".[5]

The majority of the multi-ethnic people of Uganda live in villages, with the minority living in urban communities and scattered trading centres. The unemployment rate at such urban centres is alarmingly high and successive macro-economic measures made over the years look overwhelmingly lacking. The quality of life remains lukewarm in the general population as a result.

According to the published statistics of the Mo Ibrahim Index of African Governance, for the year 2011, there is no marked improvement in the areas of corruption and transparency. This portrays the poor "good-governance" credentials and the consistent impunity in the area of eliminating state-tolerated corruption. The World Bank country profile reports thus on this Mo Ibrahim Index[6]:

> In terms of accountability of public officials, Uganda and its East African neighbours scored poorly, with a low rating of 33.3. Uganda also scored poorly in the area of corruption of public officials, while its score of 40 was higher than Kenya and Burundi's 20. Regarding prosecutions of related abuse of office, Uganda's performance deteriorated from 71.4 to 57.1. The data related to corruption and bureaucracy – which measures petty and grand forms of corruption, as well as "capture" of the state by elites and private interests – shows that the performance of most East African countries, including Uganda, has been declining over time.

---

[4] www.worldbank.org/country/uganda

[5] www.worldbank.org/en/country/uganda/overview

[6] www.worldbank.org/en/country/uganda/overview
www.moibrahimfoundation.org/uganda

The Legal System

Uganda inherited the British common law and is therefore is a common law country and since gaining its Independence in 1962, attempts are being made to enact laws with domestic cultural values and aspirations.

An anachronistic national law governs the regulation and management of sports in Uganda. Whereas there cannot be a single legislation to regulate sports given the various areas of its outreach, tort, tax, contract, employment, intellectual property law, constitutional law, commercial law, administrative law, it is imperative that the administrative and constitutional aspects have to be dealt with in a "one-stop" law to avoid ambiguity.

Most international sports bodies, FIFA, IOC, IAAF usually pay respect to the national laws in regard to the establishment and affiliation of the national Associations and peaceful co-existence so long as there is no political interference in the management of national Associations by the state governments.

The specific law governing sports is mainly the National Council of Sports Act, Cap 48 that was passed in 1964 and commenced on 25th June 1964. It noteworthy that the said Act establishes the National Council of Sports, popularly known as "NCS". The stated objects of the NCS are under S. 3 of the Act.

(1) The objects for which the Council is established shall be:-

    (a) To develop, promote and control all forms of amateur sports on a national basis in conjunction with voluntary amateur sports organizations or associations by providing:

        (i) training and other staff
        (ii) grants –in-aid to National Associations or organizations;
        (iii) stadiums, playing fields and other facilitations;
        (iv) sports equipment and other sports items as may be necessary for the accelerated development of sports.

    (b) To encourage and facilitate cooperation among the various national associations.
    (c) To approve international and national sports competitions and festivals organized by national and other associations.
    (d) To organize, in consultation with the national associations, national, international and other sports competitions and festivals as means of exchanging experience and fostering friendly relations with other nations and
    (e) To do all such things as are incidental or conducive to the attainment of the above objects or any of them as may be approved by the Minister.

The Act stipulates the duties of NCS under S. 3(2) which include stimulating general interest in sport at all levels, plan the general policy of sports promotion.

The underpinning objective to the Act, and the Regulatory body, NCS is therefore **"voluntary amateur sports"**, and S. 10 of the Act gives powers to the line Minister, by Statutory Instrument, to make regulations for the NCS, to carry out its supervisory mandate. It states that:

The Minister may, after consultation with the Council, by statutory instrument, make regulations for better carrying into effect the purposes and provisions of this Act and in particular, for the following matters:-

(a) The establishment of national association and the registration of the associations with the Council.

(b) The functions of national associations.
(c) The establishment and composition of national committees, including sub-committees, other than committees of national associations.
(d) The promotion and encouragement, in consultation with the Minister responsible for education, for sports and games in schools and colleges.

The Minister has to-date never made the Statutory Instrument but, factually, many sports bodies exist, and these include the Federation of Uganda Football Associations, with the acronym, FUFA. How have these sports Associations been affiliated to NCS or in case of football, to FIFA internationally?

The NCS guidelines to National Associations/Bodies, 2009 and Requirements for Affiliation, which exist, are not enough in the creation of National Sports Associations as they have no foundation in law.

There are two scenarios currently in place: **Dejure** and **Defacto**. Black's Law Dictionary, Eighth Edition defines these terms as:

  (i) Dejure: "As a matter of law": "existing by right or according to law"
  (ii) Defacto: "In point of fact":

1. Actual; existing in fact: having effect even though not formally or legally recognized.
2. "Illegitimate but in effect"

The existence and operation of sports associations in Uganda is therefore defacto and largely dependent on the goodwill and general acceptance of the players in that particularly sports discipline. This applies to FUFA.

The Amateur and Semi-professional Sports

The law in Uganda is therefore purposely made and exists to regulate amateur and voluntary sports organizations. Generally speaking, what is not specifically proscribed by a given law is not outlawed. By default, therefore, semi-professional and professional sport exists in Uganda, and is only emerging.

The major and popular disciplines of sport in Uganda are Football, Athletics, Boxing, Rugby, Basketball, Motorsport, Cricket and Netball. It is mainly Football, Boxing and Athletics with aspects of semi-professionalism and professionalism affiliations.

This author has argued, in a different forum, on the state of sport in Uganda thus[7]:

Note should be made of the fact that the NCS Act does not govern or regulate professional football. This is primarily because sport, in the past, the pre-1964 Uganda, was mainly amateur, for feel-good factors, voluntary association and for recreational purposes, and players and officials participated out of the spirit of voluntarism. There was no expectation of prize money, salaries or wages and commercialism was absent. Some of these aspects also apply now and would be ever-present in the modern sport but it is inescapable that the tide has changed and there is need for an overhaul of the law and government policy.

---

[7] Mulema Mukasa Richard: Football Administration Structures in Uganda and the Need for Reforms; 2012.

Funding Sports Disciplines

Ideally sports funding would be the responsibility of both on the Government and the members of the voluntary amateur sports organizations. The Government has mainly concentrated on the building of the sports infrastructure like stadia, courts, playing fields, and the sports Association or the Clubs on the training of athletes/players, payment of salaries, wages or allowances to its players and officials. This has not been easy owing to the voluntarism and the lackadaisical interest of successive Governments.

Sports, in Uganda, today in line with the market – liberalization policies discussed above, has been left to private hands and occasional grants from the international sports bodies. The advent of semi-professionalism and the lack of a definitive purpose – made law has largely engendered the increased participation of the private sector. The Government only steps in intermittently when there is international participation and the pride and sovereignty of the country has to be exhibited for the international community and often times, the funding is meagre.

Despite the law and current Government policy not being conducive to private individual funders to support sports, especially by offering tax holidays or debates, the private companies have markedly sponsored different disciplines. This has been so majorly because of the advertising platform it provides and not the return on investment into the sports business as a commercial venture.

In this context, funding of sports in Uganda and indeed many Sub-Saharan African countries is exposed to a myriad of possibilities and sources. These could lead to the involvement of self-seeking and criminally-minded.

The Nature of Match-Fixing and Corruption

Corruption broadly includes match-fixing and all forms of unfair practices that undermine the rules of any sports discipline, and fair play, particularly to football. An authoritative legal definition of corruption is: "Depravity, perversion, or taint; an impairment of integrity, virtue, or moral principle, especially, the impairment of a public official's duties by bribery".[8]

On the other hand, a non-legal and broader definition of corruption more acceptable to researchers in the sports realm especially sports betting is: "any manipulation of a result or aspect of a game with the aim of enrichment on the sports betting market. In fact, the action of corrupting a sports person is only relevant if it is carried out in parallel with the placement of sums of money in form of bets in licensed betting outlets, or more specifically online betting sites."[9]

---

[8] Bryan A. Garner, Black's Law Dictionary, Eighth Edition.

[9] Iris, University of Safford (Manchester), Cabinet Praxes-Advocates, CCLS (Universite' de Pekin), Sports Betting and Corruption: How to Preserve the Integrity of Sport, 2012.

Examples and Methods of Corruption

Corruption in sport varies and Transparency International attempts to shed light on the definitional issues:

> Sport is a multi-billion dollar business. It has intricate ties to political and private interests. This means rich opportunities for corruption yet across the sporting sector, most deals and decisions take place behind closed doors. This allows corruption to go unchecked and unpunished.
>
> Corruption in sport has many forms. Referees and players can take bribes to fix matches. Club owners can demand kick-backs for player transfers. Companies and governments can rig bids for construction contracts. Organized crime is behind many of the betting scandals that have dented sport's reputation. And money laundering is widespread. This can take place through sponsorship and advertising arrangements. Or it may be through the purchase of Clubs, players and image rights. Complex techniques are used to launder money through football and other sports. These include cross-border transfers, tax havens and front companies.[10]

Match-fixing is the commonest form of corruption in Uganda and this is not specifically restricted to football. This involves the national Association/Federation, Referees, Coaches/Manager, Clubs officials, athletes/players, technical staff, league managers who in one way or the other abuse their positions for personal gain or for the benefit of the corruptor for varied reasons.

Some of the rampant methods and examples of match-fixing and corruption in Uganda are:

  (i) "Through fixture pile-up for unfavoured clubs or conversely, regularly spread schedules for favoured clubs to demotivate or wear down a club and on the other to encourage a club".

 (ii) "Blatant giving away of matches" by clubs or their officials and players especially when there is no aim in such a game, e.g. at the end of the season.

(iii) Money exchanging hands, usually at the tail-end of the season when there is no impetus to play matches of honour games and throw them away. For this club officials receive about US $75 each, players US.$10 to US.$20 each and coaches/technical staff US.$38 each. This could involve all the categories of a number of people or any of them

 (iv) The Federation/Association appoints the match official/referees and if the corruption is initiated by them it will be felt in the decisions of such match officials at the particular match.

  (v) Club official to Club official match-fixing corruption: "It is about relationships at the official level and not any persons on the Board can be approached lest it fails".[11]

 (vi) Technical level; coach-to-coach and usually amongst coaches with a degree of collegiality.

---

[10] www.transparency.org/topic/detail/sport

[11] Interview with former club official, 26th October, 2012.

(vii) Coach to players; some coaches maintain good relations with their former players or those in rival clubs.
(viii) Club officials to players of opposite teams usually through friendship built as during periods spent playing with the corruptor club.
(ix) Match official/referees approach club officials in coded or explicit language and a deal is struck. The match officials/referees ask for between US. $75 to US.$108 for the four officials who form a set to share after match-day.
(x) Overzealous fans of big or popular clubs mobilize money and meet and pay the match officials or players of rival team to fix matches.
(xi) Matches are also fixed for the purpose of causing change in the technical/coaching setup or at the Board or Federation level. These are usually political manipulations that are unfortunately manifested at the field of play.
(xii) Influencing referees by looking after their personal welfare or that of their families or contributing in kind or monetary means in case of referee's bereavement.

The "Arrow Boys" Football Scandal: Case Study

The country's premier competition, the Super League, ran by The National Football Committee, then saw the league denigrate into a farce in 2003 majorly due to the split loyalties the two Ugandan big and popular clubs, SC Villa and Express FC, generate in Ugandan football, who were running neck and neck to the championship that season. This is not to discount that behind the scenes, there were shenanigans being orchestrated by football politicians who wanted to capitalize on the nadir the game had plummeted to throw their names in the hat for the top leadership of the National Football Association. There are at least three most prominent incidences of the legacy of this league that stand out and portray the dare-devil nature of the referees, officials and how the processes of the football institutions were manipulated.

(i) SC Villa Vs Akol FC 22 – 1: Case Study
     One of the most abiding memories of the "Arrow Boys" Scandal is the "22 – 1 win" of SC Villa over Akol FC, a team from the Northern region of Lira, a distance of about 344 km from Kampala, the capital city, where the match was to be hosted. SC Villa and Express FC, traditional football giants in Ugandan football with mass followings, were running close to each other in the season-ending matches on points, at some times level on points and it looked most likely that the league was to be decided on goal difference.
     With about ten matches to complete this 2003 league championship, the pressure and anxiety had began to show; FA officials, league managers, club officials had been involved in the clearest forms of match-fixing highlighted above.[12]

---

[12] The Observer report, Op. Cit, P. 7.

With this game one of the penultimate ones for SC Villa, with Express marginally leading on goal difference and with Akol FC, assured of relegation, under hand methods were devised to ensure that SC Villa emphatically wins this game with a generous goal tally. Dan Obote, a Villa player hailing from Lira region had traveled to Lira prior to the match, ostensibly to visit his family. and it was understood he met key players and officials of Akol FC to influence them to throw the match. The National Football League/FUFA dispatched a FUFA bus to pick the players from Lira on the eve of the match. Another bus was also sent to pick the Akol FC players by SC Villa officials/supporters. There was divided opinion in the Akol FC camp whether they should honor the game and this had torn their camp into two sides: pro and against. The ones for playing were influenced by SC Villa and the other, Express FC.

The bus carrying the players set-off on the 5 h journey to Kampala and meanwhile the other bus was trailing, and at every refreshment stop, it would stop to ensure that no players abscond and jump off the bus. An ominous air hanged around the players' bus with heated disagreements about honoring the match, and bribery allegations. The officials and players kept receiving calls about their head way to Kampala or decision to play.

Within a distance of the outskirts of Kampala, Police Patrol vehicles were dispatched by the authorities, to provide safe passage of the team bus to the stadium, given to the traffic congestion in the city but also to oversee, on behalf of SC Villa, that the players make their way to the field of play. SC Villa had contacts with high ranking police personnel to their aid. At about this time, at Kawempe, some players of the originally 20 or so players who began the Lira – Kampala journey jumped off the bus, leaving eight or so players on board. The majority got another smaller commuter mini-bus and went to the FUFA head-quarters where they were apparently detained and were not to honor the match.

The group of eight or so players remaining on a bus got on a different commuter van at this point of dispersion, escorted by police vans and turned up at the stadium. They were joined by another hastily organized "players" from a school, Standard High School, Zanna, to make the requisite 11 players and the substitutions. The eight or so players were not renowned members of the first 11 and Akol FC had already been relegated. The hastily organized players were never licensed or registered players for the top league, and no attention was paid to this before the match by the officials. Akol FC was massacred 22 – 1.

Thereafter, the public was enraged, the media gave the league a black-out and the Government, through the Ministry of Education and Sports, and NCS intervened. One of the league sponsors who was rewarding each goal scored in the league a sum of US.\$38, M/s Property Masters Ltd, pulled out of the sponsorship. The Referees Chairman, Mr. Aggrey Kibenge, resigned.

The League Committee met and nullified the game on grounds that Akol FC did not show up at the game, and the game was forfeited to SC Villa with a 2–0 win. The Inquiry Report was released but no action taken to execute its recommendations and therefore no sanctions implemented.

Surprisingly one of the memorable things in this event was the death of the Akol FC goal-keeper who took part in the "nullified" game. He died mysteriously shortly after medication at a heath facility before he could appear at the Inquiry where he was a key witness.

(ii) Express FC Vs Uganda Revenue Authority, URA: Case Study

This match was played before the SC Villa Vs Akol FC match and as provided this 2003 League fiasco one of its endearing visual images: A centre referee pictured kicking at one of the many players he physically fought in that match! The first half had ended 1 – all and when second half restarted, URA took the lead. It was tension – packed, seeing that, it was one of the last games, and the league was in a home straight between SC Villa and Express FC. Express FC equalized to make it 2 – all and then all hell broke loose.

The centre referee gave two undeserved straight red cards to URA players and before this; he had boxed and manhandled the very players he sent off. He then unusually, and perhaps unprecedented anywhere in Association Football Rules jurisdiction, extended the game to have a total time of 120 min only to ensure that Express FC wins. When Express FC scored the third goal, he stopped the match; it ended 3–2. The result stood and was reckoned in the final league standing.

(iii) Express Vs Top TV FC: Case Study

In this case, the coach/Manager of Top TV FC ordered his team off the field upon conceding two suspicious goals from the centre line. This match took place after the Akol FC fiasco, and Express FC had to win to keep pace with SC Villa and/or maintain the competition on goal difference. This was the last game of the season while Villa played Kinyara FC at the same time.

The Top TV FC goal keeper conceded twice from the centre line in the first 20 min, and the Top TV coach forced a walk-off of his team from the field. Express FC had thought of maximizing the situation by scoring many goals against this relegation threatened team. The match was adjudged abandoned and a two goals win given to Express FC. The coach was accused of having made the rare decision to favor SC Villa.

SC Villa won their game 2–0 and the title on goal difference but Express FC blamed Villa for the termination of their match as they would have scored more and beaten Villa to the title.

The dying embers of a once popular league were marked in the 2003 edition with low fans turn-up, increased political wrangling that later culminated into the dissolution of the FA by Government. The culprit referees were sidelined by the FA for some months and curiously, some are still serving and holding FIFA badges.[13]

The coinage of the name "Arrow Boys" was by the Ugandan media; this was solely inspired by the on-going insurgency in the Teso Region of Northern Uganda that had experienced infiltration from the Acholi and Lango Regions

---

[13] Interview with Dhakaba Muhammad, ex referee, 31st October, 2012.

of the brutal armed groups of Lords Resistance Army, LRA, led by Joseph Kony. This armed rebel outfit was gallantly and tenaciously repulsed in the Teso region by hired and organized community vigilantes/militias who were using rudimentary arrows in defending their communities, and they were paid a stipend for this until the regular national army reinforced them.

For their fearlessness, impunity and bravado, the referees involved in this league scandal were only comparable to the "Arrow Boys" referees and the term has since been embedded in Uganda's football lexicon for a derogatory reference.

The Incidence of Corruption in Other Sports Disciplines

As noted before, other big and popular games are afflicted by the match-fixing and corruption scandals, with the only differentiation being the regularity, degree and consequences of their occurrence.

In Amateur Boxing and to some extent international professional bouts organized in Uganda, there are many forms of corruption. An interview with a boxing official revealed the following list:

> 1. Boxing moguls paying money to boxers from opposition Clubs to lose matches or bouts. 2. Boxing moguls creating fake clubs or teams and registering them on the eve of a tournament with a hidden agenda of dominating the tournament. 3. Bribing referees and judges to stop matches on "TKOS" (Technical Knock-Outs) etc... 4. Disqualifying boxers on flimsy grounds. 5. Changing Constitution with the intention of eliminating opponents from vying for the available positions. 6. Undue interference and nepotism in national team selection. 7. Administrators wanting to be the stars of national teams instead of letting the players take the spotlight. 8. Bribing delegates and scribes whenever administrators want to, or after they actually do, push through certain selfish motions and constitutional amendments.[14]

UABF has been bedeviled with endless wrangles just as FUFA has been owing to the aspects of corruption, not only in regard to match-fixing or lack of fair play, but also other financial corruption.

The Secretary of NCS had a general comment of integrity in sport and said: "Integrity loss in sports is a common dilemma in Uganda sports exhibited under practices like match-fixing".[15]

A Senior Sports Tutor, Department of Recreation Games, at Makerere University and the current Secretary General of UOC opined thus on Integrity in Sport.

> This is an issue we tirelessly fight while we train our students in different games and Sports Science. However, it is a big issue that is very difficult to fight both at national and international level. We have instituted rules and regulations that we pass on to our students at Makerere University Sports Science Department. This is because the nature of sports is such that it is very competitive and the more it gets competitive, the higher the chances of employing crude practices to win the game.[16]

---

[14] Interview with Gimugu Kenneth, Boxing Administrator, 2nd November, 2012.

[15] Interview with Jasper Aligaweesa, General Secretary, NCS, 30th October, 2012.

[16] Interview with Penninah Kabenge, 30th October, 2012.

In motor racing, there have been rampant disagreements emanating from unfairness and cheating at motor rallies and closed circuit routes, and this has had, often times seen some drivers retire early or others withdraw or boycott some motor race events. The former Vice President of Federation of Motorsport Clubs in Uganda, FMU, confirmed this:

> There is disquiet about the integrity of results posted by time-marshals during competitive events. Marshalls have been known to post more favourable results of crews that they support.[17]

The lower leagues or competitions have not been spared. In football, match-fixing is rife in second Division, First Division, Big league, and even in the leisure tournaments at the village levels, corruption has permeated.

In Buganda Kingdom, which is the central region of Uganda, the Masaza Cup Competition, organized by the said institution, is usually attended and patronized by throngs of spectators. One investigative sports journalist, observed on their integrity:

> At the Masaza Cup, team managers and officials fix games; they tell players to dive in the box to win penalties or to score goals from off-side positions as the goals would stand thanks to referees.[18]

The game of Cricket, is also bedeviled into forms of match-fixing and corruption. The President of UCA, states them as:

> Influencing the result of a game, giving information about your players or match conditions to bookmakers, corrupting match officials and fixing events during a match.[19]

Another equally popular game, basketball, is reported to experience problems of biased refereeing, match-fixing, favouritism of some clubs exercised by FUBA and corruption during the play-off-stages.[20]

The match-fixing problem has no specific legal framework and no specific regulatory body, other than the Disciplinary Committees, and one of Uganda's respected coaches argues that prosecution in ordinary Courts should be one of the proposals to stop the vice. With regard to the integrity of the coaches or technical personnel, he notes:

> Professional integrity has failed significantly as coaches, through fear or neglect, refuse to take professional decisions. There is lack of self esteem, timidy. Poor revenue and dishonest contracts have significantly influenced decision-making. In a recorded number of instances, coaches have been known to ask for bribes from players to include them on match day team sheets. There is a general deficit of integrity that would require a lot of work, legal structures and career guidance to address.[21]

---

[17] Interview with Oscar Kihika, 7th November, 2012.

[18] Interview with John Vianney Nsimbe, The Observer, 30th October, 2012.

[19] Interview with Richard Mwami, President Uganda Cricket Association, 7th November, 2012.

[20] Interview with Dennis Mbidde, President/Chairman of Falcons Basketball Club, 8th November, 2012.

[21] Interview with Mike Mutebi, former national team coach and SC Villa Manager, 13th November, 2012.

Integrity, Ethics and Disciplinary Bodies of Associations

Invariably every sports Federation/Association has an Integrity, Ethics or as most usually called, a Disciplinary Committee. These bodies and acts serve as the primary enforcers of the rules of the sport. The referees, umpires, judges or match officials are supposed to interpret and ensure that the rules of the sport are abided by on the field of play on the other hand. However, the referee can also be brought on charges by such Disciplinary bodies for what they do on the pitch or off it, just like other sports people, players/athletes or officials.

The statutes of major International Sports Federations/Associations encourage and obligate their affiliate members around the world to incorporate them in their constitutions or legal documents. However, the problem is not their presence in the constitutions or the physical existence of such bodies but the doubt that still lingers about their credibility, strength, reliability and independence. In the midst of match-fixing and corruption, oft-times with the participation of the Association or Disciplinary body members, how can discipline or integrity be kept?!

It is important and desirable that sports governing bodies should jealously guard their rights to govern and control their sport. This is called self-regulation; that is, members of the governing body agree through their membership of the body, to be regulated and sanctioned by that body. This is done in many ways like mediation and arbitration, compliance checks, fines and surcharges, suspensions, etc....[22]

The opening of specialized courts like The Court of Arbitration for Sport (CAS) as an appeal mechanism is welcomed but it will largely remain a far cry for most disputants from sub-Saharan African and other regions with poor sports economies.

These specialized bodies, municipal or international, can only do so much. The State Governments through the national laws have a vital role to play and to assist, and in most cases, take over the cases involving fraud and massive corruption. This is due to the fact that Governments have the facilities, expertise and the sovereignty in the community of nations in case of transnational cooperation to fight crime. INTERPOL is one example of such a medium.

Understanding the Problem and Culture

Innumerable problems exist in Uganda's sports and it can be argued that they are, perhaps, beyond the reach and solution of the Federations/Association. These are national problems to be solved by the State Government.

In February, 2012 in the USL semi-professional football season, 2011/2012, the Uganda Footballers Association organized a nationwide strike over poor pay and the lack of credible FIFA standard contracts for their members. It paralyzed two rounds of the game and most Clubs were caught unaware and terribly affected.

---

[22] Mulema Mukasa Richard; Football Administration Structure in Uganda and the Need for Reforms, 2012.

The FA acted in an incredulous and nonchalant manner. This however, was not the first time it had happened. Previously, there had been players' strikes over poor or delayed pay at the big and popular clubs; SC Villa, Express FC and Kampala City Council (KCC).

Dan Walusimbi, the chairman of UFA says of the current situation:

Players are suppressed upon putting across their grievances; asking for better remuneration is taken to be indiscipline. Players are not empowered, not educated or exposed, they are not motivated. An average pay for a Super League player is about UShs.150,000/= (US.$59=) to U.Shs.200,000/= (US$78=) per month. It is not enough and it comes in arrears.

He goes on:

When it comes to FUFA, it has not done and put much attention to the players. There exists some contracts between players and Clubs but they are not "footballing contracts". The FA has not done much to endorse and supervise these contracts as required by the FIFA standard contracts. The Clubs at times tamper with these contracts, and in most cases the players are not given copies to keep for records.[23]

Football in Uganda is a mass game and is a source of employment for most youths who play in the Regular Leagues. Cricket, basketball and rugby on the other hand, have most of the players engaged in regular jobs elsewhere with playing the sport being more of a pastime. The players in these latter disciplines are more educated and exposed. Boxing is also played on an amateur and professional level in Uganda but is restricted in its outreach.

Sports has unfortunately been affected by the general level of moral degeneration in society such that it is not far fetched to state that it mirrors the endemic corruption at the national level. There is a palpable sense of resignation and apathy to fight corruption by the state and the community, and this has allowed corruption to fester.

However, the ethos and culture of Uganda as a multi-ethnic country, betrays the current spate. The traditional culture bides the people and their societies to be well behaved and abhors cheating or any form of selfishness and greed.

The phenomenon or the new emergent culture of cheating is eloquently espoused in the following excerpt:

Match-fixing/malpractices: This starts at a lower level. You find adults passing weighing tests to play in kids' matches. It is gross and I have seen this throughout my stay in sports training. I was involved in Post Primary Schools competitions in 2000 in Kapchworwa where I saw adults being screened to compete in games and since they are small-bodied, they fit in easily. Some times it is hard to protest this since your own colleagues, district officials and teachers are involved. In 2012 in Mbarara, the under-12 teams in athletics had those from 16 teams compete. Teachers only change bibs. This is brought about by the desire to accumulate points. This business starts at lower levels and treating this cancer should not be reserved for professional players. In 2009, in Gulu, during the National Post-Primary Sports Games, mercenaries were beaten up. So the focus on winning medals, prestige, having money is the root cause of this vice. Coaches want to be known as the "best coach". Cheating is massive in schools at all levels.[24]

---

[23] Interview, 29th October, 2012.

[24] Interview with Charles Mukiibi, Lecturer Department of Sports Science and In-charge Athletics, Kyambogo University, 2nd November, 2012.

Engendering Integrity in Sport Through Education

INTERPOL has placed emphasis on education as a means to achieve their goals in the integrity in sport program. Indeed the training of match officials, technical persons and other stakeholders in sport, is focused on the adherence or following of the rules of the sports discipline. The intensity of the training may differ from region to region or from sport to sport but the common denomination is that players/athletes or the other sports stakeholder are given lessons on "respecting and playing to the rules". The tendency has been that to most sports people these rules are seen as mundane and rite of passage process rather than a means to a fair play end.

There is no particular course unit on integrity aimed at referees. A former football referee states:

> There is no course unit on integrity in sport in the training of a referee but there is emphasis on high integrity as a person because a referee is looked at as someone who is fair in society.

He goes further:

> To qualify as a referee one undertakes a short course, one week, and one has to score at least 75% of the theory: the 17 laws of the game, and the orals. From here you undergo a fitness test which you have to pass. It all however depends on how you apply and interpret the laws in a practical match situation after all the above.[25]

Similar situation can be observed in the other popular games in Uganda. The referees/judges/umpires are hastily trained in those capacities and allowed to past the tests. The out-put has been wanting in many instances and has led to disastrous ends like fan violence, abandonment of matches, protests, boycotts. A leader of a football Fans Association opines:

> The refereeing standards are so low, a referee comes to officiate a match with the sole aim of making a team win or lose at all costs. We have seen many dubious decisions over the years and we highlight them.[26]

In Uganda, today, there are two elite educational institutions that have significant focus on sport as an academic pursuit, and include integrity in sport as a course unit in their academic curriculum and awards. Two interesting and edifying facts can be found in the interviews with the Administrators/Academic staff at these institutions, Kyambogo University and Makerere University.

(i) "This Department originated from another which was called P.E (Physical Education) under then ITEK (Institute of Teacher Education Kyambogo), a teachers' only training institution. That was 10 years ago. It therefore changed the name when we became a university. Originally under ITEK, the motive was to train teachers who would then go and give knowledge to school children to appreciate sports as a leisure activity and how they can better manage their

---

[25] Interview with former referee, Op. Cit, P. 19.

[26] Interview with Yusuf Kasule, President NAFUSO, 31st October, 2012.

leisure time. We then introduced the Bachelor of Science in Sports and Leisure Management. Most of our offerings teach the schools health clubs. We have also a diploma in Sports Management (P.E and Sports Management), a Post Graduate in Sports, Management and Masters in Sports Science".[27]

(ii) "It is not that everyone has studied sports and its moral obligations. Generally, the country is wanting on the issues of morals. There needs to be a complete remolding of the nation in the different sectors so that people can be more responsible. We run a module that covers ethics and responsible behavior in sports (Ethics in Sports Science). We are organizing new programs targeting people in the system and this will operate effectively in the next academic year (2013/2014). This is where people that are already in service and management of sports will be much more welcome to be able to reinvigorate their knowledge on the ever changing trends in sports. We feel we are responsible because we have the expertise; we are part of the problem. Therefore, we are designing programs to have all people enroll and have more avenues of entry to access this knowledge that we disseminate in the programs. We are also working with Sports Associations in the country to ensure that they are delivering quality; we ensure that our input is felt through training and other forums of skilling. In some instances, we participate in awarding Certificates to those who pass set targets in sports. Currently, we run only one program, Bachelor of Sports Science, thus we feel the need to have more programs tailored to suit our target group".[28]

At a national level, the Government put up a full cabinet Ministry of Ethics and Integrity and has its vision stated as: "A well governed and prosperous society that cherishes moral values and principles and the mission." "To coordinate national efforts against corruption and empower Ugandan society to uphold moral values and principles."[29]

This is a herculean mandate placed on this Ministry and many times its impact is not felt but the idea behind its creation is appreciated.

Legal Structure and Nature of Gaming and Sports Betting

Organization of gaming, sports betting gambling and all forms of pool betting in Uganda is seen more as a positive or leisure activity in the entertainment industry than an activity to increase the passion and interest of the population or investors in sports. The latter is the primary reason sports betting is legalized with all the

---

[27] Interview with Charles Mukiibi, Lecturer Department of Sports Science and In-charge Athletics, Kyambogo University, 2nd November, 2012.

[28] Interview with Deogratius Bamweyana, Coordinator of Programmes, Department of Biochemistry and Sports Science, Makerere University, Kampala, 31st October, 2012.

[29] http://mak.ac.ug/prospectus/Science/Bachelor%20of%20sports%20science.pdf. www.dei.go.ug

positive spin-offs in a society.[30] In some countries gaming, pool betting and lotteries are used to create endowment and charity funds to aid the vulnerable, disprivileged and for humanitarian purposes.

Tracing Gambling, Gaming and Betting

In Uganda, as indeed in most societies the world over, games of chance have existed for centuries. This is as old as the human specie itself, and in Uganda, they existed in pre-colonial times. Often times a bet, stake or wager would be put in place for winning upon chances of something happening or not happening. This would be in form of money, article, property or any worthwhile thing. It could be on any event or the African pastimes or games in pre-colonial epoch like running, canoeing, "omweso" (board game), wrestling, hunting, fishing, etc.

With the era of colonialism in Africa, in the nineteenth century, this pastime of games of chance took on a new dimension, as with all other spheres of life, and then transformation is felt to this date in a myriad ways.

Understanding the Legal Regulatory Framework

The law governing sports betting is primarily "The Gaming and Pool Betting (Control and Taxation) Act", Cap 292[31] and this law came into place in 1968. The law is enforced majorly by the Ministry of Finance, Planning and Economic Development. The long title of this Act clearly defines the intention of the law:

> Act to make provision for the licensing of and the imposition of a tax on gaming and pool betting and for other matters incidental thereto and connected therewith.

The key commercial activities the law seeks to regulate are Gaming and Pool betting, and the latter bears relation to sports betting. They are interpreted as follows in Section 1:

> (b) "Gaming" "means the playing of a game of choice for winning in money or money's worth."
> (c) "Pool" "means any competition organized for the gain of the promoter in which for a monetary of other material regard the public are invited to foretell the result of any game, race or event, and includes a pool operated on the system known as a fixed odds betting pool on the result of any such game, race or event."

The licensing is done in three categories; Promoters license, Principal agents license and an Agents license. The latter two mainly being agents. The first category does promotion of gaming and pools within Uganda, the second is aimed at gaming

---

[30] See www.onlinecasinosuite.com/gambling/uganda/

[31] www.ulii.org:ugandalegalinformationinstitute

and pools done outside Uganda, and the third agent's license is for both categories (Sect. 3 of the Act).

This licensing is supposedly the responsibility of the Minister but there is little regulation and the Ministry has to improvise in so many respects. There is no designated regulatory body and regulations made under this antiquated law. The only regulation by Statutory Instrument available touches on taxation of the betting houses since the Government policy and outlook is to take the industry as an economic activity.[32]

Recently, the Government raised the taxes for sports betting from 15 % of the total amount received or of the total amount of bets to 20 % in the financial year 2012/2013.[33] The betting houses had through their body, Uganda Sports Betting Association, petitioned the national Parliament, through the Committee of Finance, Planning and Economic Development, proposing that they pay Value Added Tax (VAT), which is a consumer tax, instead of being charged on each bet or pool of bets. They contended that the current taxation, unless changed, would chase their customers away.[34]

The law makes provision for examination of books of accounts, documents relating to gaming and pools; unauthorized advertising and general offences and sentences in regard to flouting of laws on licensing, taxation, books of accounts, transfer of monies outside Uganda. Other than the regulations on tax referred to above, there are no regulations to govern the other aspects made by the Minister under S.11. The fines are so low, they range from under US.$1 to US.$4.

The law, in its text, is more prohibitive than permissive yet, it is to provide for the legalization and regulation of a commercial activity. Hence, the permitted activity is found more in exceptions, default clauses or the provisions on the Sections than in the purposive parts of the Sections.

The weakness of the law is corroborated by Government functionaries themselves; the Commissioner Tax Policy and member of the Licensing Board says:

> The industry is minimally regulated since we are still running on the old Gaming and Pool Betting Act of 1968, Cap 292, and as such, we do everything we do within the framework of the current law.[35]

Owing to the inadequacy of the law, the Government is using a law of a sister activity, lotteries, to regulate sports betting. This is because there is no standing Board, or for the reason that the Act does not provide for it. The National Lotteries Act[36] provides for the creation of the National Lotteries Board in Sect. 8(b). What is

---

[32] The Gaming and Pool Betting (Control and Taxation) (Gaming and Pool Bets Tax) Order, No. 31/2009.

[33] www.parliament.go.ug/news/images/stories/speeches/budget12.pdf
www.observer.ug/index-php?option=com-content

[34] www.ugpulse.com/uganda-news/.../betting.../2455.aspx

[35] Interview with James Mpeirwe, Ministry of Finance, Planning and Economic Development, 5th November, 2012.

[36] www.ulii.org:ugandalegalinformationinstitute

inescapable though is that, just like the law regarding gaming and pool betting, lotteries are schemes or indulgencies of chance.

The National Lotteries Act is also implemented by the same Ministry as the gaming and pool betting law and this is why, for convenience sake and not out of following the designated law, the Ministry uses the same Board as a regulator for gaming and pool betting. This research has discovered that all complaints of fraud, non-payment by betting houses among others, are handled by this Board.

There is eminent confusion in the regulation of the industry; one administrator with a renowned betting house in Kampala and its environs revealed the following:

> We have been given regulations like opening business at midday every day of the week, not accepting those less than 18 years and having enough security detail at our premises. But these regulations are not practical because there is no law. For example, I do not have to wait for midday to open my premises yet I need to maximize profits. I have heard Uganda Police will put up a monitoring team to effect these regulations but they cannot charge me for any criminality since there are no laws to guide the betting industry yet. We have a regulatory framework under the Ministry of Finance, the Lotteries Board, where we should get a license but they still ask us to register with URA (Uganda Revenue Authority). URA also tells you to go back to the Ministry, or Lotteries Board. This seems a calculated move to limit the business expansion in the country since Government still views it with a negative attitude. It is thought to be creating idleness and lawlessness among the youth. However, if they do not make real by-laws, the regulations are not of any importance.[37]

The Ministry, through the National Lotteries Board or the Commissioner Tax Policy, issued a "Guide for Application for Gambling and Pool Betting License" which is a checklist on what to carry or lodge when applying for a license under the Gambling and Pool Betting (Control and Taxation) Act. This "Guide" has no foundation in the law from which it purports to derive. The powers to regulate reposed on the Minister are to make by-laws in form of Statutory Instruments which is a legally recognized way of legislation but this has not been done save for the Statutory Instrument setting the taxation referred to previously.

In the makeshift Guidelines aforesaid, there are curious ones; requiring the Applicant to "demonstrate experience in gaming and pool betting in the third world", "show responsible gambling measures i.e. protection of vulnerable groups of society like minors against evils of gambling"; "attach serial numbers, makes, origin and proof of certification by recognized gambling standard of the equipment intended to be used". The others are in regard to proof of incorporation, address of business, tax compliance, personal details of directors/shareholders, financial details of the company and its shareholders.

The fact that the Guidelines have no force of law and are at the whim of the Board, Ministry or its Commissioner, compounds the fact that they cannot be respected and/or enforced. Refusal to grant the licence, on basis of these Guidelines can also result in a successful legal challenge in Courts of judicature.

---

[37] Interview with Administrator of a Betting House, 31st October, 2012.

The Parliament of Uganda has realized the paucity of an effective legislation and there is clamoring for introduction of a robust and definitive law. At the time of this study, there was no White Paper or Proposed Bill in place.[38]

In neighbouring Kenya, the regulation is more harmonized and the supervision clearly delineated by the law. This will be discussed latter.

It is worth noting that the current law comes short in light of the increased activity of online betting and cyber crime.

Consumerism and the Advent of Televised Foreign Sports

In the last decade of the twentieth century, there was increased and unprecedented interest in foreign professional sports activity in Uganda. This coincided with global changes in the realm of Information, Communication and Technology. The outreach of television, particularly the broadcast rights all over the globe, helped to bring hitherto rare sports tournaments into people's living rooms or the nearest make-shift video halls in the trading centers on a regular basis. This is the continuing trend in all emergent urban settlements.

This was also at the time most leagues were gaining semi-autonomy from their FAs so as to maximize the commercial rights of their leagues by selling broadcast rights to mega broadcasting companies.

Previously, foreign sports interest was seasonal and mainly felt amongst the urban population save for the football World Cup Olympics and Continental Sports Championships.

Uganda's population is mainly a youthful population like in all countries in Sub-Saharan Africa. The youths have been known to copy and adapt to new inventions and cultures quite easily. The effect of globalization has not spared them. Therefore, there is consumption of sports culture from more successful countries in Europe, the Americas and Asia. This has given birth to a new foreign sports urban culture and sport betting on foreign sports has festered as a consequence.

Organised Sports Betting and Outreach

Sports betting of any nature in Uganda is as a result and a function of the inadequate laws that govern these activities. They are liable to exploitation by all manner of persons with different motives, good or bad, and herein lays the hotbed for corruption and criminal activity allied to sports betting.

Sports betting companies in Uganda are spread throughout all major urban centers and in doing this they have had to adapt to the socio-economic conditions of the population. Given the popularity of the sports activities especially football, boxing,

---

[38] http://www.ugpulse.com/uganda-news/sports/mps-want-sports-betting

motor racing, this has aided its growth. The convenience brought about by the betting houses taking the smallest bets as low as less than US.$1 has also done them no harm. It is a lucrative business.[39]

Foreign football leagues have ruled the roost for most betting houses, that is the Premier League, the UEFA Champions League, the Europe League, the African Cup of Nations, Copa America, Eastern European Leagues, the other top leagues in Europe (France, Italy, Spain, Germany etc. The reason for this is that they have organized a consistent scheduling of matches. They are also popular to the punters because they are presumed to be more secure and free in terms of match-fixing and they provide better odds and money. The business is so brisk and gainful, and it is manifested that on a good day, according to a reliable source interviewed for this study, a betting house UEFA earns a net profit of US.$40,000 = on a Champions League football night.[40]

People of different shades of life are engaged in sports betting and they harbor different perspectives, some of them presented below.

(i) "I actively engage in betting. Depending on how much I have to pay for a bet, I will always wish to maximize my opportunity to get a win. Normally, I will go for several bets. On average, the bets I have taken are at US.$3. Some times you win sometimes you lose so you have to take risks like any other business. People claim that those in sports betting are idlers, but that is not a hundred percent true".[41]

(ii) "I like sports betting. I have lost some money before but I also won UShs.500,000/= (US.$200=) in one bet. If they were to start taking bets on our local football games, only U.Shs.2,000,000/= (US.$800=) would be enough for a goalkeeper to give away goals and this is very little money for the sports betting houses yet our players are paid only a small portion of that. Our local game would be gone".[42]

(iii) "I switched from the Ugandan based sports betting houses to international ones because when you would win a bet of U.Shs.6,000,000/= (US.$2,400=), it would take another 4 days to get your money just because the betting house does not have money and would take days. For the international betting houses online, like bwin, it is automatic, there and then".[43]

However, despite the fervour and enthusiasm of sports betting, stakes and/or odds have not been placed on Ugandan games. A former sports betting executive explains why.

---

[39] www.newvision.co.ug/news/635744-sports-betting-firms-milking-ugandans-dry-html/
www.observer.ug/index.php?option=com-contentview=article
www.theceomagazine-ug.com/oped/perspective/sports-betting-a

[40] Interview with Protected source, 25th October, 2012.

[41] Interview with Jemenze Joseph, University student, 2nd November, 2012.

[42] Interview with a Sowedi Kayondo, 13th October, 2012.

[43] Protected Source, interview 31st October, 2012.

The game in Uganda is very disorganized, there is no good management at FA level, club level and the league. It is a mixture of a pastime with little semblance of business. The professionalism is lacking in the game. The clubs lack financial muscle to pay and maintain players yet players are most vulnerable and susceptible to being compromised.[44]

The country's top tier management, USL, confirms that they have not heard of any incident of sports betting based on their league but they dread the time it will happen as they do not have the capacity to tackle it and the past incidences of match-fixing will fuel it. The former Chief Executive Officer of USL avers:

Our economy here is that not many homes or people can afford pay-TV, satellite television, but sports lovers go to video halls and I saw at these video halls in suburbs our USL games being advertised along with foreign games on the notice boards. Therein lays the fertile ground for betting to crip into the USL games. The USL Board has urged that we be fore-sighted and see how we can nip it in the bud so as not to destabilize the game.[45]

However, sports betting is alive and thriving in Uganda bringing with it many social problems and the main outreach is the sports fan. The vice present an umbrella football fans body states:

With the poverty looming in the community coupled with passion for the game, sports betting is an avenue to earn from it. This is why it is highlighted.[46]

Foreign Ownership of the Betting House

The law on gaming and pool betting, and the liberalized market structure of the Ugandan economy allows foreign capital investment in Uganda.

The study of the Ministry of Finance, Planning and Development, that is charged with powers to supervise this industry, reveals that there are about 20 registered betting companies and most of them are foreign owned. The reason advanced is that it requires huge investment given its risks and no average Ugandan may deal in such a venture. The upper and middle level work personnel at most betting houses is foreign and recruited from Europe and Asia where the industry is thriving.

Organised sports betting in Uganda is a foreign influence and the increased investment in this by foreigners is hinged on liberalization of economic markets, globalization and the consumerism that the Ugandan market has exhibited towards foreign based businesses and cultures. No doubt then that the Government has viewed this gold-rush market with purely commercial lenses. A retired FIFA Referee observes:

Government is looking at betting as tax revenue opportunity other than an avenue for ero-sion of moral fabric in society. It is a big risk to the youth that are unemployed. It engages the productive youths into unproductive activities and the total output of this is trouble.

---

[44] Interview with Joseph Kigozi, former administrator of a Betting House, 26th October, 2012.

[45] Interview with Jimmy Ssegawa, Ebil, CEO USL (2011–2012) 26th October, 2012.

[46] Interview with Patrick J. Kalungi, 31st October, 2012.

Betting is not a positive form of leisure or even expressing passion for the game. Instead, if it were an expression of passion, then we can form cheer clubs. This is positive since it engages an individual on the match and even energizes him or her.[47]

The fact that majority of betting houses in Uganda are foreign owned, mainly having tentacles in Europe, and are more regulated and with a more informed and activist society, means that global conventions and controls can bear upon them, and indirectly any outward and negative ramifications of their activities can be brought into check.

Money Laundering and Criminal Gangs

Money laundering is the process by which proceeds from a criminal activity are disguised to conceal their illicit origin. It is evident that regulation in gaming and betting is wanting, and people who are criminally minded can very possibly, if they have not done so already, use this lawful commercial activity to cleanse their dirty money.

Two appraisal study reports on Uganda, and the neighbouring region, give a grim picture about the lack of laws and institutional structures to combat money laundering. In August 2007, the Eastern and Southern Africa Anti-Money Laundering group made a detailed Assessment Report on "Anti-Money Laundering and Combating the Financing of Terrorism" about Uganda. It observed that:

There have been some efforts especially by the Ministry of Finance and the Bank of Uganda to facilitate putting in place an AML/CFT (Anti-Money Laundering/Combating the Financing of Terrorism) regime, although much more work is required to meet international standards. Uganda has been, and still is, the victim of domestic terrorism. As a result of Uganda's geographic position, it is also susceptible to being used as a transit point for funds and resources that may be used to destabilize Central African countries and perpetuate war in these areas. Arms trafficking involving Somalia, Southern Sudan and Eastern Democratic Republic of Congo (DRC) is prevalent. Human trafficking (including children) and smuggling (including protected species) are significant components of the cross-border criminal activity, which sometimes use Uganda as a transit stage. Drug trafficking is also emerging as a major problem.[48]

Another joint Report made in 2009 by the Institute for Security Studies (ISS), Cape Town and Peace and Security Institute of Africa (PSIA), Kampala, noted the following:

Money laundering (ML) is a serious problem in Uganda, yet the population remains largely ignorant of the fact or the impending dangers incident to it. This situation is made worse by the fact that ML is not recognized as an offence by law and those who know and understand it believe it should be left to thrive as it provides an avenue for development for both the individual and the state, which is largely a wrong theory as the dangers of ML as this Report

[47] Interview with Muhmed T. Ssegonga, retired referee and Chairman Referees Committee, 7th November, 2012.

[48] www.esaamlg.org/userfiles/UGANDA-MER1.pdf

will indicate, are more grave than the benefits that may accrue there from. By its very nature ML is concealed and may be hard to detect. The existence of ML in Uganda is therefore indicated by the incidence of offences predicate to it.

The Report notes further in regard to the regional regulation and observance:

Uganda is a founder member of the Eastern and Southern Africa Anti-Money Laundering Group (ESAAMLG). Re-cognizing the danger posed by money laundering and predicate activities, the members of ESAAMLG agreed and committed themselves in 1999 to enact AML Legislation in each of their respective member states as part of efforts to combat ML in the region. Several member states including Botswana, Zimbabwe, Tanzania, Namibia and Lesotho have fulfilled their obligations. However, Uganda and Kenya still lag behind in fulfilling this commitment.[49]

Uganda embarked on that road of enacting a law in 2002; the Anti-Money Laundering Bill, and the law has gone through many series but the edition of 2009; Bill No. 13 of 2009 was last tabled in Parliament on 10th April, 2012.[50] It however remains unpassed to this date. It seeks among other venues, to criminalize money laundering and to create two bodies; the Anti-Money Laundering Committee and the Finance Intelligence Authority.

The Uganda Police, another vital partner in fighting of sports betting related crime, has identified the problem but only in respect to crimes concerning idleness of youths, consumption of drugs and excessive alcohol, public order, affray, breaches of peace, assault and murder among others. It should be understood that the Police Force faces a multitude of problems touching capacity, professionalism, sophistica-tion, corruption, human resource, logistics, financial and expertise to tackle crimes associated with transnational money laundering and criminal gangs especially so when the laws are non-existent or weak.

The Police Spokesperson made the following comment on sports betting:

We treat sports betting like any other activity in the country. Not all people go for sports betting, and therefore, there is need to consider both parties; the goers and non-goers in our dispensation of security services. Some of those individuals that go for betting have other motives; to commit crime. The meeting we held in July, 2012 was to identify how we can better mobilize them to be security conscious so that their places are not places for organi-zation of crime. Some time back a manager of a betting company was killed in cold blood. This means that some people come to these places with criminal minds.[51]

Further, in Kampala which is the hotbed of sports betting in Uganda, and where licensed or unlicensed sports betting houses have their headquarters, the Commandant of Kampala Metropolitan Police, noted the emergent problems and lamented the lack of good laws:

We were compelled to meet the sports betting companies after receiving several complaints from the community. We therefore came up with some guidelines since the law is yet to be enacted to regularize betting and gaming apart from the gambling law, there is no other legal instrument that governs betting. The public was concerned about the age of children

---

[49] www.psiafrica.org/index.php?option=com-docman&task

[50] www.observer.ug/index.php?option=com-content&view=articl

[51] Interview with Judith Nabakooba, 31st October, 2012.

in betting, the amount one has to have. They were also encouraging house wives to bet since some could allow betting at a fee of UShs.500/= (less than a dollar). School children were betting their school fees. We also ensured that minimum operational capital is established since companies do not have enough money while others cheat their clients. All this cannot be policed and regularized because there is no effective law.[52]

Studies have shown that crimes associated with money laundering are increasing and with the surge of sports betting business in Uganda, and East Africa, it is probable that sports betting is a conduit. Their effect on the field of play and therefore the integrity of the local games is however not yet reported but it will occur when the game is better administered. The ESAALG Report observed further:

Acquisitive crime has shown a sharp rise in recent years. Duty fraud and smuggling are estimated to be of a scale that is causing serious loss of revenue to the Ugandan authorities and the size and frequency of these crimes suggest that they are undertaken by organized crime groups. Generally, the proceeds of these crimes, and corruption, are being expended on land, buildings, houses, cars, shops and other forms of businesses which are used to disguise the origins of criminal proceeds.

It notes further:

Uganda is a largely cash based economy. Only a small proportion of the population has bank accounts and the percentage having insurance policies or owning securities is even lower. As a result, the absence of effective AML/CFT controls in the formal financial sector gives rise to a major vulnerability in practice. (The CFT position is harder to access). However, there are plans for the development of the economy which would lead to more transactions being effected through the formal financial sector. The use of cash for transactions within the country and across the borders remains a significant risk area. Uganda shillings are accepted as "legal" tender in neighboring countries such as Southern Sudan, Rwanda and Eastern DRC. This encourages cross-border movement of cash and increases Uganda's vulnerability to AML/CFT.[53]

The Dawn of Information, Communication and Technology

Previously, it has been shown that in the last two decades the incidence of Information, Communication and Technology (ICT) has exponentially grown, not only in Uganda but, in the entire Sub-Saharan Africa. It was further demystified and engendered by the deep penetration of mobile telephony whose outreach is at the village community grassroots.

Sports betting in Uganda takes place online in addition to the on sport or over-the-counter transactions. This makes it even more accessible by the sports betting firms after the introduction of mobile phone betting which has popularized the activity. There are also virtual betting machines. This study revealed the following:

---

[52] Interview with Andrew Felix Kaweesi, 31st October, 2012.
[53] Ibid. P 34.

> There are so many games up for betting. These include international soccer games. We rarely deal in local matches since people are not so passionate about them. Others are horse racing, dog racing. These are controlled by our IT technicians. Of course people complain that these games in particular are not fair but they always come back to give it another try. But we have tried to explain to them that betting is all about luck.[54]

The information age has also kept the sports fans and punters updated about the sports results, news, and status of the sports events and players they are interested in or have placed bets on. Television, internet and other forms of communication have helped maintain the passion and suspense about the subject of bets. The nature of the betting requires information and electronic broadcast, most especially radio has weighed in to render support. Sports betting firms have sponsored programs on the ratio, television and newspapers about the odds. For example, there is a weekly sports newspaper, The Octopus, that publishes the bets the odds and analytical opinions by pundits.[55]

The advent of ICT has led to Uganda's premier league, USL, clinching a television broadcast deal with Super sport to telecast league games all over Africa and the environs. This has been in place since the 2011/2012 season and is set to continue for another 4 years in the broadcast contract of 5 years worth US.$5,000,000=. The stakes and interest in the league will continue and it will be left to the administrators to manage this interest and the looming possibility of sports betting companies and the likelihood of their effect on integrity of the game.

There is a need to be knowledgeable about the facts before bets are placed. A betting operator states:

> Different items are up for staking and these include: wins, draws, overs (when you predict that your team will score above say, 2 goals); unders (the opposite of overs), free kicks, half time (extra time or no time allotted to the match at hand). The winner claims for their cash within 60 days.[56]

Subsequently, The Government enacted a raft of laws to move in parity with the ICT age but their adherence, enforcement and purview is lacking and should be improved. These laws are; the Computer Misuse Act, No. 2 of 2011; The Electronic Signature Act, 2010; The Electronic Media Act, Cap 104; The Uganda Communications Act, Cap 106 and The Electronic Transactions Act, No. 8 of 2011.

However, in Uganda, little or no attention is paid to the law when commercial transactions involving ICT are being done. With an obsolete law governing gaming and betting the situation is conducive for illegal sports betting and associated negative practices of money laundering and criminal gangs.

---

[54] Interview with a Sports Betting operator, 2nd November, 2012.

[55] www.octopus.co.ug

[56] Ibid. P 36.

Regional Reflections

In the larger East African region, the socio-economic situation and the way sport is practiced, is not different from Uganda. It is largely amateurish with pockets of semi-professionalism and professionalism. Football or soccer still remains the most popular sport.

There is a correlation between corruption in society in general and the way football administration and management is.

The Case of East Africa (Uganda, Kenya, Tanzania, Burundi and Rwanda)

The said countries are part of a regional economic block, known as the East African Community, that was re-established in 1999 under the East African Community Treaty. The said community has a Parliament and makes laws.[57]

According to the most recent East African Bribery Index released in August, 2012 by Transparency International, the region's statistics are worrying. This Index is a governance tool developed to measure bribery levels in the private and public sectors in the region.

The Index reports:

> Bribery prevalence in Kenya remains high as the country moved from fourth place recorded in 2011 to third in the 2012 East African Bribery Index (EABI) with an aggregate index value of 29.5% up from the 28.8% recorded last year. Uganda registered the highest bribery levels in the region with a value of 40.7%. Burundi, the worst ranked country in 2011, recorded a significantly lower index of 18.8% down from 37% recorded last year. Tanzania recorded 39.1% respectively while Rwanda remains the least bribery-prone country in the region with an aggregate index of 2.5%.[58]

The region, it should be understood, has some of the poorest human living conditions in the world and is underdeveloped. The region's corruption statistics are largely a microcosm of the wider Sub-Saharan region where most countries feature as some of the poorest countries in the world.

This study has discovered that sports betting is prevalent in all the five East African countries with the most business in Kenya, Uganda and Tanzania, and in the countries of Rwanda and Burundi being a nascent industry. Regulation of sports betting in all the countries is poor and not up to speed with the contemporary sophistication to prevent abuse and most especially its effect on the integrity of sport.

Kenya has a more expansive legislation that has been updated by amendments over the years. The law, The Betting, Lotteries and Gaming Act, Cap. 131, was

---

[57] www.eac.int

[58] www.transparency.org/news/pressrelease/the-east-afrucab-bribery-index-2012-bribery-levels-remains-high-in-kenya

passed in 1966 and establishes the Betting Control and Licensing Board. The law is more elaborate than the Ugandan counterpart. In Uganda, licenses are given to private businesses to run lotteries yet such businesses should have been granted gaming licenses. Lotteries are mainly for raising of public funds for charity and not private gain.

Uganda has become the epicentre of sports betting in the region given that the laws are lax and the process of setting up the business are not elaborate and involve less scrutiny by the Governmental bodies. An interview with a former sports betting employee reveals that most foreign based businessmen set up shop first in Uganda and then roll out in the region. Kenya is most difficult to get a license, and with the betting operator he worked with, it took them close to 2 years to get one there yet in Uganda, it was a matter of months.

Tanzania and Kenya have put in place anti-money laundering legislations but Rwanda, Uganda and Burundi are yet to do so.[59]

These countries have a regional body, CECAFA, that brings them together and holds a number of football competitions for the senior teams, under-age competitions, and club competitions. Over the years, there have been reports of match-fixing and corruption in these competitions.

The respective FAs and leagues in these countries have also had their fair share of football administration wrangles and corruption related instances that continue to undermine the integrity of sport. Uganda, Kenya and Tanzania football leagues have television broadcast contracts and are shown all over Africa.

Confederation of African Football, (CAF) "Home Match Win" Syndrome

On the continental scene, there has been a consistent play out of incidences of match-fixing and corruption. This has been manifested especially in the qualifying matches to the final editions of the African Cup of Nations, the youth tournaments, women's championships, and also in the Club Championships.

The organizing Federation, CAF, has not however taken bold steps to stamp out these forms of corruption. They are mainly felt through refereeing decisions, fixture making, boardroom decisions over petitions made to CAF, age-cheating in under-age youth tournaments, seeding system for qualifying of groups for tournaments and hosting, and remuneration of referees for CAF fixtures, etc.

In CAF organized activities, especially in round-robin fixtures, a certain type of culture evolved, which spread around the African Continent, which make people believe that a home team in such a format of schedules has to win a game at its home at all costs. This has unfortunately become the raison d'etre for the organization of

---

[59] www.afronline.org/?p=9222

the tournaments in such format. It has been gravely abused as these three examples involving Uganda attest:

(i) Nigeria Vs Uganda, Abekouta, Nigeria, March, 2007, AFCON 2008 Qualifier
Nigeria was leading 1–0 at home against Uganda. Uganda equalized in injury time of second half through what was a genuine goal but the goal was controversially disallowed by Senegalese centre referee, Badara Diatta. Surprisingly, the Nigeria players were ready to restart the game having thought it was a legitimate equalizer. No action was taken by CAF and instead he went ahead to officiate the Africa Cup of Nations final of 2012 edition.

(ii) Uganda Vs Congo Brazaville, Kampala, Uganda, June 2012, AFCON 2012 Qualifier
The centre referee for this game, Moroccan El Ahrach Bouchaib, made so many controversial decisions in favor of the home team to help them beat their opponents 4–0. He looked biased and his decisions left many players and officials of Congo Brazaville and the neutrals wondering.[60]

(iii) Uganda Vs Nigeria, Kampala, Uganda 2007, AFCON 2008 Qualifier:
Nigeria was leading Uganda by a single goal at half time and in the second half, the centre referee awarded two dubious quick penalty spots to Uganda to lead and win the game 2–1.

CAF has a standing system where match officials are taken care of by the home Federation, their accommodation, entertainment and relaxation, allowances, travel within the home country is also footed by the host Federation. There is also a culture engrained in the people that it is okay to bribe the referee or match officials, be it for local or international games.[61]

Accordingly, the host federation pulls out all the stops to see that the game is won at whatever expense literally. It becomes a case of pay high and win your home game in CAF competitions.

Recently, in October, 2011, the home football fraternity was blaming the FA for not bribing the Kenyan officials and players, or the match officials, for Uganda to beat Kenya and qualify for AFCON 2012. Ditto, in the last edition of the USL season, 2011/2012, Express FC fans wanted, and put pressure on their officials to bribe Bidco FC's officials and players, to throw their last match of the season against Express FC such that the latter wins the title. This was after Express FC had drawn with Bunamwaya FC in the penultimate game yet Express FC needed a win in that game to win the title.

In 2010, Uganda was disqualified by CAF from the Under-19 Africa Championship qualifiers after it used over-age players in this competition against Zambia in the two legs. This illuminates a problem in Africa that is also common in South America. The Ugandan ex-referee and journalist who disclosed this to the world states:

---

[60] http://observer.ug/index.php?option=com-content-andvrew=article4id=19344:robertmadoi

[61] Interview with John Vianney Nsimbe, op.cit P. 21.

> I wrote to CAF as a whistle-blower raising many issues including referee match-fixing and use of over-age players. The whistle-blowing was out of the fact that the team had so many players in advanced stages of their careers, some were at final years at University, some were married with families, many had altered their passports, birth certificates, others had played in the top league for an average of four seasons and it was impossible in the Ugandan setting to be Under 19 years.[62]

The selection of players for the national teams is fraught with lots of problems ranging from favoritism by the technical benches of Federation officials to some players paying their way to get into the team. This is a recipe for match-fixing and possibly a fertile ground for involvement in sports betting illegal schemes.[63]

One of Uganda's foremost referee at FIFA level, now retired opines:

> Ethics is a reflection of the wider society; therefore, everything in Uganda is part of this society. Corruption therefore is not a unique practice to sports alone. It is the impact of the wider society that influences affairs in the sports industry than vice versa. It therefore takes an incorruptible personal character to refuse and say no to any forms of advances brought in one's way. Your personal character is your own defender. It is what people think of you that forms basis for their perception towards you. I am such a person, I have never allowed these temptations to come near me and therefore the entire sports fraternity knows me for this character. We have had such allegations of some referees accepting favors and this is a routine thing.[64]

On the "Home Match Win" syndrome, John Vianney Nsimbe, observes about the problem:

> CAF has not done enough to protect the foundations of the game in regard to fair play, and that has been hidden in the pretext that home teams have to always win home games. This has led to subjugation of visiting teams. This is an unwritten rule in CAF competitions based on home-and-away format. It has affected the integrity of the game.

The Zimbabwe "Asiagate" Scandal

Between the years 2007 and 2010 Zimbabwe's FA ZIFA sent their senior national team on a friendly tour in Asia to pay against national sides, Malaysia, Thailand, and Singapore. In one of these matches, ZIFA dispatched a club side, Monomotapa United FC, as a guise for the national team to pay Malaysia's national team. The Zimbabwean national team lost all these matches in circumstances that led to credible suspicions that they were part of match-fixing and betting syndicates with Asian criminal organizations.

---

[62] Interview with Dhakaba Muhammad; Ibid. P. 19.

[63] Interview with Daniel Walusimbi; Ibid. P. 23.

[64] Interview with Muhmed T. Ssegonga, Op. cit P. 32 webmail.observer.ug/index.php?option=com-content&view=article&id=13565.tobcA-madix-african-refereeing-could-do-with-moresegongas&catid=44.spc

Players admitted to taking money to throw matches and they were paid ranging between US.$500 and US.$1,500, and that US.$50,000=could have been paid for each of the matches fixed. This scam involved officials within ZIFA, and the technical team. It led to the purge within ZIFA and suspension of over 80 players and officials. The Zimbabwean Parliament has also intervened.[65]

This depicts the depth the football game can sink into when crooked football administrators get involved with betting syndicates to organize tour matches. It happens a lot in Africa when national FAs, usually with the help of international football agents, organize such dubious friendly matches. The desire to expose the players to such countries and the money on offer are usually a good stimulus to the FAs, and consciously or unconsciously, they fall prey.

The Zimbabwean Asiagate scandal is still unfinished, as that the players and officials banned in the scandal would like to appeal, in whatever forum, the sentences passed by ZIFA. They range from life bans, to bans of 6 months to 10 years from football.[66]

"Friendly Tour Matches" Outside the Region

There is a spate of activity in recent times involving top Ugandan Clubs, Villa SC, Express FC and KCC in which they are invited to tournaments in South East Asia, especially Vietnam, to play friendly matches on tour. They are meant, according to what is known to the public, to help the Ugandan Clubs to market their players for possible transfer to Vietnamese Clubs and also for the clubs to make money. The expenses of travel and accommodation are majorly met by the hosts.

In the past 3 or 4 years these top teams have gone on tour, controversy has brewed over the fact that some teams have left without authorization by the FA, they have included players from other clubs, have left in the middle of the league causing rescheduling, some players have been improperly transferred to Vietnamese clubs, disagreements within tour agents, some players staying over in Vietnam inexplicably after end of tours, etc.[67]

The existence of, an increased stimuli and vigour in such tournaments, if not well managed and supervised by football authorities, can present problems of match-fixing and corruption as the Zimbabwe "Asiagate" scandal. All the trappings of what can go wrong are all already apparent.

The interview with a FUFA official revealed that they are aware that the problem of match-fixing exists but, it is mainly amongst players and officials. In the mind of

---

[65] en.wikipedia.org/wiki/Asiagate
    http://www.voazimbabwe.com/content/zimbabwes-parliamentary-com
    http://www.guardian.co.uk/world/2012/feb/01/zimbabwe-footballers-

[66] www.newzimbabwe.com/sports-9496-FIFA warns Rushway'aOhidzambwa/sports.aspx

[67] en2eastafrica.net/uganda-vek-alliance-returns-to-fight-illegal-players—transfer/

FUFA, they believe that the game in Uganda has not reached the level of sponsoring match-fixing because the betting operators do not have the money.[68]

This study established, based on an account from one of the heads of the Clubs in Uganda attending these Asian tours, that the trips are meant to market their players and offer the clubs a commercial platform from which to build a good financial base in the changing times in which football is run as a business and owing to the fact that the Eastern African region is lagging behind.[69]

Sports betting, if well regulated in the world and in Africa where commercial investment in the game is lacking, can be a vital pillar in many respects. A football administrator opines:

> Sports betting is a modern way of attracting fans and sponsorship to the game, and is welcome in that respect because it generates interest and passion. It however has to be managed and controlled so as not to affect the integrity and fair play of the game.[70]

Conclusion and Recommendations

Numerous ways of containment, prevention and eradication of match-fixing and corruption have been put forward in this chapter. Sports betting and all its associated negative impacts, actual or likely, on the integrity of sports and avenues of how they can be surmounted in Uganda and the neighboring countries, have also been addressed by this author.

Based on the research and analysis presented in this chapter, the following measures are proposed:

(i) There is an urgent need to strengthen the regulatory framework by which far reaching laws on gaming, pool betting, lotteries are handled in a single legislation. This will involve lobbying Government to amend or better still, overhaul the obtaining lax laws.

(ii) Making the institutional framework of the FAs more credible, independent and competent especially, the Ethics & Disciplinary Committees, since they handle day-to-day issues of match-fixing and corruption involving players, clubs, officials, referees, etc. The court of Arbitration for Sport, CAS, has to be decentralized to continents on even regions to make it accessible.

(iii) Formation of Steering Committees, Monitoring or Action Committees within the regional inter-government football bodies like CECAFA, COSAFA, etc., in which to run the INTERPOL programs of training, education and prevention.

(iv) Enactment of laws at economic integration or cooperation level, for example, SADC, COMESA, ECOWAS, EAC to achieve transnational treaties or

---

[68] Interview with James Kalibbala, 6th November, 2012.

[69] Interview with Fred Muwema, Chairman/President SC Villa, 12th November, 2012.

[70] Interview with Julius Kavuma Kabenge, Chairman, USL, 13th November, 2012.

conventions to tackle sports betting related crimes especially money laundering, match-fixing and corruption, criminal gangs.

(v) Increased linkages between domestic police and the FA. This should not stop at stemming hooliganism at football events. The FAs security committees should take note.

(vi) Heighten the incorporation of sports betting related offences in the FIFA and FA statutes with stringent sanctions to players, officials, referees and other participants for whom the FA have jurisdiction.

(vii) Encouragement and creation of sports activist movements at a national and regional level. These private Non-Governmental Organizations will act as watch-dogs that critique and blow the whistle, if necessary, on match-fixing and corruption, e.g. Transparency International and those that exist in Western Europe.

(viii) Creation of Independent Governance Committees to engender transparency and good governance. They act as a self-cleaning and watch-over body on the exercise or abuse of power by office holders at FAs. The creation of such a body at FIFA recently should trickle down to FAs in Africa whose leadership is non-accountable and dictatorial. There is a correlation between bad governance and corruption, and this has exacerbated the problem, for example the "Asiagate" scandal in Zimbabwe.

(ix) Raising awareness amongst, training and education with Fans Cubs, Club Managers/Coaches Associations, Players Associations, Sports Betting Associations and other such sports related groups.

(x) Development and support of an academic curriculum for use by Academic institutions offering sports courses like universities and colleges.

(xi) INTERPOL should render technical and educational support to national police forces in detection, investigation and prevention of sports betting related crime.

(xii) Monitoring sports betting through financial transactions of the punters and the operators. No bet should be placed or taken unless such person has financial records that can be identified through bank records or any ICT platform.

(xiii) Establishment of Sports Betting Operators/Sports Associations' Forums to increase in which dialogue and understanding of issues of concern. This has worked out in cases of where sports betting firms sponsor sports activities and clubs, and it should work out as well in curbing the problems at hand.

Acknowledgments This chapter has been prepared for presentation at the Plenary Session of the Interpol Global Academic Experts Meeting for Integrity In Sport, Singapore, 2012, and its research was made possible further to this global campaigns to strengthen integrity in sport.

I am heartily thankful for the opportunity to be part of this. I am grateful as well to Mr. Allan Kyobe Ssempebwa, for the help extended in conducting some of the interviews that greatly enriched this study.

List of Acronyms

AFCON	Africa Cup of Nations
CAS	Court of Arbitration for Sport
CAF	Confederation of African Football
CECAFA	Council of East and Central African Football Associations
CESAFA	Council of Southern Africa Football Associations
COMESA	Common Market for Eastern and Southern Africa
EAC	East African Community
ECOWAS	Economic Community of West African States
ESAAMLG	Eastern and Southern African Anti-Money Laundering Group
FA	Football Association
FIFA	Federation of International Football Associations
FIBA	Federation of International Basketball Associations
FMU	Federation of Motorsport Clubs in Uganda
FUBA	Federation of Uganda Basketball Associations
FUFA	Federation of Uganda Football Associations
IAAF	International Association of Athletics Federations
ICC	International Cricket Council
IOC	International Olympic Committee
ITF	International Tennis Federation
NAFUSO	The National Association of Friends of Ugandan Soccer
NCS	National Council of Sports
NUFFA	National Union of Football Fans Associations
SADC	Southern African Development Community
UABF	Uganda Amateur Boxing Federation
UCA	Uganda Cricket Association
UFA	Uganda Footballers Association
UOC	Uganda Olympic Committee
USL	Uganda Super League
ZIFA	Zimbabwe Football Association

Appendix: Interviews Carried Out with Different Persons/Institutions

1. Jimmy Ssegawa Ebil, former Secretary Firemasters Football Club Ltd., former Chief Executive Officer, USL; 26th October, 2012
2. Joseph Kigozi, former Public Relations Officer, Sports Betting Africa and Sports Journalist, 26th October, 2012
3. Daniel Walusimbi, Chairman, Uganda Footballers Association, 29th October, 2012
4. John Vianney Nsimbe, Investigative Sports Journalist, The Observer Newspaper, 30th October, 2012.

5. Patrick J. Kalungi, Vice President, NUFFA, 31st October, 2012
6. Yusuf Kasule, President NAFUSO, 31st October, 2012
7. Dhakaba Muhammad, retired Referee and Sports Journalist, 31st October, 2012
8. Kayondo Sowedi, active punter/betting participant, 13th October, 2012
9. Jasper Aligaweesa, General Secretary, NCS, 30th October, 2012
10. Penninah Kabenge, General Secretary, UOC and Senior Sports Tutor, Department of Recreation and Games, Makerere University, 30th October, 2012
11. Judith Nabakooba, Uganda Police Spokesperson, 31st October, 2012.
12. Andrew Felix Kaweesi, Commandant Kampala Metropolitan Police, 31st October, 2012.
13. Jemenze Joseph, University Student/Active Punter, 2nd November, 2012
14. Charles Mukiibi, Lecturer, Department of Sports Science, Kyambogo University, 2nd November, 2012.
15. James Kalibbala, Administrator, FUFA, 2nd November, 2012
16. James Mpeirwe, Commissioner Tax Policy/Member, Lotteries Board, 5th November, 2012.
17. Muhmed T. Ssgonga, retired FIFA Referee, former Chairman Referees Committee, 7th November, 2012
18. Oscar Kihika, former Vice President of FMU, 7th November, 2012
19. Protected Source, former Club Official, 26th October, 2012
20. Gimugu Kenneth, Boxing Administrator, 2nd November, 2012
21. Deogratius Bamweyana, Coordinator of Programmes, Department of Brochemistry and Sports Science, Makerere University, 31st October, 2012
22. Protected Source; Administrator of a Betting House, 31st October, 2012
23. Mike Mutebi, Manager, SC Villa, 13th November, 2012
24. Julius Kavuma Kabenge, Chairman USL, 13th November, 2012
25. Dennis Mbidde, Chairman/President, Falcons Basketball Club, 8th November, 2012
26. Fred Muwema, Chairman/President, SC Villa, 12th November, 2012
27. Protected Source, Sports Betting Operator, 2nd November, 2012
28. Richard Mwami, President, Uganda Cricket Association, 7th November, 2012
29. Protected Source, former Betting Operator, 25th October, 2012

References

Anonymous, Interview with former club official, 26th October, 2012
Bryan A. Garner, Black's Law Dictionary, Eighth Edition. en2eastafrica.net/uganda-vek-alliance-returns-to-fight-illegal-players—transfer, retrieved, June 2, 2013.
http://mak.ac.ug/prospectus/Science/Bachelor%20of%20sports%20science.pdf. www.dei.go.ug, retrieved, May 24, 2013.
Iris, University of Safford (Manchester) (2012, Cabinet Praxes-Advocates, CCLS (Universite' de Pekin), Sports Betting and Corruption: How to Preserve the Integrity of Sport.
Mukasa, M. (2012). Football Administration Structures in Uganda and the Need for Reforms; Field Notes.

The Gaming and Pool Betting (Control and Taxation) (Gaming and Pool Bets Tax) Order, No. 31/2009.

The Observer report, Op. Cit, p .7. http://observer.ug/index.php?option=com-content-andvrew=ar ticle4id=19344:robertmadoi, retrieved, May 25, 2013.

www.interpol.com/News-and-media/Speeches, retrieved, May 25, 2013.

www.observer.ug/index-php?option=com-content&view=article&id=4316%3Ahb-ziwa-22-1win over-akol- retrieved, May 26, 2013.

www.transparency.org/topic/detail/sport, retrieved, May 24, 2013.

www.worldbank.org/country/uganda, retrieved, May 25, 2013.

www.worldbank.org/en/country/uganda/overview, retrieved, May 25, 2013.

www.worldbank.org/en/country/uganda/overview,retrieved, May 25, 2013.

www.moibrahimfoundation.org/uganda, retrieved, May 25, 2013.

www.onlinecasinosuite.com/gambling/uganda/, retrieved June 2, 2013

www.ulii.org:ugandalegalinformationinstitute, retrieved June 2, 2013.

www.parliament.go.ug/news/images/stories/speeches/budget12.pdf, retrieved, June 2, 2013.

www.observer.ug/index-php?option=com-content, retrieved June 2nd, 2013.

www.ugpulse.com/uganda-news/.../betting.../2455.aspx, retrieved, June 2, 2013.

www.esaamlg.org/userfiles/UGANDA-MER1.pdf, retrieved, June 2, 2013.

www.octopus.co.ug, retrieved, June 2, 2013.

wikipedia.org/wiki/Asiagate, retrieved, June 2, 2013.

www.voazimbabwe.com/content/zimbabwes-parliamentary.com, retrieved, May 25, 2013.

www.guardian.co.uk/world/2012/feb/01/zimbabwe-footballers, retrieved, May 25, 2013.

www.newzimbabwe.com/sports-9496-FIFA warns Rushway'aOhidzambwa/sports.aspx, retrieved, May 25, 2013.

Further Reading

Corruption: How to Preserve the Integrity of Sport.

Eastern and Southern Africa Anti-Money Laundering Group, ESAAMLG Report, 2007; Anti-Money Laundering and Combating the Financing of Terrorism, Republic of Uganda.

Electronic Media Act, Cap 104

Electronic Transactions Act, No. 8 of 2011

FIFA Standard Cooperation Agreement

FIFA Statutes, July 2012

IRIS, University of Salford (Manchester) and CCLS (Universite de Pekin) 2012; Sports Betting and Corruption: How to Preserve the Integrity of Sport.

Institute for Security Studies (ISS), Cape Town & Peace and Security Institute of Africa (PSIA), Kampala, Report, 2009; Report of the Anti-Money Laundering Workshop, Imperial Resort Beach Hotel, Entebbe, 14th – 16th December, 2009.

Mulema Mukasa Richard, 2012: Football Administration Structures in Uganda and The Need for Reforms.

The Anti-Money Laundering Bill, No. 13 of 2009.

The Betting, Lotteries and Gaming Act, Cap 131 (Kenya)

The Electronic Signature Act, 2010

The Gaming and Pool Betting (Control and Taxation) Act, Cap. 292

The Gaming and Pool Betting (Control and Taxation) (Gaming and Pool Bets Tax) Order, 2009

The National Council of Sports Act, Cap. 48

The National Lotteries Act, Cap. 191

Uganda Communication Act, Cap 106

Bryan A. Garner, Black's Law Dictionary, Eighth Edition

Ministry of Finance, Planning and Economic Development: Guide for Application for Gaming and Pool Betting Licence.

It Is Just Not Cricket

Hanif Qureshi and Arvind Verma

Abstract The game of cricket now stands tarnished by betting and fixing match outcomes through corrupt practices. Star players and club officials are involved and there is evidence of major matches, even during the World Cup being compromised. The spread of illegal betting in cricket has expanded with the advent of technology. Internet based betting sites coupled with unregulated nature of betting in Asian economies, particularly India, has facilitated growth of illegal gambling. This has encouraged the entry of underworld crime syndicates to manipulate games and outcomes for massive gambling profits. The result has been major corruption scandals and questions about the sports itself. This paper describes the betting phenomenon and some major incidents associated with the growing corruption in cricket. The policy responses of major cricket playing nations are presented, along with suggestions for strategies to be adopted to curb corruption in cricket.

Introduction

The prevalence of game of chance dates back to ancient times in India. There are references to gambling and betting in folklore and religious scriptures. In fact, gambling using dice to play on checkerboard was the starting point of the great mythological war depicted in the epic Mahabharata, dating back to 1500 BCE. During the

H. Qureshi (✉)
School of Criminal Justice, University of Cincinnati,
665 Dyer Hall, 2600 Clifton Avenue, Cincinnati, OH 45221, USA
e-mail: hanifq@gmail.com

A. Verma
Department of Criminal Justice, Indiana University -Bloomington,
307 Sycamore Hall, Bloomington, IN 47405, USA
e-mail: averma1978@gmail.com

M.R. Haberfeld and D. Sheehan (eds.), *Match-Fixing in International Sports:*
Existing Processes, Law Enforcement, and Prevention Strategies,
DOI 10.1007/978-3-319-02582-7_4, © Springer International Publishing Switzerland 2013

medieval period, when much of India was ruled by a succession of Islamic dynasties, gambling, along with drinking, was officially proscribed, in keeping with the requirements of S*haria* (Islamic law), which prohibits *maisir* (monetary gains from chance or speculation). Yet gambling remained ubiquitous, and was especially popular in the Mughal court. Babur, the founder of the Mughal Empire in India, is believed to have introduced *ganjifa* (a precursor to poker). Aurangzeb, the sixth Mughal, appointed *muhtasaibs* (censors of public morals) to suppress public passion for gambling and alcohol consumption without much lasting effect. In modern times, betting is widespread in both rural and urban areas in India, with activity increasing around the time of festivals, particularly, Diwali. Organized crime syndicates operating 'matka' a form of gambling based on selecting numbers from a set has also been going on for decades. Mumbai based mafia has been known to be behind these bets placed around the country with large sums involved. Horse racing has been another form of gambling attracting the rich but has been limited to few selected metropolitan cities only. Though betting takes place in many sports, for instance in soccer in Europe, in India, it has primarily affected cricket. This too has emerged in the last three decades when the shorter form of One Day International (ODI) cricket matches became more popular, especially after traditional rivals – India versus Pakistan matches attracted millions of viewers and fans.

The Game of Cricket

Cricket is a bat and ball game played between two teams each with 11 players. Each team takes turns to bat, during which it tries to make as many runs as possible. This is followed by role reversal: the team bowling gets to bat and vice versa. The traditional game was played over 5 days and was called a test match. However, many new versions of the game have been introduced over the years including One Day International (ODI) matches, T-20 and the like. Evidence suggests cricket was played in England as early as the twelfth century. In 1744, the London Cricket Club produced what are recognizably the rules of modern cricket. The game underwent major development in the eighteenth century and became the national sport of England. Betting played a major part in that development with rich patrons forming their own "select XIs". The first official international match was played between Canada and United States, at New York, September 24–25, in the 1844 (Lewis 1987).

The International Cricket Council [ICC], which has ten full members and six associate members controls cricket. The ten major cricket-playing nations are Australia, Bangladesh, England, India, New Zealand, Pakistan, South Africa, Sri Lanka, West Indies and Zimbabwe. However, the South Asian diaspora settled in South America and Pacific islands play cricket making it popular and visible in these regions. Cricket leagues have sprung up in the US too with heavy participation by diaspora of these cricketing nations. All together, there are currently 96 cricket-playing nations in the world and some like Canada, Ireland, Kenya and the Netherlands even sending teams to the World Cup.

Cricket is played on an oval grassy field, which has a 'pitch' at the center. The pitch is a flat rectangular area, about 3.3 yards across and 22 yards long, with short grass. At both end of the pitch are placed wooden targets, known as the wickets. The batsmen stand in front of the wickets facing the bowler who throws the ball towards the batsman facing him. The batsman tries to prevent the ball from hitting the wicket by striking the ball with a bat. If the ball is hit so hard that it crosses the boundary before any fielder can catch it the batsman gets four or six runs (or points), otherwise the batsmen would run between the wickets and try to score as many runs as possible before the ball is returned to the bowler. Any one of the several ways can dismiss the batsmen such as clean bold (ball hits the wickets), leg before wicket (LBW) [ball hitting the leg obstructing the wicket], or catch out etc. The first innings will continue as long as ten players have been dismissed (in a test match), or when the prescribed number of 'overs' (a group of six throws of the ball by a bowler) has been bowled (in ODIs and limited over matches). There are other ways to dismiss a batsman such as run out, stumped, hit wicket etc.

A cricket match is divided into periods called *innings*. It is decided before the match whether each team will have either one innings or two innings each. During an innings one team *fields* and the other *bats*. The two teams switch between fielding and batting after each innings. All 11 members of the fielding team take the field, but only two members of the batting team (two batsmen) are on the field at any given time. Once an entire team is dismissed, the team bowling would bat next and the one bowling would take to batting. The team scoring the maximum number of runs is declared the winner (www.cricket-rules.com).

There are many uncertainties, which can affect the outcome of the game, apart from the performance or strength of the teams. For example, a team may have an advantage batting first innings based on the condition of the pitch. A toss of the coin by the umpire decides which team plays first and this introduces an element of chance in the game. The rules of cricket only specify the size of the pitch and the field and ground. Pitch and outfield variations can have a significant effect on how the ball behaves and challenges the players. The firmness of the pitch including size of the grass affects the bounce, spin and seam movement that the bowler can exploit. Hard pitches are generally considered good to bat because of high but even bounce of the ball. Damp pitches allow good fast bowlers to extract extra bounce and help fast bowlers throughout the match, but become better for batting as the ground dries and the surface begins to crack. Thus climatic conditions can also significantly affect the play. These physical variations create a distinctive set of playing conditions at each ground. There are grounds known to be friendly to the batsmen and some known to be bowler friendly. Due to these factors cricket is sometimes called a game of chance and it is not unusual for weaker teams to defeat stronger ones due to many of the uncertainties of pitches, balls and even the weather. Further, cricket has been described as a game of 'gentlemen' and sticking by the rules, not disputing the decision of umpire and playing fairly were considered its hallmarks. Playing by the rules implied that winning was always based on stronger performance that prevailed over uncertainties. This was very attractive to the millions of followers and helped make cricket the major sport in the Commonwealth nations. However, these uncertainties proved a bonanza to the gamblers who exploited the outcomes through insider information, corrupt players and by compromising the rules. Illegal betting took roots through factors causing uncertainty and has been exploited by the bookies in collusion with players and officials including umpires (Rediff.com, 2000).

In India, cricket players are superstars and almost treated as Gods. The game has been glamorized through association with the Mumbai based glitzy world of Bollywood and advertisement commercials featuring cricket players. The marriage of leading cricket players with Bollywood superstars further enhanced this relationship. This was exemplified as early as 1969 by the romance and the subsequent marriage of the Indian captain Mansur Ali Khan, 'Nawab of Pataudi', with Bollywood actress Sharmila Tagore. The trend has continued with another Indian captain Mohammad Azharuddin marrying actress Sangeeta Bijlani. Constant gossip about affairs between players and actresses has been the staple themes in popular magazines, further expanding the fan base of the game.

Political parties too courted cricket players for their ability to attract crowds. Some players even cashed their visibility and popularity to enter politics. Mohammad Azharuddin won the Indian national elections in 2009 from Moradabad to become a Member of Parliament (MP). Navjot Sidhu, a prominent Indian opening batsman was elected to the Indian parliament from Amritsar in 2004. Imran Khan, the Pakistan captain is the president of the Tahrik-e-Insaf party, which put up an impressive show in the recent national elections in Pakistan. Sanath Jayasuria and Hashan Tillakaratne, the Sri Lankan batsmen were elected MP in Sri Lanka. Kirti Azad (India) has been another player who is now a prominent politician. Most such cases seem to be in the South Asian region; however, there are some examples elsewhere. For instance, Sir Frank Worrell (West Indies), a renowned batsman and the first black captain of the West Indies, became a senator in Jamaica. Joe Darling, Australia's captain at the turn of the twentieth century, sat for 25 years in the Tasmanian Legislative Council (Martain 2006).

Betting in Cricket

Although betting on cricket matches existed on a small scale before 1983, betting by organized groups, started only after India's triumph in the 1983 Cricket World Cup. It became more organized, and a number of bookies started operating in major metropolitan cities of India. Several series played between India and Pakistan at Sharjah, in particular, provided the opening for crime syndicates to make an entry. In particular, Dawood Ibrahim and his gang played a major role in hosting players and organizing lavish parties to celebrate with players and Bollywood stars (Burke et al. 1999). The mass adulation by millions in India and Pakistan provided the opportunities and large sums to bet on these games. Soon, players and organizers were involved to fix games and outcomes that could provide lucrative profits to the crime syndicates.

By early 1990s, betting on cricket had spread across India and had become quite sophisticated. Typically, a bookie needed a telephone connection, a television set, a notebook and a clientele who were known to the bookie through various contacts to start his business. The punter is a person who places a bet with a bookie. All transactions were effected by word of mouth. For example, if a punter wants to place his bets on a particular match, he will call up his bookie over telephone, find out the odds, and place his bets for a particular amount. No money is required at this time and the punter's bet is entered by the bookie in his notebook. After the conclusion of the match, the bet is settled by exchange of money (Burke et al. 1999). The written records are typically destroyed.

Match fixing is a term used to denote many different activities including

(i) Instances where an individual player or group of players received money individually/collectively to underperform. The Pakistani team reportedly took large sum to lose to the weak Bangladesh in the world cup held in England in 1999.

(ii) Instances where a player accepted bets in matches in which he played that would naturally undermine his performance. Three players from Pakistan took money to bowl no balls at a specific moment in a match between Pakistan and England that led to the conviction of these three players.

(iii) Instances where players or club officials passed on information to a betting syndicate about team composition, probable result, pitch conditions, weather, etc. A senior official of Chennai IPL T-20 team recently shared his insider information with bookies to earn huge sums of money.

(iv) Instances where grounds men were given money to prepare a pitch in a way that suited the betting syndicates.

(v) Instances of current and ex-players being used by bookies to gain access to other players to influence their performances for a monetary consideration. Former Indian captain Azharuddin was charged for conspiring to lose a match by prevailing upon some of the team members.

Indeed, betting includes any activity meant to alter the performance of a game using deceit or cheating.

Some Major Corruption Cases

In one of the major scandals relating to betting in the cricketing world in 2010, the International Cricket Council (ICC) prosecuted the Pakistan cricket team's captain, Salman Butt, and opening bowlers Mohammad Amir and Mohammad Asif. They were offered money by an Indian bookmaker who had taken $230,000 from an undercover reporter posing as a fixer. Subsequently, the players bowled 'no balls' as asked by the bookie at a particular time of the game. The Pakistan team lost the game by a heavy margin. Criminal charges for conspiracy were brought against the Pakistan players under the Prevention of Corruption Act 1906, Criminal Law Act 1977 and Gambling Act 2005. Contravention of the first two Acts carried a maximum penalty of 7 years' imprisonment and contravention of the Gambling Act carried a maximum sentence of 2 years imprisonment. Evidence was produced in the form of information from secret recordings and text messages from the undercover sting. The ICC tribunal found the players guilty of corruption based on undisputed video and telephonic evidence. Salman Butt received a 10-year ban from playing cricket, out of which 5 years were suspended on the conditions that he does not breach the ICC code of conduct again and participates in anti-corruption education Gardiner (2013). Mohammad Asif received a 7-year ban from cricket out of which 2 years were suspended on the same conditions as the sentence given to Salman Butt, and Mohammad Amir received a 5-year ban (Mahyera 2012).

In sentencing the defendants, Mr. Justice Cooke held:

> It is the insidious effect of your actions on professional cricket and the followers of it which make the offences so serious. The image and integrity of what was once a game, but is now a business is damaged in the eyes of all, including the many youngsters who regarded three of you as heroes and would have given their eye teeth to play at the levels and with the skill that you had. You procured the bowling of three no balls for money, to the detriment of your national cricket team, with the object of enabling others to cheat at gambling. (Mahyera 2012)

Another major case pertains to the South African Captain Hansie Cronje, who confessed to providing match-fixing information to an Indian bookmaker to rig a match for money (The Economist 2000). Wessel Johannes "Hansie" Cronje was the captain of the South African Cricket team during much of the 1990s. The Kings Commission enquiry indicted him and he was banned for life from playing international cricket. An investigation by the Delhi Police (India) revealed that Cronje was in league with Sanjay Chawla, an Indian bookmaker based in London, and together they planned match fixing. In 2000, Delhi Police charged four South Africans, including skipper Hansie Cronje, for fixing the One-Day International (ODI) series against India. Herschel Gibbs, Pieter Strydom and Nicky Boje were also alleged to have taken money to underperform and thus fixing the match to lose. The phone transcripts indicated passing of information as to who will be playing and who will not be playing and other information. Cronje later confessed to having been involved in illegal betting since 1995 and admitted to receiving around $140,000 from bookmakers (Howe 2000).

Not only cricket players but umpires have also been involved in allegations of match fixing and spot fixing. A sting operation by a local Indian television channel claimed to have exposed umpires involved in match fixing, including two Pakistanis, a Bangladeshi and three Sri Lankans in 2012. As a follow up, the Bangladesh Cricket Board (BCB) formed a three-member commission to examine the state of fixing T20 matches through umpires, as revealed by the sting operation. The umpire in question, Nadir Shah was banned for 10 years after he was found guilty. The International Council of Cricket dropped Pakistan umpire Asad Rauf from the Champions Trophy (2013) of UK after it became known that the Indian police were probing the Pakistani umpire for spot fixing. Similarly, the Pakistan Cricket Board suspended international umpire Nadeem Ghauri for 4 years for agreeing to "extend undue favours for material gain" (The Financial Daily 2013).

Although these major scandals involved Pakistani and South African players, players from other major cricketing nations have been involved too. Two of Australia's greatest cricketers – bowler Shane Warne and batsman Mark Waugh – have been involved in a betting scandal as confirmed by the Australian Cricket Board. The Board fined Waugh and Warne for providing information to an Indian bookmaker called 'John the bookmaker' during Australia's tour of Sri Lanka in 1994. It is believed both players admitted having supplied the bookmaker with information about match conditions and possible team selection. Unofficial accounts put the amount received by them anywhere from $2,500 to $15,000 (Howe 2000). India is, however, at the center of the illegal betting industry of cricket worldwide and also the main market for international 5 day, 1 day, Twenty20 and the latest IPL matches.

Reasons for Growth of Illegal Betting

Betting Procedure

The odds for a particular match are decided among bookies based on certain accepted criteria such as the relative strength of the two opposing teams, previous record, pitch and weather conditions, team composition, etc. After these odds have been decided upon, primarily by bookies based in Mumbai, Dubai or London, they are transmitted telephonically to bookies in different parts and betting starts. The punters place bets with concerned bookies over the telephone and the money is exchanged later on.

The whole betting procedure is a very flexible system in which odds keep changing during the course of the match depending on how the match is progressing and the punter can conclude and place fresh bets according to his judgement. Bookies transmit these odds by telephone to different parts of India and the punters place bets with concerned bookies over telephone. If a punter wins his bet, he would get $1.2 or $1.4 for each dollar he placed on the bet depending upon the odds offered by the bookie. The bookies are constantly in touch with actual players through agents and contact persons. They ensure that the match turn out in such a manner that no loss is caused to bookies, The odds which keep fluctuating as the match progresses, are transmitted to the bookies throughout India by mobile phone, pager or other communication medium (Bag and Saha 2011).

The premier investigation agency of India, the Central Bureau of Investigation (CBI), investigated match fixing in cricket and related malpractices in 2000. It uncovered the unholy nexus of punters, bookies and leading players of the day including Azharuddin, Nayan Mongia, Ajay Jadeja and Manoj Prabhakar among others. The CBI report revealed Mumbai as the hub of the betting in cricket in India. It observed that the 'odds' on which bets were placed in any match throughout India were determined by the bookies based in Bombay [Mumbai]. Further, it also observed that Bombay remained the base around which all betting operations in

India revolve (CBI Report, Oct 2000). Some of the CBI's most severe strictures were reserved for the Board of Cricket Control in India [BCCI], the governing body and a powerful organization. The CBI did not find the direct involvement of any of the members of the BCCI in match fixing, but there was evidence to suggest that it failed to supervise the cricket administration and allowed the massive betting to go unchecked.

Betting on cricket is today perhaps the biggest organized racket in India. According to rough estimates, the turnover for a 1-day match in any part of the world, which is being telecast in India, is to the tune of Rupees hundreds of crores ($20 millions) (Shears and Whiting 1998). One reason for the growth of this racket is the relatively liberal provisions of the Public Gambling Act, 1867. The ingredients and punishments under this Act differ from state to state within India. It is even debatable whether betting on cricket attracts provisions of this Act, since cricket theoretically is a game of skill. This is a particular legal provision for the public Gambling Act of 1867 section 12 stipulates that the "Act not to apply to certain games.-Nothing in the foregoing provisions of this Act contained shall be held to apply to any game of mere skill wherever played". The maximum punishments under the Act also vary from state to state. For instance, in Delhi, for a first offense, the imprisonment is for 6 months and a fine of Rs 1,000 ($20) and for subsequent offences the imprisonment is for 1 year and fine up to Rs. 2,000 ($40). For the bookies who deal in much larger volumes, this amount of fine is no deterrent.

The Influence of Bollywood

Lalit Modi, the Vice President of the BCCI, introduced a new form of cricket in 2008. This was called the Indian Premier League, or the IPL. This resulted in business deals with global media giants such as Walt Disney Pictures and ESPN sponsoring and telecasting the live matches (Upadhyay & Singh 2010). The revenue of BCCI increased sevenfold between 2005 and 2008 (Wade 2008). The IPL has been compared to the US Super Bowl with regard to size of advertizing as well as audiences. At present, Bollywood stars own three IPL franchises, or three teams (Kings XI Punjab, Rajasthan Royals, and Kolkata Knight Riders). Industrialists Mukesh Ambani of Reliance Industries, Vijay Mallya of United Brewery (UB) Group, N. Sirinivasan of India Cements, G.M. Rao of GMR Group, and Kochi Cricket Private Limited own five teams (Mumbai Indians, Royal Challengers Bangalore, Chennai Super Kings, Delhi Daredevils, and Kochi Tuskers Kerala), respectively. Influential media groups the Deccan Chronicle and Sahara India Pariwar own the remaining two teams (Deccan Chargers and Pune Warriors).

In 2010, ten players signed contracts with various IPL teams each for about US$1 million for a 5-week season. The IPL format is also popular among sports channels. For instance, before the start of third edition of the IPL in 2010, the Indian Cricket Board made US $1.75 billion by selling broadcast rights. Involvement of big money, the film industry, and celebrity consortiums has turned the IPL into a trendsetter in the world of cricket, and its brand value is estimated to be more than US $2 billion (Rasul 2011).

This offers a significant opportunity for Bollywood stars and entrepreneurs to invest in the IPL. Bollywood heartthrob Katrina Kaif and Deepika Padukone are brand ambassadors for Royal Challengers Bangalore; Kareena Kapoor and Anil Kapoor (of the 'Slumdog Millionaire' fame) for Mumbai Indians, and Akshay Kumar for the Delhi Daredevils. The Kings XI Punjab team was bought for US $76 million for 10 years by Bollywood actress Preity Zinta and Ness Wadia of Bombay Dyeing. For the fourth IPL season, Shah Rukh Khan created a music video with music diva Shakeera to promote his team. The cricket-Bollywood association has become a powerful mechanism for marketing products and producing enormous profits.

However, connections with Bollywood have also given rise to flow of illegal money and possible link to crime syndicates, operating chiefly in Mumbai. Prakash Chandanani, a film producer of Bollywood was arrested by Ahmadabad immigration cell in April 2012, after he landed from Dubai. Chandanani, who is a major bookie and handles Chhota Shakeel's (underworld mafia leader) betting syndicate, had purposely landed in Ahmadabad to evade arrest. However, he did not know that once LOC (Look out Circular) is issued, it is circulated to all international and domestic airports. He was charged with diverting the cricket betting money into Bollywood (S Ahmad Ali 2013). The police had arrested Kothari and Jalan in May 2012, who revealed that Chandanani and Abhichandani were the key players in the international cricket-betting racket. Chandanani and Abhichandani are well-known figure in Bollywood parties who shuttle between Mumbai and Dubai. During the course of investigations police had learnt that many Bollywood personalities paid money through a hawala operator (illegal money transfer) after they lost the bets in the IPL. They have also been linked to Chhota Shakeel though this has not been proved as a fact.

The betting however has not stopped even after multiple high profile arrests. Recently, in May 2013, Delhi Police Special Cell arrested cricketer S. Sreesanth, Ankeet Chavan and Ajit Chandila on charges of spot fixing. Seven bookies were also arrested in the major operation launched by the Delhi Police. A bookie Ramesh Vyas held the key to unraveling of this 'spot fixing' scandal. The fixing was managed from Dubai and had connections ranging from Karachi to Ahmadabad. The cricketers were booked under sections of cheating and criminal conspiracy (120B, 420 Indian Penal Code). The initial interrogation revealed that the parts of IPL matches at Mohali and Mumbai were fixed. Delhi Police commissioner stated that the police had hundreds of hours of recordings of phone conversations between the players and bookies, 14 of whom have also been arrested. The players received up to Rs 60 lakh ($110,000) for one over for giving away runs as per arrangements with bookies with underworld connections overseas (Business Line, Chennai, May 18, 2013). The investigation revealed that the bookies gave these players specific approval codes which were used to signify a compromised over during the matches. The bookies gave players instructions to communicate that they would give away these runs. The instructions were 'put the towel in your trousers', 'take time setting up the field', or, 'take out the shirt or the vests that you are wearing'. For instance, in one match- Rajasthan Royals versus Pune Warriors on May 5, 2013, the player Chandila gave 14 runs in the second over of his spell but he forgot to give the predetermined signal due to which the bookies could not bet in this match. This led to an argument and demands for return of money, all recorded by the police on their phone tapping devices.

The corrupting influence of money, glamor and media publicity has seriously affected the cricket players who have also entered the world of sleaze. The Rajasthan Royal trio of fixers induced the players through women. Transcripts of their monitored calls show that these players requisitioned the girls or availed escort services by the bookies eager to entice their prize catches in illegality. Sreesanth was in the company of three women when he was arrested outside Mumbai's RG Disco, as per police records (Hindustan Times, Mumbai, May 20, 2013). It is alleged that the bookies belong to D Company, an organized criminal gang headed by the wanted terrorist Dawood Ibrahim having operations across South Asia, but chiefly in India, Pakistan and Dubai. It is involved in arms trafficking, contract killing, counterfeiting, drug trafficking, extortion, cricket betting and terrorism. The group is responsible for the 1993 bombings in Mumbai, which killed 257 people. The U.S. designated Dawood Ibrahim as a Specially Designated Global Terrorist (SDGT) in late 2003. He is also suspected of allowing Al Qaeda to use his smuggling routes to escape Afghanistan (Burke et al. 1999). At times, the D-Company has been linked to the Bollywood film industry, as well as real estate and cricket betting businesses, from which it is said to derive considerable revenue.

The arrest of Bollywood actor Vindoo Dara Singh, the son of the Great Indian Wrestler Dara Singh, in May 2013, has further exposed the deep connection of Bollywood with illegal betting in cricket (The Economic Times 2013). The investigations show that the illegal betting is not only at a lower level, but is spread to highest levels of cricket administration and owners of IPL cricket teams. The arrest of Gurunath Meiyappan, the owner of Chennai Super Kings team takes the involvement in illegal betting right up to the top level of ownership of the teams (The Hindustan Times, May 23, 2013). It is believed that these two acted as middlemen between teams, bookies and celebrities.

The linking of cricket betting with organized crime syndicates is an ominous development, which not only involves money laundering, but also involves terrorism and violent crimes (Chandravarkar 2013). It is widely believed that Pakistan-based underworld don Dawood Ibrahim's brother Anees Ibrahim runs the entire betting syndicate through its fronts. Prominent among them are Sunil Abhichandani (recently arrested) and Suresh Nagri.

Weak Preventive Efforts by Cricket Administrators

Illegal betting has got entrenched in cricket due to the weak administration provided by the governing bodies. At the International level, the International Cricket Council (ICC) governs cricket. With 106 member countries, ICC is responsible for the organization and governance of cricket's major international tournaments, notably, the World Cup. It has set up the ICC code of conduct, which sets professional standards of discipline. The ICC takes action against corruption, and 'match fixing' through the

'Anti-Corruption and Security Unit' (ACSU). This unit investigated the cases of the South African captain Hansie Cronje and that of the Indian captain Mohammad Azharuddin and Ajay Jadeja.

The ICC revised its code of conduct in 2000 after the Hansie Cronje episode. The code is focused on investigation, education and prevention. Any attempts at fixing, or otherwise improperly influencing the result, progress, Conduct, or any other aspect of any international match or ICC event is deemed violative. If ICC alleges that an offense has been committed, the ICC Code of Conduct Commission appoints three members to form the anti-corruption tribunal, which determines whether an offense has been committed. During the pendency of the investigation, the ACSU can provisionally suspend players suspected of betting or corruption.

Once the ICC determines that an offense has been committed; it can impose two kinds of sanctions. The first is a ban on playing international cricket from 2 years to a lifetime ban. The second type of sanction is the imposition of a fine that can go up to the value of the reward received by the player in relation to the offense committed. The exact nature of the punishment depends on the seriousness of the offense as in whether only betting was involved or it was a wider corruption case.

However, even after the change in rules and strengthening of the code of conduct, instances of match fixing and betting are fairly common. The ICC banned Maurice Odumbe, Kenya's cricket captain for 5 years when it found that he received money from bookmakers in 2004. Similarly, Marlon Samuels (West Indies) was banned for 2 years from playing cricket when he was found guilty of communicating match-related information to an Indian bookie. Policing cricket is not easy and illegal betting and match fixing continue to plague the sport. Moreover, ICC does not have the sophistication to investigate vast transfers of money behind the scenes and develop insider intelligence. It can only ban players and members, but has no jurisdiction over the general population, which includes bookmakers and agents who are hidden from public view.

Influx of Black Money

Most betting takes place using telephones and through word of mouth. The high liquidity in the betting markets enables large amounts of money to enter the system without attracting attention and hence a reduced threat of being monitored by the intelligence agencies or banks. Asian markets, especially India, have large parallel economies and betting markets provide a suitable mechanism to channel them. There are ample choices for the illegal money to inflow from low yield matches to high stake international matches like the IPL.

Hawala system is often used to channel these transactions. Hawala is an alternative remittance system that exists parallel to traditional banking or financial channels (Dougherty 2006). Money is transferred via a network of Hawala brokers, or *hawaladars*. It is the transfer of money based upon trusted references. Money is given at one end to a Hawala operators who informs his counterpart in another part of the world to pay the amount without going through the banking system.

No receipts are kept and the transactions can be conducted in any currency. The system is used to facilitate money laundering, avoid taxation, and move wealth anonymously. The movement of money in illegal betting in cricket is suspected of using the Hawala route. Mumbai Police arrested one Hawala operator Alpesh Patel along with actor Vindoo Dara Singh in connection with betting mafia in the ongoing IPL. Over one crore rupees (US \$200,000) was recovered from Patel, who acted as a conduit in money transfers between India and Dubai.

Decentralization of Betting

In the past there used to be a few large bookies based in Mumbai or Delhi. The more common scenario is now bettors or punters using odds comparison services available online. This has made the bettors significant as compared to the bookies. Although big bookies still exist and transact large volumes, the growth in small bettors spread across large areas is significant. The increase in the use of mobile phones and the Internet has increased the reach of bettors even to distant rural areas.

The spread on the betting community has also given rise to spot fixing. As opposed to match fixing, where the outcome of the match is at stake, in spot fixing bets can be placed on almost all small events of the game. For instance, one could place a bet on the number of 'runs' in an 'over', or whether a player would make ten runs and the like. Live betting, facilitated by new technology favors spot fixing and appears to have become more popular than match fixing. For instance, the investigation in the Hansie Cronje affair revealed that batsmen had been paid not to score beyond a specified number of 'runs', and bowlers paid to allow batsmen to score more than a predetermined number.

Emergence of Online Betting

Betting or gambling is illegal in most of India, but there is no law that makes online gambling an illegal activity. One of the advisory websites indiatablet.com claims that they do not take bets but help their clients contact international online book makers. The question of whether it is legal to bet from India using an international bookmaker is not very clear in law. While bookmaking in India is illegal, there is no specific law in India, which bans an individual customer from placing an online bet with a bookmaker based outside India. It is difficult to catch internet gambling offenders if the websites are hosted by servers located in countries where betting is legal. Enforcing the act is a tough job if the servers are located offshore. Goa and Sikkim are two states, which have allowed regulated online betting. In March 2009, the Government of Sikkim issued a memorandum known as Sikkim Online Gaming (Regulation) Rules, 2009. This outlines the rules and regulations for online gambling licensing within that state. The Internet has made it easy for anyone to bet online. For instance, one website (cricketbetting.com) brings the latest news and has guidelines on how to bet. It has inputs on international leagues, IPL and hosts many resources, which are available to its users to learn about betting.

Limitations of Laws Governing Gambling in India

The Board of Control for Cricket in India (BCCI) is the national governing body for cricket in India. It is not only the richest sporting body in India, but also the richest cricket body in the world with revenues of US$ 160 million in 2010–2011. Apart from the regular 5 day and 1 day matches, the BCCI has recently established the Indian Premier League (IPL) in limited overs and the Twenty20 cricket matches. It is similar to the major professional leagues such as the English Premier League. The elections of BCCI office bearers have remained controversial with the Supreme Court of India directing the election of office bearers under the supervision of a former Election commissioner in November 2005. The IPL consists of nine teams comprising the best cricket players from around the world. It was the first sporting event ever to be broadcast live on YouTube, and its brand value was estimated at US$ 2.99 billion in its fifth season (India Business Insight Feb 20, 2010). However, it has been dogged by allegations of money laundering, betting and match fixing on several occasions.

Gambling in India is prohibited through the Public Gambling Act of 1867. The Act does not address betting in sports per se but prohibits all kinds of bets or gambling in general. The Act prohibits both public gambling and the "keeping of common gaming-houses." A common gaming-house is described as any house, walled enclosure, room or place in which cards, dice, tables, or other instruments of gaming are kept or used for the profit or gain of the person owning, occupying, using or keeping such house, enclosure, room or place. Prohibition on gaming-houses, on its face, prohibits activities such as card games and typical casino-style games, or games that depend on chance. The Public Act specifically does not apply to "any game of mere skill."

However, the Public Act does not define gambling or explain what a game of skill might be, and does not address betting in general or sports betting specifically. The fines provided are insignificant. For instance, anyone who owns, occupies, is in charge of, or uses such a gaming-house, is liable for a fine not exceeding Rs. 200 (US $4) and 3 months in jail. Whoever is only *found* in the gaming-house for gaming can be fined up to Rs. 100 (US $2) and sentenced to 1 month in jail. Any person found in a gaming-house "shall be presumed, until the contrary be proved, to have been there for the purpose of gaming.

The Supreme Court of India has defined gambling in '*Lakshmanan v. State of Tamil Nadu & Anr*' (AIR 1153, 1996 SCC (2) 226). It used the Encyclopedia Britannica's definition to describe gambling as "the betting or staking of something of value, with consciousness of risk and hope of gain on the outcome of a game, a contest, or an uncertain event the result of which may be determined by chance or accident or have an unexpected result by reason of the better's miscalculations".

However, because the Public Act does not define game of skill, it is unclear whether the Public Act governs gambling in cricket. Cricket is a game of skill; however, the law does not address this issue clearly and leaves the scope of the Act unspecified. The Government of India, however, considers betting on cricket illegal. Only two states (Goa and Sikkim) allow casino gambling and legal gambling in other states is restricted to horse racing. Some cities in India can also enforce their own gambling laws and make gambling, including betting on cricket, illegal. For instance, the Delhi High Court found individuals guilty of betting on a cricket match and violating the provisions of the Delhi Public Gambling Act, 1955.

Recommendations

Designing Effective Laws to Govern Betting in Sports

Not only is the law in India unclear and the penalties minor, there are problems in investigation. For instance, all offenses under the Act are bailable. This means that the arrested person is entitled to be released on bail as soon as he is apprehended. The absence of custodial interrogation does not allow investigation agencies to reach to the depth of the case. Typically, offenders would confess and get away with a minor fine, and then they are often outside the reach of the criminal justice system having gone through the entire process, albeit in a very short time. Except Sikkim and Goa, most states do not have any legislation on betting and they continue to use a colonial era law to control gambling. As pointed, Indian law is not only out of sync with its history and culture, but also is out of sync of other major cricket playing nations such as South Africa and England that have laws which regulate gambling and online betting.

The outright banning of gambling in India has driven it underground making it harder for investigation agencies and cricket managements to control the menace. There are other handicaps to investigation by law enforcement agencies and monitoring by Cricket Boards. For instance, it is difficult to obtain judicial permission to tap phones of the suspects and monitor the transactions of underground economy that facilitates transfer of money undetected through the system. It is not possible to prevent meetings in locker rooms or hotels, and there is little material evidence as everything is done through telephones and cash transactions. A provision of law, namely Section 25 of the Indian Evidence Act, 1872, makes any confession before police to be inadmissible in court. This makes it difficult to prosecute unless substantial material evidence is collected.

There have been demands from BCCI and other stakeholders to legalize and regulate betting in India. Recently, the law minister of India has mentioned that there needs to be a law to recognize match fixing and spot fixing as a criminal offense. However, he did not comment if betting is proposed to be made legal.

Lessons from UK and South Africa's Law

The UK Law

The England and Wales Cricket Board (ECB) is the national governing body of cricket in the United Kingdom. Its regulations address match fixing and betting and apply to players and employees of the ECB. No bet is allowed to be placed by the players, nor is any information allowed to be shared that would give someone an unfair advantage in placing a bet (Mahyera 2012). The Board can ban a player from playing international cricket on behalf of England, if it finds violation of its rules and regulations. ECB rules do not prevent bets by individuals who do not participate in matches, and are only spectators.

Thus, the Gambling Act, 2005, does not criminalize gambling, but regulates the betting covering all individuals, including cricketers and spectators. The Act does differentiate between legal and illegal gambling. Placing a bet on a particular outcome is considered legal, however, match fixing and spot fixing are covered under illegal betting. Penalties include imprisonment up to 2 years and fine. The Act also establishes a Gambling Commission, which permits legal gambling and generates reports about incidents and regulation of gambling.

The Commission grants licenses to individuals and betting syndicates and thereby regulates gambling activities. The commission maintains a record of all activities taking place in the gambling facilities and utilizes the authority to review betting practices before being made to ensure legal compliance. To further address illegal sports betting, the United Kingdom also developed the Sports Betting Intelligence Unit (SBIU) as part of the Commission. SBIU works with sports governing bodies to help keep corruption out of sports betting and encourage the flow of information. The SBIU does this by requiring license holders to inform the Commission anytime a bet occurs that the Commission would want to void. The license holders also have to report any violations of the laws of sports governing bodies. The SBIU collects and develops information about corrupt sports betting. SBIU also coordinates with the local police if criminal activity is suspected.

The commission has powers to revoke a gambling license, and issue a penalty. It can also limit the hours of operation of the licensee or change other licensing conditions. There are always fears that legalizing gambling make promote addiction to gambling. The Commission has established a Responsible Gambling Strategy Board (RGSB) to deal with the problem (Orford 2012). The RGSB also promotes responsible gambling by encouraging licensed operators to provide socially responsible gambling products and players to have control over their play. The licensee cannot hire an employee or allow an existing employee to engage in any work unless the employee meets the requirements of the Act.

South Africa's Law

The Cricket South Africa (CSA) is the national governing body of cricket in South Africa. The country had banned gambling initially, but started regulating gambling through the National Gambling Act, 2004. Similar to the UK Act, the South African Act also differentiates between legal and illegal gambling. Licenses are granted to individuals or entities where activities permitted or available are specified, including the premises.

In addition to the national legislation, there are nine provincial statutes (one for each province) which regulate and grant licenses for gambling. The provincial authorities conduct inspections to ensure compliance with the Act, provincial law, and conditions of provincial and national licenses. By issuing licenses, the National Gambling Board (NGB) and provincial authorities can keep track of individuals engaged in gambling.

South Africa has also established the National Gambling Policy Council to oversee the NGB and make policy recommendations to the government (Collins 2002). This system creates a free flow of information between NGB, NGPC, provincial authorities and the national government. The NGB and the provincial authorities can not only revoke licenses but award imprisonment up to 10 years or fines up to about $ 1.4 million if there is evidence of illegal gambling or betting. Thus, the South African Act does not criminalize all aspects of sports betting, but addresses the problem of betting in cricket through an elaborate arrangement of administrative apparatus and close monitoring of betting activity.

At present, the Asian markets are huge and unregulated, with India being at the center of cricket betting. In order to regulate betting, it would be prudent to draw upon the experiences of the major cricketing nations of the world and enlist the support of researchers who can attempt to find out the causes and remedies to the ever increasing threat of corruption in cricket. The following suggestions are worth considering.

Internal Supervision/Vigilance by BCCI/Clubs

The body, which controls cricket in India, is the BCCI. It is a society, registered under the Tamil Nadu Societies Registration Act. It often uses government-owned stadiums across the country. As a member of the International Cricket Council (ICC), it has the authority to select players, umpires and officials to participate in international events and exercises total control over them. Apparently, BCCI has failed to control corruption within cricket in India. It has limited powers of taking action except suspending the players. The examples of South Africa and England can be used to create bodies like the National Gambling Board, Responsible Gambling Strategy Board, and Strategic Betting Intelligence Unit to handle the education of players, monitor the betting syndicates, and develop intelligence on illegal betting and take legal action if corrupt practices are noted.

Legalizing Gambling

There is growing support to legalize gambling in the country. Betting on the outcome of sports, other than racing, continues to be illegal, except in Sikkim, the only state to legalize betting on cricket, including the Indian Premier League (IPL) and other sports such as football, tennis, golf and chess. Illegal gambling on the outcome of sports events, especially cricket, remains an unregulated, huge and lucrative market. Online gambling operators, both domestic and offshore, operate with impunity in India, thanks to inadequate legislation; lack of enforcement and an indifferent judiciary that allows unregulated and untaxed gambling. In recent times, there has been a growing opinion that the government needs to examine ways to legalize the activity. A provincial court judgment even suggested that sports betting should be made legal and the revenue generated used for public welfare. The International Cricket Council chief executive recently urged the Indian government to legalize cricket gambling in the country. The government is reportedly looking into the possibility of legalizing sports gambling seeking directions from parallels in other countries, particularly Britain's Gambling Act of 2005. The government is seen driven by the prospect of huge revenues, which could ostensibly be used to fund public good including sports development. Arguments for legalizing and regulating gambling include:

(i) Increased revenue generation for states potentially amounting to around 2 % of the nation's gross domestic product;
(ii) Reduced funding to criminal and terror-related activities, as most of the illegal betting activities are run by the Mumbai-based underworld and the profits are suspected to fund drugs, illegal arms-deals, boot-legging and terror activities; and
(iii) The possibility that regulation would provide avenues for preventing and treating problem gambling.

Empowering Law Enforcement Agencies

The criminal justice system in India is under considerable strain and faltering. Insecurity, growing violence and criminality are evident in every part of the country. Further, terrorist threats originating from across the border to instigate secessionism and threaten stability of the country are also serious challenges to the security agencies. In such a state, the ability of the police to deal with white-collar crimes and in particular gambling in major sports is limited. The police lack basic resources, training and personnel to deal with this menace. The police continue to function under an antiquated legal and organizational system where local accountability is absent and politicization is rampant. The police need to undergo major reforms, upgrade their capabilities and incorporate modern management systems to become more effective. The police also need to be empowered with greater legal powers to keep surveillance over the activities of bookies and collect evidence about financial transactions. Furthermore, the police and the cricket authorities need to work together to face this problem of betting and advent of syndicated mafia in major sports of the country.

Enhancing Public Disapproval

Sport is a mass entertainment activity with millions of dedicated supporters and fans. Team fortunes and players in particular are followed closely and adulation matches that of film stars and politicians. Hence, fudging games and violating rules of the games is a major let down for the fans and one that has the potential of damaging the sport. For this reason alone it is imperative that illegal betting in cricket be controlled and eliminated quickly. One possible method is to involve the fans in condemning the players and officials involved in illegality. Public shaming could be a powerful mechanism to deter offenders (Harris and Murphy 2007). This may even be a more effective instrument than policing the sport. As described above, cricket provides a large number of avenues to bet on the outcome and it is next to impossible to supervise everyone involved in the game. Only public censure and condemnation can be effective mechanisms to control such illegal betting in the game. Loss of prestige and face may be the best deterrence to keep cricket the gentleman's game.

Encouraging Research into the Issue of Corruption in Cricket

Corruption occurs in all sports including cricket as does it occur in all spheres of life and all over the world. The World Bank estimates more than US$1 trillion is paid in bribes each year (Judge 2011). Corruption significantly deters the development of markets, increases uncertainty, undermines the rule of law and turns away fans from the sports. Sponsors may also withdraw if they feel sports are not generating the energy required by them. For instance, Sahara India recently announced its decision to withdraw from the IPL's costliest franchise of US $ 370 million by pulling out of T20 cricket matches (Times of India, May 21 2013). This has come after a series of scandals where the police arrested three cricket players of Rajasthan Royals cricket team for match fixing.

There is a need to systematize the knowledge available so far on corruption in sports, particularly cricket. Researchers can fulfill that need by examining which strategies works and those, which do not work. This would prevent duplication of efforts and repetition of mistakes. While a commoner may suggest one system of governance as better as compared to the other, extensive research can go into depth and analyze the effectiveness of strategies to deal with the issue of corruption. For instance, INTERPOL has entered into a 10-year initiative with the Fédération Internationale de Football Association (FIFA) in May 2011 to develop and implement a Training, Education and Prevention Programme in regards to raising awareness around the key role of organized crime in match-fixing and corruption in football (Forrest 2012). This would hopefully create a body of knowledge, which can be used to deal with betting and other problems in sports. Researchers can also identify target groups in the education sector who can assist in raising awareness of the problems associated with match-fixing and illegal betting. Thus researchers can present the issues and the way to move forward in a holistic fashion drawing from the best practices the world over.

References

Bag, PK & Saha, B. (2011). Match-fixing under competitive odds, *Games and Economic Behavior,* 73(2), 318–344.

Burke, J., Campbell, D., & Mitchell, K. (1999). Revealed: Godfather of cricket's scandals. *The Observer (London),* 12–13.

Businessline, 2013. 'IPL spot-fixing: Delhi police teams to track money trail', May 18. http://www.thehindubusinessline.com/news/sports/ipl-spotfixing-delhi-police-teams-to-track-money-trail/article4727028.ece viewed May 31, 2013.

Chandravarkar, Rohit. 2013. 'IPL spot-fixing: Proceeds from T20 betting used to fund terrorist outfits, says police', *The Economic Times (Online),* May 24. http://articles.economictimes.indiatimes.com/2013-05-24/news/39502315_1_crime-branch-shobhan-mehta-bookies viewed May 31, 2013.

Collins, M. F. (2002). *Sport and Social Exclusion.* Routledge Ltd.

Dougherty, JM. (2006). Hawala: How terrorists move funds globally, *Corporate Finance Review,* 10(6), 28–36.

Dr. K.R. Lakshmanan v. State Of Tamil Nadu And Ors (1996) Supreme Court of India: AIR 1153, 1996 SCC (2) 226

Forrest, D. (2012). The threat to football from betting-related corruption, *International Journal of Sport Finance,* 7(2), 99–116.

Gardiner, S. (2013). R v Amir & Butt [2011] EWCA civ 2914, *Leading cases in sports law* (pp. 287–303) Springer.

Harris, Nathan and Murphy, Krista. (2007). Shaming, Shame and Recidivism: A Test of Re-integrative Shaming Theory in the White-Collar Crime Context, *British Journal of Criminology,* 47(6), 900–917.

Howe, Darcus. (2000). Cricketers must have known of the cheats for years, *New Statesman* 129, No. 4483

Judge, WQ. (2011). The antecedents and effects of national corruption: A metaanalysis. *Journal of world business:* JWB (1090–9516), 46(1), p. 93. doi: 10.1016/j.jwb.2010.05.021.

Lewis, RM. (1987). Cricket and the beginnings of organized baseball in New York City, *International Journal of the History of Sport,* 4(3), 315.

Martain, (2006). Grave plaques honour Tassie cricket legends. *Mercury* (Hobart, Tas.), 13.

Mahyera, R. (2012). Saving cricket: A proposal for the legalization of gambling in India to regulate corrupt betting practices in cricket, *Emory Int'l Law Review,* 26, 365–489.

Orford, J. (2012). Gambling in Britain: The application of restraint erosion theory, *Addiction,* 107 (12), 2082–2086.

Rasul, A. (2011). Bollywood and the Indian Premier League (IPL): the political economy of Bollywood's new blockbuster. *Asian journal of communication,* 21(4), 373–388. doi: 10.1080/01292986.2011.580851.

Rediff.com (2000). Report on cricket match fixing and related malpractices, October, Central Bureau of Investigation, New Delhi. http://www.rediff.com/cricket/2000/nov/01full.htm viewed May 31, 2013.

S Ahmad Ali (2013). IPL Spot-Fixing: Cops may have names of Bollywood celebs into betting [ET Cetera]. *The Economic Times (Online),* p. n. Ahmad Ali (2013).

Shears, R & Whiting, M. (1998). 'Waugh and Warne in betting scandal; Two fined for helping bookmaker', *Daily Mail (London)* December 9. http://www.questia.com/library/1G1-110693622/waugh-and-warne-in-betting-scandal-two-fined-for viewed May 31, 2013.

The Economic Times, (2013). IPL spot-fixing: Cops may have names of Bollywood celebs into betting, May 19. http://m.economictimes.com/news/news-by-industry/et-cetera/ipl-spot-fixing-cops-may-have-names-of-bollywood-celebs-into-betting/articleshow/20119602.cms viewed May 31, 2013.

The Economist. (2000). Heads, you lose. May 4. http://www.economist.com/node/333216 viewed May 31, 2013.

The Financial Daily. (2013). PCB bans Ghauri for corruption charges, April 15. http://www.thefinancialdaily.com/NewsDetail/161243.aspx viewed May 31, 2013.

The Hindustan Times, (2013). Vindoo was invited to match by Gurunath: Police, May 23. http://www.hindustantimes.com/Specials/Cricket/T20/Chunk-HT-UI-T20-SpotFixing/Vindoo-was-invited-to-match-by-Gurunath-Police/SP-Article10-1064564.aspx viewed May 31, 2013.

The Times Of India. (2013). Illegal Betting in IPL Could Be worth 40 k Crores' May 17. http://articles.timesofindia.indiatimes.com/2013-05-17/news/39334935_1_indian-premier-league-ipl-old-delhi viewed May 31, 2013.

Upadhyay, Y & Singh, SK. (2010). When sports celebrity doesn't perform: how consumers react to celebrity endorsement? *Vision, 14*(1), 67–78. Retrieved from http://search.proquest.com/docview/649038880?accountid=2909.

Wade, M. (2008). The tycoon who changed cricket. *The Age* (Melbourne, Vic.), 2008-03-08, p5.

Match Fixing: Case Studies from Greece and Ireland

Nikolaos (Nick) Petropoulos and Ronan Maguire

Abstract The purpose of this chapter is to provide an overview of the current status of soccer match-fixing cases and allegations in Greece and Ireland. It will introduce the reader to the historical background of Greek and Irish football. Further, it will examine cases that have been investigated to date by the football associations, law enforcement and judicial authorities. Match-fixing is a global problem. Greece and Ireland are exposed to this threat no different than any other country. Finally, we will evaluate the effectiveness of the available legislation and administrative tools to combat match-fixing in Greece and Ireland respectively. It will be argued that the legal systems are not robust enough to deal with match-fixing in an efficient manner.

Introduction

The football leagues in Greece and Ireland attract a strong following of supporters. Continuous allegations of match-fixing in any of these leagues could lead to permanently damaging its reputation and ultimately to its demise. This could have further repercussions for the already fragile Greek and Irish economies. As a result, this chapter explores a number of avenues to combat match-fixing. Such avenues include reform of governance mechanisms, as well as accountability and organizational

N. Petropoulos (✉)
John Jay College of Criminal Justice, 20-14 43rd street, Astoria, NY 11105, USA
e-mail: npetropoulos@jjay.cuny.edu

R. Maguire
John Jay College of Criminal Justice,
21, Forest Close, Kingswood Heights, Dublin 24, Ireland
e-mail: ronanmaguire3@hotmail.com

M.R. Haberfeld and D. Sheehan (eds.), *Match-Fixing in International Sports:*
Existing Processes, Law Enforcement, and Prevention Strategies,
DOI 10.1007/978-3-319-02582-7_5, © Springer International Publishing Switzerland 2013

structures. Investigations into match-fixing are time-consuming endeavors and owing to the cross-border nature of this crime, this chapter will argue that effective stream-lined legislation is a priority. Finally the authors will also posit that there should be greater collaboration between law enforcement and academia in an effort to find solutions to match-fixing. Education in this area is vital.

Greece: Case Study

Over the past decades, often times other sports have received a lot of attention and support by Greek fans, the most prominent being basketball which has been repeatedly characterized as "the national sport of Greeks". However, football has been diachronically Greece's most popular sport mainly due to its unrivalled social, economic and political dimension (Alexopoulos and Senaux 2011).

The first Greek Football Association (Greek abbreviation: EPO) was established in 1926 and a year later it joined FIFA. In 1954, EPO became a member of the Union of European Football Associations (UEFA). However, despite its longstanding popularity, it was not until 1979[1] that football in Greece became professional (Alexopoulos and Anagnostopoulos 2010). That year, the Union of Professional Football Companies was established (Greek abbreviation: EPAE). The new Union, operating under the auspices of EPO, was primarily aiming to "promote the interests of the newly established football clubs" that were subject to the rules and regulations of the Ministry of Development (Anagnostopoulos and Senaux 2011). EPAE was charged with running the three professional football national divisions, namely the first (or premier), second and third division.

Over the past three decades, Greek football has been gradually moving towards professionalization and football clubs, quite often struggling with economic viability issues, sought to establish professional standards, boost public interest and subsequently, their revenue. In 2006, the chairmen of three of the major Greek football clubs (namely, AEK Athens, Skoda Xanthi and Panathinaikos Athens) took the initiative to break away from EPAE and create a new league, in line with the English Premier League standards. The new Super League would include 16 teams. The major goal of this initiative was to better organize football in Greece and make it a product that could attract more customers by benefiting from an unprecedented, tremendous achievement of Greek football: The winning of the European Championship by the Greek national team in 2004. In fact, it was suggested that the national team's success in EURO 2004 was the turning point for football business to grow and attract more customers/supporters (Anagnostopoulos 2011).

---

[1] Law 789/1979.

Allegations regarding match fixing cases in Greek football have been very common since day one of its professionalization. However, the vast majority of allegations would never reach the trial stage and would be dismissed well before any person was charged with criminal charges. Not surprisingly, newspapers and sport websites would quite often refer to match-fixing allegations as the best-kept secret of Greek football.[2] Furthermore, frequent allegations of referees' malpractice and widespread reputation of match fixing were often cited as among the main causes responsible for the financial instability of Greek football clubs (Avgerinou and Giakoumatos 2009).

Unfortunately, studies on Greek football have attracted limited academic interest in Greece. Moreover, match fixing-related studies and articles published in academic journals are nonexistent. However, given that the football sector in Greece has grown increasingly since the 1980s it does not come as surprise that according to the Greek Institute of Sport Business in 2011 it accounted for 65 % of the €2.5 Billion of the annual worth of the sport industry in Greece (Anagnostopoulos 2011). With multiple allegations around various football officials and huge amounts of money involved, it was just a matter of time before the first match-fixing scandal struck Greek football.

Indeed, in June 2011 UEFA published a list of 41 match results from the 2009–2010 period that were characterized as suspicious and were, allegedly, related to match-fixing. Greek law-enforcement and judicial authorities immediately launched an investigation that ended up involving scores of Greek football club officials, players, businessmen and other individuals.

Initially, the investigation involved around 70 people. Among the suspects that were named in connection with the alleged match-fixing scandal were the presidents of two of the Super League, with the most prominent of the suspects being Vangelis Marinakis, Greece's number one league official and president of Olympiakos Piraeus football club who has repeatedly denied the charges. Police investigations led to the arrest of ten people, including Achilleas Beos and Makis Psomiadis; presidents of Olympiakos Volou and Kavala respectively, both Super League teams. Olympiakos Volou had finished in fifth place of the Super League during the 2009–2010 season, while Kavala finished seventh.

What is particularly interesting about this investigation is that most suspects were charged with a variety of offences. That is, the charges included illegal gambling, fraud, extortion as well as money laundering. According to the Associated Press (Washington Post 2011) details of the match-fixing scandal were provided in a 130-page document drafted by the special prosecutor for football-related offences. Greek newspapers and media[3] would refer to the match-fixing scandal as "Koriopolis", a combination of the name Calciopoli that refers to the Italian match-fixing scandal in 2006 and the Greek slang word for wiretapping "Korios".

---

[2]http://www.sport24.gr/football/ellada/anamenontai_kai_alles_syllhpseis_foyntwnoyn_oi_fhmes_gia_to_sthmeno_ntermpi.1112461.html (in Greek).
[3]http://www.gazzetta.gr/article/item/204308-calciopolis-vs-korio-polis (in Greek).

On July 28, 2011 the disciplinary committee of the Super League decided to relegate both Olympiakos Volou and Kavala to the football league (former second division), whose presidents have already been put in pre-trial detention while they were both banned for life from any involvement in football. The decision was based on the fact that both clubs' officials were charged with illegal gambling and money laundering. Additionally, the two clubs were fined €300,000 each. Although both teams appealed the relegation, in August 2011 they were ultimately relegated to the fourth division[4] due to their involvement in the match-fixing scandal. It is also worth mentioning that Olympiakos Voloy which had reached the Europa League play-off round, was excluded from the competition by UEFA[5] due to the match-fixing accusations.

The ongoing investigation which is now conducted by two special prosecutors includes a number of 188 suspects who will be brought to trial no sooner than 2014. Although most defendants will face felony charges, the investigation has been proven extremely time-consuming and labyrinthine, demonstrating the complexities law-enforcement and judicial authorities face when investigating match-fixing cases. Not surprisingly, given that the maximum length of pre-trial detention in Greece is 18 months, only one of the pre-trial detainees remains in jail and he is likely to be released in November, 2013 if the trial does not start soon. It should also be noted that, according to the Greek Code of Penal Procedure, the details of any on-going criminal investigation conducted by the judicial authorities are not publicly disclosed until the case reaches the trial stage. Thus, more detailed information on the match-fixing scandal is not currently known to the larger public.

Concerning the legislative framework in Greece, match fixing – related offences are covered in specific provisions of the Greek criminal law (Sports Law). In particular, Art. 132.1 and 2 Law 2725/1999 considers active and passive bribery with the purpose of manipulating results in favor of a club, an Athletic Societe Anonyme (AAE) or a Remunerated Athletes Section (TAA) as a misdemeanor (art. 132.1).[6] Both active and passive corruption is punishable with penalties of at least 3 months imprisonment. This may be increased to 6 months in cases where the perpetrator achieves the intended results. The scope of the provision is limited to the alteration of results in favor of a club, an AAE or a TAA. Furthermore, the law contains exonerating provisions for those who provide information on the sports crime. It specifically refers to the necessary autonomy and independence of the criminal and disciplinary proceedings in case persons involved are sportsmen – athletes, coaches, trainers, administrative agents or members of sports clubs, TAA or AAE- (132.5). Modified art.

---

[4] http://www.novasports.gr/news.aspx?a_id=200162&Sport=1&Competition=1713&Season=100 081&Country=82&Period=252785 (in Greek).
[5] http://www.uefa.com/uefa/footballfirst/matchorganisation/disciplinary/news/newsid=1658759. html.
[6] http://ec.europa.eu/sport/news/documents/study-sports-fraud-final-version_en.pdf.

132[7] of Sports Law made betting related match-fixing a felony punishable by up to 10 years in prison. However, it should be noted that the defendants of the match fixing scandal were not charged according to these provisions. Instead, most of them will likely face charges for illegal gambling, fraud, extortion and money laundering.

However, after an EU study on match- fixing on sport was published, a new Law was passed and article 132 of the Law 2725/99 was replaced. In particular, article 13[8] of the L.4049/2012 (Official Gazette 35A) "Confrontation of violence in the

---

[7]Law 2725/1999 as amended by Law 3057/2002 Article 132: "Corruption – bribery for alteration of the result of the Football Game 1. Anyone who demands or accepts gifts or other benefits or promise thereof, in order to manipulate -in favour or against a sports association, an Athletic Anonymous Society (AAS) or a Department for Salaried Athletes (SAD) – the results of a match, of any team or individual sport that is conducted or is to be performed shall be punished by imprisonment of at least three (3) months and a fine of at least €2.934.

2. The same penalty shall be imposed to anyone under paragraph 1 who offers, gives or promises to an athlete, referee, administrative agent or any other person connected in any way with the athlete, the referee, the union, the AAS or SAD, gifts, benefits or any other benefits.

3. If from the punishable action under the preceding paragraphs the result intended by the perpetrator is achieved, then he is punished with imprisonment of at least six (6) months and a fine of at least €5.869.

4. In addition to the above penalties, to the persons who commit offenses under paragraphs 1–3 of t his article, disciplinary sanctions are imposed, in accordance with the provisions of Article 130, for violation of sportsmanship.

5. If the persons prosecuted for offenses in paragraphs 1, 2 and 3 of this article are athletes, coaches, trainers, administrators, or members of a sports association, an AAS or a SAD, disciplinary sanctions of either the removal of points from the league table of the ongoing or upcoming championship or of the near championship, in which they will participate, or the relegation of these to the next lower category are imposed by the competent disciplinary body of the relevant sports federation or the relevant professional association to the association group, the AAS or the SAD that these persons belong to. In accordance with the precedent paragraphs, the disciplinary proceedings, prosecution and sentencing g, are autonomous and independent from the criminal trial in which the culpable persons are referred to, because of the performance of the above offenses."

[8]1. Anyone intervening with illegitimate actions, with the intention to influence the evolution, the form or the result of a game of any team or individual sport is punished with imprisonment of at least one (1) year and cash penalty from one hundred thousand (100,000) up to five hundred thousand (500,000) Euros.

2. Anyone who, with the same intention, demands or accepts gifts or other benefits, or any other allotment or promise of them is punished with imprisonment of at least two (2) years and cash penalty from two hundred thousand (200,000) up to one million (1,000,000) Euros.

3. By the same penalty of paragraph 2 of the present article is also punished anyone who, with the same intention according to this paragraph, offers, gives or promises to an athlete, trainer, referee or administrator, or to any other person associated in any way with the athlete, the referee, the club, the Sport Incorporated Company, the Department of Paid Athletes, gifts, benefits, or any other allotments.

4. If by the punishable action of the previous paragraphs 1–3, the aim pursued by the perpetrator is achieved or if the game, of which the result is distorted, is included in bets placed at national level or abroad, then the perpetrator is punished with imprisonment up to ten (10) years.

For the punishable actions of the paragraphs 1–4, the investigation and the interrogatory actions can also include all the proceedings of article 253A of the Code of Penal Procedure, under the conditions mentioned therein.

During the criminal procedure for these crimes, measures of protection of witnesses can be taken, according to the article 9 of the L. 2928/2001.

stadia, Doping, match-fixing and other provisions" reinforced criminal sanctions for the sport offence of bribery and replaced article 132 of the L.2725/99.

As far as the football sector oversight and inspection is concerned, in 2003, the Greek government established an inspection body, the License Commission for Professional Sport (Greek abbreviation: EEA) which was responsible to deal with transparency and legality issues of professional sport in Greece (Anagnostopoulos and Senaux 2011). EEA is mainly responsible for granting all football clubs a license to participate in the league and is given the status of an independent authority in an effort to become as efficient as possible. However, EEA has yet to deal with a sketchy regulatory framework under which Greek football operates (Anagnostopoulos and Senaux 2011).

Ireland: Case Study

Although there have been no celebrated cases of match fixing in Ireland, it would be foolish to state that the country is immune from this growing epidemic that threatens the integrity of football worldwide. This case study will focus on the background to the league of Ireland, recent allegations of match fixing and the legal and educational tools available to deal with it. The island of Ireland comprises of two football leagues. Historically, the Irish Football Association (IFA) governed football for the entire island of Ireland. After the Irish War of Independence, a decision was made by the clubs in the south of Ireland to form their own league. This led to the formation of the Football Association of Ireland (FAI) in 1921.[9]

For the purposes of this case study, the chapter will focus on the Republic of Ireland (hereinafter "Ireland") which comprises the 26 counties of the south of Ireland. The league of Ireland is the national association football league of Ireland (FAI website). It originally began with 8 teams in 1921. It now consists of 20 teams. There are 12 teams in the premier division and 8 teams in the first division. The league is currently sponsored by "Airtricity" and hence it is officially known as the Airtricity League (2012). Before 2006, the league was governed by its participating members. Since 2006 the FAI has been charged with the running of the league with a view to improving standards, governance and funding.

In 2007, the league of Ireland became the first domestic league in Europe to introduce a salary cost protocol (Airtricity League website). This entails that clubs in the league of Ireland cannot spend more than 65 % of their income on players' wages. It follows that clubs have to keep their finances in check and can only spend the set percentage of income on players and salaries. In the past, a number of league of Ireland clubs encountered major financial difficulties. Some clubs sought the protection of the courts and entered into examinership (Independent News website). High wages for players was a big burden on club finances to the extent that players were

---

[9]The Football Association of Ireland History. Retrieved from http://www.fai.ie/fai/history.html.

earning 1,000 Euros per goal in bonuses (Independent News website). This was at a time during Ireland's economic prosperity. Since the recession, players' wages and contracts are no longer as attractive as they once were. Like any football league in the world, one cannot overlook the possibility that clubs, players and officials in Ireland might be tempted or coerced into match fixing.[10]

Betting on football has come a long way from when one was only able to bet on whether a team would win or lose. Online betting has become a huge phenomenon. Punters are now able to bet on a variety of outcomes. Live betting allows punters to make bets even as the match is in progress. Irregular betting patterns usually alert the bookmaker to question why such bets are being made. When large amounts of money are placed on matches that are not necessarily high profile, suspicion is aroused. However, not all irregular betting movements are a cause for concern. There are syndicates who happen to know more about a certain match than the bookmaker (Darby 2012).

As a result, it can be very difficult to discern between genuine legal betting and illegal match fixing. The following examples of allegations of match fixing in Ireland are outlined below. These examples are intended to show the complexity of uncovering whether a genuine bet is placed or if there is a more sinister motive behind it.

On May 4, 2012, the Airtricity League of Ireland informed the Union of European Football Associations (UEFA) of irregular betting patterns. This concerned a football match between Shelbourne Football Club and Monaghan United.[11] The irregular betting patterns revolved around the probability of a penalty being awarded during the game which was played at Shelbourne Football Club's home ground, Tolka Park in Dublin. It subsequently transpired that a penalty kick *was* awarded to Monaghan United early in the second half of the match. Monaghan United pulled out of the premier division of the Airtricity League of Ireland in June 2012, citing financial reasons as the main factor for their decision (Irish Examiner website).

In August 2011, during the fourth round of the FAI cup, allegations of match fixing arose. A football match between Shelbourne Football Club and Sheriff Youth Club aroused suspicion with irregular betting patterns. Sheriff Youth Club which are a non-league side caused huge upset and controversy when they beat Shelbourne Football Club 3 goals to 2 goals. Initially, Sheriff Youth Club were losing by 2 goals. This result caused immediate suspicion. In the days prior to the match and right up to half time, large bets were being placed that Sheriff Youth Club would win. These bets were placed even though Sheriff Youth Club were losing at half time. It transpired in this case that Sheriff Youth Club were disqualified from the FAI cup for playing an ineligible player (Darby 2012).[12]

---

[10]Rebel wages 'outrageous'. Retrieved from http://www.independent.ie/sport/soccer/league-of-ireland/rebel-wages-outrageous-26554475.html.

[11]United seek full examinership. Retrieved from http://www.independent.ie/regionals/droghedain-dependent/news/united-seek-full-examinership-27128229.html.

[12]Darby, J. (2012, May 10). Spectre of match-fixing haunts Ireland's Airtricity league. Retrieved fromhttp://www.goal.com/en-ie/news/3942/ireland/2012/05/10/3092839/spectre-of-match-fixing-hauntsirelands-airtricity-league.

The most recent allegation of match fixing in football in Ireland was reported in April 2013. Longford Town Football Club, who, at the time of writing, are currently the first division Airtricity league leaders; had to suspend a player in order to carry out an investigation into match fixing. Longford Town Football Club issued a statement to the effect that a player was suspended pending an investigation into possible involvement of activities that could be construed as conspiring to influence the outcome of football matches.[13] An internal inquiry was launched by Longford Town Football Club and a separate investigation was undertaken by the FAI's Disciplinary Control Unit (at the time of writing, this matter is still under investigation). Details surrounding the incident were communicated to UEFA and FIFA as per standard protocol.[14] An Garda Síochána were also notified about the incident (Independent News website).

Ireland is policed by An Garda Síochána, who are the national police force responsible for carrying out all criminal investigations and are also responsible for the preparation of all criminal court files. A police investigation into allegations of match fixing is a complex matter and can be difficult to prove. There are no specific criminal laws in Ireland aimed at match fixing regardless of the sport involved. However, there are various laws in the Irish Statute Book that can be utilized to prosecute individuals for match fixing, some of which are outlined below.

The Criminal Justice (Theft and Fraud Offences) Act, 2001[15] consolidated and updated the law relating to theft, dishonesty and fraud in Ireland. Section 6 of the Criminal Justice (Theft and Fraud Offences) Act, 2001 is directed at "making gain or causing loss by deception". It states: "A person who dishonestly, with the intention of making a gain for himself or herself or another, or of causing loss to another, by any deception, induces another to do or refrain from doing an act is guilty of an offence". This is an arrestable offence and carries a maximum sentence of 5 years in prison (Irish Statute book).

The Criminal Justice Act, 2006 was enacted to enhance the powers of An Garda Síochána in the investigation and prosecution of offences. It provided updated legislation to deal with organized crime. Section 70 of the Criminal Justice Act, 2006 as amended by Section 3 of the Criminal Justice (Amendment) Act, 2009 defines a criminal organization as: "A structured group, however organized, that has its main purpose or activity the commission or facilitation of a serious offence". A structured group means: "A group of 3 or more persons which is not randomly formed for the immediate commission of a single offence, and the involvement in which by 2 or more of those persons is with a view to their acting in concert, for the avoidance of doubt, a structured group may exist notwithstanding the absence of all or any of the

---

[13] Longford town player suspended as FAI launches probe into match-fixing. Retrieved from http://www.independent.ie/sport/soccer/longford-town-player-suspended-as-fai-launches-probe-into-matchfixing-29172204.html.

[14] UEFA informed of 'irregular' bets. Retrieved from http://www.irishexaminer.com/archives/2012/0507/opinion/uefa-informed-of-aposirregularapos-bets-192965.html.

[15] The Criminal Justice (Theft and Fraud Offences) Act, 2001. Retrieved from http://www.irishstatutebook.ie/2001/en/act/pub/0050/.

following: (a) formal rules, or formal membership, or any formal roles for those involved in the group; (b) any hierarchical or leadership structure; (c) continuity of involvement by persons in the group" (Irish Statute book).

Section 73 of the Criminal Justice Act, 2006[16] as amended by Section 10 of the Criminal Justice (Amendment) Act, 2009[17] is directed at individuals who commit offences for a criminal organization and it states: "(1) A person who commits a serious offence for the benefit of, at the direction of, or in association with, a criminal organization is guilty of an offence. (2) In proceedings for an offence in *subsection (1)*, it shall not be necessary for the prosecution to prove that the person concerned knew any of the persons who constitute the criminal organization concerned. (3) A person guilty of an offence under this section shall be liable on conviction on indictment to a fine or imprisonment for a term not exceeding 15 years or both" (Irish Statute book).

Although there are legislative provisions in place that can deal with match fixing in Ireland, it would be more prudent to have specific sports fraud legislation. Match fixing crosses many borders and jurisdictions and hence a streamlined approach from all countries affected should be put in place.

Education is also vital to combat match fixing. It is important that clubs, players and officials are made aware of the serious consequences that may unfold should they partake in such activity. They must realize the personal risk they take which could result in imprisonment, fines and lifetime bans from the sport. They must also realize the long term damage it can cause to the integrity of the sport as a whole, where fans lose faith and no longer support the respective league resulting in its demise. There are a wide variety of sports related courses in third level institutions in Ireland. However, sports integrity does not receive great prominence in most curriculums. The role of academia cannot be overstressed in helping to find solutions to prevent corrupt practices in sport and greater collaboration should take place with law enforcement.

The football leagues in Ireland are equally vulnerable to match fixing as any league throughout the world.[18] Interested parties should remain vigilant to signs of corrupt behavior. Education is a priority to ensure that all key actors are fully conversant in recognizing and resisting corruption. Although match fixing is complex to detect, members of An Garda Síochána are highly trained police officers who are exceptionally competent and have a proven track record in dealing with cross border crime. Continued co-operation and the sharing of information from football clubs and the FAI is vital in order for An Garda Síochána to carry out a successful investigation of the crime and prosecution of offenders.

---

[16]The Criminal Justice Act, 2006. Retrieved from http://www.irishstatutebook.ie/2006/en/act/pub/0026/.

[17]The Criminal Justice (Amendment) Act, 2009. Retrieved from http://www.irishstatutebook.ie/pdf/2009/en.act.2009.0032.pdf.

[18]Match fixing is alive in GAA. Retrieved from http://www.sundayworld.com/top-stories/crime-desk/donal-macintyre-s-crime-cafe/match-fixing-is-alive-in-gaa.

Ireland remains committed to combating match fixing in sport. From January 2013 to June 2013, Ireland held the Presidency of the European Union. Holding the Presidency allows the Member State an opportunity to shape and influence European Union policy and legislation. The Minister of State for Tourism & Sport said he would focus on the integrity of sport as Chair of the European Union Council of Sports Ministers (Irish Government news website).[19] This was done with a view to addressing issues of common interest across the Member States, sharing best practices and speaking with one voice at an international level. As we look to the future, continued cross border co-operation and a uniformity of laws to deal with match fixing are essential in combating this global crime. The Council of Europe is cognizant of the problem and it has taken steps to negotiate on an International Convention against manipulation of sports results (European Commission website).[20] For the moment, and with existing laws in place, An Garda Síochána stands ready to investigate and prosecute individuals engaged in match fixing in Ireland should the need arise.

Conclusion

This brief chapter has attempted to present a picture of match-fixing cases and allegations in Greece and Ireland and how the Greek and Irish authorities have dealt with them over time. Although it is apparent that the Greek legal framework is more than efficient and coherent, nevertheless law-enforcement and judicial authorities struggle with time-consuming procedures and delays that jeopardize the effective and comprehensive investigation of allegations and accusation concerning football match-fixing.

While the legislative measures seem sufficient, the Greek state should seriously consider addressing the issue of match-fixing with additional regulatory interventions. For example, introducing a new more flexible betting legislation or amending the existing one could be a preventive measure. The ultimate goal should be to make the investigative stage of any match fixing-related criminal case less time-consuming and, subsequently, more effective. In the case of Ireland, more specific sports related legislation would be beneficial for law enforcement and judicial authorities. It is important to bear in mind that match fixing crosses many borders and jurisdictions. As a result, streamlined legislation should also be considered. Furthermore, the lack of accountability of football clubs and officials who, as it has been proven by recent match-fixing scandals, can easily operate below the radar, lacking any form of integrity should be addressed both in Greece and Ireland.

---

[19]Minister Ring to focus on match-fixing during Irish presidency. Retrieved from http://www.merrionstreet.ie/index.php/2013/02/minister-ring-to-focus-on-match-fixing-during-irishpresidency/.
[20]Commission negotiates convention against match-fixing. Retrieved from http://ec.europa.eu/sport/news/20130613-convention-match-fixing_en.htm.

Last but not least, further research on the issue of match fixing is needed. Thus, Greek and Irish academics should focus more on the issue of match fixing and conduct empirical studies, collect and analyze data and, eventually, produce a series of proposed policies that could help the Greek and Irish state launch effective preventive measures. After all, as Hippocrates, the father of Western medicine, stated nearly 25 centuries ago *"prevention is better than cure"*.

References

Airtricity League clubs vote unanimously in favour of FAI stewardship. Retrieved from http://www.airtricityleague.ie/index.php/about/presoffices/2112-airtricity-league-clubs-vote-unanimously-in-favour-of-fai-stewardship

Alexopoulos, P. & Benoît Senaux (2011). Transforming top-tier football in Greece: the case of the 'Super League'. *Soccer & Society*, 12, 6, 722–736

Alexopoulos, P., & C. Anagnostopoulos (2010). *The Business of Football in Greece: The Structure and Organisation of the Greek Professional Football* [in Greek]. Athens, I. Sideri.

Anagnostopoulos, C. (2011). Stakeholder management in Greek professional football: identification and salience. *Soccer and Society*, 12, 2, 249–264.

Avgerinou, V., & Giakoumatos, S. (2009). *Price, Income & Unemployment Effects on Greek Professional Football*. IASE/NAASE Working Paper Series, No. 09–07.

Darby, J. (2012, May 10). Spectre of match-fixing haunts Ireland's Airtricity league. Retrieved from http://www.goal.com/en-ie/news/3942/ireland/2012/05/10/3092839/spectre-of-match-fixinghauntsirelands-airtricity-league.

The Washington Post (2011, June 24). Greek league chief linked to corruption scandal after UEFA identified suspect games. Retrieved from http://www.washingtonpost.com/

Match Rigging in Italian Professional Soccer: The Economic Determinants of Corruption

Tito Boeri and Battista Severgnini

Abstract In the last decade the Italian professional leagues were involved in several police investigations. The episodes uncovered were connected with two of the largest match fixing scandals in Europe involving criminal organizations, soccer players, team managers, and referees. These investigations, also known as *Calciopoli* and *Scommessopoli*, offer unique case studies to understand the mechanisms behind match fixing in professional football.

In this chapter we exploit the information collected in these investigations to evaluate the economic determinants of corruption in sports. We proceed in three steps. First, we offer a brief overview of the main facts and probes of the Italian scandals showing that *Calciopoli* and *Scommessopoli* are two completely different types of corruption with changing actors and mechanisms. While in the *Calciopoli* scandal corruption is a tool to obtain a particular sport result (*corruption for sport results*), in *Scommessopoli* the fixing is strictly related to bias and to illegal gains from betting markets (*corruption for betting results*). Secondly, we explain the differences of the cases reported by the police using the tools, notably the decision trees, provided by economic theory. Finally, we draw from our analysis to present

This chapter is inspired by the presentations during the session *Where do we go from here-what Interpol wants?* And at the following discussion at the conference *Interpol Global Academic Experts. Meeting for Integrity in Sport*, held in Singapore, November 28–29th, 2012. We also benefitted from informal conversations with Simone Farina, John Foot, and Daniela Giuffrè. All errors are our own.

T. Boeri (✉)
Igier-Bocconi University and CEPR, via Roentgen 1, Milan, Italy
e-mail: tito.boeri@unibocconi.it

B. Severgnini
Copenhagen Business School, Porcelænshaven 16A, Frederiksberg DK – 2000, Denmark
e-mail: bs.eco@cbs.dk

some suggestions as to how to detect and prevent future episodes of match rigging. Particular emphasis is put on the first type of corruption, while most of the literature to date on devising measures to reduce corruption concentrates on illegal gains from betting markets.

Introduction

The relationship between sports and corruption has deep historical roots.[1] However, the scientific literature, notably the empirical literature on match rigging is relatively recent. This is rather unfortunate as the effects of corruption are somewhat easier to identify in sports than in other activities, and hence there is potentially much to learn from in-depth analyses of match rigging. Unlike other activities where performance is often difficult to measure, productivity in sport competitions is readily observable and can be measured according to metrics that are generally agreed upon. Detailed data on the characteristics of athletes and on the conditions in which sport events take place are also generally available. However, economists only recently started investigating corruption in professional sport industries.

The first theoretical contributions in economics concerning rigging in sportive events can be found in Konrad (2000), who considered match fixing as a particular type of sabotage in sport, and in Preston and Szymanski (2003), who defined a methodological framework for studying how actors in a gambling environment can bias and fix results of sportive events. The empirical identification of match rigging episodes made significant progress with the pioneering works of Duggan and Levitt (2002) and Wolfers (2006), who exploited advanced econometric techniques in assessing match fixing in Japanese sumo wrestling and in American basketball, respectively. Despite all these relevant contributions, the identification of match fixing episodes still represents a very challenging task for scholars.

Detecting and quantifying corruption in sportive events is extremely difficult. The intangible nature of corruption makes it hard to detect. According to an *International Monetary Fund* report (Tanzi 1998), corruption is like an elephant that is difficult to describe in isolation, but easy to recognize on the damages. This prevents economists from obtaining the type of loops between theory and empirical work, via the guidance that theory provides to data analysis and the evaluation of the empirical relevance of models via the testing of their assumptions and implications, which are essential for advances in our method.

---

[1] A large number of scandals of corruption affected sport participants and biased results. Scholars claim that episodes of organized corruption can be traced as far back as the Olympic Games in Ancient Greece (Harris 1964). More recently, the most striking events in the last centuries happened in 1896, when a group of cyclists was accused of using doping during the *Bordeaux-Paris* race (Rosen 2008), and in 1919, when investigators found gamblers bribing *Chicago White Sox* baseball players to intentionally lose games during the *World Series* (Cook 2001).

At the same time, understanding the characteristics and determinants of match fixing is of great potential interest not only to criminologists but also to other social scientists. Firstly, these phenomena have a negative impact on the society at large, as sport events keep on reaching larger and larger audiences worldwide. To give an example, football is the professional sport that was most successful in penetrating the developing world. The South African World Cup was broadcasted in some 200 countries with a potential audience of 25 billion persons. The final match was watched by some 700 million individuals across the globe. Secondly, the study on match fixing can provide important insights on more general criminal events as well. Indeed, some of the mechanisms behind match fixing and betting are contiguous to other illegal activities and often involve criminal organizations operating well beyond the professional sports industry. Thirdly, match fixing is a topic of interest also from a strictly economic point of view, since sport activities contribute to a significant share of GDP, i.e., up to 2 % of EU GDP (Boeri and Severgnini 2012). Several statistics also document the large negative impact of corruption on economic activity. According to recent studies (Lambsdorff 2007), every year corruption reduces the level of yearly productivity by about 4 % and a country net annual capital inflow by some 0.5 % of GDP. Match rigging, in particular, has a relevant cost for the society. To give an example, according to *Interpol* Secretary General, Ronald Noble, match fixing has a value of hundreds of billions of Euros per years, a sum which can be compared to the total revenues of *Coca Cola* (Fritzpatrick 2013).

Ongoing investigations on corruption in professional sports provide a wealth of data to researchers. In-depth analyses based on these data can then provide relevant support to police investigations. Several international police inquiries shed light on very important aspects of the socio-economic environment of corruption in sports and on the main actors involved in match fixing all over the world. Furthermore, the evolution of technologies adopted in the investigations (for example, the extensive use of tapped phone conversations) gives to the researchers the opportunity to obtain not only qualitative information, but also hard data, which can be used to measure the extent of the phenomena to be analyzed. Mass media also play an important role in denouncing and describing some negative events in sports, helping scholars to understand cross-country differences in the levels and characteristics of corruption.

The purpose of this chapter is to analyze the characteristics of match fixing in professional football exploiting the information provided by two important police investigations. In particular, we shall develop and use economic tools for understanding match fixing for sportive purposes, i.e. when team managers bias the sportive results without the influence of illegal betting. We think that this type of rigging is relevant since it has occurred in several important Championships like the Italian and the Russian first division tournaments, and it has not been as yet duly investigated by researchers. We will also suggest some alternative approaches, which could be useful not only for understanding the main mechanisms of fixing but also for trying to prevent corruption episodes in the future. Our methodology does not substitute for other models and techniques proposed by criminology and by other fields in social science, but offers a complementary point of view on match fixing, since it provides a quantitative estimate of the probability that a match can be rigged, and identifies the role played by the characteristics of the match, of the referees and of the teams involved in affecting this probability.

More precisely, in this chapter we shall concentrate our attention on two recent scandals of match fixing in Italian football, also known as *Calciopoli* and *Scommessopoli*. Having access to the records of the police investigations, we have the opportunity to exploit a unique overview on these episodes of match fixing.

We proceed in three steps. At first, in section "*Calciopoli* and *Scommessopoli*: A Tale of Two Scandals", we illustrate the two Italian case studies, providing a brief overview of the two scandals. Next, we look into the black box of match fixing trying to understand and explain the dynamics of corruption using some economic tools. This is done in sections "Winning or Betting? Two Types of Corruption" and "The Economic Toolbox for Explaining Match Fixing", where we analyze the analogies and differences between corruption for sportive results and corruption for betting results and we show how economic tools are useful for describing and quantifying match fixing. In section "How to Prevent Future Episodes of Match Fixing", we highlight the implications of our work for both police investigations and prevention of crimes, notably in terms of improvements in the detection of matches potentially rigged. Finally, section "Conclusions" provides a summary and suggestions for further research.

Calciopoli and *Scommessopoli*: A Tale of Two Scandals

Corruption in Italy is perceived to be widespread. The rankings of the *Corruption Perceptions Index 2012* (Transparency International 2012) places Italy at the 72nd position, just before Liberia and after Brazil. Although one may question such rankings, there is little doubt that widespread perceptions tend to provide support to social acceptance of illegal activities, whereby individuals behaving illegally believe that they are just replicating actions of many other individuals.

Criminal organizations seem also to play an important in role in match fixing and betting. According to media reports, a number of meetings and phone calls between mafia members and soccer players have been taking place. In some cases, members of *Camorra* apparently asked a football team manager to exert pressure on doctors in a local hospital to support an illegal trade of organs (Saviano 2012).

Match fixing is not a new phenomenon in Italy (Foot 2007). The practice of rigging matches has deep cultural roots. In 1927 an attempt of corruption during the match between *Torino Calcio* and *Juventus* induced the Italian fascist regime to revoke the Championship won by *Torino Calcio*; in 1982, players of *A.C. Milan* and *Lazio Rome* were condemned for being part of illegal gambling on soccer games, which led to the relegation to the Second Division (*Serie B*) of the two teams. Furthermore, despite the fact that there were no official judicial inquiries on match fixing in Italian football before 2004, Italian media investigations suggested several fixing episodes involving referees during the 1990s (Boeri and Severgini 2008).

In recent years, more precisely in 2006 and in 2011, Italian prosecutors brought to light two different scandals, known as *Calciopoli* and *Scommessopoli*. In May 2006, during an investigation on the use of doping in *Serie A*, the Italian first Division, tapping phone conversations revealed a large system of match fixing during the 2004–2005 Italian Championship, which was won by *Juventus*. In particular, the prosecutors found that general managers of major and minor soccer teams, such as *Juventus, A.C. Milan, Fiorentina, Lazio Rome*, and *Reggina*, had exerted pressure on referees and officials of the football federation in order to fix 78 out of 380 matches of the first league Championship. Although the judicial inquiry is still pending, the sport justice revoked the 2004–2005 Championship of *Juventus* and relegated the team to the Second Division (*Serie B*) with a reduction of nine points in the 2006–2007 Championship. Furthermore, *A.C. Milan* was penalized with a reduction of eight points; *Fiorentina* was excluded from the *UEFA Champions League* with a reduction of fifteen points; *Lazio Rome* experienced a reduction of three points and was prevented to play in the *UEFA* cup; *Reggina* experienced a reduction of fifteen points in *Serie A*. Finally, in 2012 the former general manager of *Juventus*, Luciano Moggi, was banned for life from all Italian football positions.

In June 2011, the investigators of the two Italian cities, Cremona and Bari, who started the judicial inquiry of the *Operation Last Bet*, discovered several fixing episodes in the professional Second, Third, and Fourth Divisions (i.e. *Serie B, Lega Pro Prima Divisione*, and *Lega Pro Seconda Divisione*). This investigation, known as *Scommessopoli*, also involved several former Italian players. The retired footballers Giuseppe Signori (former national player during the 1994 *FIFA World Cup*), Mauro Bressan (midfielder for *Fiorentina* during the 1999–2000 Championships), Cristiano Doni (attacking midfielder during the 2002 *FIFA World Cup*) were all arrested. Furthermore, other tens of people connected with episodes of match fixing were accused of rigging several minor matches finalized to illegal betting.

In the following section we shall highlight common features and differences between the last two scandals.

Winning or Betting? Two Types of Corruption

The investigations carried out in Italy by the local police and by *Interpol* provide ample material for studies of the determinants and mechanisms behind corruption in football. Tapped phone calls allow to observe the decisions and the actions among the corruptors, offering to researchers a large amount of information. Like in a large scale version of a reality show, we can observe the peculiar characteristics of *Calciopoli* and *Scommessopoli* in a very detailed way. For instance, these phone call registrations report the timing of the fixing, the identity of all the fixers, their favorite targets, the reasons for fixing a particular match and which type of games were corrupted.

The facts that emerged from *Calciopoli* and *Scommessopoli* underline two different types of match fixing. In the first scandal, we observe *corruption for sportive results*, i.e. team managers who are active in order to manipulate the

Table 1 A comparison between *Calciopoli* and *Scommessopoli*

Characteristics	Match fixing scandals	
	Calciopoli	*Scommessopoli*
Motivation for fixing the game	Modify the sportive results	Illegal bettings
Agents acting as corrupter	Team managers	Criminal organizations
Corruption target	Referees	Soccer players
Timing	Middle of championship	At the end of the championship
Type of games rigged	Games relevant for the championship	Relatively minor games and *Coppa Italia* matches

outcomes of a tournament by altering results of games involving directly or indirectly (e.g., penalizing potential competitors) their team. In the second scandal, *corruption* occurs to secure *betting results* for criminal organizations, that are the main fixers of the game. The tools of economic theory are quite useful to explain the decision trees and the underlying mechanisms involved in these two kinds of corruption episodes. Table 1 summarizes the main characteristics and differences between the two types of match fixing.

In this section, based on the material provided by the police, we particularly emphasize the mechanisms behind the first scandal, i.e. *Calciopoli*, for two main reasons. Firstly, there are several economic studies related to betting scandals in football (e.g. Forrest 2012), while there has been to date relatively scarce scientific work on the type of scandal exemplified by *Calciopoli*. Secondly, recent studies (e.g. Buraimo et al. 2012) show that the 2004 scandal has not only reduced the credibility and the attention for soccer, but also the revenues of teams. A large number of supporters, shocked by the results of investigations on match fixing, stopped either attending matches at the stadium or watching the games on TV, which has lead to a drastic decrease of the teams' revenues and of welfare. In other words, this type of corruption seems to exert long-lasting negative externalities on wellbeing of individuals interested in sport events and on the financial conditions of the clubs, including those not involved in match fixing.

A template of the characteristics of *Scommessopoli* is presented in Fig. 1, displaying a typical example of corruption related to betting scandals.[2] The figure illustrates how illegal money are invested in match fixing in different countries, and how the interactions involve several players. Criminal organizations decide to invest their own massive amount of liquidity[3] obtained from their illegal activity into betting syndicates for money laundering purposes and -at the same time- to obtain a high return on investment. These syndicates use to diversify their investment asking

---

[2]Foschini and Mensurati (2012) describe the mechanisms of the Italian *Scommessopoli* in a detailed fashion; Hill (2010) illustrates the mechanism of organized crime and betting at an international level.

[3]For the role played by liquidity, see Forrest (2012).

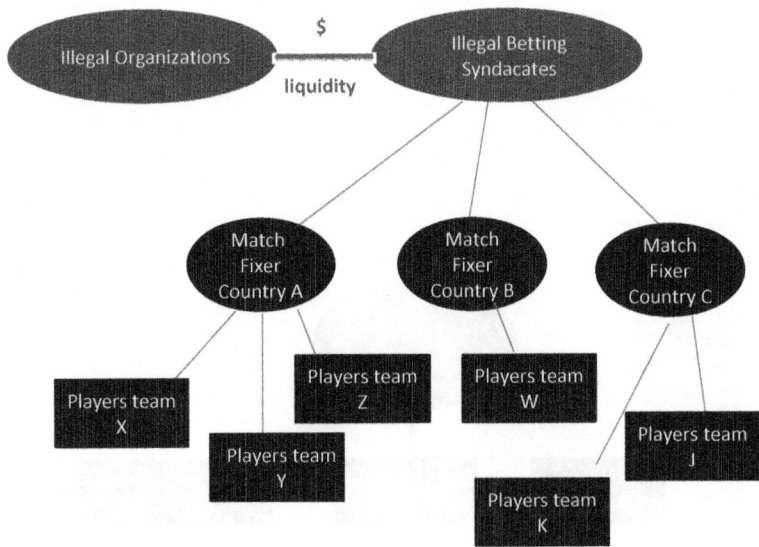

Fig. 1 A stylized representation of corruption for betting results

match fixers to manipulate the number of goals scored, by bribing or blackmailing football players in order to obtain substantial revenues from the rigged matches.

Investigations show that the main targets of corruption were football players, some of whom had been famous in the past and were at the time of the fixing competing in rather minor teams during the final part of their career and/or were playing in teams with financial difficulties. In order to minimize the risk of being discovered by police investigations, match fixers usually choose events covered by very low media attention. The types of rigged matches are often games of lower divisions (most of them are played in *Serie B* and *Lega Pro*) or qualifying rounds of the *Italy Tim Cup* (*Coppa Italia*), non-relevant for the Championship, usually played at the end of the season, once the winner is already decided.

The tapped phone calls in *Calciopoli* suggest that the main goals of match fixing type I was to obtain precise sets of sportive results. Figure 2 displays a stylized representation of the scandal. In these corruption episodes, sport managers[4] were the main source of fixing. During the 2004–2005 Italian Championship, we observed *Juventus* and *A.C. Milan* competing for the final victory in the *Serie A*; while *Fiorentina* and *Lazio Rome* were competing for a position qualifying them in one of the international competitions; *Reggina* was instead struggling to avoid relegation in *Serie B*.

---

[4]Unlike some English *Premier League teams,* coaches in Italy are different from team managers and have just sporting tasks.

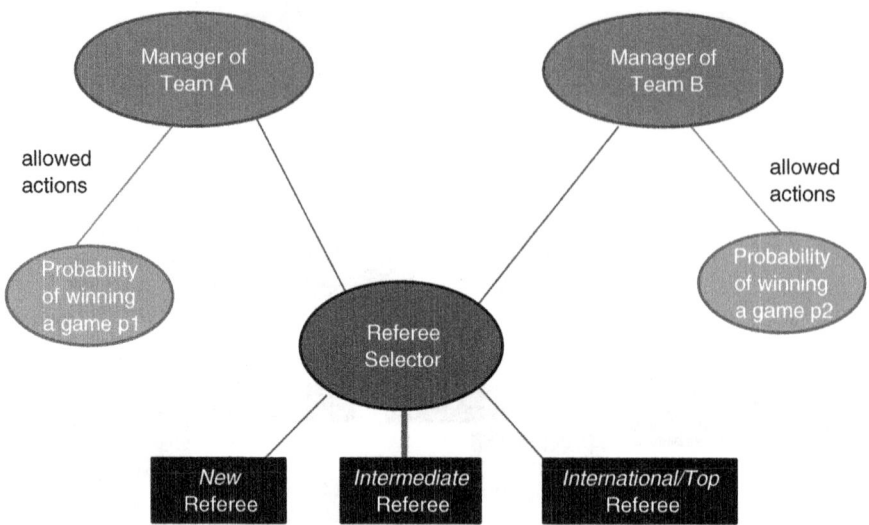

Fig. 2 A stylized representation of corruption for sporting results

The Economic Toolbox for Explaining Match Fixing

Figure 2 describes the interactions among managers, the referee selector and different types of referees in the fixing of games for sportive results. The main goal of the team managers involved in match rigging was to alter the outcome of a game in order either to win a Championship or to allow their own team to reach a particular position during the competition (e.g., *Uefa Cup*, avoiding a relegation, etc.). In this case, the corrupters, however, had a *limited* amount of resources to allocate to bribes or pressure (capture by threat) in order to attain this goal. Figure 2 describes the relevant interactions and the decisions of the managers of the teams. The limited budget, at the disposal of club managers can be allocated to two different types of activities. The first activity is enhancing the competitive strength of the team by legal means, i.e. buying and selling good athletes, hiring a new coach, investing in game strategy, etc. Those activities are positively related to the managers' competences. The second type of activity relates to spending money and effort in match fixing.

The decision of managers' over investing money and energy in regular activities or match fixing, is based on a continuous evaluation of the costs and benefits of the legal versus illegal activity. Economics and, in particular, the field of research of *Price Theory* introduced by the Nobel Prize Gary Becker, is very useful for explaining this phenomena and in predicting the decisions of the different economic agents. We show below how these techniques can be applied to the *Calciopoli* scandal.

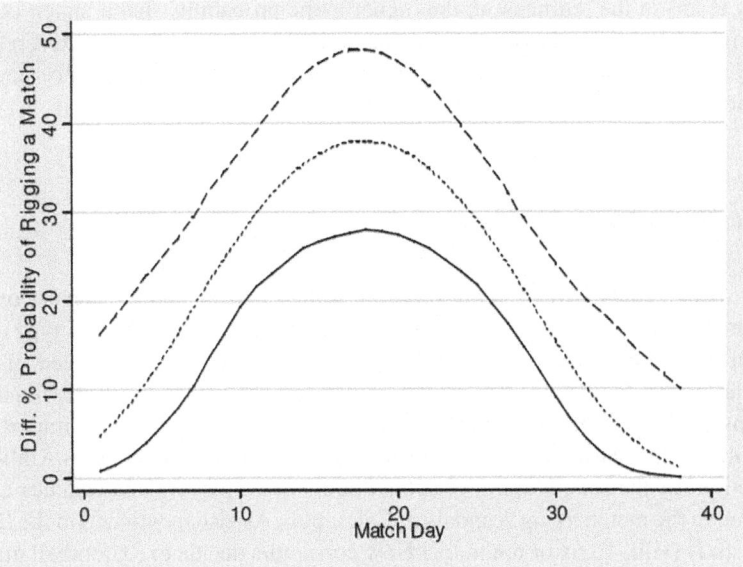

Fig. 3 Difference probability of rigging a match (Source: Boeri and Severgnini 2008)

Econometric Techniques for Studying Match Fixing

In one of our publications (Boeri and Severgnini, The Italian Job: Match Rigging, Career Concerns and Media Concentration in Serie A 2008) we investigate the main determinants of match fixing, exploiting the massive information provided by the registered phone calls and by sportive statistics. More in detail, from the judicial records, we have information on which matches have been rigged, which team manager have exerted pressure, which referees have been involved and on the timing of corruption. Furthermore, we merge this type of information with the personal characteristics of the referees, the yearly financial situation of each team and the sportive performance of the players during each match.

Applying advanced econometric techniques, we find that the main drivers of match fixing relate to the sportive performance of teams. More precisely, we find that the number of matches rigged is much higher in the second half of the Championship than in the first and that the probability of match rigging increases as the challenge of the competitors becomes more serious. This suggests that there is an option value in waiting to know the relative performance of the team before deciding upon the allocation of resources to either legal or illegal activities. Figure 3 provides a graphical representation of the pattern of the difference of probability of fixing a match along different match days according to our empirical model: halfway throughout the tournament, we can observe an increase of about 35 % in the probability of match fixing. Furthermore, we find that the higher is the competition among teams in the tournament, the higher is the probability that a match is going to be rigged. In other words, a team manager is much more likely to exert pressure on the referees once the main competitor is improving its performance and may become a very serious obstacle on the way to attain the desired outcome.

Career Concerns and Match Fixing

In our second study (Boeri and Severgnini, Match rigging and the career concerns of referees 2011), we observed that the typical strategy followed in this type of corruption was to exert pressure on referees in a systematic way.[5] Instead of using financial bribes, team managers preferred instead to influence the professional promotions of the referees, drawing on their own career concerns. It is important to stress that in this case it is the referees to be the target of the corrupters. Unlike the corruption for the sake of betting results, both soccer players and coaches are not involved in the match fixing scandals of Calciopoli. As also mentioned in the Declan Hill's study (Hill, To fix or not to fix? How corruptors decide to fix football matches 2009), referees-with their own decision on faults, penalties, cards and off-sides-provide an implicit guarantee that match fixing will be successful. Furthermore, it is much cheaper to involve referees, as opposed to players, in corruption episodes. Indeed those players, who, with their own performance, can potentially bias the results of a football game, usually have much higher earnings than referees have, and, in the case of superstar players, they have a salary which is about 100 times higher than the average earnings of an Italian referee.

The targets in *Calciopoli* were referees who were at a crucial step in their career, i.e., just before an international promotion (also defined *intermediate* referees). According to the data on Italian referees' characteristics and salaries that we collected, we found that the increase of lifetime earnings associated to an international promotion can be quantified in about 2.2 million dollars. These career concerns of intermediate referees contribute to explain why both referees at the early stage of their career (*new* referees) and experienced referees (*international/top* referee) were not involved in Calciopoli.

How to Prevent Future Episodes of Match Fixing

Based on the analysis of the two recent match fixing scandals in Italy, our results provide some suggestions as to how to detect and prevent future episodes of match fixing. First of all, our findings suggest that judicial investigations should be concentrated on matches played during the second half of the Championship, especially

---

[5]Cheloukhine (2012) describes a similar type of corruption in Russian soccer.

when the competition is getting tougher, and the uncertainty as to the final sportive outcome is somewhat lower, i.e., the probability of success is better defined. Secondly, we learned that at least in the case of referees, career concerns can be a substitute for financial bribes. Thus, we suggest that policies for detecting and preventing corruption should especially control the referees who can, potentially, be promoted in the near future. Therefore, more transparency on referees' designation rules and evaluations may reduce the probability of match fixing. Furthermore, incentives are important: a compensation scheme for referees with relevant flat-rate salary components could make referees less vulnerable to the decisions of the referee selectors and to the pressure exerted by the team managers.

Conclusions

In this chapter we analyzed the match fixing phenomenon, devoting particular attention to corruption aimed at altering sport results. Unlike several studies on corruption in sports, we find that we can exploit the judicial investigations of two major scandals in Italian soccer in 2006 and 2011, i.e. *Calciopoli* and *Scommessopoli*, to analyze the determinants of match fixing. Theoretical models and empirical (econometric) estimates converge in pointing out that time before the end of the tournament and the proximity of competitors in the ranking do affect the likelihood of match rigging. Furthermore, we find that referees who are likely to be promoted are the most important targets of corruption. More transparency and better incentives for referees, e.g., in terms of flat compensation schemes, can be useful to reduce episodes of match rigging in the future.

References

Boeri, Tito, and Battista Severgnini. "Match rigging and the career concerns of referees." *Labour Economics*, 2011: 349–359.

Boeri, Tito, and Battista Severgnini. "The Decline of Professional Football in Italy." *IZA Discussion Papers, 7018*, 2012.

Boeri, Tito, and Battista Severgnini. "The Italian Job: Match Rigging, Career Concerns and Media Concentration in Serie A." *IZA Discussion Papers, 3745*, 2008.

Buraimo, Babatunde, Migali, Giuseppe, Simmons, Robert. *Corruption does not pay: An analysis of consumer response to Italy Calciopoli's scandal.* Working Paper, Lancaster: Lancaster University, 2012.

Cheloukhine, Serguei. *Fixing Match in Football: Organization, Structure and Policing. The Russian Case.* Singapore: Paper presented at conference Interpol Global Academic Experts. Meeting for Integrity in Sport, 2012, 353–374.

Cook, William A. *The 1919 World Series: What really happened?* Jefferson NC: McFarland, 2001.

Duggan, Mark, and Steven D. Levitt. "Winning isn't everything: Corruption in sumo wrestling." *American Economic Review*, 2002: 594–605.

Foot, John. *Calcio: A history of Italian football.* New York: Harper Perennial, 2007.

Forrest, David. "The threat to football from betting-related corruption." *International Journal of Sport Finance*, 2012: 99–116.

Foschini, Giuliano, and Marco Mensurati. *Lo zingaro e lo scarafaggio. Da gioco piu' bello a gioco piu' sporco del mondo: Viaggio tra le macerie del calcio italiano*. Milan: Mondadori, 2012.

Foschini, Giuliano, og Marco Mensurati. *Lo zingaro e lo scarafaggio. Da gioco piu' bello a gioco piu' sporco del mondo: Viaggio tra le macerie del calcio italiano*. Milan: Mondadori, 2012.

Fritzpatrick, Nick. "Bets on - tackling illegal gambling." *Legal Week*, 2013.

Harris, Arthur Harold. *Greek athletes and athletics*. London: Hutchinson, 1964.

Hill, Declan. *The Fix: Soccer and Organized Crime*. Toronto: McClelland & Stewart, 2010.

Hill, Declan. "To fix or not to fix? How corruptors decide to fix football matches." *Global Crime*, 2009.

Konrad, Kai. "Sabotage in Rent Seeking Contest." *Journal of Law, Economics, and Organization*, 2000: 155–165.

Lambsdorff, Johann Graf. *The institutional economics of corruption and reform: Theory, evidence and policy*. Cambridge: Cambridge University Press, 2007.

Preston, Ian, and Stefan Szymanski. "Cheating in contest." *Oxford Review of Economic Policy*, 2003: 612–24.

Rosen, Daniel M. *Dope: A History of Performance Enhancement in Sports from the Nineteenth Century to Today*. Washington: ABC-Clio, 2008.

Saviano, Roberto. *Supersantos*. Milan: Feltrinelli, 2012.

Tanzi, Vito. *Corruption Around the World. Causes, Consequences, Scope, and Cures*. IMF Staff Papers, Washington: International Monetary Fund, 1998.

Transparency International. *Corruption Perceptions Index 2012*. Berlin: Transparency International, 2012.

Wolfers, Justin. "Exposing cheating and corruption: Point shaving in Basketball." *American Economic Review: Papers and Proceedings*, 2006: 279–83.

Match Fixing in Soccer: Organization, Structure and Policing. A Russian Perspective

Serguei Cheloukhine

Abstract Fixing soccer games is a thriving business which will continue in the near and far future, unless some extreme mechanisms of control are put in place and implemented. All these illegal activities are derived from a social nature of human being, mercantile ambition, and thirst for glory and, of course, struggle for power. Every fixed match has its own character and goal. We will examine this phenomenon in three categories. First is aimed at receiving illegal profit. Second one is usually organized by club presidents and owners. Many of them are politicians, tycoons or "Russian Oligarchs" whose living credo is "victory by all costs". The third one is splitting game scores. Soccer in Russia is not a sport competition but rather a business to make big money; buying and selling players, millions of dollars in advertisement contracts, television and the internet shows. This chapter attempts to investigate the nature and depth of match fixing in the Russian football and offer possible solutions to curb its growth.

Fixing Soccer Matches

Soccer – the game loved by the entire world – is currently experiencing a tragic moment in its history. These situations can occur when the world of sport and business collide in a manner which may bring the game into disrepute[1]. In the contemporary sports world these types of games can be compared to a theater play,

---

[1]Since this article is intended for publication in the United States, the author will be using term "soccer" rather than the broadly used "football" in Europe and Russia.

S. Cheloukhine, Ph.D. (✉)
Department of Law, Police Science and Criminal Justice, John Jay College
of Criminal Justice, City University of New York, New York, USA
e-mail: scheloukhine@jjay.cuny.edu

M.R. Haberfeld and D. Sheehan (eds.), *Match-Fixing in International Sports:*
Existing Processes, Law Enforcement, and Prevention Strategies,
DOI 10.1007/978-3-319-02582-7_7, © Springer International Publishing Switzerland 2013

in which teams play a match where the result was determined before the game even begins and according to the script, the final scene is stipulated in advance. This syndrome is commonly know as "match fixing." Several questions arise in this situation, amongst them: who benefits from match fixing and who suffers the most consequences?

According to rates quoted by various bookmaker offices, estimates of the financial implications of match fixing vary from league to league and game to game. However, conservative estimates are that match fixing organizers can profit from hundreds of thousands to millions of dollars for a single match. Although even though the low end of the scale may seem like a lot of money, one may question how that profit is achieved (Matveev 2009).

Though there are many various methods of match fixing, all of them are united by one common principle – to earn money in any manner possible by betting on soccer. As an example, in a given situation Club representatives could conceiveably work on an agreement between themselves and then bet on the pre determined result. Such an agreement can have several outcomes and beneficiaries. It could be favorable for both parties or for one of them who could, in addition to other benefits, pay or forfeit an amount to the other party for losing the game or any other component of the bet. When organized in a pre determined manner, the bets are then staked and the subsequent result of profits made.

Soccer, in recent years, has come under scrutiny in the media for having a darker side involving million of dollars in illegal match fixing and questionable business operations, often be compared to an organized criminal empire (Matveev 2009). Recent cases have been highlighted showing some leagues or teams are ruled by the same laws of the black market as any other sphere of a profitable, semi-legal business (Ibid). The only difference is that the players in the sport serve as commodities and the role of a supplier is played by some entity that could be compared to a sort of "labor union." The history of threats indicate that revealing names or potential identities could have severe repercussions and that in disclosing and discussing these relevant activities related to this business, that it must be done with due diligence.

The evolution of match fixing in Russia has seen the Captains of the Russian post-Soviet soccer business having already grown out of their "crimson jackets",[2] having replaced a habitual gangster type attribute with one more reflecting of a European glamour model. These "entrepreneurs" have demonstrated they prefer to steer clear of violence against soccer magnates. Certainly it would do those involved no good to have Russia maintain the status of one of the last islands of "the wild capitalism." A further development of the most favorite national sport is therefore quite predictable.

In setting out a plan for complete domination (or having set a plan for complete domination), several components must come together. First, the richest clubs would

---

[2] After introducing market in post-soviet Russia, many small business entrepreneurs were connected to Organized Crime groups and leaders whose fashion and way of affiliation was to wear colorful jackets. colorful jackets.

divide the remaining and lucrative resources amongst themselves, which are the players and sponsors. Then a number of notorious "unfriendly absorption" transactions would follow. Finally, a soccer branch of Russian business would start acquiring western clubs, taking away rival awards and titles and delivering talented players in exchange.

For several years soccer championships in Russia are accompanied by continuous accusations of the complete selling of matches and/or the bribing of soccer officials. Further issues have arisen about the imperfection or lack of legislation required to combat match fixing effectively in Russia. In its current form, Soccer officials diligently delegate the responsibility for investigating accusations of match fixing to law enforcement agencies. However, traditionally, the police do not want to become involved as historically such investigations denote a lack of evidence, perpetrators, and willing victims to come forward in order to open a criminal case.

The legislation of the Russian Federation in this area is far from perfect with the only current legal article in the Criminal Code of the Russian Federation being Article 184, which allows punishing the participants and organizers of "match fixing." This Article, however, is limited for enforcement purposes in that it states the responsibility is only for cases of bribing athletes, sports judges, trainers, team managers, and other participants or organizers of professional sports competitions in regards to the transferring of money in exchange for desired results. It is clear that the current legislation considerably lags behind the new and current complexities of match fixing facing the game of soccer today.

There is no doubt that fixing soccer games has always been a thriving business, and as long as there is an opportunity for lucrative profits, always will be. This derives from social nature of the humans, their mercantile ambitions, thirst for glory and, of course, struggle for power. In contemporary soccer, fixing match is one of the three existing evils. Every fixed match has its own specifics and goals. This chapter will examine this phenomenon in three categories and how it is affecting the game of soccer in Russia.

Fixing Matches for Pure Profit

It occupies the smallest share, but is the most disgraceful and dangerous in the area of fixing matches. Soccer players, judges, trainers or team owners pre-determine a deliberate result in favor of an outcome of a match, or any part of same. The follow up through underground bookmakers, or by bribing the rival club itself, results in an illegal profit and tarnishes the integrity of the game. One may question how this method can account for only a small share of the lucrative business of match fixing. In reality, arrangements occurring at the player, trainer or judge level rarely take place on a regular basis. Also, there is a club owner who is certainly not the simplest person on a planet, after all (Dogovornye matchi, http://www.dogovornoymatch.org/).

Therefore this type of arrangement is a distinctive feature for matches that preclude an absence of sports motivation through an outcome of a championship or

Table 1 "True fixed matches" (http://www.dogovornoymatch.org/)

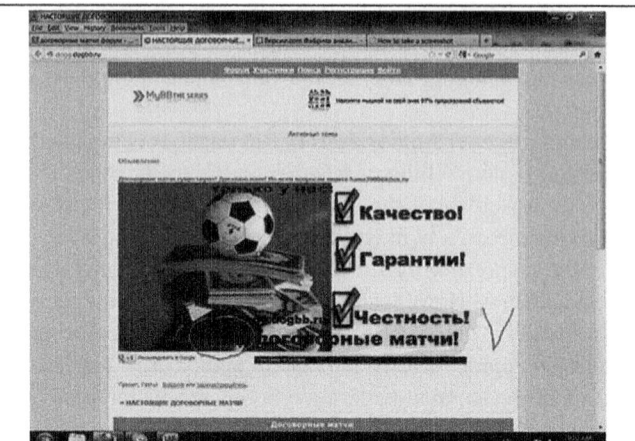

a cup, or the change of a tournament outcome given it does not have an historical adherence to principles of opposition. Moreover, soccer players have the potential to earn a high awards and bonuses for a victory. This method is both dangerous and disgraceful because underground betting, more often than not, is connected to organized crime, the underground casinos, and non illegal lotteries. Not all of these activities are under vigilant control of law enforcement and pursued by law enforcement.

For example, by checking Russian search engines, in 0.18 s, there are 150,000 hits with fixed matches and betting options. This image below (see Table 1) suggests 100 % guaranteed return in betting promising quality and honesty in fixing matches.

Fixing Matches Among Owners and Club Presidents

The second category is the organization of fixed matches amongst owners and club presidents. Many of them are financial tycoons, high-ranking politicians and businesspersons. For them, a steady positive result of a game is the corresponding card of their success indicators in society. Their vital credo is "Victory by all cost!" Therefore achievement of positive results, gaining a champion title, prize-winning placement and successful games in the international cups, is vital. Thus, the possibility of arrangements taking place at the highest level are highly possible with little desire to override that (Matveev 2009).

It is more often than not, the benefit of the arrangement is not solely financial, but other spheres of influence, favorable business contracts, as well as political motivations are high motivations for involvement. Information on such arrangements seldomly emerge and are not very well known. It could be something as small as a trainer or manager entering a change room to state "the president considers the victory in this game not to be in our best interest". This type of method therefore also precludes the first category (*fixing matches for profit*) as they are practically excluded.

Dividing Points

The third and the most dangerous category is dividing points. The large majority of soccer clubs play at the average level and do not have the opportunity to set themselves to compete at the Premier League championships or international cups. Soccer to them is the instrument of doing business at a highest possible level that they can achieve. Clubs acquire most of the profit from sale-purchase of players, advertising contracts, television and internet of show (Newsru 2012). Hence, in order to support and develop these tracks it is absolutely necessary to support the higher level of the game. For this purpose teams agree among themselves about the necessary distribution of points (Matveev 2009).

As an example, Team *A* has arrangements with four other teams in the same league for a principle victory at home and a defeat on a competitor's field. Thus, each team has already accumulated 12 points for the championship that greatly reduces chances of either team leaving the league as a bottom tier relegation. Such arrangements can exist for years and rarely cause suspicion, as both teams are approximately equal and sit somewhere in the middle of the standings. This phenomenon in soccer is universal and has the tendency to increase as soccer is increasingly becoming a business rather than a sport (Ibid, 2009).

Increasing Use of Dirty Technologies

With the increased nature of technologies involved in sports, practically all people acting in soccer, – players, trainers, officials, judges, and team's sponsors have access to same to facilitate illegal activities in soccer. Moreover, the atmosphere of players and judges purchases and sales, having flourished for decades in Russian soccer, adds to the provocation of shady business practices for uncontrolled and non enforced actions. They feel uninhibited and without obstruction and are not under scrutiny from the law enforcement. With limited budgets and staff, Police have more serious state crime to investigate and match fixing or criminality in football is not considered a high priority.

According to some experts, the scale of this ugly phenomenon has the potential to increase as fixing matches allegedly decreases (Matveev 2009). It's became more and more difficult to agree on some issues and the money for this is not always available. Therefore, there is a thought that yesterdays schemers should play fairly. That said, match fixing has not disappeared. It is felt the evolution of these technologies, if utilized properly, could gradually increase the eradication of crime in soccer. To start, we will explain the essence of the problem.

As an example, team representatives, before the actual start of a soccer match, come to an agreed upon arrangement for a fixed result which satisfies both parties. In fact, it is not obligatory, nor for that matter necessary, that in an orbit of secret negotiations all soccer players, trainers, and club managers need to be involved. Sometimes there may be two or three people from each party to make a deal or transaction. The result, for a certain price, is that these unfortunate masters, in the face of thousands of fans, imitate an honest game on the field which almost always reaches the required results.

There are tens, if not hundreds of fixed games delivery combinations. For example, the defender whose services are paid prior to the match's beginning, can fall accidentally in the penalty square, having opened a passageway for a rival pass. Or, out of the blue, violate a rule and receive a penalty. Sometimes rivals silently play for a beneficially drawn game, with the audience once again deceived, all while the interests of *the high parties* are observed. This does not happen in every domestic match, however, according to analysts, 20–30 % of soccer games, in every season, are fixed (Matveev 2009).

Some Scenarios of "Match Fixing"

There are several options to potentially fix a match, the first being the simplest one: selling points. Representatives of one club can, and do, reach out to the representatives of the other with a proposed specific amount of money for an agreed upon outcome. At the beginning of the season, the amount could start at 100 thousand dollars and by the end of the season reach 400–500 thousand dollars (Matveev 2009). When it appears everything is set, a new element or surprise could be introduced. A few players players could be bribed (most likely defenders or the goalkeeper), or the coach could be involved and makes replacements and substitutions with poorly trained or unqualified players.

A second option is the most widespread: "three-three" score. Teams at the beginning of a season agree upon mutual victories. Usually, as a rule, it takes place at the level of weakest and average clubs with the outcome being everyone wins at the home field.

The third option is six points for the next season. For example, the victory is vital to some losing team. They ask the rival to fix the game and in return an agreement is made, promise to lose twice the following year.

The final option and perhaps the most exotic one, involves three points for the player. At an agreed upon point once in the season, in addition for the transfer, sell or trade of a good player, one solid and well performing stronger team have to pay with their own defeat in a match.

These arrangements do not always go as planned and sometimes the business transaction ends with outrage and a dissatisfied party. For example, one of the first leagues matches in Russia this year, which was not expecting any publicity, suddenly ended with fist fight in the back room. A soccer team had to fix the game over to a southern team and everything was negotiated: the trainer released a semi-reserve team and the judge, for reliability was "loaded" with money. As a result, the southerners – according to the scenario – planned for a 2:1 outcome and acquired the right to a penalty, but did succeed in making it. Moreover, at the last minute suddenly gave up a questionable goal. The score was 2:2, and instead of and "easy" three points, the southern team received only one. The altercation then took place due to the pending obligations (Sport-weekend 2012).

In another example, a team, trying to avoid exit, asked another team to fix a game over for six points in the following year. The proposal was encouraging as the club was in the second class and would lose nothing in the current season. However, in the following season, the club could gain potential to climb into the highest league, so any reserved points would be of help. The only condition was a guarantee that the hopeful team, would survive, otherwise it would be impossible to determine who would give the six points back. The game ended according to the plan – 1:2, but at the finish the unfortunate club took off, having brought the contractors into bewilderment and frustration (Matveev 2009).

This scenario is an exception rather than the rule. With such a scheme, fixing a match is usually always insured via advance payment. Even though the next season is yet to come, the money must be transferred at the moment and yet the club still must and shall lose twice, as agreed in order to receive advance payment in return.

There was another, highly suspicious incident in Russia. A Trans-Ural team approached rivals on their field and demanded pay for a loss (a case to admit this is extraordinary). Otherwise, they stated they would play hard. This was very understandable as when this incident took place, the team had nothing to lose given even a potential departure from a league would not affect the club (Sport-weekend 2012).

And the last, most shocking example, is the way in which representatives of the southern criminal group prevented match fixing. A recently created club was planning to fix a match over to a team fighting to enter the premier league. Everything was ready to go when some influential people, from the competitors club, suddenly interfered (they represented the interests of two southern teams which had combined efforts for a joint move into a premier league) and persistently stated the game had to be played fair. The outcome of the game was not as expected as it was a draw. However it was clearly in the best interests of all parties to come to a mutual agreement to avoid repercussions (Newsru 2012).

All in all, the origin of money in soccer and its progress after all is the principle issue. Criminal money brings criminal customs and, in the case of the Russian championship, it is very difficult to get rid of once instituted in the game. Longevity of the game's imminence is also critical as the young soccer players, who are constantly being approached and participating in match fixing, will have a very difficult time becoming future stars.

Spartak Vodka with Coca-Cola

A history of the popular soccer club "Spartak", illustrates it is not just a smaller circle of criminal linked to match fixing. The national team always enjoyed admiration of all top-bottom level authorities and in hard times could be counted on to collect the various benefits. This benefits included allocation of free of charge land plots to granting tax exemptions. According to the Ministry of Internal Affairs of the Russian Federation, for this particular reason, "Spartak" drew the attention of *Alazansky*[3], a criminal group and one of its leaders Ruslan Atlangeriyev (who subsequently was kidnapped and disappeared in Moscow).

As field investigators revealed, criminal groups helped implant one of their members in "Spartak" and the club began to act as the guarantor under many contracts for and with the *Alazanskaya* organized criminal group. Thus, as one of their underground business enterprises, vodka "Spartak" and the soft drink "Spartak Cola" were introduced. Moreover, using the club's "roof", a network of the gas stations were constructed in the Moscow area. During this period of transition and unexpectedly, "Spartak" received a new general manager, Larissa Nechaeva, who was brought in by the coach Oleg Romantsev.

Mrs. Nechaeva decided to not only stop doubtful schemes, but also fired the mafia's person from the club. Right after these strong actions, in the summer of 1997 Larisa Nechaeva was killed in her Vladimir's country house. Police quickly identified the suspects, – Alexey Zdor and Vladimir Tenashvili, however, they too, "went missing" in the Chechen Republic. Later, both were killed for "an unsuccessful assassination attempt" of Aslan Maskhadov[4] which was allegedly ordered by the Chechen criminal group leaders originating from Chechen Republic (Matveev 2009).

The elimination of people resisting criminal organizations is an everyday occurrence in the underworld environment In Russia. Such an unfortunate fate did not spare soccer agents either. Yury Tishkov, the former Torpedo and Dinamo player, was killed in the yard of his house in January 2003 and became the one of the most known victims. One of the motives was that Mr. Tishkov was closely watching young perspective soccer players, who in fact, are currently playing leading roles for the Russian national team. Mr. Tishkov's friend, the former goalkeeper Valery Sarychev, met Yury shortly before the murder. Mr. Tishkov informed Valery of receiving menacing calls from unknown persons, but did not pay attention to them. The crime still remains unsolved today (Ibid, 2009).

---

[3]Chechen criminal group under leadership of Lom-Ali Gaitukaev was active in 1990s and involved in a range of fraudulent financial charges in banking.
[4]Aslan (Khalid) Aliyevich Maskhadov, was a leader of the Chechen separatist movement and the third President of the Chechen Republic of Ichkeria.

Stealing Budget Money

The considerable part of any regional soccer clubs survival is the expense of state or a region's budget. This also attracts attention of the criminal groups. For example, the Voronezh regions "Fakel" club management, from the beginning of 2001, became a target of criminal investigation. Investigators found out that the considerable amount of money allocated to the club was received by people officially unrelated to "Fakel" (Table 2).

A similar situation happened to Grozny "Terek". The head of "Chechentransgaz" Mr. Umar Yasayev received Power of Attorney from the President of Chechnya Republic Ahmad Kadyrov[5], granting the right to work independently with revenues associated to the club. As a result, a considerable amount of money "Chechentransgaz" collected passed through suspicious business, and disappeared. Based on that, the Investigative Committee at the Ministry of Internal Affairs of the Russian Federation brought a criminal case forward against "Chechentransgaz". What surprised investigators was that when interrogated, Mr. Yasayev admitted that the millions of dollars were not stolen at all, but in fact were all used with permission of the Republic Leader (Kadyrov, [S.C.]) for "Terek" needs.

With the arrival of vast capital investments into soccer clubs and teams, it became difficult for criminals to implement "the 1990s mafia's methods", although, they were not all completely eliminated. Among the soccer representatives there are still people allegedly connected to crime. For example, In 2002, Osman Kadiyev, the president of the soccer club "Dynamo", Makhachkala, Republic of Dagestan, was red flagged and put on the international wanted list by the FBI. He was suspected of extortion and forgery from former USSR natives. Mr. Kadiyev was considered person No. 3 in 'the Russian mafia list" in the USA – after "thieves in law" Vyacheslav Ivankov (*Yaponchik*) and Alexander Bohr (*Timoha*). Kadiyev simply ignored these charges (Russian Mafia 2012).

Mr. Kadiyev became one of the persons involved in an attempt of match fixing between "Terek" and CSKA, in Grozny. As Judge Alexander Gvardis acknowledged after the game, during break time three persons, including Mr. Osman Kadiyev, attacked him in a changing room. The three threatened the referee that "if he will not judge the way they want, they will find him everywhere" (Ibid, 2012).

Threats to fair play that criminal groups presented in recent years have grown to such proportions that they became a subject of close attention of intelligence services, including INTERPOL. In Germany, for example, the Croatian criminal group was investigated for bribing judges. Similar investigations took place in Finland, the Czech Republic and Austria. Business activity of bookmakers is being monitored

---

[5] Akhmad Kadyrov was the Chief Mufti of the Chechen Republic of Ichkeria in the 1990s during and after the First Chechen War. At the outbreak of the Second Chechen War he switched sides, offering his service to the Russian government, and later became the President of the Chechen Republic from 5 October 2003, acting as head of administration since July 2000. http://en.ria.ru/russia/20091215/157250277.html RIA Novosti, Vladimir Vyatkin "Chechnya establishee Kadyrov peace award". 12/15/2009, accessed 19/10/2003.

Table 2 Fixed matches in Europe and Russia

Fixed Matches in Europe	Fixed Matches in Russia
1. Mafioso finds a person well connected to soccer players. Usually this is a former player having some money, alcohol or women problems. 2. Former player agrees to talk to some key players and judge that a potential result could be dependent on. In the second German Bundestag League, a soccer player was offered 10-20.000 Eu and judges 9-15.000 Eu 3. Mafioso betting on a particular team and score. Not attract law enforcement bids are not too large. For example for German Championship match between Paderborn - Hamburg betting was about 80.000 euros, but winners took a few hundreds thousands[1]. 4. Criminals involve more participants; as in case of German's referee R. Hoizer	1. Club's President who needs team victory meets rivals President; price tag: first division – 50-60.000 euros; premier League – 100-250.000. They can also trade points for the next season. 2. Cash to bribe competing club managers and players comes from the club funds misallocation and often from criminals interested in a particular club. 3. Before the match both parties meet with involved handling money; rarely it's done after the fact. 4. In case negotiation fails due to unexpected disagreements, or request is too high, a judge will be targeted to fix the match.

and investigated by a special task force at INTERPOL, with controls on how authorities should report matches where the greatest interest among club players is affected. Along with negative publicity, Soccer officials are also being compelled to react. As a proactive measure, the Union of European Football Association (UEFA) created a special department to identify cases of fixing matches. However, in Russia, where almost daily discoveries cause outrage on match fixing and corruption is reported, it appears little or no proactive activity is taking place to prevent or follow it up on the national scale.

It is not a secret that representatives of many, if not all Russian soccer clubs, are compelled to approach Mafia, given they do not have the business experience to make a profit and the club's maintenance is a significant investment. In soccer, as in a mirror, all troubles of modern society are reflected. That is why one of the reasons the budgets of approximately 80 % of Russian teams consist of criminal money. It would be a mistake to think that Mafiosi-fans supply clubs with money just for the love of soccer (Rusarticles 2011).

Head of teams generously offer much needed financial support for clubs, but with extraordinary conditions or interest stipulated. In a simple plan, they would permit running the Mafia's commercial operations under the club umbrella, which usually enjoys tax exemptions and are rarely audited. For example, a criminal ring could ask the club managers to sell loads of expensive imported sports clothing in a domestic market, where 70–75 % of revenues goes back to the criminal organization and only about 30 % remains with a soccer team (Russian Mafia 2012). No taxes are paid and although it is said 30 % is not a large profit, it is still significant enough to pay everyone in club and the possibility of bribes (Ibid, 2012).

Although there is no doubt most clubs do have legal sponsors, even with including funds that come from government and the Ministry of Sports, these funds are small and typically not enough for a club to remain financially viable. Therefore, without mafia and criminal financial support, clubs simply cannot endure. There are always a few people on club lists traveling to European, Asian or World cups. Naturally these people can travel themselves, but a benefit of team travel is that the soccer teams baggage either is not examined at all, or informally checked. And the *"businessmen"* sponsoring the club, do not declare for example, diamonds, precious metals and cash. Mafia's slang would dictate it as traditional laundering, an old and reliable method with nobody interrupting the chain of illegal activity. Law enforcement knows about such "small" crimes, but simply closes its eyes or are not staffed to combat this (Ibid, 2012).

Frequently, at soccer games, these *"businessmen"* meet government and city officials where mutually advantageous deals are often discussed. Per chance, if it happens an official is a soccer fan, everything from acquiring property to federal or city contracts are made available. All that is required is financial support with a transfer to the club account (Russian Mafia 2012).

There are also other sources of shadow financing for example. Huge clothing markets in every city with soccer clubs have commercial potential. Many are cash transactions only, with neither cash registers nor verifications. All profit goes to the businessmen supervising or controlling soccer's paraphernalia sale for the clubs.

The entire Russian soccer is huge shadow chasm. However, these are the "rules of the game" in any country with underdeveloped laws in match fixing which could result in a lack of rule of law and a corrupt economy. City and municipal officials look for all possible scenarios to ensure the local team will not become stagnate and to at least simply survive, not to mention mythical prosperity. Thus odd decisions are often passed at the local legislative assemblies meetings, such as granting tax exemption status to some enterprises in return for a cash money transfer to soccer clubs.

Is there any solution to this deadlock for Russian domestic soccer? How does one stop the inflow of illegal money into the popular game?

In principle, it is easy to trace money transfers on the accounts, providing government decided to be proactive and create some inspection program to conduct both total and random inspections. The results would be that bribery, corruption and match fixing would be become more difficult to facilitate and thus decrease the occurrences.

For example, well-known Victor Ponedelnik, a former center forward of the Rostov SKA and USSR national team concurs: "We are witnessing the developed industry of purchase and sale of soccer matches. For this purpose some average clubs use the illegal cash "donated" by doubtful commercial structures. This money spent on bribing arbitrators, rival clubs managers and players as well as government or law enforcement officials. And the most terrible, vast majority of team trainers suits a present situation, they already got used to such "quagmire" (Nikitchenkov 2012).

Except the elite clubs, which are quite sustainable and profitable, there are about 80 % of financially unsuccessful or struggling teams. Those are most often in control of semi-legal, and illegal commercial structures, incorporating mafia-like small and joint ventures to sponsor soccer clubs every season.

Certainly, businessmen and criminals are financially concerned in a team's success and simply will not invest money in it otherwise. Therefore, the result is to often use blackmail and threats, bribing judges and in some cases trainers and soccer players of the rivals team in order to succeed. These transactions are not necessarily and only financial and sometimes include the offering of services in the acquisition of scarce goods, benefits and other resources.

Black market cash exists in all clubs which comes in from different sources. As an example, for club and management needs, the state and municipal sports agencies allocated, free of charge, four Lexus RX 570 SUV vehicles. Three of them are used by the club and the fourth is sold for 150,000 dollars. This money is used for bribing and fixing matches (Nikitchenkov 2012).

There are numerous ways in which to approach a judge. They can be approached on the street, airport or in a hotel room or at a dinner. There are an increasingly amount of opportunistic judges which collect money from the home and guest teams at the same time. If the home team wins, a portion of money goes back to guest's team, and vice versa. In case of a draw, there is a different option: if it suited the guests, the money remains with the judge (Ibid, 2012).

In some, if not in all soccer federations, there is a rigid and very peculiar "tax" system developed. There is well-known price list for fixing match (Ibid, 2012).

All trainers and players, are involved in some negotiation and agreements. Especially, this type of business turns out well for former team players who approach rival clubs and provide necessary results or recommendations for a concrete match outcome. Not all players have to be bribed, with as little as two-three from each party being a sufficient number.

Refereeing Matters

It is with great shame for the game, judges often can, and do, play a direct role in carrying out fixed matches.

As a rule, the so-called club's sponsors and the home team manager can try to bribe a judge and, if needed, endless and total blackmail will be used. Most judges do not report this to police for fear of that a lack of security and protection would be provided. Who to trust in coming forward remains a large problem for those with a desire to combat matchfixing.

Certainly, in a totally corrupt system of fixing matches it is not only judges who are the main characters of this performance but the soccer players themselves. Following are some episodes which remain behind the scene for the majority of fans, but demonstrate the integration of match fixing in Russian soccer: "If you will move to Moscow, a whole family will be slaughtered". This was local Mafiosi reacting to Dmitry Loskov's possible departure from Rostov "Rostselmash" to Moscow's CSKA (Nikitchenkov 2012). In fact, the transition of the halfback to CSKA never took place. Only later the senior club board members agreed to Loskov's departure to Moscow's "Locomotive". Similar stories accompanied Ruslan Nigmatullin, while at "Kazan" club and Oleg Veretennikov who plaid for Volgograd's 'Rotor" and some other well-known soccer players (Ibid, 2012). The threat or potential threat to benefit crime is clear.

One of the explanations for such tactics is that in almost each large city, where matches for the Russian championships take place, underground and illegal gambling are very prominent. Mafiosi make outstanding bets on results of actual matches (according to some police data, each gambler takes in 300–500 thousand dollars in bets from the Russian championship; the sum of 50 thousand dollars will be considered as failure) (Ibid, 2012).

Undoubtedly, gambling organizers are interested that club's leading players remain in their city and play a key role in their "gain or profit". For mafia, negotiations on the match desired results are often conducted with leading soccer players who then "work" with team associates. Such developed "*business*" of purchase and sale of soccer matches prospers for a long time and many club managers and law enforcement are turning a blind eye on it (Russian Mafia 2012).

This type of benefit can help explain why there is anyone who would voluntarily and without compensation permit soccer players to be transferred to other cities and clubs. Hence, mafia's influence for the best players in the league results in the best possible seasons proceeds. The following table (Table 3) below compares pays to top players and trainers.

Table 3 Comparing the top five paid players and trainers

Top 5 Players pay	Top 5 trainers pay
1.Miguel Danni («Зенит») 23 Mln Euro	1. Dick Advocate (Russia) – 7 Mln Euro
2. Bruni Alvesh («Зенит») 18 Mln Euro	2. Lucciano Spaletti («Зенит») – 4 Mlm Euro
3. Igor Akinfeev (ЦСКА) ninth place in the most expensive gatekeepers	3. Miodrag Bojovich («Динамо») – 2 Mln Euro
4. Vagner Lav (ЦСКА) 16 Mln Euro	4. Rud Gullit («Терек») – 1,5
5. Carlos Eduardo (Рубин) 15 Mln Euro	5. Leo Slutsky (ЦСКА) – 1,2

This table was designed for global experts meeting for integrity in sport. INTERPOL, Singapore 28–29 November 2012 by Dr. Cheloukhine

For desired match results, representatives of gambling structures can and do offer substantial bribes to soccer arbitrators. The sums can appear very impressive. For loyal refereeing the minimum rate is 5,000 dollars and depending on the match's prestige a potential offer of 30–50 thousand dollars would not be an unreasonable limit. Judges are offered money and advised "not to offend" their soccer players and club. Resisting or stubborn judges are "tenderly" met at the airport or approached anywhere else and suffer the threats of violence for disobedience of Mafioso's direction or the desire for refereeing. Family members are also at constant pressure, stress and blackmail (Russian Mafia 2012).

In all leagues, most trainers admitted involvement in some dirty tricks in relation to match fixing. They speak openly about it because there is no punishment. In the event Commissions or committees with respected people are not able to bring any order into game, anti-soccer proponents will prosper in Russia and internationally. One proactive approach to this in order to de-criminalize activity in soccer would be to ensure police and security agencies become involved and assigned to investigate suspicious games.

Currently, however, there is little involvement of law enforcement agencies being assigned to be present in the judges' room. However, some clubs started contracting police to guard judges from strangers and shady dealers at the time of match. These proactive measures should be looked at and adapted as best practices in Russia.

In the 2012 season, for example, Mafiosi tried to dictate their rule and desire for the outcome of the game at the Moscow's stadium "Dynamo". In the match's break time they went to judges' room, but were escorted out by police. This incident occurred in Moscow where the police have some power, however as of yet it has not become the norm in the rest of Russia. It can be noted other city clubs are contracting police officers to block access to judges and accompanying them to the soccer field and back. This is a spontaneous attempt to isolate judges from external influence. Some clubs are even contracting police officers for meetings and are present at the same hotel as the arbitrators. This all intended to prevent fixing match and possibly protect young players from likely communication with shady businessmen and it is essential these practices expand.

> There were three of them and they beat him together, carefully consider each blow. Street fight was played according to the classical scenario: he was met at night near home and asked for a cigarette, then light, and then, they tried to drag his girlfriend into their car. All was well planned, the client asked to bit him carefully but hard: rising star of Petersburg soccer club "Zenit" Oleg Kozhanov was needed alive but cooperative to Mafia. (Gataulin 2006)

The Connection Between Sychev, Arshavin and the "Podolsk" Organized Criminal Group

Beaten and injured, Oleg Kozhanov was not the Russian first soccer player who suffered from the hands of criminals. Stars of domestic soccer were *"educated"* all the time. The conditions were always the same: night, dark yard and a baseball bat. The attackers tried not to hurt the victim's legs. Thoughtful fans and informed professionals noted one common feature uniting all similar cases. As a rule, attacks were made on the eve of the soccer players transition to other club (Russian Mafia 2012).

The clear flaws of the law in Russia prevent honest people from the ability to live freely. Instead, some criminal entrepreneurials prefer to derive a profit from the lack of clear laws and enforcement. Russian soccer, as mentioned before has been poorly built into capitalism. According to the existing Russian labor legislation for all workers, 15 days notice is required to notify an employer about leaving employment. Soccer players, as well as all other salary receivers, are considered as ordinary workers. Based on this, the soccer player, for whom the club has paid millions of dollars, can leave at any time and subsequently leave the club with no return on investment to the club. Similar cases had taking place earlier, until resourceful people paid attention to the potential profitability and abuse of such employment laws.

For example, Mister A[6], a well-known peson in the soccer world, was the first man who executed unauthorized players transitions from club to club. At the time, he was the head of the lowest division club near Moscow. National team players Arshavin and Kerzhakov, the forward of "Spartak" Pavluchenko and the halfback of the same club Bystrov, did not escape his attention. While in the lowest division, Mr. A quickly became accustomed to a semi-criminal environment and top clubs

---

[6]The name is not reviled for security reasons

Table 4 Football billionaire's club

16 Russian clubs, in the Summer 2011, spent
250 Mln Euros buying football players

- "Spartac/Спартак" - Mr. Fedun, (Billionaire) VP "Lukoil" oil company

- "Zenith/Зенит" – Mr. Golubev, Gazprom (Billionaire)

- "Anzhi/Анжи" – Mr. Kerimov, (Billionaire)

- "TsSKA/ЦСКА" – Mr. Giner, (Billionaire)

This table was designed for global experts meeting for integrity in sport. INTERPOL, Singapore 28–29 November 2012 by Dr. Cheloukhine

managers, where he united all in an informal association which someone sarcastically called it "labor union" (Ibid, 2012).

The "labor union" methods are quite traditional. For example, there is a soccer player who gets paid very little. This occurs very often, especially if the player is young. A long-term contract could be signed for about 5 years for a small salary. Usually, the player willingly, or has to borrow money from everyone and in the event is unable to re-pay the loans, the possibility exists the player becomes a slave to the loan provider. When this type of situation arises, the player can be sold to another club and play as needed and obligated in order to pay off the debt.

A similar situation happened to Mr. Sychev from the "Lokomotive" club. His close relative borrowed 175 thousand dollars for a sports school in Omsk. It was very evident that the soccer school could not pay this amount off in 1 year, if at all. The debt was transferred to Sychev after he was traded off to another club for four million euros (Ibid, 2012).

Another tactic is a *promise*, not less effective and usually accompanied with an intimidation aspect. Thus, "Spartak" fans still recall and question Mr. Sychev's bizarre situation when he left while other clubs were ready to pay him from four to six million euros. Subsequently the club signed contracts with Pavluchenko and Bystrov as well as intended to buy Arshavin. Many claimed that this was unusual "kickback" for Sychev. However, those who signed the contracts, in every possible manner, showed discontent and persistently called Mister A "the Podolsk criminal group member" (Russian Mafia 2012) (Table 4).

The Premier League Is Supervised by "Criminal Authorities"

The arrival of the so called "labor union" has troubled many soccer club owners and officials in Russia. For example, Mr. Mutko, the present head of the Russian Sports Federation, in the middle of outrage with player Sychev, carried on intense negotiations with "Spartak" management on behalf of Romantsev and Chervichenko. Mr. Mutko even arrived in Moscow in spite of the fact that he was the president of "Zenit" club. The skilled manager realized that he was now under the same pressure that Sychev was, as well as their leading players Kerzhakov and Arshavin.

The murder of the well-known "Torpedo" player and then soccer agent Yury Tishkov, is linked, by many soccer experts, to a transfer of one young soccer player. However, there was not enough evidence for a full investigation and the murder case is still unsolved. Since the soccer environment is not very open for media and cooperation, clubs try not to quarrel openly. And when there was a conflict, it is usually settled cordially. It could account for the reason, by different estimates, that there are about eight supervising authorities presiding over 16 teams in the premier league and all are members of "labor union" (Gataulin 2006).

The potential for huge financial gain is evident. Investing 1,000 dollars for 100 perspective players each potentially results in five soccer stars with the potential resulting value being several million euros each.

Respectively, "labor union" revenue increases as well when they represent individual players. And the personal agent, in the domestic semi-shadow soccer business, is everything, the patron, the "roof", the mediator and the beneficiary. The Russian agents, at the time of player's transfers, quite often ask for a quarter of the agreed amount plus salary and bonus. An agent can represent up to one dozen players in different leagues making it a very lucrative business.

Corruption and a crime in soccer, in spite of the fact that there are only a few complete investigations, are all present and available for fixing the game. Soccer fans can see how soccer and sports motivation is falling and this is much more evident as the corruption could decompose Russian society as a whole.

"Saturn's" Criminal Figures

In Russia, soccer and crime were never closer to one other than at the end of the 1990s. The outcome of many matches were discussed and the destiny of a match could be decided at gangsters meetings.

In one case, investigators in Moscow's Regional Unit Combating Organized Crime (RUBOP) closely connected successes of the local soccer club "Saturn" with its charismatic leader, "thief in law"[7] Mr. Oleg Shishkanov, of the *Ramensky*

---

[7] A career criminal who is respected, had informal authority and an elite status within the organized crime environment in the Soviet Union, and currently in the post-Soviet states and respective diasporas abroad.

criminal group. Mr. Shishkanov was constantly bragging about his role and financial support in the teams' success to become the Premier League club.

Further, "Saturn" changed owners more than once until it was eventually bought by businessman Evgeny Giner (*see table above*). Mr. Giner, besides soccer, is also involved in the energy and automobile business (Vershov 2008). Law enforcement officials, however, believe that Mr. Giner was closely connected to the clothing markets in "Luzhniki" and those on the property of CSKA sport center. Moreover, the Ukrainian Ministry of Internal Affairs, on the request of the Russian intelligence services, were informed about Mr. Giner's criminal records. The CSKA president called it nonsense (Vershov 2008).

In February, 2005 Evgeny Giner "Mercedes" was shot by unknown assassins, as police claimed. The businessman himself was not in the car, but his son Vadim, who also worked for the club, was seriously wounded.

Mr. Evgeny Giner became CSKA's president in 2001 and 2 years later he headed the Russian Football Premier League (RFPL). He then quickly appointed Mr. Tatevosa Surinova as general director of RFPL. By the end of 2004, Mr. Surinov was charged with fraud in the CSKA club. Along with Surinov, Mr. Ibrahim Suleymanov, known to law enforcement as the person running the underground gambling business in regards to selling tickets for Euro Cup match tournaments which include Russian national team participation, was also arrested. Later, both, Surinov and Suleymanov received long prison sentences (Vershov 2008).

However, history repeats itself. In May of 2008 in Kazan, Moscow businessman Mr. Radik Yusupov, known to law enforcement under the nickname Dragon, was detained. Soon after, Mr. Yusupov's best friend Rustem Saymanov was behind bars. Mr. Yusupov was the sports director of the Kazan "Rubin" soccer club. During the investigation, old facts emerged where friends, in the mid-90s, were active Sevastopol's criminal group members.

Both, Yusupov and Saymanov faced three murder charges in Sevastopol. Though, in "Rubin", few believed the criminal past and accustations against their sports director. The "Rubin" press secretary, Mr. Lopukhov, characterized Saymanov as a very successful businessman in achievements: "acknowledging Mr. Saymanov efforts, "Rubin" received excellent soccer players, such as Sergey Semak, Sergey Rebrov, Savo Milosevic and Gökdeniz Karadeniz; that is precisely Mr. Saymanov made the team one of the best and strongest in Russian championship" (Vershov 2008).

Solutions

Article 184, Statue 22 of the Criminal Code Russian Federation reads: "Bribing participants and organizers of the professional and commercial sport competitions" (Criminal Code of Russian Federation).

1. Bribing sportsmen, sport referees, trainers, head of teams and other participants or organizers of professional sports competitions, in order to influence on results of these competitions is punished by the penalty of 200,000 rubles (about $6,000)

or at a rate of salary or other income for the period of 18 months, or obligatory community work for up to 360 h, or jail term for up to 3 months.

2. The same act conducted by organized (crime) group, – fine 100,000–300,000 rubles ($3,000–$10,000) or at a rate of salary or other income earned from 1 to 2 years, or imprisonment for up to 5 years.

3. Illegally receiving money, securities or other values (property), as well as illegally using property as a payoff for assisting or influencing on results of the specified competition, – punished by fines of 300,000 rubles ($10,000) or at a rate of a salary or other income for the period of 2 years, or restrict to occupy certain positions for up to 3 years, or imprisonment for up to 6 months

However, despite these Criminal Code sections existing, very few people or clubs were ever investigated or charged.

As the Russian Soccer Association claims, they have a representative working undercover in almost every region. They receive classified information on each point that is taking place around and during soccer games, as well as outside the game in a lobbies and with players. At present time most club owners, gamblers and other people have departed from the principle of bribing the team. Historically if they were previously spending up to one million dollars or on bribing a team, now they are better investing money with more precise results, – 50–100 thousand euros bribes to judges and a desired result is delivered.

The Russian State Duma has introduced the president's bill on strengthening criminal and administrative charges for the organization in fixing matches and bribing participants. The bill was brought to the State Duma in November 2012 and already passed the first reading. Accordingly, the bill brings a number of changes into gambling and the organization of various betting. The bill proposes punishment for up to 7 years of imprisonment, and penalties increase from 200 thousand rubles to 1 million rubles.

Proposed Bill "Combating Match Fixing" to Russian Government/President Putin November 6, 2012; Amendments to Federal Law on Physical Culture and Sport, Taxation and Criminal Laws:

- "...organizers of fixed matches are facing seven years of incarceration
- team players and referees the monetary penalties (*increase from*) 300.000 to 1 million rubles ($33.000)
- Law Enforcement are allowed to use eavesdrops investigating cases
- The bill requires disqualification of persons whose involvement in the match fixing is proven; teams or federations are subjects to the above charges
- Russia is forming a unit to investigate soccer games fixing. Law Enforcement involvement (full investigation) is a mandatory because the National League Committee for the Fixed Matches Enquiry cannot charge those involved unless there is criminal investigation underway. For these matters the bill requests to establish: Training Law Enforcement assignment and creating units in charge; Anti-Corruption education of sportsmen and trainers at all levels (local, state, university); Forbid betting to trainers and players on soccer results (must ID proves at registering bids + tax); Use of informants prior/post games Use of eavesdrops
- Since INTERPOL, Europol and FIFA have limited investigative powers, they should rely on countries' governments and law enforcement agencies to pursue cases at their domestic level and according to their Criminal Code.

In conclusion, case studies, criminal charges, media and law enforcement reports have shown the issue of match fixing and crime in soccer needs to be addressed. Although some clubs and associations have introduced some preliminary, proactive measures (police in judge's rooms, etc.), there is still a long way to go to re-instill integrity into the game of soccer in Russia. A combined, aggressive approach involving legislation, law enforcement, intelligence gathering, media and strong cooperation with programs in prevention, education and training, especially with youth, would demonstrate that Russia is sending a clear signal that it wishes to clean up the game of soccer and bring integrity back into the national game.

References

Article 184, Statue 22 Criminal Code RF: Bribing participants and organizers of the professional and commercial sport competitions. Criminal Code of Russian Federation. http://www.russian-criminal-code.com/

Cheloukhine, S. "Fixing Match in Football in Russia". Global Experts Meeting for Integrity in Sport. INTERPOL, Singapore 28–29 November 2012

Gataullin, R. "Argumenty I fakty", 06.07.2006

Dogovornye matchi. http://www.dogovornoymatch.org/, Accessed August 7, 2013

Matveev, A. Dogovrnyak. Kak pokupayut I prodayut matchi v rossiiskom futbole. *Sport v detalyakh*, 2009. Accessed http://lib.rus.ec/b/215006/read

Nikitchenkov, A. Korruptsionery v butsahk. Rosbalt. 30/03/2012. Assessed http://www.rosbalt.ru/main/2012/03/30/963498.html

Newsru. Uroven korruptsii v rossiskom futbole. December 3, 2012. http://newsru.com/sport/03dec2012/radar.html, Accessed August 7, 2013

Podorvanyuk, V. Dostatochno esli futbolistam budet stydno? http://gazeta.ru 13.12.2006

Pri MVD planiruyut sozdat otdel po bor'be s dogovornymi matchami. http://izvestia.ru/news/538963#ixzz2CaJsGvh7 Russian Mafia. 10.19.2012 http://rumafia.com/material.php?id=540

Russian reporter. (Русский репортер), 23.10.2008 http://www.compromat.ru/page_23490.htm Vershov, Y. Kriminalnye igry. "Russkiy reporter" 23.10. 2008

Dogovornye matchi, pravda i lozh. July 2011. Rusarticles.com http://www.rusarticles.com/futbol-statya/dogovornye-matchi-pravda-ili-lozh-5072715.html. Accessed August 7, 2013

Sport-weekend. Penalti b Nalchike ot 50 do 100 tysyach Evro? September 10, 2012. http://sport-weekend.com/Premer-liga/50-100-6897.html. Accessed August 7, 2013

http://www.compromat.ru/page_23490.htm

Part II
Preventing Match-Fixing: Contemporary Approach

Safeguarding Sports Integrity Against Crime and Corruption: An Australian Perspective

Ashutosh Misra, Jack Anderson, and Jason Saunders

Abstract Safeguarding the integrity of international sports has assumed greater urgency the world over. Sports bodies, associations, clubs, national teams, sports officials and law enforcement agencies are today dealing with a variety of threats ranging from match-fixing to corruption, illegal betting and use of performance and image enhancing drugs in sport. The Australian sporting world is not immune from these threats, and lately, the revelations of the involvement of organised criminal identities in sports, the world over, and in Australia shows the seriousness and complexity of the challenge international sport confronts. This chapter presents an Australian perspective on the nature of integrity threats that various sporting codes in Australia are facing and measures that can help deal with them. The authors discuss a number of match-fixing cases in the National Rugby league, A-League Football and cricket in Australia and identify different variants of sports

This research is supported by a Leverhulme Study Abroad Research Fellowship, 2011.

The research team acknowledges the support received from the Australian Research Council in funding this research.

The authors would like to thank Professor(s) Simon Bronitt and Melissa Bull, Director and Associate Director, CEPS, respectively, for their invaluable comments and suggestions on the paper.

A. Misra (✉)
Australian Research Council Centre of Excellence in Policing and Security (CEPS),
Griffith University, 3.01, M10, 176 Messines Ridge Road, Mount Gravatt Campus,
Queensland 4122, Australia
e-mail: a.misra@griffith.edu.au

J. Anderson
School of Law, Queen's University of Belfast, 27-30 University Square,
Belfast BT7INN, UK
e-mail: jack.anderson@qub.ac.uk

J. Saunders
Professional Development Unit, Education & Training Command, Queensland Police
Service, Griffith University, CEPS, 3.01, M10, 176 Messines Ridge Road, Mount Gravatt
Campus, Queensland 4122, Australia
e-mail: Saunders.JasonP@police.qld.gov.au

M.R. Haberfeld and D. Sheehan (eds.), *Match-Fixing in International Sports:*
Existing Processes, Law Enforcement, and Prevention Strategies,
DOI 10.1007/978-3-319-02582-7_8, © Springer International Publishing Switzerland 2013

corruption and vulnerabilities of professional sports to transnational and organised crime. The authors analyse how sports corruption from being a blind spot of the law enforcement agencies in Australia, until some years ago, has become one of their top priorities, yielding encouraging outcomes on various counts. This chapter takes a roll call of measures undertaken by the Commonwealth and state institutions, sports bodies and federations, clubs and national associations, and the law enforcement agencies to curb match-fixing, corruption and drug use, and preserve the integrity of sport in Australia. The recommendations furthered by the authors could be relevant for other countries as well.

Introduction

Preserving the integrity of sport has become a major concern for sports bodies and law enforcement agencies alike worldwide and the transnational nature of threats to sport integrity has made the task all the more challenging. The growing involvement of organised crime syndicates in match-fixing, illegal betting and distributing prohibited drugs among athletes has grown alarmingly in Asia, Europe, Latin America and the United States (US). In February 2013 following the biggest ever investigation, European Police Office (Europol) in a shocking exposé revealed that around 380 suspected matches including the World Cup, European Championship qualifiers and Champions League were fixed by an organised crime syndicate in Asia, involving around 425 match/club officials, players and criminals across 15 countries (Guardian Staff and agencies 2013). Deeply concerned with growing corruption and criminal activities in football, Fédération Internationale de Football Association (FIFA) and International Police Organisation (INTERPOL) signed a 28 million Euros 10-year agreement in May 2011 to curb and prevent Asian based match-fixing and illegal betting in sports (Media Release 2011).

Australia is no exception to this trend of growing corruption and involvement of organised criminal identities in sports. In February 2013, a startling report of the Australian Crime Commission (ACC), 'Organised crime and drugs in sport: New generation performance and image enhancing drugs (PIEDs) and organised criminal involvement in their use in professional sport", revealed "the involvement of organised criminal identities and groups in the distribution of new generation PIEDs" (Australian Crime Commission 2013). The report was a consequence of a 12-month investigation conducted by ACC with the support of the Australian Sports Anti-Doping Authority (ASADA)[1] and the Therapeutic Goods Administration (TGA). It concluded that organised crime syndicates posed a serious threat to the integrity of sports in Australia.

---

[1]ASADA was established in 2006 by the Australian Government to eliminate doping in sport in Australia. It also spearheads anti-doping efforts at the international level in collaboration with National Doping Organisations, the World Anti-Doping Agency and other stakeholders.

In 2011, the President of the International Olympic Committee (IOC), Jacque Rogge, identified gambling-related corruption as the biggest single threat to the integrity of international sport. The ACC report highlighted that Australian sport is not immune from this corruptive influence. Moreover, the threat posed is not confined to sport. By utilising online gambling platforms, recognised international crime syndicates have the capacity to launder money and engage in assorted secondary criminality of a financial nature that includes identity theft, economic conspiracy and fraud. According to the ACC's conservative estimate serious organised crime costs the Australian community up to $15 billion each year (Lacey 2012). Shane Neilson, National Manager, ACC argues that globalisation, increased cross-border movement of people, goods and money, international markets and rapidly developing technology facilitate organised crime. Groups offend in one jurisdiction, launder in another, and enjoy the proceeds in a third country (Neilson 2011).

In the above context this paper has been divided into seven broad segments. The first provides a brief overview of the meaning of 'integrity' in the context of sporting events. The second segment discusses instances of match-fixing in four Australian sporting codes: the National Rugby League (NRL), Australian Football League (AFL), A-League Football and cricket. The third segment identifies the key patterns and variants of sports corruption in Australia. The fourth segment traces the involvement of transnational and organised crime syndicates in the Australian sporting domain. The fifth segment traces the altering priorities of the law enforcement agencies and their growing focus on crime and corruption in sport. The sixth segment examines the evolving national policy on the development of codes of conduct and anti-match-fixing measures in Australia. And the last segment offers recommendations and suggestions for preserving integrity in sport, from the Australian perspective.

Overview and Meaning of 'Integrity' in Sport

Cheating in, and the fixing of, sports events have a history that is almost as old as organised sport. Modern sports organisations have developed quite sophisticated, if largely private, self-regulatory mechanisms in identifying cheats and fixers. In particular, the manner in which international sport, as directed by the World Anti-Doping Agency (WADA), monitors, internally prosecutes and sanctions those who take prohibited performance enhancing drugs is instructive as to how sport might deal with the integrity threat posed by illicit, online gambling and match-fixing. In addition, the relationship between gambling and sport has a long history. The manner in which the oldest organised professional sport, the horse racing industry, monitors, internally prosecutes and sanctions those associated with gambling-inspired corruption is again highly instructive as to how sport deals with betting-led conspiracies (Glesson review of sports betting regulation in the state of Victoria 2011).

This institutional history is the combination of cheating and betting in sport, based on inside information supplied by officials or players and placed upon online and offshore gambling platforms. It poses a significant integrity threat to modern sport and also reveals certain regulatory vulnerabilities within international sport. Today certain sports betting platforms are being used as a conduit for transnational financial crimes, cross border money laundering and associated economic criminality or fraud.

In this context what does then "integrity" threat in sport imply? Borrowing from the Australian Sport Commission's (ASC) definition of the "Essence of Australian Sport, integrity in competitive sport has four essential elements: fairness; respect; responsibility; and safety (The Australian Sports Commission 2012). Put simply, integrity in this regard concerns an "on-field" respect for the core values of fair and open competition in the game or event in question. "Off-field", integrity extends to the procedural fairness of investigative procedures, tribunals and other forums in which allegations against sports professionals are considered. In the context of modern professional sport, however, integrity has, for sports governing bodies, a meaning that extends beyond the above and this is related to modern sport's business model and branding.

Revenue streams – gate receipts, associated merchandising, sponsorship and, crucially, television and media rights deals – in the world's and Australia's leading sports leagues remain relatively robust with the primary financial stability threat tending to be internal (in the form of spiralling player wages) rather than external (in the form of the global economic downturn); nevertheless, sports governing bodies across the world are acutely aware that this "robust" business model is based fundamentally on an implied contract of trust and confidence with its spectators and sponsors. Further, that contract or bond is predicated on supporters and sponsors believing in the "controlled unpredictability" of what occurs on the sport field. Accordingly, if that trust is undermined because, for instance, supporters and sponsors suspected that players' actions are motivated for nefarious reasons, then consumers and sponsors will quickly move their money elsewhere and thus destabilise that sport's financial viability. In this, leading sports governing bodies are aware that in today's highly competitive sports market (epitomised by the various codes in Australia) there are a number of alternatives for this support and money.

Similarly, the integrity threat emerges where doubts or suspicions arise about, for example, an unusually slow run rate in cricket or a high number of dropped balls in the field; a decision by a player to take a tap rather than a kick at goal in rugby; a tennis or snooker result that is at odds with the form or ranking of those involved; idiosyncratic positional moves by a coach; or the inconsistent decision-making of a referee during the course of a game. Although all of the above may be underpinned by perfectly rational explanations, recent gambling related events suggest that on occasion certain happenings on the pitch may be driven by a more sinister rationale or, at the very least, warrant the suspicion of betting-led conspiracy influencing the behaviour of players.

In sum, it is the credibility or integrity of the brand that is of the utmost importance to sports bodies and thus the associated anxiety of leading sports bodies, as led by the IOC through its Founding Working Group (FWG) on the Fight against Irregular and Illegal Betting in Sport established in March 2011 (Founding group 2013).

This can create pressures for organisational cover-up or minimisation strategies that render the industry and regulators potentially complicit in the wrongdoing. Analogies abound from the world of sport about the corrosive impact that (lack of) integrity issues can have on a sport's brand and goodwill and, as a corollary, on the difficulties a sport can have in trying to regain that trust and confidence of supporters and sponsors. The regulatory corruption that has led to the demise of professional boxing as a mainstream sport is noteworthy (Anderson 2007). The allegations of corruption surrounding the administration of the Indian Premier League (IPL) have seen turnover figures for that cricket tournament decline markedly in the last year. The reputational difficulties that athletics and professional cycling have with regard to doping continue, despite recent progress in cleaning up the sports in question. The shocking doping confessions of the ace cyclist Lance Armstrong is a case in point. The International Cyclist Union (ICU) has asked Armstrong to return $4 million earned from the seven Tour de France titles and also stripped him of those titles (O' Keeffe 2012).

Key Australian Match-Fixing Cases

National Rugby League (NRL)

Two minutes into a NRL game between the North Queensland Cowboys and the Canterbury Bulldogs in August 2010, the Bulldog's Ryan Tandy was penalised for a delaying offence. Ordinarily, the Cowboys would have taken a kick at goal but elected to tap the ball and eventually scored a try. Irregular betting patterns involving significant amounts of money were identified by betting operators on a Cowboys' penalty goal to be the first scoring play. An investigation by the NSW Casino and Racing Investigation Unit has led to four arrests including Ryan Tandy and his agent. The charges were based on economic conspiracy and obtaining money by deception and, in the player's case, relate to providing false and misleading information to a parallel investigation by the New South Wales Crime Commission (NSWCC). In December 2011, Tandy was found guilty on the "knowingly providing false evidence" charge and received a 6 month, non-custodial sentence.

Australian Football League (AFL)

In July 2011, Heath Shaw a player with leading AFL club Collingwood was suspended for eight matches and fined a $20,000 after being involved in a betting scandal also involving Collingwood captain Nick Maxwell. Shaw and a friend bet a $10 each on Maxwell kicking the first goal of a league game against Adelaide, knowing that Maxwell was to start the game not in his usual position but in the forward line.

Shaw also passed the information to friends who also laid a series of minor bets. Maxwell was fined a $5,000. Three members of Maxwell's close family also placed bets. There was evidence that betting odds in the markets on Maxwell scoring came in from 100 to 1 for the first goal to 25–1.

In early 2013 press reports again put the spot light on AFL over the alleged use of PIEDs by some players. The AFL and ASADA interrogated the Melbourne Football Club 'Demons' doctor Dan Bates based on the exchange of mobile text messages with Stephen Dank, a sport biochemist, who also ran the club's supplement programme in 2012, over his possible role in arranging PIED for some players (News Limited Network 2013). Similarly, Essendon, another Melbourne based club has also been mired in an alleged doping scandal. As a result the club's high performance manager Dean Robinson Essendon was suspended who once noted the existence of the 'seedy underworld of the sport' (Clark 2013). Essendon is also conducting its own investigations and the club coach James Hird is expected to dispose before ASADA and acknowledge having received two injections from Dank, for 'health reasons'. Hird is reportedly 'absolutely shocked' at the scandal describing it as a 'terrible disturbing situation' (Dampney and APP 2013). The Fox Sports News commentator Mark Robinson believes, "Criminal figures, criminal gangs, organised criminal gangs are infiltrating sporting codes, including the AFL". Dean Robinson was closely associated with Stephen Dank, who is alleged to have injected calf blood in some of the Manly club's players in the National Rugby League during his tenure with the club. ASADA is currently continuing the investigations in close cooperation with both the AFL and NRL (ASADA Media Statements 2013).

A-League Football

The February 2013 EUROPOL exposé of widespread match-fixing done by the Asia based organised crime syndicates, in over 380 football games, also allegedly included an A-League match played in 2012 in Melbourne, involving as much as A$40 million in legal and illegal betting from Asian agencies. The Football Federation Australia and Victoria Police denied any such possibility. However, the Victoria Police Deputy Commissioner Graham Ashton struck a note of concern over potential match-fixing in Australia. He said, "Any sport that is attracting significant betting offshore is at a major risk. This thing is coming down the highway and we have to be prepared" (Gatt 2013).

Cricket

The 75-page International Cricket Council (ICC) cricket 2011 report prepared by Sir Paul Condon, director of the ICC Anti-Corruption Unit (ACU) revealed that the

ICC had failed to take any substantive action against two top Australian test cricket players, Shane Warne and Mark Waugh, who were allegedly paid by Indian bookies (Report on Corruption 2011). In the 1990s the Indian subcontinent saw match-fixing cases proliferating with the arrival of cell phones, live telecasts and computerisation in which the Australian cricketers have been implicated. The Indian Central Bureau of Investigations (CBI) which investigated the match-fixing allegations of the 1990s revealed that the one bookie had paid $20,000 to Mark Waugh for providing 'information about pitch, weather, team strategy, and morale prior to Australia's matches (CBI's report 2000). The report also mentions Dean Jones being offered $40,000 by the bookies, but refusing after allegedly sensing having seen by Alan Border, the captain, meeting the bookie Mukesh Gupta. Now Asian betting syndicates are also allegedly betting on Big Bash cricket matches (premier league) in Australia (Gatt 2013). According to press reports Australian junior cricketers aged between 15 and 19 are also at risk of corruption and could be groomed by overseas bookies. However, Cricket Australia (CA) spokesman Peter Young denied having any evidence of the practice within Australia but acknowledged that CA's Anti Corruption Unit head, Sean Carroll was aware of such grooming practices overseas (Dowsley 2013).

Key Patterns and Variants of Sports Corruption

In Australian sports the following patterns and variants of corruption are discernible:

1. Evolving sophistication of the betting market

Traditional forms of gambling fixes, for example, a boxer 'taking a dive' or the 'nobbling' of the favourite in a horse race, appear somewhat quaint to the contemporary eye. In horse racing, for instance, the fix had to be quite elaborate: the horse in question had to be interfered with physically; the money placed on the favourite or backing another horse or both had to be put on in a conspiratorial manner so as not to attract the suspicions of an irregular betting pattern by the relatively small and highly risk aware bookmaker community; and finally the fix had to be effective, in the sense that the favourite had to lose.

Contrast this with today's online betting environment. The 'where, when and what' a gambler can bet on is virtually unlimited. Wireless and telecommunication developments mean that a customer can, and on various multimedia platforms, incessantly bet and do so from home or in the sports bar or at the event itself. This flexibility and anonymity lends itself to betting conspiracies. Moreover, while in the traditional form of betting, the punter gambled on the final outcome of the event i.e., who might or might not win, the various different in-play forms of betting now available mean that punters can engage in bets on much more defined aspects of the game itself such as spot-bets or spread-betting (pertaining to just one particular aspect, such as the first free kick, foul or a penalty in soccer and first no ball or a boundary in cricket, and not the final outcome of the match).

The match-fixing cases discussed earlier and the investigations of Declan Hill and others suggest that if a third party can convince a player to do something particular at a specific time in a game, which need not necessarily impact on its final outcome (and thus cause no great moral hesitancy for the player), this inside information can be used to the advantage of that third party on betting exchanges (Hill 2008). Again it must be stressed that, although bets of the kind outlined appear somewhat "exotic" in nature, a quick perusal of online betting exchanges and spread betting facilities illustrates that the combination and category of bets available to the modern punter are bewilderingly broad. Put simply, no matter how exotic a bet appears, there is nearly always a market online for the customers' money.

2. Vulnerable players

Player education and awareness, supplemented by strict enforcement action and sanctions against wrongdoing, is a central preventative measure in dealing with this activity. Players are sometimes unaware that seemingly innocuous information, such as positional or tactical changes for a forthcoming game, may be used to the betting advantage of third parties (leave the footnote).

Players also need to be educated as to the undue influence that might be placed on them for such information, whether it is through a commercial agent or their wider social network. Matters such as the profiling of vulnerable players (like those from countries where corruption is already a facet of everyday life) and the regulation of sports agents is important here. The proper regulation of sports and financial accountability is essential in the wake of entry of private equity into sport and ownership of individual clubs by private entities.

Elite players in well-paid leagues, for example the English Premier League (EPL), are unlikely to be targeted in this regard, unless they have a gambling problem or related debts. These players are well paid but players further down the league or working in semi-professional leagues may be more susceptible. Further, note that in a league that has salary caps where, although leading players are well paid, the remainder of the team may not be, the resulting inequality might heighten the vulnerability of the latter to illicit betting approaches.

3. Vulnerable games

Sports that attract high betting volumes, such as football, may be targeted by illicit betting syndicates in an attempt to hide otherwise irregular betting patterns in the general weight of money bets on the particular game or event.

Episodic games, such as tennis or snooker, where an individual player can exert a significant amount of control over whether a particular set or frame is won or, more likely, lost, have been known to have resulted in betting-related conspiracies.

Similarly, games where there is little at stake, for example, so-called "dead rubbers" or games between teams who are untroubled by the play-offs but safe from relegation, can be vulnerable.

4. Referees

As some case studies also demonstrate a referee can control the point spread in a high scoring game and thus aid those who bet on spread-betting or points handicap betting markets. In a relatively low-scoring game, such as football, one decision (the award of a penalty kick) can decide or materially change the outcome of a game – and there have been celebrated examples of this. In Germany in 2005 a scandal was reported based on the confessions of a second division referee, Robert Hoyzer, who confessed to fixing and betting on matches in league and cup football matches which led to a large scale review of match-fixing in that sport.

Overall, in games as diverse as cricket, rugby and boxing how the referee "calls" a game can be of the utmost importance and therefore protecting referees who, in professional sport are usually the least paid person on the pitch, is critical.

5. Poor regulatory ethos

Where a sport's central governing authority is weak or sets a poor example, this may lessen the impact that its integrity regulations have on participants and open that organisation to targeting by criminal syndicates. The Secretary General of Interpol, Ronald K Noble, noting that corruption in international football is "widespread", argued that a key challenge in addressing the problem was that "public confidence in FIFA's ability to police itself is at its lowest" (Noble 2011). In August 2011, the Transparency International published a document entitled "Safe Hands: Building Integrity and Transparency at FIFA" in which it sets out an "integrity audit" agenda for FIFA (Transparency International 2011). The recommendations include the creation of a multi-stakeholder group, an independent investigation of the past and a 'zero tolerance' policy towards bribery.

Similarly, in a 2011 review of corruption in Great Britain by the Transparency International, a survey ranked sport as the second most corrupt sector in British society – political parties were ranked first; parliament third (Transparency International 2011). In Australia, however, notwithstanding the growing concern with corruption in sport, the history of enquiries of drugs in sports by ASADA and the current legislative and regulatory gaps, international policing agencies, such as the INTERPOL perceive the country's international image as positive and admirable. Dale Sheehan, director, capacity building and training at INTERPOL said that Australia's betting regulations, law enforcement and executive response mechanism are considered of a high standard for preserving integrity in sport (Sheehan 2013).

Sports bodies also have to reconcile their integrity anxiety relating to gambling with the heavy amounts of sponsorship accepted by such bodies from online betting companies. In addition, there may be a potential conflict of interest in a betting company sponsoring a club or league on which it takes bets (Liga Portuguesa 2009).

Vulnerability of Professional Sport in Australia to Transnational and Organised Crime

In 2011 the Australian Crime Commission published a report entitled, 'organised crime in Australia' which illuminated the contemporary manifestation of organised crime in Australia. The report although did not reflect sufficiently upon organised crime involvement in sports, it did list 'sports and fitness' as one of the impact areas of organised crime. The report revealed that PIEDs were being used by body builders and elite athletes. The report also said these drugs were:

> readily available through social networks of like-minded individuals, individuals within legitimate business such as gyms, sporting clubs and fitness centres, forged prescriptions, compliant doctors and pharmacists, thefts from medical sources (such as hospitals), the veterinary industry and Internet sales...Because of inconsistencies in the legal status of PIEDs internationally, these substances are readily available overseas and are relatively cheap compared with the illicit market price in Australia. (Australian Crime Commission 2011a, p. 69)

According to the report most PIEDs trafficked into Australia from Hong Kong, Thailand, Eastern Europe, the United Kingdom, India, The People's Republic of China, South Africa, the United States and Canada' (Ibid). The report stated that organised crime cost Australia between 10 and 15 billion dollars annually with an overall social cost exceeding a $8 billion' (Ibid, 3).

The 2013 ACC report has delved deeper into the involvement of organised crime in sports in trafficking of PIEDs and illicit drugs based on the 12 month investigation in conjunction with ASADA. The report observed that organised criminal identities supplying PIEDs by exploiting their interaction with professional athletes, pose a serious threat to the integrity of Australian professional sport. The report said, 'Relationship between athletes and organised crime identities can be exploited by criminals to corrupt the athlete and give a form of social status to the criminal, in the same way that the steroid market has been used by organised crime to corrupt law enforcement officers'(Ibid, 31). According to the report, organised criminal groups involved in match-fixing are increasingly targeting sub-elite athletes because they are easier to exploit and also draw lower levels of scrutiny from integrity authorities. These criminal groups would develop their relationship with athletes over the years and then exploit it for match-fixing, says the report (Ibid). The report has identified four key threats to the integrity of professional sport in Australia. *First*, organised criminal infiltration of unregulated markets; *second*, infiltration through legitimate business, contractors and consultants; *third*, illicit drug use and criminal associations; and *fourth*, differing levels of integrity oversight in professional sport in Australia (Ibid).

Organised crime identities are also involved in gambling and can potentially use sports and illegal betting for laundering the proceeds of their crime further. Australian Transaction Reports and Analysis Centre (AUSTRAC), the agency in Australia tasked with anti-money laundering and counter-terrorism financing responsibilities, closely monitors movements of money through gambling, including gambling on sport. It lists betting accounts as one of the most common methods of money laundering and gaming in general as a sector that is closely monitored. Cash still remains the most prominent in the money laundering process. The nature and medium of gambling is often cash and methods of money laundering include 'structuring' of transactions, i.e. moving smaller amounts of money which fall under the cash transaction threshold of a $10,000. Exchanging cash into foreign currency is also popular. An emerging form of money laundering technique is 'cuckoo smurfing' which involves moving money through an unrelated third party account, often without the third party knowing the full extent of transaction which can potentially be used in sport as well (Australian Transaction Reports and Analysis Centre 2008, p. 7). The ACC's submission to the Australian Parliament's Joint Select Committee into Gambling Reform on 23 June 2011 concluded that "Online gambling is an identified money laundering risk and increasingly is also acknowledged as a risk for revenue and taxation fraud"(Australian Crime Commission Submission 2011, p. 4).

Australia, like many countries has increased its compliance of financial institutions, particularly since 9/11, and the Financial Action Task Force (FATF) anti-money laundering and counter-terrorist financing standards are being developed and adopted. Simultaneously, the globalisation of financial markets and the development of information technology have gradually boosted the criminal economy and expanded possibilities for organised crime. FATF recognises that the sporting industry is one of the many sectors that is attractive for criminals for money laundering (Financial Action Taskforce Report 2009).

In a recent review by FATF on money laundering in the football sector, FATF highlighted that in order to facilitate such activities international crime syndicates were establishing their own online gambling platforms on which to take a wide variety of bets (Ibid). Unlicensed betting operators operating online and offshore have caused problems for the proper regulation of the industry in the UK, other EU states, and United States and in Australia breaches of the *Interactive Gambling Act 2001* (Cth) have been brought to the attention of the Australian Federal Police (AFP) with increasing frequency.

The ACC 2013 report claims that the threat to Australian sport from organised criminal groups is now assuming systemic characteristic. As mentioned earlier, associating with a local sports star sometimes provides a medium for criminal elements to enhance their social, community and business status and thus engender them with an air of legitimacy. Further, as online betting in Australia grows rapidly – from an industry worth a little over A$100million in the mid-1990s to one that is projected to reach A$3billion by the end of this decade – the systemic risks increase, as aggravated by the online nature of the industry. As with any financial service offered online, the danger is that at the margins of the industry, it can be difficult to police and regulate effectively, if at all, given the offshore, relatively anonymous nature of such activity and the huge resources needed to trace money flows through various identity theft and customer identification traps.

Sports, Crime and Fraud Linkage: From Law Enforcement's Blind Spot to High Priority

Law enforcement responses to gambling led corruption in sport within Australia have historically been reactive and have been given low priority. It was reported in 2011 that the AFP had failed to act on 15 complaints since 2009 of criminal breaches of the Interactive Gambling Act 2001 (IGA) because it had considered them to be of low priority (Smith 2011).

Fraud and corruption investigations have also traditionally not had the same level of commitment of police resources or the level of expertise as have other types of organised crime investigations and often involve jurisdictional issues. This is not unique to Australian law enforcement. Gambling led corruption in sport investigations are basically fraud related investigations. As noted by the 2006 Fraud Review in the UK, most police agencies do not prioritise fraud or include it in their strategic planning. There are a number of reasons for this, not the least jurisdictional and multiplicity issues (Button et al. 2008, p. 243).

Until recently there was a lack of intelligence concerning the links of organised crime and gambling led sport corruption in Australia. Whilst it was recognised, through overseas events, that gambling led corruption could be a serious organised crime issue, it was viewed that this was more of an 'international' problem, particularly in places where betting was legally prohibited and that as a result, there was a large underground market.

With limited attention given by public policing, nationally or internationally, monitoring and intelligence gathering has remained largely within the domain of sport controlling bodies and regulators. Police would become involved only on a reactive basis to particular incident/s of gambling led corruption. There was also a high level of suspicion and lack of information sharing between law enforcement and the sports controlling bodies.

A Growing Priority

In recent years, like other places in the world, the traditional view and priorities of Australian law enforcement agencies have changed, including those relating to gambling led corruption in sport and its relevance to and potential impact upon organised transnational crime. Similarly, with rapid advancement in technology, cyber-crime and online fraud has also been seen strategically as a priority issue. The proliferation of online betting and gambling and the rapid development of exotic or spot betting have exposed sport to vulnerabilities of transnational and organised crime involvement. Police agencies in Australia now recognise the threat in the light if the emerging instances of gambling led corruption in sports in Australia. In February 2013 the Victoria Police created a Sporting Integrity Intelligence Unit

(SIIU) and a specialised squad to investigate the allegations of organised crime in sport (Premier of Victoria 2013).

Earlier in 2011, the ACC's strategic intelligence assessment had also found significant vulnerability of the sector to infiltration and exploitation by organised crime and some links between organised crime and individual sports and individuals. The ACC provided several briefings to partner law enforcement agencies, major sporting bodies and regulators and government (Australian Crime Commission Annual Report 2011–2012, chapter "Match Fixing in Western Europe"). A number of converging vulnerabilities in the sector were identified. Convergences include the exponential growth of the online wagering market, the appeal of 'spot betting', inconsistent approaches to market monitoring and surveillance, the continued internationalisation of sport, and the natural attraction the sports and leisure market has for organised crime (Lacey 2012. An additional $A3.6 million was allocated by the government in the 2013–2014 budget for the ASADA and National Integrity in Sports Unit (NISU) to help with the current investigations and also help strengthen integrity systems in various sporting codes. The government currently invests $A169 million in high performance sports system through the Australia Sports Commission and with another $A1.76 million for ASADA and $A 1.7 million for NISU through 2014–2015 it seeks to further safeguard the integrity of sport in Australia (Senator Kate Lundy 2013).

National Policy on the Codes of Conduct and Anti-Match-Fixing Measures in Sport in Australia

Several sports organisations at the national and international levels, in light of emerging integrity threats, are already implementing sophisticated risk assessment strategies to address the problems of corruption in sport. Many of these strategies are based on those which were first established in the horse racing industry and typically combine programmes that have three central elements: education, investigation and sanctioning.

Dedicated player education programmes; codes of conduct; moral clauses in player contracts; anti-corruption compliance and investigative units; and lengthy sanctions are essential to the anti-corruption policy of any leading sports governing body. In Australia's highly regulated horse racing industry, requirements that jockeys do not bet, statute-based investigative units and lengthy sanctions, epitomised by the "warning-off" penalty, are well established, as is the fact that administrators within racing's integrity units provide specialised advice, and even personnel experienced in compliance matters, to other sports.

The horse racing industry was also among the first to reach out to the licensed betting operators, entering into memorandum of understanding with them so that both early warning could be provided on a potential race-fix and further investigation facilitated. In April 2013 the Racing Victoria also approved of several initiatives for integrity enhancement in the industry. These include *jockey betting declaration* which prohibits them from betting on thoroughbred racing anywhere in the world in the previous season; *form analysis declaration* which requires the jockeys to identify persons that they will call upon to provide professional advice on form analysis, speed maps and race tactics, to get annual license renewal; and new *stand down powers* via its Local Rule 72 C which provides the stewards with an express power to stand down a person from further participation who has been charged with a serious offence that may be detrimental to sports integrity and image (Further Victorian Integrity 2013).

The mutual benefits of the relationship between sporting codes and the law enforcement agencies remain central to the effective policing of match-fixing. As was seen to good effect in the Ryan Tandy case study outlined earlier, where substantial bets are taken on unusual, exotic bets, this can alert the receiving operator and that information can be passed onto the rest of the betting community and to the sports authorities in question. It is in the licensed betting operators' interest that their industry is not taken advantage of by match-fixers, as much as it is in the interest of sport itself.

In June 2011, all Australian sports ministers endorsed a National Policy on Match-Fixing in Sport (Australian Government Department of Regional Australia 2012). Under the policy, Commonwealth and state governments agreed to pursue:

I. Nationally consistent approach to deterring and dealing with match fixing in Australia;
II. Information sharing arrangements and highly efficient networks between governments, major sports, betting operators and law enforcers;
III. Consistent code of conduct principles for sports; and
IV. Active participation in international efforts to combat corruption in sport including an international code of conduct and an international body.

In September 2011, sports ministers endorsed a model to give effect to this policy. The model incorporates the following elements:

I. Sports organisations can apply to the relevant state regulator to become a sports controlling body (SCB);
II. SCB can enter into integrity agreements with betting agencies which provide for information exchange, a return of revenue to the sport and a right of veto on bet types; and
III. All sporting organisations receiving government funding will be required to meet integrity benchmarks as agreed under the national policy.

Individual state and territory governments are pursuing this national agenda in developing the proposed nationally consistent criminal offences and sanctions as per the national policy. Australia is a federal system in which the responsibility for criminal law and policing is shared across the Commonwealth, States and Territories. The federal agencies have limited jurisdiction, confined to the fields of legislation competence granted under the Constitution. With no general power to enact national criminal laws (unlike other federations, such as Canada), the federal parliament can only enact national criminal legislation where the Commonwealth Constitution confers that power by a head of power, either expressly or by implication. Thus federal drug law, for example, is based on the combined power of the federal parliament to regulate imports and exports (customs power), and also to implement international treaties including the various United Nations treaties on drugs to which Australia is a signatory. The States individually or collectively can also refer its powers in the criminal law field to the Commonwealth Parliament under the Constitution, but this is rarely done, exceptionally reserved for dealing with matters on which there is an urgent consensus, such as measures to counter terrorism in the wake of the 9/11 and Bali bombings (Bronitt 2010, p. 81).

The upshot of this patchwork model is a general lack of harmonisation in law enforcement approaches across Australia, inconsistent and inadequate policy responses particularly in relation to criminal activity that crosses internal jurisdictional borders. Attempts to promote uniformity through law reform (such as a Model Criminal Code) have been met with varying levels of enthusiasm. The issue of sports corruption has shared a similar fate, until recently, with only New South Wales referring the matter to its Law Reform Commission for consideration in 2011, which released a Report finding that the present law in NSW was inadequate and recommending (i) the adoption of new offences dealing with cheating and corruption in sport; and (ii) the desirability of adopting a national uniform approach.

The latter recommendation was given recent impetus with the launch of the *National Policy on Match-Fixing in Sport* 2011 following a meeting of the Australian Sports Ministers. As a result, the Standing Committee of Attorneys-General established a Standing Council of Law and Justice working group to develop a proposal and timetable for a nationally consistent approach to criminal offences relating to match-fixing. On 18 November 2011, Australian Attorneys-General at the Standing Council on Law and Justice supported the development of consistent national match-fixing offences with a maximum penalty of 10 years imprisonment. As noted by the New South Wales Law Reform Commission this penalty is in line with general fraud offences (New South Wales Law Reform Commission 2011). Offences will include corrupting the betting outcome of an event and also using inside information about an event for betting purposes.

As a part of the National Policy, the Australian Government has already established NISU which will be a non-regulatory body focused on implementation of the National Policy, including a number of integrity measures and processes. Such a unit could also liaise and be the conduit between Sports Controlling Bodies and Law Enforcement, overcoming some potential conflict of interests and inherent suspicions.

In 2011, the federal minister for sport in Australia, and his state and territory counterparts, had various meetings and correspondence with Malcolm Speed, the former chief executive of the ICC and now chairman of the Coalition of Major Professional and Participation Sports, a union of chief executives from the AFL,

NRL, Australian Rugby Union (ARU), CA, Tennis Australia (TA) and Netball Australia (NA). The policy that has emerged from this initiative is based largely on the model that exists in Britain and in the state of Victoria. It is five fold in nature.

I. The adoption of codes of conduct by sports;
II. The possibility that federal funding of sports would be made contingent on sports bodies implementing appropriate anti-corruption policies and practices;
III. That legal and licensing arrangements would be developed between betting companies and sports bodies that include obligations to share information and veto bets, as overseen administratively by a newly established NISU;
IV. That agreement would be pursued on achieving nationally consistent legislative arrangements and specifically with regard to a criminal offence of cheating at gambling, which would assist in targeting those involved in such conspiracies but who do not come within the regulatory remit of a sports body.
V. A commitment on behalf of all parties to continue to pursue an international solution and further international co-operation in the area.

The policy is a welcome development though still in its early stage. Moreover, problems can be envisaged in terms of obtaining, for example, a national consensus on the legislative framework (Consultation Paper 2011). In this regard three additional points are noteworthy about the proposal.

First, central to the policy will be to appropriately fund the NISU which has been created in 2012 to safeguard integrity in sports in Australia. The NISU type institutions are likely to be quite resource intensive, requiring a diverse body of expert personnel from law enforcement agencies (economic crime units) and those with experience in sports administration (compliance units) and the betting industry (integrity units). A long-term, stable funding model would be central to NISU's credibility and operational effectiveness. To promote sustainability, sports bodies should be given the right to exploit betting rights to their sport and that part of the revenue raised by sports bodies from the betting industry in this regard would then be siphoned off to fund the NISU. Moreover, assets confiscation under proceeds of crime legislation, which relate to sports corruption, could be earmarked to the funding of NISU.

Another problem is that without clear legislative powers to investigate and gather evidence (by telecommunications interception or controlled operations) the NISU would operate merely as a 'feeder' of intelligence to the relevant federal, state and territory law enforcement agencies. Its personnel would cultivate close working relations with law enforcement officials and provide the essential expertise needed to prepare compelling briefs of evidence, but the lack of its 'own motion' powers to investigate and prosecute limits its likely regulatory impact. The operation of NISU should be premised on full cooperation from betting industry, in terms of supplying information on irregular betting patterns, and it would also have to have certain accountability mechanisms imposed on sports bodies to ensure that the information supplied to them by NISU would always be properly pursued, irrespective of the consequences it might have for the sport in question. Without full compliance (from the betting industry) and accountability (from the sports industry) it is unlikely that law enforcement agencies such as the ACC would feel comfortable in, or be permitted to, supply any sensitive data or information that they might have, and thus the effectiveness of any putative NISU would be limited.

The solution preserving integrity in sport generally lies in greater international and regional cooperation between sports bodies and law enforcement agencies. Nevertheless, it is only when a country has its own "house in order" can it contribute materially and with due moral authority at the international level. In this, the recent national initiatives are of the utmost importance and ensure that Australia plays an influential role in the international resolution of this problem, and potentially in the formation of a World Anti-Corruption Agency (WACA).

Moreover, it must be stressed that in countries such as Australia and the UK, where sports industries such as horse-racing are deep-rooted, have an important cultural education role to play in enriching the debate on preserving sports integrity. In many jurisdictions, such as in continental Europe, sports administrators do not have an intuitive or cultural understanding of betting and this may be resulting in leading sports bodies underestimating this integrity threat. In contrast, the integrity threat emanating from drugs in sport is clear to all and thus a settled ethical stance on it among all stakeholders was achievable, as manifested in the establishment of the WADA. The ethical stance towards, even the understanding of, gambling and the associated risks to integrity, is not widely appreciated. For instance, there are problems in many countries in Asia where integrity threats originate from betting's illegal and thus unregulated status, due to cultural reasons, making it difficult for the authorities to legalise it for better regulation.

Conclusion and Recommendations

Corruption in sport needs to be recognised as part of an overall national anti corruption plan rather than simply an aspect of sport governance or integrity or organised crime strategy. The problems of international corruption, organised crime and self-regulation have been identified by the Transparency International in its recent review of corruption in UK sport. These risk factors equally apply to Australia, as identified in this chapter. It is of interest that even in the UK, where the matter of corruption and crime in sport appears to be well-regulated, and a sports betting integrity unit is already in operation, Transparency International nevertheless recommended "a full independent enquiry into corruption in UK sport commissioned by the UK governing bodies of major sports, with a view to setting up a coordinated response to corruption across all UK sports" (Corruption in sport). Building on that Transparency International (2013) recommendation, research should be conducted as a matter of priority into sport's vulnerability to gambling-led corruption and informing a coordinated and more effective response by sport and relevant government agencies in an effort both to underpin the integrity of sports events and undermine the illicit, online behaviour of criminal syndicates.

Second, does the close relationship between betting and sport lend itself to corruption? The answer to this question is no, or rather not *necessarily* so, and certainly not always. These common features, which have also been referred to in other research–notably the research commissioned by the EU Sports Platform, *Examination of Threats to the Integrity of Sport* (2010)–can assist sports governing bodies both in identifying and isolating their regulatory vulnerabilities to the threat and in instigating preventative and investigative mechanisms to address the problem (Oxford Research 2010).

Third, it is recognised that there is need for strong partnerships between industry, sports authorities and law enforcement. Coordination, collaboration and information sharing between the number of law enforcement and monitoring agencies, sporting controlling bodies and other stakeholders, including gambling industry and NISU will be crucial in controlling gambling-led corruption in sport. Too often agencies can work in a silo or at the best bi-laterally without partnerships across all agencies and stakeholders. The threat of organised crime infiltrating this sector identified by the ACC, has been the catalyst for some recent and rapid developments in law enforcement of gambling led corruption in Australia. The nature of professional sport in the modern era regularly crosses international boundaries. The collaboration needs to extend globally. Having officers and staff who can champion this work is always beneficial with emerging types of crime such as gambling led corruption.

Fourth, law enforcement resources are finite and local law enforcement agencies have many competing priorities, often dictated by government, media and the general community. The importance of the integrity of sport nationally and internationally is vital in an industry worth billions of dollars. In today's economic times, many things are about efficiencies and the focus law enforcement has tended to be very much on frontline policing and community perceptions of safety. Having said that, organised crime has become an enduring priority for law enforcement and governments. It is important to recognise how the markets for organised crime are elastic and crime groups are adaptive moving from established markets in illicit drugs to exploiting new opportunities such as corruption in sport. The threat of organised crime infiltrating professional sport and impacting on its integrity will ensure that gambling led corruption in sport is not merely a niche area of law enforcement. Leveraging off partnerships with sport controlling bodies, regulators and such bodies as the NISU could ensure an effective law enforcement response. The possible future establishment of a World Sport Anti-Corruption Agency or similar body would also facilitate a global response and raise the profile of this issue in the global community, including the law enforcement community.

Fifth, combating gambling-led corruption should also focus on all parts of the corruption process and the enablers of the crime. As coined by David Lacey, Executive Director, ACC, 'corrupters who corrupt the corruptible', corruption involves three actors/events - the corrupters, the act of corruption and the enablers being the corruptible (Lacey 2012). The corruptible can often be the professional athletes, referees and officials. A recent media report in Australia reported that sports betting by AFL players have reached troubling levels (Ralph 2012). The combination of easy access to betting websites, 24 h televised sport and high incomes is blamed for the escalating issue. Target hardening of players and officials through education and awareness focused on the potential 'corruptible' should be a priority strategy. A NISU in collaboration with Sport Controlling Bodies is best placed to implement these strategies. Partnerships such as FIFA and Interpol provide funding for implementation of these education and prevention strategies.

Sixth, Michael Jeh, founder of *Life Skills* professional sports consultant organisation, in his interview (October 29, 2012) with Inspector Jason Saunders (one of the authors of this chapter) shared that many professional sport controlling bodies provide significant resources to educating athletes and run programmes aimed at strengthening life skills of sportspeople with the view to encourage a better conduct from them on and off the field. Jeh, a former cricket professional, who played for the Oxford Blue, now provides life skills training to young athletes in Australia. He is currently engaged in a training programme with the ARU. He said that the focus to date on these types of programs has been on drugs and alcohol and lifestyle choices. These programs could incorporate more about gambling led corruption and the corruption process. As gambling led-corruption is financially motivated, financial affair management of athletes would be an important part of life skills training, assisting athletes to maximise their returns on their legitimate income. This type of proactive work by the sporting industry can prevent the corruptible being corrupted by the corrupters. This will also alleviate the use of finite law enforcement resources.

References

Anderson, J. (2007). *Legality of boxing*, London: Routledge.

Australian Crime Commission. (2011). Submission to the Australian Parliament's Joint Select Committee into Gambling Reform. Reference 11/106554, Canberra, June 24, 2011.

Australian Crime Commission. (2011). *Organised crime in Australia 2011*. Commonwealth of Australia. Canberra. Retrieved July 29, 2012, from http://www.crimecommission.gov.au/sites/default/files/files/OCA/2011/oca2011.pdf.

Australian Crime Commission. (2012). *ACC annual report 2011-12*. Retrieved July 3, 2013, from http://www.crimecommission.gov.au/sites/default/files/files/annual_reports/1112/ACC_AR_2011-2012.pdf.

Australian Crime Commission. (February 2013). *Organised crime and drugs in sport: New generation performance and image enhancing drugs and organised criminal involvement in their use in professional sport*. Commonwealth of Australia. Retrieved February 17, 2013, from http://www.crimecommission.gov.au/sites/default/files/files/organised-crime-and-drugs-in-sports-feb2013.pdf.

Australian Government Department of Regional Australia, Local Government, Arts and Sport. (2012). *Media release: National policy on match-fixing in sport*. Retrieved May 9, 2012, from http://www.regional.gov.au/sport/programs/files/national_policy_match-fixing.pdf.

Australian Sports Anti-Doping Authority (ASADA). (March 20, 2013). ASADA Media Statements: Organised crime and drugs in sport. Retrieved March 27, 2013, from http://www.asada.gov.au/media/organised_crime_and_drugs_in_sport.html.

Australian Sports Commission. The essence of Australian sport. Retrieved November 8, 2012, from http://www.ausport.gov.au/__data/assets/pdf_file/0011/312869/A4_brochure_7_05-V5.pdf.

Australian Transaction Reports and Analysis Centre (2008), *Money laundering methodologies, Typologies and case study reports*. Canberra. Retrieved June 3, 2012, from http://www.austrac. gov.au/files/typ_2008_mlm.pdf.

Bronitt, S. (2010). The criminal law of Australia. In M. Dubber & K. Heller (eds), *The handbook of comparative criminal law* (pp.49–96). Stanford: Stanford University Press.

Button, M., Johnston, L and Frimpong, K. (2008). The fraud review and the policing of fraud: Laying the foundations for a centralised fraud police or counter fraud executive? *Policing*. 2:2. 241–250. Retrieved November 3, 2012, from http://policing.oxfordjournals.org.libraryproxy. griffith.edu.au/content/2/2/241.

CBI's's report on cricket match-fixing and related malpractices. (October 2000). *Central Bureau of Investigation*. New Delhi. Retrieved July 4, 2012, from http://www.rediff.com/cricket/2000/ nov/01bet.htm.

Clark, J. (February 6, 2013). Fox footy expert Mark Robinson believes organised crime infil-trating AFL and more is to be revealed'. *Fox Sports*. Retrieved February 6, 2013, from http://www.foxsports.com.au/afl/afl-premiership/fox-footy-expert-mark-robinson-believes-organised-crime-infiltrating-afl-and-more-is-to-be-revealed/story-e6frf3e3-1226571909062 ? from=public_rss#.UXC8SrWmjLk.

Dampney, J. and APP. (April 12, 2013). Drugs allegations "a terribly disturbing situation", says Demetriou. *AFL News*. Retrieved April 17, 2013, from http://www.afl.com.au/news/2013-04-12/terribly-disturbing-situation.

Dowsley, A. (February 16, 2013). AFL players caught on phone taps with drug dealers. *Herald Sun*. Retrieved February 17, 2013, from http://www.heraldsun.com.au/news/law-order/afl-players-caught-on-phone-taps-with-drug-dealers/story-fnat79vb-1226579152457.

Financial Action Task Force Report. (July 2009). *Money laundering through the football sector*. Retrieved November 5, 2012, from http://www.fatf-gafi.org/media/fatf/documents/reports/ ML%20through%20the %20Football %20Sector.pdf.

Founding group on fight for irregular and illegal betting calls for a universal monitoring system. (May 14, 2013). *International Olympics Committee*. Retrieved June 4, 2013, from http://www. olympic.org/news/founding-group-on-fight-against-irregular-and-illegal-betting-calls-for-a-universal-monitoring-system/199073.

Further Victorian integrity enhancements. (April 8, 2013). *Thoroughbred News*. Retrieved June 12, 2013, from http://www.thoroughbrednews.com.au/Australia/default.aspx?id=65883.

Gatt, R. (February 8, 2013). A-League fights off match-fix reports. *The Australian*. Retrieved March 11, 2013, from http://www.theaustralian.com.au/sport/football/a-league-fights-off-match-fix-reports/story-fn63e0vj-1226573016528.

Guardian Staff and agencies. (February 4, 2013). Europol: investigators identify 380 fixed football matches. *The Guardian*, Retrieved March 8, 2013, from http://www.guardian.co.uk/foot-ball/2013/feb/04/europol-investigation-football-matchfixing.

Hill, D. (2008). *The fix*. Toronto: McClelland & Stewart.

Lacey, D. (August 15, 2012). Corrupters who corrupt the corruptible. *Australian Crime Commission address to the national public sector fraud and corruption congress*. Retrieved November 12, 2012, from http://www.crimecommission.gov.au/media/address-to-national-public-sector-fraud-corruption-congress.

Liga Portuguesa de Futebol Profissional and Bwin International Ltd, formerly Baw International Ltd v Departamento de Jogos da Santa Casa da Misericórdia de Lisboa (2009) C-42/ECR I-7633, para 71. Retrieved September 12, 2012, from http://eur-lex.europa.eu/LexUriServ/ LexUriServ.do?uri=CELEX:62007J0042:EN:HTML.

Media Release. (May 9, 2011). FIFA makes historic contribution to INTERPOL in long-term fight against match-fixing. Retrieved November 24, 2012, from http://www.interpol.int/News-and-media/News-media-releases/2011/PR035.

Neilson, S. (2011). Threats to the integrity of professional sports in Australia. *International confer-ence on Combatting Serious Crime and Corruption in Sport, Centre of Excellence in Policing and Security*. Brisbane. July 27.

New South Wales Law Reform Commission (2011) (NSWLRC 130). *Cheating at gambling.* Retrieved August 3, 2011, from http://www.lawlink.nsw.gov.au/lawlink/lrc/ll_lrc.nsf/pages/ LRC_reports.

New South Wales Law Reform Commission. (2011). *Consultation paper on cheating at gambling.* CP12. Retrieved October 3, 201, from http://www.lawlink.nsw.gov.au/lrc.

News Limited Network (April, 19, 2013). AFL demands Melbourne tell truth after allegations emerge over links with Stephen Dank. *Fox Sports.* Retrieved June 7, 2013, from http://www. foxsports.com.au/afl/afl-premiership/director-of-exercise-and-sports-science-australia-calls-into-question-the-qualifications-of-stephen-dank/story-e6frf3e3-1226623973899.

Noble, R. K. (July 20, 2011). On the right path. *The New York Times.* Retrieved November 11, 2012,fromhttp://www.nytimes.com/roomfordebate/2011/07/19/how-can-fifa-address-corruption-in-soccer/fifa-is-on-the-path-to-rooting-out-corruption.

O' Keeffe, M. (October 26, 2012). Lance Armstrong asked to return nearly $4M in Tour de France prize money by cycling's international governing body. *Daily News.* Retrieved November 7, 2012,fromhttp://www.http://www.nydailynews.com/sports/i-team/lance-asked-return-4m-tour-de-france-prize-money-article-1.1193242.

Oxford Research. (April 2010). *Examination of threats to the integrity of sport.* Retrieved October 12, 2012, from http://www.eusportsplatform.eu/Files/Filer/examination %20 of% 20threats% 20to%20sports%20integrity.pdf.

Premier of Victoria. (February 7, 2013). *New Victoria police sporting integrity intelligence unit.* Retrieved March 5, 2013, from http://www.premier.vic.gov.au/media-centre/media-releases/5991-new-victoria-police-sporting-integrity-intelligence-unit.html.

Ralph, J. (2012). Sports betting by AFL players has reached troubling levels, key figures say. *The Advertiser.* Retrieved October 28, 2012, from/sports betting-by-afl-players-has-reached-troubling-levels-key-figures-say/story-e6freck3-1226504893702.

Report on corruption in international cricket. (2011) *International Cricket Council.* Retrieved November 4, 2012, from http://www.icc-cricket.com/anti_ corruption/condon-report.php.

Review of sports betting regulation. (March 31, 2011). *Glesson review of sports betting regulation in the state of Victoria.* Retrieved October 4, 2012, from https://assets.justice.vic.gov.au/jus-tice/resources/5c9236e3-f37e-440d-ae53-4dc5fbdef7ef/sports_betting_review_ 2011_report. pdf.

Senator Kate Lundy. (May 4, 2013). *Anti-doping and sports integrity funding boost.* Retrieved May23,2013,fromhttp://www.katelundy.com.au/2013/05/04/anti-doping-and-sports-integrity-funding-boost/.

Sheehan, D. (2013). Transnational cooperation. *International working group meeting on "Preserving sports integrity: Combating crime and corruption".* CEPS. Brisbane. June 5.

Smith, P. (2011). Rogue operators make battle to maintain integrity of sport more difficult. *The Australian.* July 16. Retrieved November 9, 2012, from http://www.theaustralian.com.au/sport/ opinion/rogue-operators-make-battle-to-maintain-integrity-of-sport-more-difficult/story-e6frg7t6-1226095581959.

Transparency International (2011). *Safe hands: Building integrity and transparency at FIFA.* Retrieved June 11, 2012, from http://www.transparency.org/whatwedo/pub/safe_hands_ building_integrity_and_transparency_at_fifa.

Transparency International (2013). Corruption in sport. *Transparency International UK.* Retrieved June 23, 2013, from http://www.transparency.org.uk/our-work/corruption-in-the-uk/sport.

Which Factors Favor Betting Related Cheating in Sports? Some Insights from Political Economy

Luca Rebeggiani and Fatma Rebeggiani

Abstract In recent years, cheating scandals connected with betting activity have shown to be a major concern for professional sports. From an economic point of view, such scandals threaten the integrity of sport and put the whole commercialization of this good (regarding e.g. sponsoring, broadcasting) in danger. This chapter the incentives for cheating connected to traditional and new bet types in the sports betting sector and how they might affect the behaviur of sportsmen, coaches, and officials. We develop a simple theoretical model and derive from it some political implications which we recommend, among others, for the ongoing reform of the German sports betting market. Our recommendations should contribute to an effective prevention of scandals like those unveiled in European football in the last years.

Introduction

Since their early days, professional sports have been accompanied by cheating scandals connected with betting activity. During the last years, a rising number of such scandals affected even sports traditionally considered as "noble", like tennis or sumo. Especially the innovations in the field of information technologies, which led to the development of live bets and other types of online gambling, and the increasing commercialization of sport are being made responsible for this. From an

L. Rebeggiani (✉)
International Research Institute for Gambling and Gaming, Business Campus Rhein-Sieg GmbH Grantham-Allee 2-8, 53757 Sankt Augustin, Germany
e-mail: rebeggiani@forschung-gluecksspiel.de

F. Rebeggiani
Bremen International Graduate School of Social Sciences, University of Bremen, Wiener Straße/Ecke Celsius Straße, 28359 Bremen, Germany
e-mail: rebeggiani@bigsss.uni-bremen.de

M.R. Haberfeld and D. Sheehan (eds.), *Match-Fixing in International Sports: Existing Processes, Law Enforcement, and Prevention Strategies*,
DOI 10.1007/978-3-319-02582-7_9, © Springer International Publishing Switzerland 2013

economic point of view, these scandals threaten the integrity of sport which represents the background of each sort of commercialization of the respective sport event (besides betting, in particular this relates to sponsoring, merchandising, and selling broadcasting rights). Therefore, they constitute a major risk that gambling regulation policy should target instead of focusing on addiction issues only, as has traditionally been the case in Germany and other countries.

This chapter analyzes the incentives for cheating related to traditional and new betting types in the sports betting sector and how they affect the behavior of sportsmen, coaches, and officials. First, we adapt a simple theoretical model developed by Forrest and Simmons (2003) and derive from it a classification system for different types of sports. The various kinds of bets as well as their placing modalities are then being analyzed and classified accordingly. The model yields five general results displaying the linkages between detection probability, expected gains from successful cheating, probability of success of the planned fraud, and expected financial losses in case of detection on the one side, and cheating propensity on the other side.

We then present AsTERiG as a new tool for the empirical evaluation of the risk potential of sport bets. The tool has been developed in cooperation with one of the largest German public lotteries (*Aktion Mensch*) and is currently used to assess the addiction potential of online games. AsTERiG assigns an individual risk score to each bet type by combining different weighted criteria and allows for a comparison between various bet types. We discuss a first classification of the risk score of some of the most popular sports bets including football.

Based on these results, we derive a list of political recommendations for the ongoing reforms of the European sports betting markets. Among others, we advise the close supervision of certain types of bets and the reorganization of some tournament settings. Especially in the German market, which is currently being completely re-regulated, politicians and officials should take account of these insights. The measures should help ensure a more effective prevention from scandals like those unveiled in European football during the last years.

Political Background

The German Gambling Market

The German gambling market has traditionally been under strong regulation, and the degree of regulation has even increased in the last years, when a new state treaty (*Glücksspielstaatsvertrag* – GlüStV) was put into place by the federal states in 2008.[1] The declared motive for this strong regulation was the supposed inherent addiction potential of gambling (§1 GlüStV). The period during which the GlüStV

---

[1] In the German federal political system, gambling market regulation is part of the federal states' (*Länder*) responsibility.

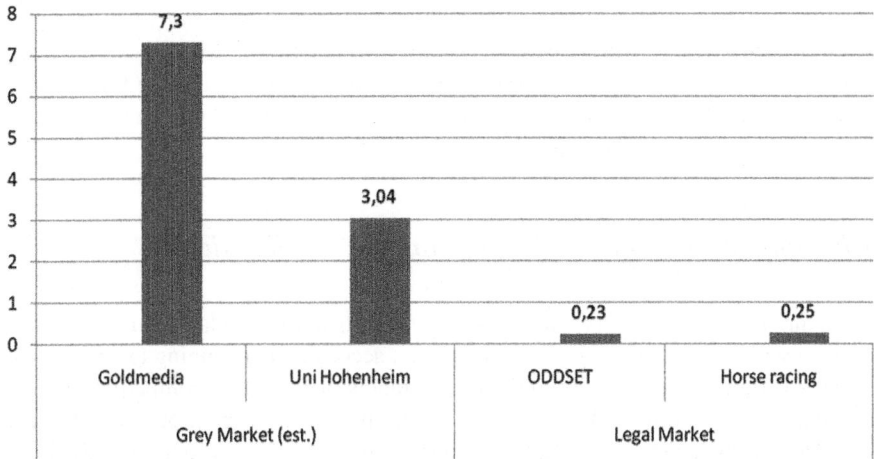

Fig. 1 German sport betting Market 2009 – turnover in bill EUR (The Goldmedia data are taken from Goldmedia (2010). The other comprehensive estimation of the size of the German grey gambling market from the University of Hohenheim is more conservative but still assesses its size at 87.4 % of the total market (Becker and Barth 2012))

was in force, from 2008 until the end of 2011, was thus characterized by a strict state monopoly with the publicly owned *Oddset* being the only legal provider of sports betting. Furthermore, advertising for gambling was highly limited,[2] and online gambling was entirely forbidden. These restrictions on advertising and online distribution additionally reduced the attractiveness of *Oddset* betting products, which were already characterized by lower payout ratios and less variety than those offered by private companies. As a consequence, the grey (i.e. unlicensed) market for sport betting grew significantly in Germany – to up 95 % of the total betting volume (Fig. 1) – while the turnover of *Oddset* sharply decreased.[3]

Due to a decision of the European Court of Justice which declared the state monopoly as an unjustified restraint of competition,[4] the German *Länder* were forced to liberalize the gambling market starting from 2012. Since they could not agree on central issues of the reform, especially on the extent of liberalization of the sports betting market and on the permission or prohibition of other types of online gambling, there currently exist two different models. The *Land* Schleswig-Holstein implemented a rather liberal one, while the other 15 federal states introduced a more

---

[2]However, this ban on advertising was not always observed in practice, especially by state lotteries (Albers 2008). This considerably threatened the credibility of the state treaty.

[3]See Rebeggiani (2010) for a detailed description of the evolution of turnovers and tax revenues before and after the implementation of the state treaty in 2008.

[4]Decisions of the ECJ of the 8th September 2010 regarding the cases C-316/07, C-358/07, C-359/07, C-360/07, C-409/07, C-410/07 (Markus Stoss et al.), C-409/06 (Winner Wetten GmbH), and C-46/08 (Carmen Media Group Ltd). For an overview of the legislative procedure leading to the modified state treaty in 2012 see Rebeggiani (2011).

restrictive policy.[5] The majority model, the *1. Glücksspieländerungsstaatsvertrag* – GlüÄndStV (First Modified State Treaty on Gambling), still preserves many aspects of the old monopolistic setting and guarantees a dominant role for the governmental institutions. Both models do, however, allow private companies to enter the German betting market via a licensing process.

Cheating in the Contest of Gambling Market Regulation

Germany is one of the European gambling markets that in the last years were confronted with the need to adapt their regulation according to changing technological standards on the one side and to the requirements of European competition policy legislation on the other. The old monopolistic frameworks seem obsolete, but for cultural reasons a rapid opening of the markets to private (and often foreign) enterprises faces strong resistance among politicians and also in the public opinion.

Still, the liberalization of the sports betting market has been going on in several European countries over the past years.[6] Given the international supply of online betting products and the seemingly unlimited access to these via the internet, the case for a national monopoly seems rather difficult to uphold. In Germany, the rise of the grey market and the descent of *Oddset*'s market share and turnover in real terms have proven that the monopoly could not be enforced properly. Market liberalization might therefore help to reduce the share of the grey market of sports betting by allowing government-controlled private market activities. On the other hand, liberalizing the market might promote private market activities and thus enlarge the betting market, which in turn could provide an incentive for cheating activities and worsen the already existing cheating problem.

The issue of betting related cheating is not only a legal one but affects the economic dimension of both betting regulation and professional sports. When looking at the negative effects of cheating behavior in the sports betting market, the following mechanisms – both individually and in their joint effect – are threatening the market for and the provision of sport offerings.

- Cheating threatens the **credibility of sport contests**: The very nature of a sport contest focuses on determining the better team or individual in terms of ability, skills and mastery of the discipline. Therefore, fairness is inseparably implied in its concept. Cheating as opposed to this concept threatens the credibility of sport contests and thus damages the integrity of sport in general.
- Being a problem in itself, the loss of credibility additionally undermines the **spectators' interest** in the sport event. Sport events live on the interest of the public, both in terms of immaterial support and economically.

---

[5] After elections and the formation of a new government in June 2012, Schleswig-Holstein joined on 8th February 2013 the regulation implemented by the other *Länder*. However, it is still unclear what will happen with the licenses already issued under the previous liberal regulation.
[6] For an overview of gambling regulation reforms throughout Europe see Rebeggiani (2012).

- A shrinking interest in a sport contest thus leads to a less successful commercialization and less **economic investment by the private market**. This affects each business sector related to professional sports, especially sponsoring,[7] broadcasting, and merchandising. The last years have shown many examples of economic declines of sports after scandals which undermined their credibility. In the next session, we discuss the case of the Italian *Serie A* which, compared to the 1990s, has suffered a substantial loss in spectators' interest followed by a general drop in economic potential due to a series of scandals in the last years (*Calciopoli* 2004–2006, *Calcioscommesse* 2011–2013).
- Perhaps the most striking example of what happens when the credibility of the sport is being severely damaged has been provided by professional cycling during the last decade: Starting with the *Festina* case in 1998, a series of doping scandals came to light, leading to retroactive corrections of race results and to the "fall" of previously acclaimed top stars like *Marco Pantani* or *Lance Armstrong*. All in all, the impression given to the public was that of a thoroughly corrupted sport, where no result is really definitive and where especially exceptional performances (that are usually at the core of the spectators' interest) are to be seen sceptically. This not only led to a significant drop in public interest, but also to the exit of most of the traditional sponsors, worried to be associated with a corrupt environment. In Germany, public opinion even forced public TV to stop broadcasting the *Tour de France*, because the coverage of such a scandal rigged event was regarded as incompatible with a publicly funded institution.
- A loss in credibility and a shrinking public interest necessarily makes the case for **public sports funding** harder: Due to the image damage, the sport might no longer be considered a "merit good" which the state should fund. Public funding is however one of the major financial sources of many sports. Even professional sports like football are highly dependent on public monies especially with regard to their facilities, which in most cases are at least co-financed by local governments.[8]
- The loss of credibility is detrimental for the **sports betting sector** itself because, obviously, no punter agrees to invest money in a system which he cannot trust. One reason for the shift of Asian betting syndicates towards European sports at the end of the 1990s was the widespread corruption in Asian football leagues. Today, betting operators still refuse to accept bets on matches of certain particularly corrupt leagues like minor divisions of Eastern European countries (IRIS et al. 2012, p. 31).

---

[7]Sponsoring in the face of match fixing scandals does not only suffer from diminishing spectators' interest: few enterprises will be interested in engaging in a corrupt environment, thus reducing or withdrawing completely their sponsorships.

[8]The issue of public financing of professional sports and sports mega events has been widely debated in the sports economic literature. See for an overview Coates and Humphreys (2008). Rebeggiani (2006) analyzes in detail the particular case of the FIFA World Cup 2006 in Germany: Even for this responsibly planned and well organized event, public subsidies amounting to more than half a billion Euro were necessary to co-finance the venues – plus other securities given by the government and the costs of infrastructure measures which were fully borne by public coffers.

For all these reasons, in economic terms cheating should be considered a negative externality which harms both professional sports and the sports betting market. This externality in our view justifies regulatory interventions by the government much more than the "addiction prevention" motive. Match fixing prevention should be kept in the core of gambling market regulation, in Germany and elsewhere. Indeed, along with the recent scandals, the awareness among politicians and regulators has risen significantly and cheating prevention is now mentioned as a central target in both the French and the German gambling regulation bodies.[9]

Sports Betting and Cheating: A Long-Time Relationship

The history of cheating scandals connected with betting activities is remarkably long. People have always tried to help fortune along. The processes of cheating have, however, changed throughout time, taking into account developments in the means and resources available for cheating as well as external and implicit restrictions to it. Part of the most significant recent developments influencing cheating activities is the internationalization of betting markets and the high liquidity in them. The enlargement of the betting market results in increasing competition among betting companies which then leads to the expansion of their product portfolio and to higher payout ratios. The technological development has not only integrated markets but also fostered innovations resulting in new products. New types of online betting products have been established such as live bets and betting exchanges, but to name a few. We will come back to these issues in section "Policy Recommendations".

Although these developments went along with efforts to increase transparency and to strengthen cheating prevention, the number of scandals increased. Furthermore, the cheating problem spread to formerly unsuspicious sports such as tennis (e.g. the *Davydenko* case in 2007). Forrest et al. (2008) provide a list of 42 cheating scandals connected with sport betting, discussing some "classical" cases like the 1919 baseball World Series scandal or the 2000 *Hansie Cronje* case in cricket in more detail. Hill (2009) presents the results of a comprehensive study about gambling corruptors fixing football matches that were drawn from personally conducted interviews as well as from the analysis of newspaper articles and police transcripts. The white paper by IRIS et al. (2012) contains a detailed discussion of recent corruption cases with particular emphasis on the impact of new bet types.

For illustrating the points made above, we will briefly present two prominent investigations, which recently uncovered a bunch of allegedly rigged matches. The investigations are still ongoing while in many cases proceedings have already been instituted against several involved actors, some of which have even been convicted (Europol 2013). Both investigations are characterized by the "new" factors described above:

---

[9]This is e.g. the case in the very first article of the German 1. GlüÄndStV.

Table 1 Recent major investigations in professional football

	Extent of match fixing	Role played by the betting market	Peculiarities
EUROPOL-investigations 2011–2013 (still ongoing)[a]	More than 380 suspicious matches in Europe, further 300 in the rest of the world. 425 match officials, club officials, players, and alleged corruptors, from more than 15 countries involved	Over €8 million in betting profits, over €2 million in corrupt payments to those involved in the matches	Even World Cup and European Championship qualification matches, as well as two UEFA Champions League matches among the allegedly fixed ones. Many operations were run out of Singapore with bribes of up to €100,000 paid per match
The *Calcioscommesse*-scandal 2011–2013 in Italy (investigation still ongoing)	Six legal proceedings examining over 100 suspicious matches (2008–2012), more than 160 involved persons, 200,000 phone calls analyzed. Some of the trials concluded with bans for several players and officials, and three relegations (Alessandria, Ravenna for the season 2011–2012, and Lecce for 2012–2013)	Investigations revealed a worldwide network, mainly orchestrated from Singapore (prominent role of businessman *Tan Seet Eng*) and administrated in Italy through contact persons from Eastern Europe and the Balkans (e.g. *Almir Gegić*) who then approached Italian players and officials. Many cases of (prohibited) insider betting by players were uncovered[b]	Many prominent former players (e.g. *Stefano Bettarini, Giuseppe Signori*) and end of career players (e.g. *Cristiano Doni, Stefano Mauri*) indicted. Additional relevance was given by the involvement of *Juventus*-coach *Antonio Conte*, who in 2012 had just won the national championship with his team

[a]For details see Europol (2013)
[b]Prosecutor *Roberto Di Martino* estimates the percentage of players betting on their own sport at 70 % (Gazzetta dello Sport 2013)

(1) Globalized betting and match fixing networks; (2) Importance of new technology and related bet types (e.g. live bets); (3) Damage for the sport itself and its commercialization and thus high relevance for regulation efforts. The cases are summarized in Table 1.

In order to generalize our analysis, we follow IRIS et al. (2012) by defining betting related cheating as *any type of manipulation, successful or attempted, of a result or aspect of a game with the aim of enrichment on the sports betting market.*[10] These cheating activities are usually characterized by the following particular traits:

- **Cheating to lose instead of cheating to win**: While the doping problem is about illegal activities aimed at improving an athlete's or team's performance, usually no one is able to significantly improve his/her performance after being bribed. Therefore, most of the money is spent by corruptors in order to reduce performance of key players of one team. In individual sports, the athlete can deliberately choose to reduce his/her performance or to give up (as happened in the *Davydenko* case in 2007) in order to achieve the desiderated result. Bets are then placed on the loss of the team or the athlete.
- **Fixing matches in a proper way**: Preference is given to results that are more easily to achieve, like draws, or to results yielding high odds on the betting market, like losses with unusually high scores.
- **Cheating without harming too much**: As we will show in the next section, the loss of sporting glory by losing deliberately is one key deterrent for sportsmen to agree on fixes. Many of the corruption cases happen therefore in friendly or end of season matches. Even more easy is the possibility offered by new types of bets to punt on single events (e.g. first goal scored, first throw-in, number of goals scored) or on partial scores. One of the most frequent "anomalies" regularly detected by the early warning system *Sportradar* in football is the pattern of the weaker team leading at half-time but losing the match at the end (Sportradar 2013, p. 25). Another type of this kind of "painless fixes" are those connected to spread betting (Wolfers 2006), where players can agree on a fix without having to lose the match.

Which mechanisms favor the emergence of cheating behavior among athletes, officials and bookmakers? And which measures can policy put into place in order to combat this? In the next section, we will develop a formal politico-economic model to get deeper insights into the nature of the problem.

Theoretical Model

In modern economics, there are several approaches to model cheating behavior in sports. One strand of the literature explores the emergence of cheating in the framework of classical contest theory without connecting it to betting activities (e.g. Caruso 2009). Only few attempts exist to set up models linking sports betting to match fixing. In an influential paper, Preston and Szymanski (2003) analyze three types of cheating in sports: sabotage, doping and match fixing. They present a model of match fixing, where the agents (bookmakers, sportsmen) choose rationally

---

[10] See IRIS et al. (2012), p. 6. According to this definition, some very prominent cheating cases are not included in the scope of this analysis. This is e.g. the case for the *Calciopoli*-scandal in Italian football (Boeri and Severgnini 2011), since it was not connected with betting activities.

to cheat or not depending on their given preferences and the decisions of the other agents. Their results are similar to those we will present below. Bag and Saha (2011) employ a sophisticated microeconomic model in order to study the conditions under which briberies organized by influential punters may occur even in an environment where bookmakers compete with each other. Finally, Dietl and Weingärtner (2012) explain the rise in cheating scandals as rooted in the non-existence of certain property rights which make the commercial use of football fixtures and match results costless for betting operators.[11]

Because of its clarity and its practical employability, we apply the model introduced by Forrest and Simmons (2003) to the political discussion described above. In the model, betting related cheating is modelled as a rational decision involving the consideration of costs and benefits while being embedded in moral preferences. Assuming rational decisions is central to economics and we regard it as an important contribution to the understanding of the corruption problem.[12] On the one hand, this avoids looking at cheating only from a legal or "moral" perspective, the first being often too narrow, the second suffering from a lack of practical employability. On the other hand, this view will allow us to single out different factors influencing the behavior of the involved actors and to evaluate their respective contribution to the cheating decision.

In the model, agents (athletes, referees or officials) cheat if and when their expected payoff is higher than their expected costs. Expected costs do involve both monetary and non-monetary costs. Partly, these non-monetary costs of cheating relate to moral principles. For players, we assume that these differ regarding their moral principles as well as their expected income from sport. The model framework is summarized in Table 2, which explains in detail the central equation of the model.

Assuming that agents are risk-neutral (that means, not particularly inclined to the thrill of risky actions neither particularly scary of risks), they will cheat if $E(U_{fix}) > 0$.[13] Being different in their personal values of F and $U(C)$, they will e.g. require different amounts of G in order to engage in a fixing attempt. Thus, the equation allows analyzing which variables in which way affect the probability of agents to cheat. All in all, the model yields five major implications for cheating attempts to decrease:

1. The higher the **probability of detection** (p), the fewer cheating attempts will be undertaken. Therefore, market transparency and cooperation between the involved actors (betting companies, sports regulating bodies, regulators) are highly important.

---

[11]Other economic contributions include Strumpf (2003), Wolfers (2006) as well as Winter and Kukuk (2008).

[12]Indeed, the model by Forrest and Simmons (2003) builds on the seminal work by Ehrlich (1996), who provides a systematic analysis of criminal behavior from an economist's point of view, based on "the assumption that offenders, as members of the human race, respond to incentives" (Ehrlich 1996, p. 43).

[13]This assumption might be contested since agents involved in the sports market are expected to be rather risk prone. However, this would only increase the number of cheaters, not the mechanisms involved and thus the factors that favor cheating activities (Forrest et al. 2008, p. 10).

Table 2 Model framework for betting related cheating

$E\,(U_{fix}) =$	The expected utility increase from the fix is equal to…
$(1-p)\,[qU\,(Y+G)]$	The utility from profit, if the fix is successful
$+\,(1-p)\,[(1-q)\,U\,(Y)]$	Plus the utility from current wealth, if the fix fails
$+\,p\,[U\,(Y-F-R)]$	Plus the loss of utility, if the fix is being detected (negative)
$-\,U\,(Y)$	Minus the utility from current wealth
$+\,U\,(C)$	Plus the intrinsic utility from cheating itself (may be positive or negative)

With:
p = probability of being detected
q = probability of successful cheating
Y = current wealth
G = wealth increase through successful and undetected cheating
F = wealth loss due to cheating detection
R = loss of reputation due to cheating detection
$U(C)$ = intrinsic utility from cheating

From this viewpoint, the growing importance of online betting has indeed some advantages, because data processing allows for a constant monitoring of stakes and odds movements. This applies, of course, only to the case where there is a gambling authority in charge of the betting market or when there exist a cooperation with a fraud detection operator like *Sportradar* or the *Early Warning System GmbH*. At the same time, today's extensive TV coverage of sports provides a deterrent against fixing attempts through extended visibility.

2. The lower the **probability of cheating being successful** (q), the fewer cheating attempts will be made. This implies an enormous variance between different sports and different bet types, explaining why individual sports like tennis may be particularly in danger and why bets on single events (both can be easily be manipulated by a single person) do also offer more incentives to cheat.

3. The lower the **profit** (G) from a successful, undetected manipulation, the fewer the cheating attempts; thus, the liquidity in betting markets plays a decisive role. Larger markets per se may increase cheating activity because the financial potential for bribing activities grows exponentially. This aspect has become of central importance due to the globalization and enlargement of the betting market, which we will discuss below. For regulators, this is a given fact which they can hardly influence. Reducing the market size in European countries by controlling access to it via a licensing process does not really provide a solution, because profits made by fixers are mainly realized with Asian betting operators.

4. The higher the **financial loss** if the fix is detected (F), the lesser the incentive is to cheat. Regulators can on the one side discuss appropriate fines as deterrent for match fixing. On the other side, the main financial deterrent in professional sports is given by the athlete's loss of future income from salaries and sponsoring revenues due to a possible ban or, at least, reduced market value. The salaries of players and referees therefore play a central role in cheating probability: the higher the (regular) income potential cheats would lose if they are detected, the less

they will engage in cheating attempts. This issue has been discussed extensively in studies on match fixing (e.g. Preston et al. 2001), especially because in former days fixing scandals were frequent in sports with low remuneration for athletes (cricket, US college sports). Today, major European football leagues pay such high wages that for most players the threat of losing those hardly makes engagement in fixing attempts lucrative, even when they are being promised high amounts of money for it. Problems arise with athletes at the end of their careers, for which the endangered future income streams are low, or with retired ones (the former Italian star *Giuseppe Signori*, involved in the *Calcioscommesse* scandal, is a prominent example). The same applies to lower divisions and to minor leagues with low earning standards. Also crucial is the remuneration of referees: as shown by the *Hoyzer* scandal in Germany 2005, the practice of European top leagues to employ amateur referees within the contest of highly paid professionals turned out to be hugely problematic. When the disparity in earnings between players and referees becomes too large, this goes along with envy (especially among young referees)[14] and with insufficient fraud protection due to the fear of losing (significant) future income streams when found involved in match fixing.

5. The lower **the intrinsic utility from cheating** $U(C)$ among athletes and officials, the fewer will be the number of cheating attempts. A positive intrinsic utility from cheating is a concept contrary to the ambition of most professional athletes since cheating involves match fixing by scoring less than possible. Thus, one can assume the $U(C)$ will be negative for most sportspeople. There can, however, exist significant differences regarding personal preferences and even between cultural backgrounds. Without engaging this argument too far, there is a matter of fact that in nearly all match fixing cases occurring recently in European sports (the *Bochum* trial, the scandal, other cases reported by Sportradar 2013) players and "businessmen" from the Balkans and Eastern Europe were disproportionally involved (IRIS et al. 2012). The change of personal and cultural preferences is not a task that can be achieved immediately, but nevertheless it is possible to induce significant changes in the long run, as shown by the educational campaigns against fan violence, racism and other negative phenomena in football. In the same way, individual sports like cycling or athletics have developed a much more critical attitude towards doping, which was silently tolerated in practice until only a few years ago.

Another possibility for athletes to escape the dilemma between sport's ethics and the prospect of extra income from cheating is switching to fixes which do not heavily affect one's sporting glory, like throwing matches of low importance (friendly and end-season matches) or fixing single match events, which is nowadays easily possible with live bets or different types of spread betting.

---

[14] Seeking a higher living standard was the main reason *Robert Hoyzer* declared in his confessions for agreeing in match fixes.

Empirical Evaluation of Risk Potentials of Bet Types Using AsTERiG

Which bets on which matches are most likely to involve cheating behavior? Are there bet types that differ on the above mentioned probabilities of fraud detection? In the following, we introduce the AsTERiG tool (*Assessment Tool to Measure and Evaluate the Risk Potential of Gambling Products*) and adapt it to assess the specific risk potential of different sport bets regarding betting related cheating. AsTERiG has been developed with a major German public lottery (*Aktion Mensch*) and is currently used to evaluate the addiction potential of online games (e.g. Clement et al. 2012). Here, the different sports bet types will be examined and classified as high or low risk bet, respectively. One major advantage of the tool is the visualization of the risk potential in one single value, which can be helpful in the communication with politicians, regulators and other stakeholders.[15] Besides, it also enables a direct comparison to be drawn between the risk potentials of different betting products.

The assessment of AsTERiG implies the combination of different weighted criteria (identical for all bets examined) with an individual point score for each bet and thus allows assigning a comparable individual risk score to each bet type. The ten criteria comprised within the tool are based on the theoretical model presented in section "Theoretical Model" and expert interviews with professionals from the field of gambling and fraud prevention. They cover market criteria such as liquidity in the market or financial endowments of referees and players, factors related to the manipulation of match outcomes like e.g. the feasibility of the fix or transparency in the field, as well as criteria related to the relative relevance of the match within the respective tournaments (Table 3). The criteria are each assigned a different weight, which depends on their relevance for match fixing purposes.

In a second step, different experts are asked to assess a point score to each criterion, evaluating the specific threat of a bet type. The point values are finally multiplied with the weighted criteria and summed up. Points are then standardized to "scores", which provide a better basis for visualization (e.g. bar charts). The specific score allows the assignment of the bet to specific risk classes, which we will denote by letters. Hence, AsTERiG allows for a comparison of different sport events and the related bets, classifying them according to their score as high or low risk potential (Table 4).

The results presented in this paper are still preliminary and serve as a first step to introduce AsTERiG in the context of match fixing. For a correct use of the tool, the process of criteria validation and points' assessment must be described in detail (such as in Clement et al. 2012). This work is still ongoing and further results will be presented in a forthcoming companion paper.

Without going into calculation details, below we show some examples for football and tennis bets that give a first impression of the functioning of AsTERiG,

---

[15] AsTERiG also offers many modes of visualization, like scorecards or spider charts (see e.g. Clement et al. 2012, p. 722).

Table 3 AsTERiG general weights and individual scores

Criterion	Weighting	Points	Value (maximum)
Market liquidity (G)	2.2	0–4	8.80
1. Feasibility of the fix (q) – successful enrollment of cheats necessary for the fix	1.5	2–4	6.00
1. Transparency (p) – media coverage	2.5	1–4	10.00
Financial endowment of possible cheats (players and referees) (F)	1.5	0–3	4.50
Relevance of the match (U(C))	1.7	2–4	6.80
2. Transparency (p) – experts' scrutiny	1.3	1–3.5	4.55
Loss of sport glory ($U(C)$)	1.5	0–4	6.00
2. Feasibility of the fix (q) – cheats' probability of success	2.5	0.5–4	10
General moral principles in the country/ in the sport ($U(C)$)	1.0	0–4	4.00
Totals	**15.7**		**60.65**

Table 4 Classification of bet types according to AsTERiG

Points	Score	Risk class	Risk potential
<21.45	<1.366	A	Very low
21.46–31.25	1.367–1.990	B	Low
31.26–41.05	1.991–2.615	C	Moderate
41.06–50.85	2.616–3.239	D	High
50.86–60.65	3.240–3.863	E	Very high

illustrating the bets' different risk potentials. For football, the following examples highlight the different risk classes of some of the most common bet types:

- Standard bets on the outcome of one (high interest) game in European top leagues: **Risk class B** (low risk potential)
- Standard bets on the outcome of one (low interest) game in European top leagues: **Risk class C** (moderate risk potential)
- Standard bets on the outcome of one (low interest) game in minor European leagues: **Risk class D** (high risk potential)
- Combination bets on the outcome of at least three matches in European top leagues: **Risk class A** (very low risk potential)
- Live bets on other aspects than the final result (minor European leagues, low interest games): **Risk class E** (very high risk potential)

High interest matches in European top leagues are characterized by high visibility and high relevance for the careers of the involved persons. This makes them less vulnerable for fixing attempts, even if market liquidity in terms of money wagered may be extremely high. With diminishing competitive interest, even in top leagues cheating risk rises (e.g. for end of season games). This risk turns out to be even higher in minor European leagues, where there is less visibility and low financial endowment of players and referees. Combination bets offer the best protection against cheating, because the feasibility of fixes is at its lowest here. On the contrary, live bets are subject to high risk because of the relatively easy feasibility of cheating activities. When live bets are placed on low interest games in minor leagues, we obtain the highest AsTERiG risk score.

Similar bet types as listed above may yield different results regarding their risk potential when taking into consideration a different sport. For tennis as an individual sport, the following examples make this clear:

- Standard bet on the final result of one (high relevance) game: **Risk class A** (very low risk potential)
- Standard bet on the final result of one (low relevance) game. **Risk class B** (low risk potential)
- Live bets on other aspects than the final result (of low relevance games): **Risk class E** (very high risk potential)

Due to the proportional prize money in tennis, the incentive to fix the final result is rather low, especially in important games. Hence, a much greater cheating risk lies in fixing other aspects of the match such as partial scores. The risk grows substantially in matches with low visibility, like first round matches in minor tournaments.

Policy Recommendations

General Considerations

We have argued that the prevention and detection of cheating in sport should be the utmost concern of gambling regulation policy. From a regulator's point of view, there are some empirical developments which, in the light of the model presented above, give particular reason for concern. These developments call for specific regulation measures which will not always be easy to conceive properly and to implement effectively. Following the model, we focus our attention on two particularly problematic aspects: the enormous growth of liquidity in the worldwide sports betting market and the influence of the new types of bets.

The first aspect is not easy to quantify: estimations of the global sports betting market vary from €50.7 billion (*H2 Gambling Capital*, cited from IRIS et al. 2012, p. 37)[16] to more than €750 billion per year (Sportradar 2013, p. 13). Undisputed is the fact that these values have rocketed in the last years and that this growth was closely related to the rising importance of the Asian betting market.

---

[16]This value refers only to internet bets in the year 2012.

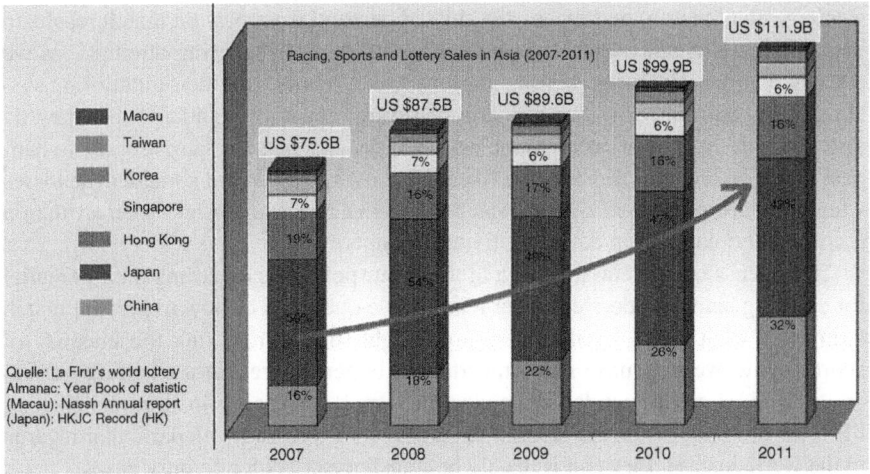

Fig. 2 Gambling turnover in Asia in $bill (Source: Sportradar 2013, p. 21)

As shown in Fig. 2, the overall size of the Asian market has increased by almost 50 % from 2007 to 2011, with especially China fuelling this growth. The structure of the supply side of the market, characterized by only few operators collecting bets, additionally enlarges the concerns we have regarding their threat to the integrity of sports. Asian operators like *188bet.com*, *sbobet.com*, and *ibcbet.com* do not only offer a wider range of bets than their European counterparts, they also accept by far larger stakes. Finally, they are able to offer better conditions, especially higher rates of return, than the Europeans, which is largely due to their enormous turnover. Up to 97 % of the amount staked is returned to bettors as winnings, compared to 92–94 % offered by the most "generous" European companies.[17] According to the third implication of the model described above, all these aspects enormously increase the profits corruptors can potentially realize on the (less regulated) Asian betting market, and thus also their margin for briberies.

Sportradar estimates the amount of bets placed worldwide on German sport events at €16.2 billion, €15 billion of which being put on football and almost €1 billion on tennis (Sportradar 2013, pp. 13–14). In Europe, the growth of the sports betting market has in the last years been driven by live bets, which by now amount to 70 % of the total betting volume in football and up to 90 % in tennis (IRIS et al. 2012, p. 38). This value illustrates rather well our second major concern: the rising share of live bets and the proliferation of betting exchanges. Both pose particular challenges for cheating prevention: the diffusion of live bets goes along with a multiplication of betting opportunities (operators offer odds for dozens of events in a

---

[17]In continental Europe, where gambling regulation is usually stricter, these rates are even lower. In France, for example, rates of returns to wagers are by law set at 85 % of the stakes.

single football match) and means the shift of demand from bets on match results to bets on single match events, which bear higher threats for fixing attempts, as we discussed above. Exchange betting platforms like *Betfair* with their monitoring systems have contributed to the detection of several cheating scandals,[18] but they do also foster the spread of problematic betting types like bets on "an event not to happen",[19] which could more easily be fixed. Moreover, they do not shoulder the losses when bets are placed on rigged matches, having in principle less interest than a traditional bookmaker in detecting fixing attempts.[20]

The discussion and classification of different sports bets regarding their potential for cheating activities derived so far leads to the questions of how to prevent match fixing and what kind of policy measures might support restoring the integrity of sport. Below, we will make recommendations targeted at regulating betting providers as well as recommendations concerning sport governing institutions such as FIFA for football. While the recommendations are expressed with particular regards to the German case, they can be easily be transferred to other country cases.

The Role of the Government

The controversial debate about the proper regulation of the German sports betting market has been outlined in section "Political Background". Although there are still some shortcomings from our view, many aspects which we criticized regarding the old regulation[21] have been included in the new modified state treaty: the inclusion of cheating prevention as a general aim of the legislation, a controlled opening of the sports betting market through a licensing process, and the proposition to cooperate with other important players like betting companies and sport governing bodies.

A key institution we still regard as missing, in particular with respect to match fixing prevention, is the establishment of a central "gambling authority" entitled to fight the negative externalities of gambling. This authority should work at the federal level – a crucial point within the German federal system – and oversee the whole process: from issuing licenses to private companies to the collection of taxes, and finally to the coordination of measures against the "dark side" of sports betting, especially the addiction issue and the integrity problem.[22] Only with the establishment of such a central authority the measures we discuss below can be properly enforced.

---

[18] One example was the *Davydenko* case in 2007.

[19] In principle, every sort of bet who finds a counterpart can be placed on such a platform.

[20] While the bookmaker has to pay out the winnings to the (corrupted) punter, a betting exchange platform only charges a commission, while the loss is suffered by the bettor who holds the bet.

[21] See Rebeggiani (2010), section "Theoretical Model" for a detailed discussion of the shortcomings of the old German regulation. Most of them apply to monopolistic regulations in other countries as well, as argued in Rebeggiani (2009).

[22] Similar central gambling authorities exist in other European countries, like the AAMS (*Amministrazione Autonoma dei Monopoli di Stato*) in Italy or, for online games, the ARJEL (*Autorité de Régulation des Jeux en Ligne*) in France.

Regulating Betting Companies

In recent years, private betting operators have been entering markets from which they were traditionally banned by monopolistic regulations. Together with publicly owned companies like *Oddset* in Germany, they are key players in the pursuit of market transparency and integrity of sports. However, an efficient market regulation requires some well defined policy measures to be implemented and enforced by public authorities:

1. In order to observe betting behavior and related suspicious activities, betting companies and sport federations should engage in the exchange of relevant information on stakes and odds movements, thus implementing an **early warning system** to detect fraud. The efficiency of market monitoring systems like *Sportradar* or *Early Warning GmbH* has been recently questioned by the chief prosecutor of the *Bochum* trial, especially because they do not cover illegal betting.[23] We, on the contrary, regard them as a fundamental tool for detection of suspicious odds and stakes movements, especially because in a nearly-perfect market like the worldwide betting market, information from illegal betting operators is likely to influence even the odds of legal ones. The recording of final scores and single match events is also a powerful monitoring tool, which can be used to detect frauds even at later times.
2. The consent to provide information on (suspicious) betting activities to a public monitoring authority should be a **prerequisite** for granting **betting market licenses** to private companies.
3. **New bet types** and their inherent cheating potential should be closely supervised; the regulator should be entitled to impose explicit restrictions on some types of bets, to the point of banning them altogether, a measure which should be taken into consideration with some live bets. However, prohibiting bet types always entails the danger of a shift to the grey market (especially to Asian operators). Therefore, a certain limitation of the offerings in combination with a close supervision should be the more effective strategy.[24]

Sport Governing Institutions

Sports governing bodies like the national Olympic committee (*Deutscher Olympischer Sportbund* – DOSB in Germany) and sports federations such as the DFB (*Deutscher Fußball-Bund*) for football play a central role in the organization

---

[23] See the interview given by *Dieter Althans* to Spiegel Online (2013).

[24] In "good old days", gambling operators could more easily avoid risky betting types, e.g. in Great Britain by not accepting bets on single football matches (only combination bets on three matches were possible, see Forrest and Simmons 2003, p. 606). In times of internet and globalization, such strict limitations would only have small positive effects in preventing cheating behavior, because major frauds are organized through Asian operators. They would, however, negatively affect the affairs of European companies by reducing the attractiveness of their offerings.

and marketing of professional sports. Including them in the policy aimed at combating match fixing is crucial for it to be successful. Based on our theoretical and empirical findings, we particularly suggest the following measures:

1. **Educational programmes** highlighting the dangers of match fixing for the sport and for the individual careers of players should be offered to (young) players in order to raise their awareness and thus prevent their involvement in match fixing activities. Experiences that have been made with anti-doping educational programmes should be taken into consideration to ensure the effectiveness of these measures. The programmes should include general courses in sports ethics but also the communication of potential income and reputation losses when found cheating as part of a policy of deterrence.
2. The abuse of **insider information**, i. e. the betting on their own sport by players and referees should be strictly prohibited. Such clauses already exist in professional sports in many countries. Furthermore, similar laws can be adapted from financial markets, where insider trading is punished as a major offence.[25]
3. The **referee compensation** should be adequate to players' wages. In professional sport, referees should be remunerated appropriately for the vital role they play for the course and the outcome of the match. In return, referees may be required to agree to controls on their financial flows. Recent plans of the German football federation to raise referee compensation therefore show in the right direction.
4. **Referee decisions** should be tightly monitored through expert commissions set up by the sport federations. Suspicious cases should early be reported to authorities entitled to check odds' and stakes' movements in the betting market.
5. **The appointment of referees** should be conducted secretly and under close temporal proximity to the respective assignment.
6. Where possible, the **redesign of contests** should be considered. This issue has been the subject of a long debate, especially in order to avoid irrelevant and uninteresting end of season matches in football ("dead rubber"). There have been proposals to hold play-off and play-out matches like in American sports, and this has been implemented with success e.g. in minor leagues of Italian football. On the other side, political developments in the last decades leading to a multiplication of participating countries have brought to a multiplication of qualification matches for European cups, which are particularly often object of fixing attempts (Sportradar 2013). A perfect solution is not in sight: as we did for live bets above, we simply suggest a close monitoring of risky matches, identifying them e.g. by using the AsTERiG score system.

---

[25] See the Directive 2003/6/CE of the European Parliament and the Council of 28th January 2003 regarding the integrity of stock markets.

Conclusion and Outlook

This chapter has developed a detailed analysis of the incentives for betting related cheating activities in sports and has then presented some concrete policy measures to be put in practice in order to fight the problem. The next steps should focus on implementation: These insights should be considered in the ongoing political debate about the re-regulation of the German gambling market, but can also offer valuable insights for the regulation of the sports betting market in other countries. As shown in section "Policy Recommendations", the model delivers many practical recommendations to be implemented directly by the governmental authorities, sport governing bodies, and other stakeholders in the betting markets, in particular by the betting companies.

On the agenda for future research, our main focus will be on the further development of the criteria and of the point system of AsTERiG in order to refine the tool for the specific purposes of cheating risk analysis. By transferring the insights of our theoretical analysis to practice, we hope to provide with AsTERiG an effective contribution to a better prevention of betting related cheating activities in sports.

References

Albers, N. (2008): Die Markenstrategie des Deutschen Lotto-Toto-Blocks unter dem Einfluss des Bundesverfassungsgerichts, Discussion Paper No. 408, University of Hannover, School of Economics and Management.

Bag, P., & Saha, B. (2011). Match-fixing under competitive odds. *Games and Economic Behavior* 73 (2), 318–344.

Becker, T., & Barth, D. (2012). Der deutsche Glücksspielmarkt: Eine Schätzung des nicht staatlich regulierten Marktvolumens, Newsletter 02/2012 of the *Forschungsstelle Glücksspiel* at the University of Hohenheim.

Boeri, T., & Severgnini, B. (2011). Match rigging and the career concerns of referees. *Labour Economics* 18 (3), 349–359.

Caruso, R. (2009). The Basic Economics of Match Fixing in Sport Tournaments. *Economic Analysis and Policy* 39 (3), 355–377.

Clement, R., Goudriaan, A. E.,van Holst, R. J., Molinaro, S., Moersen, C., Nilsson, T., Parke, A., Peren, F. W., Rebeggiani, L., Stoever, H., Terlau, W. & Wilhelm, M. (2012). Measuring and Evaluating the Potential Addiction Risk of the Online Poker Game Texas Hold'em No Limit. *Gaming Law Review and Economics* 16 (10), 713–728.

Coates, D. & Humphreys, B.R. (2008). Do Economists Reach a Conclusion on Subsidies for Sports Franchises, Stadiums, and Mega-Events? *Econ Journal Watch* 5 (3), 294–315.

Dietl, H., & Weingärtner, C. (2012). Betting scandals and attenuated property rights – How betting related match fixing can be prevented in future. University of Zurich, Institute for Strategy and Business Economics Working Paper No. 154.

Ehrlich, I. (1996). Crime, Punishment, and the Market for Offenses. *Journal of Economic Perspectives* 10 (1), 43–67.

Europol (2013). *Update – Results from the largest football match-fixing investigation in Europe.* RetrievedJuly21,2013,fromhttps://www.europol.europa.eu/content/results-largest-football-match-fixing-investigation-europe

Forrest, D., McHale, I., & McAuley, K. (2008). *Risk to the Integrity of Sport from Betting Corruption*, Report for the Central Council for Physical Recreation, University of Salford.

Forrest, D. & Simmons, R. (2003). Sport and Gambling. *Oxford Review of Economic Policy* 19 (4), 598–611.

Gazzetta dello Sport (2013). *Calcioscommesse, Di Martino: "L'inchiesta è un pozzo senza fondo"*. Retrieved July 21, 2013, from http://www.gazzetta.it/Calcio/Speciali/Calcio_Infetto/23-04-2013/calcioscommesse-martino-l-inchiesta-pozzo-senza-fondo-20282388962.shtml

Goldmedia (2010). *Glücksspielmarkt Deutschland 2015*, Berlin.

Hill, D. (2009). How gambling corruptors fix football matches. *European Sport Management Quarterly* 9 (4), 411–432.

IRIS (Institut de Relations Internationales et Stratégiques) et al. (2012). *Sports betting and Corruption*, Paris.

Preston, I., Ross, S.F., & Szymanski, S. (2001). Seizing the moment: A Blueprint for Reform of World Cricket, Working Paper, University College London.

Preston, I., & Szymanski, S. (2003). Cheating in Contests. *Oxford Review of Economic Policy* 19 (4), 612–624.

Rebeggiani, L. (2006). Public vs. private spending for sports facilities – The case of Germany 2006. *Public Finance and Management* 6 (3), 395–435.

Rebeggiani, L. (2009). The *Liga Portuguesa* Decision of the European Court of Justice – An Economist's View. *Rivista di Diritto ed Economia dello Sport* 5 (3), 111–122.

Rebeggiani, L. (2010). *Deutschland im Jahr Drei des GlüStV - Reformvorschläge zur Regulierung des deutschen Glücksspielmarktes*, Report for the German Lotto-Association (*Deutscher Lotto-Verband*), Hannover.

Rebeggiani, L. (2011). *Die Vorschläge der Länder zur Reform des GlüStV – Eine ökonomische Analyse*, Report for the German Lottery Association (*Lotterie-Initiative*), Hannover.

Rebeggiani, L. (2012). Regulierung des deutschen Sportwettenmarktes in komparativer Perspektive – Glücksspielgesetze in der Europäischen Union. In: M. P. Büch, W. Maennig, & H.-J. Schulke (Eds.), *Sport und Sportgroßveranstaltungen in Europa – Zwischen Zentralstaat und Regionen* (pp. 51–78), Hamburg: Hamburg University Press.

Spiegel Online (2013): *"Wir brauchen den Straftatbestand des Sportbetrugs"*. Retrieved July 21, 2013, from http://www.spiegel.de/sport/fussball/friedhelm-althans-bochumer-chefermittler-ueber-kampf-gegenwettmafia-a-902211.html

Sportradar (2013). Die Bekämpfung von wettbezogener Manipulation im Sport, presentation given by A. Krannich (Sportradar) at the Federal Ministry of the Interior, Bonn, 4th February 2013.

Strumpf, K. (2003). Illegal Sports Bookmakers. Working Paper, Department of Economics, University of North Carolina at Chapel Hill.

Winter, S., & Kukuk, M. (2008). Do Horses Like Vodka and Sponging? - On Market Manipulation and the favourite-longshot bias. *Applied Economics*, 40 (1), 75–87.

Wolfers, J. (2006). Point Shaving: Corruption in NCAA Basketball. *American Economic Review Papers and Proceedings*, 96 (5), 279–283.

Match Fixing: An Economics Perspective

David Forrest

Abstract The chapter employs a simple supply-demand framework to account for the evident step increase in the incidence of match fixing in sport since the Millennium. The supply of fixes comes from players and other sports insiders and the demand from betting interests seeking an edge in wagering markets. The contemporary epidemic of fixing may be accounted for by developments in the betting sector, in particular by the rapid increase in liquidity in effectively unregulated markets. These developments have made fixing more lucrative and increased the demand for fixes. Policies to mitigate the resulting problems involve addressing both the supply and demand sides of the market for fixes. Responsibilities for different policies fall variously on governments, law enforcement agencies, gambling regulators and sport governing bodies. For sport, protecting integrity is argued to be part of the wider issue of good governance.

Introduction

Match fixing to serve betting interests is certainly as old as organised sport itself, for example it is believed to have been common in the case of eighteenth century professional cricket in England. And in the twentieth century, the history of sport even at its most elite levels was punctuated by high-profile scandals, including fixes in the baseball World Series of 1919 and in the South Africa-England cricket series in 1990. For football (soccer), Hill (2010) gathered credible documentary evidence

D. Forrest (✉)
Salford Business School, University of Salford, Salford, M5 4WT, UK
e-mail: d.k.forrest@salford.ac.uk

M.R. Haberfeld and D. Sheehan (eds.), *Match-Fixing in International Sports:*
Existing Processes, Law Enforcement, and Prevention Strategies,
DOI 10.1007/978-3-319-02582-7_10, © Springer International Publishing Switzerland 2013

that fixing was far from infrequent in the supposedly Golden Age of the game in England in the 1950s.[1]

So, match fixing is nothing new. On the other hand, reports of fixing appear to have become much more frequent in the twenty-first century and the sheer number of proven instances points to a step increase in incidence over the last decade. IRIS (2012) documents some of the most prominent cases. The most important, in terms of its producing rich evidence about the modus operandi of the fixers, was that revealed in a criminal trial in Bochum, Germany in 2012. The defendants, Croatians resident locally, had manipulated more than 300 football matches in 13 countries. Since then, football has been tainted by further revelations of fixing in all parts of the World. In 2013, Europol named nearly 300 matches between national teams which it alleged to have been the subject of fixing; and criminal trials of players and officials took place in countries such as Italy, Hungary, South Korea and China.[2] 2013 also saw a continued flow of scandals in cricket, including seemingly credible exposés of manipulation of international matches and in the very high profile Indian Premier League. Outside football and cricket, proven cases emerged in 2012–3 in sports including tennis, snooker, handball and sumo wrestling.

It is a sorry tale. Of course, as with many types of crime, the majority of cases may have gone undetected and therefore it is impossible to construct a meaningful time-series to demonstrate the extent to which fixing has increased. But the consensus that fixing has become much more frequent over just the last 10 years does carry conviction. This chapter employs a simple economic framework to account for why there should have been a step increase in the incidence of fixing (and why this might have been predicted ex ante in light of developments in World betting markets). The framework is also employed to suggest possible policy responses by such as sports federations, betting regulators and law enforcement agencies.

The need for a systematic policy response to increasing corruption stems not only from a desire to protect the cultural role of sport and its values but also from the potential threat fixing poses to the economic and commercial interests of the sports industry. China, Singapore, Malaysia and Albania are among the countries where national football leagues effectively collapsed following betting-related scandals which had undermined the faith of the public in the authenticity of the competitions and had deterred existing and potential sponsors from associating with a now disreputable sector. For example, the withdrawal of the sponsor, Pirelli, from supporting the Chinese League was a key factor in the competition's loss of viability. The importance of sponsorship in the business model of modern professional sport in fact puts a greater premium than before on sports maintaining a good reputation such that sponsors continue to value association with them.

---

[1] Forrest, McHale and McAuley (2008) provide a tabulation of some prominent twentieth century cases.

[2] In addition to cases which have been detected, evidence of extensive match fixing in football is also found in survey data. From a large sample of professional footballers, the international federation of player unions reported that 24 % were aware of fixes and 12 % had been approached to take part (FifPro 2012).

An Economics Framework

A Supply–Demand Model

This chapter adopts the most familiar of all economic models, that of a market where prices and quantities are determined by supply and demand. In a landmark contribution to the economics of crime, Ehrlich (1996) introduced the notion of the supply and demand of offences. In the present context, the offence is the fix. The word 'fix' here refers to manipulation of the result or any other aspect of a sporting contest. Fixes may be purchased in order to achieve sporting success (for example, winning a championship) but here the analysis relates exclusively to fixes intended to generate gains in the betting market.

As with any other market, the price and quantity of fixes will be determined by the behaviour of sellers (supply) and buyers (demand). Any increase in quantity must be the result of a 'shift to the right' in supply or a 'shift to the right' in demand. By a 'shift to the right' is meant that sellers (buyers) are willing to sell (buy) a greater quantity than before at any given price of a fix.

The Supply of Fixes

Fixes are supplied by sports insiders. Most commonly these are players or referees but a range of other actors may also have the capacity to deliver a fix. For example, coaches can influence the result (by team selection[3] or by decisions on player substitutions during a match) and so can club medical staff (who can use their positions to impair the physical performance of players, for example by incorrect dosage of pain killers). In 1997, in English football, even stadium technicians were found to have accepted payments to make the floodlights fail and cause the abandonment of a number of matches.[4]

But, although a wide variety of actors may be involved, archetypically it is referees or players who supply the fix. The efforts of German prosecutors in the Bochum trial enable some insight to be gained into the relative frequency with which referees and different types of player are employed. Referees supplied the fix on occasions and, in a low-scoring sport like football, they have an obvious capacity to influence match outcomes, by awarding penalties or sending off players. On the other hand, these decisions are somewhat dramatic and liable to be scrutinised closely, such that referees may be reluctant to participate because the chance of detection is relatively high. In fact, the most common means of fixing football matches, according to

---

[3] Playing a weak team was one of the techniques used at the Finnish football club, AC Allianssi, to ensure poor performance. The Club had been purchased by criminal interests (IRIS 2012, p. 29).

[4] In Asian betting markets, bets are honoured according to the score at the time a match is abandoned.

evidence from Bochum, is by defenders making small errors. In the professional game, small defensive errors, such as allowing an attacker a few extra inches of space, have a high probability of resulting in a goal and so defenders can supply fixes with low detection risk: innocent errors are the most frequent reason for a goal in football and a deliberate error carries limited risk of attracting suspicion.

Detection risk is only one factor which would be taken into account by a player when he has the opportunity to sell a fix. According to the general model of Ehrlich (1996), a potential offender will decide whether or not to commit the crime by comparing the expected gain with the expected loss. This representation of the potential criminal as *homo economicus*, committing or not committing offences according to rational appraisal of benefits and costs, has been employed successfully to explain crime trends in a variety of settings.

The general model was adapted to the context of match fixing in Forrest and Simmons (2003). There, the expected gain is the bribe that has been offered, weighted by the probability that the fix can be successfully delivered (and the bribe therefore collected). Expected cost depends on the probability of detection, the consequences of detection (in lost income, for example from being banned from the sport), the value to the player of performing badly (loss of prize money or performance-related pay, loss of glory), and the psychic cost of living with having betrayed the sport. A risk-neutral individual will decide to sell the fix if the expected benefit exceeds the expected cost. Otherwise the bribe will be rejected.[5]

Players will be heterogeneous in terms of all of the components of expected cost (and the same player will have different costs in different situations and at different times in his career, for example veteran players have little left to lose in terms of future earnings). This will generate the familiar upward sloping supply curve of economic theory, with successively more players willing to sell a fix as the price of fixes increases. The supply curve will shift position if there are changes in detection risk, size of future earnings put at risk, loss from underperformance or moral disquiet about cheating.

To summarise the hypotheses concerning the supply of fixes, willingness to supply will be highest where:

- Detection risk is low (for example, where, technically, it is easy to influence match outcome without behaviour seeming unusual, or where sports have no system of monitoring for cheating)
- The penalty for being detected is low (for example, if athletes are poorly paid and ejection from the sport would lead to little financial loss)
- There is insignificant loss of sporting glory or in terms of prize money from deliberate underperformance (for example, Preston et al. 2001, pointed out that

---

[5]A *risk-loving* individual may sell the fix if the expected cost is not much greater than expected benefit Successful sportsmen may include a relatively high proportion of risk-lovers compared with the general population: there is evidence that willingness to engage in risky strategies is a feature of success in sport (for example, Sullowag and Zweigenhaft 2010). Sports players who are successful enough to advance to the professional ranks should therefore include many risk-lovers. It is also known that professional sportsmen are disproportionately interested in gambling, another indicator of risk-love.

international one-day cricket matches are often 'meaningless' because so many are scheduled, and this may create integrity risk)
* Sportsmen feel little moral unease if they let down their employer because they are resentful at how they are treated (for example, this was a factor in the Chicago team that 'threw' matches in the Baseball World Series in 1919).

Consideration of the supply side of the economic model of fixing provides an effective framework for thinking about the pattern of fixing at any point in time and therefore for understanding and identifying where integrity risk is highest. Many proven cases of fixing have emerged in college sport in the United States and, from application of forensic economics, Wolfers (2005) alleged that about 1 % of results of NCAA basketball matches were 'manufactured'. Such high prevalence of fixing, if true, would be understandable in terms of the supply analysis. Players in college sport are not paid at all and (except for the few who have prospects of being drafted by a professional club) would lose little if ejected from the sport. In American basketball, handicap bets are the norm, i.e. relate to the margin of victory of the favourite team, and thus betting interests require not that the favourite team actually loses but only that it does less well than the bookmaker spread. Hence the form of corruption in which athletes engage (point shaving) does not have to deprive them of the satisfaction of winning or of a championship. And it is plausible that many players will experience no costs of conscience from the act of corruption because they feel exploited by a system which pays them nothing but generates very substantial income for universities, broadcasters and other commercial interests. In short, all the conditions relevant to supply point to high integrity risk. Similarly, in contemporary European football, targets for buyers in the market for fixes might include suppliers such as low-paid African players in minor national leagues or players whose clubs miss wage payments (FifPro 2012): such players have little to lose financially and may (with reason) be resentful against employers.

The Demand for Fixes

As with supply, the demand for fixes may be derived from several possible sources. Some may be within sport itself. An owner may find it more profitable to require his players to lose a match than to win it. Such was the case with the Macedonian football club, Pobeda, where the Chairman arranged for his players to lose a Champions League Qualifying Round tie, enabling a profit of €300,000 when the financial pay-off from a victory was unlikely to exceed €30,000 (IRIS 2012, pp. 24–25). Similarly, players themselves may be the originators as well as the executors of a fix because they or their families see the opportunity to make personal betting market gains. This appears to have been the case at the French handball club, Montpellier, in a fixing case in 2012.

All the major contemporary cases of fixing have, however, been instigated by external betting interests. They seek to buy fixes because fixes give them an edge in the betting market. A fix may be interpreted as a specialised form of inside information.

For example, the information may be that players or referees will attempt artificially to bring about victory for a particular team. The buyer of the fix then knows that the probabilities of the various possible outcomes are different from the probabilities implicit in market prices (odds), which are based on public information. Of course, sometimes, a fix will not be executed successfully; but, in the long-run, criminals who pay regularly for fixes will make profit on the betting market given that they will be trading with the advantage of additional information relative to the market. A fix is therefore an economically valuable commodity and this is why there is a demand for fixes.

Inside information is an advantage on whichever side of a financial market one is trading. Therefore, the demand for fixes may come from either bookmakers or bettors. In cricket, recent scandals appear commonly to have implicated illegal Indian bookmakers whereas in football the high-profile trials have related to bribes by betting syndicates who profit from the fix by placing wagers in 'grey' betting markets in Asia.[6] In these high-profile cases, such as at Bochum and in the Italian *Calciosommesse* scandal, the syndicates have been linked to international organised crime based in Asia or Eastern or Southern Europe. Analysis below takes this model as the norm but could be readily adapted to the case where bookmakers rather than betting syndicates instigate the fix.

Betting syndicates purchase a fix in order to make profit on betting markets. The demand for fixes therefore depends on the size of profit that is available. In turn, this will depend first on the degree of liquidity in the betting market associated with the particular sporting event. In a market with a higher volume of trading, higher stakes can be placed without attracting undue attention and without shifting the odds in a direction unfavourable to the syndicate. Operators will be more relaxed about accepting a large liability on one outcome of an event because they will be able to hedge more easily with other operators. Liquidity is therefore the 'friend of the fixer'. It is key to how profitable buying a fix is and therefore how much it will be worthwhile to pay a player to execute the fix.

A second factor is the risk of detection and punishment for traders in the betting market who have instigated a fix. This is not the same detection risk as referred to in the discussion of detection risk for players. Sports administrators may proceed against players if there is a correspondence between unusual turns of event on the field and odds shifts in the betting market. But by then the instigators of the fix are likely to have realised their gains and, in a grey or an illegal or unregulated betting market, there will be no means for investigators to trace the origins of suspicious bets. Therefore, the twin desiderata for fixers are first a highly liquid market and second a considerable proportion of liquidity residing in the unregulated (or minimally regulated) sector. From demand analysis, these are the important integrity risk factors.

---

[6] The term 'grey market' has been used in debate to refer to betting markets where the sports book is maintained by a bookmaker which holds a licence issued by a legitimate jurisdiction but where that jurisdiction applies minimal or no regulatory oversight. The largest Asian operators are licensed in the Cagayan Special Economic Zone, Philippines.

The Quantity of Fixes

Neither supply nor demand factors *alone* can generate the corruption we observe. If players were low-paid, resentful and amoral, there may be abundant supply of fixes. But, if there were not abundant demand as well, fixing would not be extensive. Similarly, a very liquid betting market outside the control of reputable regulation would not induce corruption in an event where all the participants had strong incentives to perform to their maximum ability: there would be abundant demand but no supply. Therefore, *both* supply and demand factors are relevant. This applies certainly to the analysis of cross-sectional variation in the prevalence of fixing (for example, why fixing affects different competitions and sports to different degrees). Here, integrity risk may be assessed by considering the degree of disparity between the level of player wages (supply side) and the liquidity in the betting market (demand side). Highest risk exists where wages are only modest (players relatively willing to offend) but betting markets sufficiently liquid for potential profits from instigating a fix to be rather substantial. This is consistent with the evidence from the criminal trials concerning corruption in European football where the highest frequency of fixes has been in the second tiers of national leagues and in minor national leagues, such as that of Finland.[7] Of course, this is not to imply that higher levels of football are totally immune. In sport, as in any sphere, there will be a small number of employees who will be sufficiently risk-loving to be corruptible even though they apparently stand to lose a lot if they are caught.[8]

The focus of this chapter is, however, not on understanding the cross-sectional pattern of corruption but rather the time-series. Why can the prevalence of corruption change over time?

Hill (2010) considered the evident 'cleaning-up' of English football from the 1960s and linked it to both a supply shock and a demand shock. The supply shock was the abolition of the (very low) minimum wage in the sport in 1960. The subsequent sharp rise in player wages will have reduced the number of them willing to risk taking bribes. On the supply side, sports betting became legal in Great Britain in 1961, shifting the liquidity in betting markets from illegal and unregulated street bookmakers to reputable and well-monitored high street outlets. Both these changes would have been predicted from the economic model to be effective in reducing the quantity of fixing (even if this was not the overt objective of either policy).

In the present case of the evident step *increase* in fixing across many sports since the Millennium, it is hard to see much role for a shift in supply. Player wages have

---

[7] Finland attracts exceptional betting interest from international markets because it plays part of its season in months when most other countries are on their summer break: it is 'the only game in town'. It is fair to add that awareness of potential fixing is now high amongst the Finnish public and the country's media, which one might hope would prevent repetition of past problems.

[8] Levitt and Venkatesh (2000) for drug-dealing and Strumpf (2003) for illegal street bookmaking found lower returns in these sectors than in alternative, legal opportunities. This is consistent with criminals exhibiting risk-love such that there is a risk-discount rather than a risk-premium attached to such activities.

not fallen, the pattern of competitions has not changed radically, there is no reason for supposing a new generation of players to be less subject to moral qualms than its predecessor. Since there is no reason to suspect that factors affecting supply have changed systematically and across sports, the residual explanation is that there has been a shift in the demand for fixes. Demand for fixes depends on conditions in betting markets, which have changed substantially and, it will be argued below, in ways which make a fix a more valuable economic commodity than in the past. It is the demand shock stemming from developments in sports betting markets that appears to be responsible for the increase in the quantity of fixing.

Developments in Sports Betting Markets

Sports betting is one of many economic sectors to have been transformed since the Millennium by the possibilities offered by e-commerce. Across the economy, the impact of the internet on product markets has been greatest where services can be supplied without transport costs. Then, consumers, who may previously have been able to buy only at a local monopolist, are newly enabled to purchase from a multitude of suppliers, regardless of geographical location. This makes for a much more competitive environment than before in the markets for financial services such as insurance, stockbroking, ...and bookmaking. Here, greater competition has, entirely predictably, dramatically eroded bookmaker margins. Forrest (2012) reported that football odds, on results of matches in the English Premier League, had become so much more generous that random betting with a single bookmaker was associated with an expected loss of only 6.1 % in 2011, compared with 11.1 % in 2001.[9] Further, using comparison websites to place each random bet at the best odds offered for that bet (across a small number of reputable operators) reduced the expected loss in 2011 to a mere 0.7 %.

The radical improvement in odds essentially represents a (very large) fall in the price of betting. This would be predicted to stimulate demand by leisure bettors in Europe, where consumers had often previously had to bet with a state-owned monopolist (or, in some jurisdictions, had no means of betting on sport at all).[10] For professional bettors as well, the sector now offered far more opportunity than in the past. Professional bettors rely on bookmakers and markets making 'mistakes' in odds setting. However, the bookmaker's margin provides protection against professional bettors, who seek only bets with positive expected value. For mispricing to generate an expected profit for the better, the mistake has to be very large if all odds include an implicit commission as high as 11.1 %. But, if effective margins are as low as 0.7 %, a bookmaker's misestimating of outcome probabilities may be only 1 % but it still provides an opportunity for the professional bettor. Hence betting markets became more attractive both to leisure bettors and to would-be professional bettors.

---

[9] Similar results were noted for other European football leagues.

[10] A literature survey in a report for the European Commission by the Swiss Institute of Comparative Law (2006, Second Part, Chap. 8) pointed to strong findings of high elasticity of demand (sensitivity to price) in gambling markets.

These were factors boosting demand for sports betting in Europe post Millennium. At the same time, personal incomes in some of the most important betting countries in Asia- especially China- were exhibiting very high rates of growth, stimulating demand in that region as well.

Not only did betting volumes increase in both Europe and Asia, the two previously separated markets also became integrated. New technology made it possible for large European bettors to place bets in Asia, an appealing option because of relatively low maximum bet limits imposed by European operators. In turn, Asian operators, and a variety of arbitrageurs, could hedge into European markets for the first time. The betting market became globalised and the extent to which it is now a World market is illustrated by the speed (less than 1 min) with which odds quotes in Europe respond to shifts in odds in Asia. Odds shifts in football typically originate in Asia, which has higher volumes than Europe and, as noted, is where professional bettors will typically trade.

From this betting revolution, then, has emerged a World market the liquidity of which has been increasing very fast. Exactly how fast betting volumes have increased is hard to assess because much trade takes place either illegally or through operators licensed in jurisdictions with minimal reporting requirements. But commercial consultancies, with analysts experienced in the betting industry, attempt to produce "best estimates". H2 Gambling Capital, quoted by RGA (2010), suggested, for example, a doubling of the size of the global e-betting market, from stakes of €16.4b to stakes of €32.6b, just between 2004 and 2008, with a projection of €50.7b for 2012. These figures relate to stakes. *Gross gaming revenue* (GGR) is the amount won by bookmakers/lost by bettors, which is of course much less since most stakes are passed back to clients as winnings. Estimates by CK Consulting, in Sport Accord (2011), point to a more than tripling of the GGR from sports betting between 2000 and 2010, to €19b, including this time both land-based and internet operators. On either measure, there is clear empirical support for the popular conception that sports betting exploded in volume after the Millennium.

High liquidity was argued above to be the friend of the fixer because it enables large wagers to be placed. But it was also noted that it is important for fixers to be able to place those bets without regulatory supervision of transactions. This condition is also satisfied in the contemporary betting environment where Asia dominates in terms of volume. In most Asian countries, including China and India, sports betting is subject to legal prohibition and therefore proceeds with no regulation at all. Bets are typically passed on to higher-level operators, to pool risks, and may reach trans-national operators who do have licenses but still face no regulatory requirement to record or even to know the identity of bettors. These very large-scale operators accept aggregated bundles of bets through agents. Agents, who are often effectively franchisees, have no strong disincentive to deter dealing with suspected fixers because, by dealing with them, they acquire the inside information second-hand and can then personally profit from it by betting on their own account. External agencies can observe odds movements which may be judged as suspicious but cannot investigate where the money driving those movements originated. Thus the whole environment is conducive to fixing with large bets and little risk.

Just how great the liquidity is in these illegal or grey markets may be discerned from answers put to experienced Asian traders for the IRIS (2012) Report. How much could an agent, splitting the amount between Asian operators, bet safely for a client in respect of the outcome of a Belgian Second Division football match (a modest level of competition)? The consensus was €200,000–300,000. This does not seem fanciful given the levels of bet identified as having been made by defendants in the Bochum trial. Even on a Turkish *Fourth* Division match, the syndicate had, according to records located by prosecutors, wagered €36,000. With liquidity at a level where the market can absorb such large bets, the Bochum gang was found to have made a single-year profit of €19.5 m trading on Asian betting markets, of which €12 m was paid over to players/referees in bribes.

The notion that increases in liquidity have increased potential returns to fixing is consistent with a particular feature of recent corruption cases, namely that international organised crime is frequently implicated. Small-scale ("petty") fixing, such as when players personally bet that they themselves will underperform, no doubt continues as it always has done. But fixing on an industrial scale, as observed in several contemporary cases, indicates that organised crime now finds fixing sufficiently lucrative that it has added it to its portfolio of illicit activities. Indeed, some prominent cases have come to light as an incidental result of police investigation of crimes outside sport (as at Bochum and in a referee corruption scandal in American professional basketball).

Other Developments in Betting

Increases in liquidity in betting markets increase the demand for fixes and the growth in the size of markets may therefore be sufficient to account for greater prevalence of fixing. But increases in liquidity have not been the only significant development in betting. Again as in other sectors where e-commerce has driven change, innovation in terms of the product and its mode of delivery has also been substantial. Product development may be linked both to the increased size of the market (which makes it economical to serve niche sub-markets[11]) and to the technology lying behind market growth.[12]

How much additional sports integrity risk may be associated with these developments in betting?

---

[11] For example, most people may want to bet on the result of a football match, where competitive balance restricts the range of odds on offer to not very far from even money. But less conservative bettors (risk lovers) may seek longer-odds bets. When there are enough of them, long-odds products will be supplied to meet their preferences, for example bets on which player will score first. So there is product proliferation.

[12] For example, in-play (live) betting was very restricted before the internet because neither clients nor odds-setters could respond fast enough for a viable market to be conducted as events unfolded on the field. Now clients with a fast internet connection can place bets almost instantly and computer algorithms move odds automatically as different incidents occur in the match.

Betting Exchanges

One innovation in betting has been the emergence of a person-to-person model similar to e-Bay. *Betting exchanges* are platforms where customers bet with each other by posting offers to bet (buy) or lay (sell) a particular proposition, for example "Juventus will beat Dortmund". Offers to buy or sell are matched by system algorithms and the operator collects a commission from each transaction rather than earning its profit by being a party to each bet. One particular betting exchange, Betfair, dominates all others. 'Network effects' explain its dominance: it is advantageous for any one trader to choose the most popular market because this will maximise the chance of finding others with whom to trade, hence all the liquidity gravitates over time to whichever market place takes an initial lead in terms of volume.

The development of the exchange model has naturally been extremely unpopular with traditional bookmakers, whether in the private or state sectors, because it has exerted yet greater competitive pressure: an exchange allows private individuals to act as bookmakers by 'laying', without facing the entry barriers of having to acquire a licence, obtain premises, and so on. Those who lobby against regulators permitting an exchange to operate in their jurisdiction have argued that a betting exchange creates additional integrity risk for sport.

Since there is an element of special pleading, the argument that betting exchanges are dangerous for sport should be scrutinised carefully. In the case of horse racing, there are indeed strong a priori grounds, supported by empirical observation of disciplinary cases in Great Britain, for accepting that the exchange model provided a new opportunity for corrupt trainers to profit from 'nobbling' their horse. It is technically easy for a trainer to ensure that his horse will lose, for example by inappropriate feeding. But in the past, it was hard to profit from this action because there were usually several other horses which could win the race instead and betting on each of them would eliminate the potential financial gain. But now the corrupt trainer can 'lay' his horse on the exchange and collect the stakes from the accounts of those who unwittingly bet with him. Effectively, he is enabled to wager that his horse will lose.

However, this argument holds only because a horse race has multiple potential winners. In many sporting events, for example a tennis match, there are only two potential winners. If player x were to agree to lose, a fixer could profit by 'laying' the player on the exchange. But, equally, he could just bet on the player's opponent at a traditional bookmaker. Thus the existence of the exchange creates no new opportunity for profitable fixing and therefore no additional integrity risk in this case. Moreover, advocates for the idea of the exchange would claim that it is safer than traditional bookmaking to the extent that all trading is electronic and all trades are traceable back to source in the event of any suspicion of fraud.

In any case, betting exchanges account for a rather small proportion of global betting activity. According to CK Consulting, exchanges had GGR of about €500 m in 2010, relative to its estimate of €19b of GGR in the global sports betting sector (Sport Accord 2011). Further, in the evidence from the criminal trials to have taken place to date (outside racing), none of the corrupt bets were placed in the betting exchange sector, consistent with the notion that corrupt money will usually be channelled into more liquid markets where monitoring is weak. Therefore, a degree of scepticism is appropriate concerning claims that the emergence of betting exchanges has been one of the important factors in the increase in fixing over the last decade.

The Subjects of Betting

Betting exchanges, but also traditional bookmakers, have been enthusiastic partici- pants in a second striking development in the betting sector in recent years, namely the proliferation of subjects for betting. In every sport, operators now offer a large number of possible bets on a match, beyond the identity of the winner. For example, in tennis, all operators routinely offer 30 or more bets such as: which player will win? what will be the final score in sets (2-0, 1-2, etc.)? how many points will player x win (over- or under- a specified number)? how many aces will player y serve? Bets other than on the winner of the match have come to be known as *proposition bets* or *derivatives*.

Proposition bets have been alleged by organised sport to be a substantial source of integrity risk. The Integrity Guide published by Sport Accord notes that 100 propositions may be available on a single football match and comments that "Some of these betting types are structurally easier to influence which may do serious harm to sport" (Sport Accord 2011, p. 29).

The fears of sport appeared to be validated by the case of three Pakistani cricket- ers sentenced to prison for accepting very substantial bribes to bowl no balls in an international against England in 2011. No balls, called by the umpire when the bowler's foot overreaches the line from which he bowls, incur a one run penalty, which makes them pretty inconsequential for the outcome of matches where aggre- gate scores by each team are routinely 500 or more. The willingness of each player to accept a large payment for bowling a no ball on a particular delivery is therefore readily understandable in terms of the supply side of the economic model: it is easy to execute and makes little difference to his team's chance of winning. The case contributed to perceptions that fixing minor aspects of a match is common. The term *spot fixing* was coined to describe such fixes and it was natural to blame the oppor- tunity to bet on very specific events within a sporting contest.

However, it should be borne in mind that there was no actual betting behind the affair of the Pakistani cricketers. The bribes were paid by undercover journalists posing as bettors. It shows the willingness of the players to be bribed but cannot demonstrate that spot fixing is a serious problem in practice.

Evaluation of the notion that proposition betting carries particularly high integ- rity risk can proceed only through, first, a priori reasoning based on the economic model and, second, examination of evidence of how real world criminals have set about fixing in the cases we have been able to observe.

In terms of the model, it is insufficient, for demonstrating that proposition bets are dangerous, to focus only on the supply side, as in Sport Accord (2011). There may be abundant willingness to supply among athletes but there will not necessarily be corresponding demand. Demand depends on high liquidity in the relevant betting market and this is seldom present in markets on very specific events. For example, to support the bribes offered to the three Pakistani cricketers, it is implausible that sufficiently large wagers on the no balls could have been placed with any book-maker. Large bets in a limited market are suspicious, and unwelcome because volumes are low and bookmakers' books become very unbalanced, exposing them to risk. Similarly, football markets on such specifics as the number of red cards in the match hold little liquidity.

A priori reasoning, that proposition markets, at least at present, are too illiquid to pose a high risk is supported by empirical evidence generated by corruption cases which have come to light. In none of the many football matches fixed by the Bochum gang was associated betting conducted in an esoteric market. Always the bets were placed in a market on the final result of the game (either raw score or margin of victory) or on the total number of goals. These are the highly liquid markets in football.[13] Criminals may find it worthwhile to buy spot fixes if the specific occurrence is likely significantly to influence the probabilities of the possible final results or the numbers of goals in the match (this would gain them the edge they seek in those markets). But this does not imply that spot fixing is linked to the existence of relatively minor proposition betting markets. Thus far at least, there is no strong evidence that proposition bets add further to the growing integrity risk associated with growing volume in the overall sports betting market.

In-Play Betting

The third, and final, major development to be considered is the emergence of *in-play* (or *live*) betting as the most common form of wagering on many sports.[14]

Again, organised sport is hostile to the very notion of in-play betting; and it has successfully lobbied for its prohibition in countries such as Australia and Spain. Of course, the relevance of banning trade in individual countries when the bulk of trading takes place in international markets is questionable. And governments should take into account also that leisure bettors may gain considerable entertainment value from pitting their wits against the market as the twists and turns of a match unfold. But on the narrower argument, that in-play betting has contributed to elevated integrity risk, sport does appear to have a point.

In-play betting appears to create extra scope for criminals to profit from fixing and thereby increases the demand for fixes. Providing markets are sufficiently liquid, it becomes technically possible to place higher stakes because the money can be 'dripped' into the market over time. Potentially, it also allows a greater return on the stakes if the order for the fix specifies when in a match it is to be executed. For example, the syndicate plans to bet on a high number of goals in the match. As the

---

[13] In basketball, liquidity is high in the handicap result market and in that on total points. Cricket betting is by far heaviest in markets on the match outcome or the total number of runs in a session.

[14] At industry conferences, insiders tend to agree that about 70 % of football and 90 % of tennis on-line stakes are now placed during rather than before a match. However, no published statistics are available to verify these exact figures.

match proceeds with no goals scored, odds against a high number of goals in the final result will lengthen. Betting during rather than before the match is therefore at better odds and the syndicate will find it advantageous to specify that, for example, its suppliers should deliver the goals in the final 20 min. This is a priori reasoning but again it is supported by observation of actual cases (as documented, for example, in IRIS 2012).

In-play betting also creates scope for profiting from manipulation of just one phase of a match even though there is insufficient liquidity in the market for the outcome of a single part of a contest. Forrest, McHale and McAuley (2008) provided an example from tennis. A player might be willing to accept payment more readily if he is required only to lose the first set: he then retains the possibility of coming back to win the match in the end. How can the betting syndicate make money from the transaction? It will be able to anticipate that, between the start of the match and the end of the first set, odds against the player winning will lengthen. It can then 'sell' the player (bet that he will lose the match) before the start and 'buy' the player (bet that he will win the match) after the first set. Because the offsetting trades will be at different prices (odds), the syndicate can lock into a profit regardless of the final result. The same principle could apply, for example, if the syndicate could arrange for a red card in a football match at a particular stage in a match. News that a team has had a player excluded from the field will lengthen the odds against its winning. As in any financial market where a trader has inside information about relevant news, trading at different prices either side of the release of the news permits profit from the possession of the inside information. Note that this provides a motive for 'spot fixing' but only, of course, if the actions required of the suppliers of the fix are sufficiently consequential to be likely to shift odds in the markets (such as that on the final result) where the betting trades will take place.[15]

Policy Perspectives

Taxonomy of Policy Options

Wherever there is a market for an illicit product, the economic model suggests three broad policy approaches to trying to reduce the scale of the activity: attempt directly to disrupt transactions between buyers and sellers, *or* attempt to reduce supply, *or* attempt to reduce demand. For example, many jurisdictions choose to employ a mixture of all three approaches in the case of illicit drugs. Transactions are disrupted through intelligence operations and interception of cargos. The entry of new suppliers is deterred through harsh sentences for sellers who are detected and

---

[15] It should be emphasised that this is a different argument from that which represents spot fixing as a new phenomenon related to new and novel proposition betting markets. The point was made above that many proposition markets are too illiquid to support large wagers; but some spot fixes may enable profit to be made on the more established markets around the final result.

convicted. Education programmes seek to show potential buyers that use of drugs is dangerous for health.

These three broad policy approaches apply equally to the case of match fixing. But who in society should bear the responsibility for policy? In the case of illicit drugs, the authority vested in the state (legislators, the police, the judiciary, the educational system) is necessary for policy to be effective under any of the three approaches. But in the area of sports corruption, there are potentially more actors. To be sure, the authority of the state is relevant (for example, sport cannot confront international organised crime on its own). But some impact can also be made, for example, by sports federations and legitimate betting operators (which should have a shared interest, since a perception that corruption was endemic would endanger the demand for both their products). It will be argued below that different actors would naturally take the lead under each of the three broad policy approaches.

Before proceeding, it is perhaps worthwhile to note the reality that potential actors in any systematic attack on fixing may exhibit a degree of ambivalence in their approach to deciding on their level of participation in relevant policies. Law enforcement may be reluctant to become involved because the nature of the crime is such that convictions are particularly hard to obtain. For example, UK police invested heavily in investigations in football and horse racing but the evidence still proved insufficient given standards of proof required in the courts. Sports federations themselves may desire the objective of eradicating match fixing but fear that the process of achieving it carries too much risk of damaging their product as revelations emerge. It would be understandable if they held back to some extent from doing everything they could.

As a practical matter, the formulation of a comprehensive policy is also handicapped by disputes between the actors regarding the allocation of any economic rents that may be up for competition. For example, organised sport lobbies for governments to require betting companies to pay sports promoters (such as leagues) for the use of their fixtures (Sport Accord 2011) whereas bookmakers argue that they do not have the capacity to absorb additional costs when they are competing in a global market. Again, state betting providers in Europe argue, as incumbent monopolists would, that only they, the national lottery operators, can be trusted to safeguard the integrity of sport and that this justifies governments prohibiting on-line private sector companies marketing betting products to their citizens. These sorts of arguments can be conflated with the important and central question of what different actors can do to attack the phenomenon of fixing. At best they may be distracting, at worst they may lead to policy proposals which may be counter-productive in the attack on corruption.[16]

---

[16] Allowing foreign companies to enter a previously monopolistic national market only if they accept a (low) cap on the proportion of stakes paid out as winnings is clearly in the interests of the established monopolist. The policy may be claimed to be based on making fixing less lucrative. A more obvious argument is that integrity issues require that as much liquidity as possible should be retained within a well-regulated national market rather than induced to migrate to grey markets offshore. This outcome is not promoted by offering consumers poor value-for-money.

Disruption of Transactions

Under this heading sits a variety of policies which require the involvement of law enforcement. For example, only it has the resources and powers to trace and disrupt movements of fixers and of associated flows of funds across international borders. But under this heading there are also policies which lie within the competence of sport itself. For example, fixers require access to players both to recruit them as suppliers and to give their instructions once they are on the payroll. Tennis is among the sports to have imposed bans on visits to and use of mobile telephones in player dressing room areas. Referees are also potential suppliers of fixes. Robert Hoyzer in the German Bundesliga and Tim Donaghy in the National Basketball Association were referees found guilty of manipulating large numbers of matches in return for payments from betting interests. Both leagues subsequently adopted a policy of selecting match officials from a group of possibles only shortly before start time. This is a protective policy because the syndicate cannot easily plan and execute its placement of funds into the betting market until it knows that its agent has control of the game.

Supply Side Policies

These policies seek to make the potential suppliers less willing or less able to offer a fix. Again, some measures require intervention by agencies of the state. For example, in deciding whether or not to offend, suppliers must consider the costs to be borne if detected- and only the state can put deterrents like prison sentences into place. However, supply side policies are principally the responsibility of sports themselves.

Making suppliers less *able* to offer a fix involves mainly working on the powers of referees, judges and umpires. Here, technological solutions may present themselves in that the responsibility for making important decisions can sometimes be removed from officials and allocated to technology instead. In international cricket, umpires' influence on match results has been enormously reduced by permitting players to appeal against on-field decisions to off-field reviewers, who use camera and other evidence (for example, 'hawkeye') to reach their conclusions in a wholly transparent way.[17] Similarly, boxing and figure skating have revised their scoring systems to limit the influence of a single judge on the outcome of the competition (Maennig 2009). Competition in the technology sector will likely lead to the continuation of this trend to other sports; but the cost of using it routinely is likely to be bearable only at the highest tiers of competition.

And what of the players, the more commonly employed suppliers of fixes? What might make them collectively less *willing* to supply?

---

[17] The screens used by the reviewer are available to broadcasters and shown also at the stadium.

The sports sector places great weight on player education programmes. The International Olympic Committee "recommends that all constituents of the Olympic Movement (the IOC, international sports federations and National Olympic Committees), under their respective competences, implement a Communication, Education and Prevention Programme" (Sport Accord 2011, p. 40). UEFA has devised a training programme for young footballers. In tennis, all players taking part in the major tournaments must have completed all modules of "the Uniform Tennis Anti-Corruption Programme". In the UK, three betting operators, Betfair, Ladbrokes and William Hill, have agreed with the umbrella body for player unions to fund an education programme for players across all sports.

Though there is no formal evidence on the efficacy of such education programmes in combating corruption, the rationale for providing them is plausible. Players may be naïve in failing to recognise when they are being cultivated on behalf of a criminal gang. They may lack awareness of the long-term consequences of involvement with criminals, for example that it is hard to escape from participation in fixing after even one corrupt action since gangs will enforce continued fixing by threatening to expose earlier transgressions. So, providing fuller information appears indeed likely to cause many players to set themselves against any flirtation with fixers.

At the same time, it should be recognised that education is unlikely altogether, or even very substantially, to eradicate supply. Even with full information, and particularly if he is tolerant of risk, *homo economicus* will still sometimes reason, and correctly from his perspective, that the expected returns outweigh the expected costs.[18] Education programmes should indeed shift supply to the left; but there will still be supply and in fact the bribes available to those still willing to consider them would be predicted to be higher than before.

Protecting sports integrity therefore requires additional measures, which may be harder than education for sports to accept because they may be more costly to implement or else involve trade-offs between reducing corruption and other commercial goals. Recalling the elements important in the decision to supply, additional measures could focus on raising detection risk or directly working on the financial penalty if a player's transgression should come to light.

At the international level, cricket and tennis invest significant resources in intelligence units whose activities are intended to deter and investigate fixing. In cricket, international players must provide bank and telephone account statements, raising their awareness that suspicious transactions may lead to further inquiry. In football, UEFA funds expensive monitoring of betting markets and its contractor compares irregular movements in odds with subsequent events on the field. All these measures

---

[18] Public health campaigns often have disappointing results because too much faith is placed in education. Information about the deleterious effects of smoking has been disseminated to the point where survey evidence (since Viscusi 1990) indicates that a large majority of smokers actually perceive risks as considerably greater than they in fact are. Nevertheless, even buttressed by strong measures on price, participation-rates in Europe have only halved in 50 years.

raise detection risk.[19] Cost though is likely to be a barrier to their imitation by less well resourced sports.

Apart from detection risk, another major element in the supply decision, as modelled above, is the player's assessment of what is placed at risk should he offend and be detected. Here, higher pay offers some insurance (though not total immunity) against corruption. Of course, few sports would have obvious means of increasing wages across the board. But they could consider reform of the structure of the financial rewards offered to players.

Lessons could be drawn from other sectors because sport is not alone in facing the risk that its employees will be exposed to bribes. The possibility of bribes places the issue in the broader class of principal-agent problems extensively considered by economists. Agency problems refer to situations where a principal hires an agent but then the agent may pursue his own interests rather than those of the principal. The general solution is to restructure an agent's incentives so that they are aligned with those of the principal, which implies restructuring employee rewards where the context is employment rather than some other form of relationship. In a number of spheres of employment, such as the police and the civil service, the restructuring has often involved the introduction of deferred pay (Lazear 1979), for example replacing part of current salary with a pension. Sports could offer part of the remuneration of players and referees in the form of end-of-career bonuses or pensions (Maennig 2002), with payments contractually conditional on non-violation of integrity codes throughout a playing career. This could be particularly effective in deterring veteran players from involvement in fixing, where current reward systems provide little financial incentive for them to turn down proposals for fixing. In some sports, perhaps, sounder governance might be necessary to make the system credible to players.

In sport, rewards may also take the form of prize money or indeed just of the joy of sporting success. Sports should therefore also consider corruption issues when determining prize structure and tournament design.

Decisions for sports on how to allocate prize money must take into account various, and potentially competing, goals. Concentrating the prize money on the winner and runners-up in a tournament may promote commercial goals by attracting the best players to enter. Sporting goals may include maximising performance levels and achieving this goal involves designing a prize structure which incentivises athletes to try harder, and for longer, to advance one more place in the contest finishing order. But prize structures are also relevant to the goal of eradicating corruption. The early rounds of elimination tournaments may carry higher integrity risk than the final stages on account of supply side considerations. A relatively low-ranked professional tennis player at a major tournament has little chance of proceeding through to the rounds where the stakes in terms of prize money and reputation are high. With a low prize for

---

[19] Research would perhaps be appropriate to validate their role. Monitoring systems can provide an indicator for a fix but the statistical algorithms may not necessarily be judged by the courts to have been shown to be sufficiently robust to comprise admissible evidence. Further consideration of how criminals adapt their betting strategies to combat the monitoring systems might also prove valuable.

advancing from the first to the second round, the player might decide to supply a fix since there is a strong chance he will lose in the second round anyway and it matters little whether he exits at round one or round two. More even distribution of prize money across the tournament would provide extra incentive to try hard in round one rather than sell the fix. Similar considerations arise in major football competitions. In both tennis and football, many players have reported receiving proposals for fixing in the early stages of important championships. At such a major event, betting market liquidity will likely be high even in early rounds. Hence there will be a demand for fixes- insufficient care in creating appropriate incentives is likely then to lead to this demand being satisfied. More generally, sports can help themselves in resisting corruption by minimising the number of 'meaningless' matches, such as in 'dead rubber' situations.[20] In other words, implications for corruption should be included as a consideration in taking quite a wide range of decisions in sports management, even where these appear largely 'technical' in character, as with scheduling.

Most fundamentally, sport's capacity to resist corruption requires good governance across the board. The governing body must itself be set up so that fixers cannot take control of it and use it to organise (or turn a blind eye) to fixing.[21] The governing body must also guard against infiltration of individual member clubs by criminal interests by applying rigorous fit-and-proper-person tests when clubs are bought and sold (in Belgium and Finland, criminals purchased financially failing football clubs and installed their own personnel to supply fixes, IRIS 2012, pp. 29–30). It must impose financial discipline on clubs, currently lacking in much of European football where many clubs are so weak that they fail regularly to pay wages on time (FifPro 2012), making players more receptive to offers from fixers because they need the money and because they feel betrayed by the club. More generally, a tendency in owners and administrators to engage in any sort of malpractice would be predicted to make players more willing to supply fixes since they will have low conscience costs when they see the owners exploiting the sport for their own gain. Supply side policies to address fixing therefore include reforming sport more widely and reducing the scope for corruption in other areas of the business.

Demand Side Policies

Although sports themselves can take direct responsibility for addressing the supply side of the market for fixes, they are generally unable directly to influence demand.

---

[20] A 'dead rubber' is where a match takes place after the winner of the series has already been determined. In the infamous case of the South African cricket captain 'selling' the last match of the 1990 series v. England, his team had in fact already won the series. When members of a French handball team appeared to arrange to underperform in an end of season league match, they had already been assured of finishing in first place in the standings.

[21] China is an example of a football federation where an active fixer reached the head of the organisation, facilitating his manipulation of football throughout the league (IRIS 2012, p. 45).

Demand comes from betting markets and may be anticipated to be strong wherever there is a substantial volume of betting on a sporting contest and where much of this passes through either grey or totally illegal markets.

Whatever the details of policies may be, to be effective they must either decrease liquidity or else shift liquidity from poorly monitored to well regulated markets. Given this, the role for regulators in currently well managed jurisdictions is limited. To be sure, measures such as requiring domestic operators to notify the regulator whenever a suspicious pattern of transactions occurs, and requiring domestic operators to record the origin of all substantial transactions, are valuable in detecting and investigating domestically organised and relatively small scale fixes. But all recent large scale fixing is known, from the evidence in the cases which have come to light, to have involved wagers being placed in Asian markets where transactions are effectively anonymous. This limits what national regulators can achieve.

Attempts to reduce liquidity by imposing restrictions in domestic betting markets may, if anything, prove counter-productive. For example, if certain bet types are prohibited, or if domestic operators are constrained to offer 'unattractive' odds, serious bettors, who are responsible for a disproportionate share of volume, may shift their activities to the international market, further enhancing liquidity in the part of the market where regulatory supervision is weak or non-existent. This appears to be the opposite of what is needed. There is a prima facie argument for *improving* choice and value for bettors willing to trade in a supervised environment because, where they do so, this will reduce liquidity in the unsupervised sector.

The most extreme form of regulation of course is prohibition of sports betting, which applies in China, in India and in most of the United States. That prohibition is incapable of being enforced effectively (or, at the least, that there is insufficient political will to do so) is testified by the huge volumes of bets reaching the pan-Asian operators, by the continued existence of offshore internet operators serving the American market, and by the large scale of illegal neighbourhood bookmaking in the United States (Strumpf 2003).

These countries, and others, particularly in Asia, contribute greatly to global liquidity but the illegal status of betting in these countries leads to the liquidity necessarily being channelled through operations where activity is unsupervised and non-transparent. Arguably the demand for fixes could most effectively be shrunk by regularisation of betting in the largest betting countries. But a precondition for legalisation to have the desired effect would be that bettors be offered good value for money. Otherwise, many may choose to continue to patronise the illegal sector and the key goal of taking liquidity out of grey and illegal markets would not be achieved. Governments should not therefore regard legalisation as achieving both the goal of addressing the corruption of sport and that of providing a significant additional source of income for the state (through betting taxes, for example) because these goals conflict.

Legalisation of online sports betting has been actively considered in a number of American states and is newly the subject of national debate in India, following accusations and revelations of extensive fixing in that country's domestic cricket. In the long run, regularisation of these betting markets may allow fixing to be curbed somewhat.

The history of sport suggests that fixing will always be with us; but the epidemic of fixing associated with the recent remarkable growth of sports betting need not necessarily continue indefinitely. Legalisation offers hope of a reversal of trend, as happened in Great Britain in 1961. But meantime, several measures are open to the various interested parties. These may each make only a marginal difference but collectively the efforts may contribute to significant mitigation of the fixing problem.

References

Ehrlich, I. (1996) 'Crime, punishment and the market for offences', *Journal of Economic Perspectives*, 10:43–67.

FIFPro (2012). *Black Book*, available from www.fifpro.org

Forrest, D. (2012). 'Online gambling: an economics perspective' in Williams, R., Wood R. & Parke, J. (eds.), *Routledge Handbook of Internet Gambling*, Routledge, pp. 29–45.

Forrest, D. & Simmons, R. (2003). 'Sport and gambling', *Oxford Review of Economic Policy*, 19:598–611.

Forrest, D., McHale, I. & McAuley, K. (2008). *Risks to the Integrity of Sport from Betting Corruption*, Central Council for Physical Recreation, London.

Hill, D. (2010). 'A critical mass of corruption: why some football leagues have more match-fixing than others', *International Journal of Sports Marketing and Sponsorship*, 221–235.

IRIS (2012). *Paris sportifs et corruption: Comment préserver l'intégrité du sport,* IRIS éditions, Institut de Rélations Internationales et Stratégiques, Paris.

Lazear, E. P. (1979). 'Why is there mandatory retirement?', *Journal of Political Economy*, 87: 1261–1284.

Levitt, S. D. and Venkatesh, S. A. (2000). 'An economic analysis of a drug-selling gang's finances', *Quarterly Journal of Economics*, 115: 755–789.

Maennig, W. (2002). 'On the economics of doping and corruption in international sports', *Journal of Sports Economics*, 3: 61–89.

Maennig, W. (2009). 'Corruption in international sports and how it may be combated', in Rodríguez, P., Késenne, S., and García, J.(eds.), *Threats to Sports and Sports Participation*, pp. 83–111, Ediciones de la Universidad de Oviedo, Oviedo. Spain.

Preston, I., Ross, S. & Szymanski, S (2001). 'Seizing the moment: A blueprint for reform of world cricket', working paper, University College, London.

RGA (2010). *Sports Betting: Legal, Commercial and Integrity Issues*, Remote Gambling Association, London.

Sport Accord (2011). *Integrity in Sport: Understanding and Predicting Match Fixing*, Sport Accord, Moudon, Switzerland.

Strumpf, K. (2003), 'Illegal sports bookmakers', working paper, University of North Carolina at Chapel Hill.

Sullowag, F. and Zweigenhaft, R. (2010). 'Birth order and risk-taking in athletics: A meta-analysis and study of Major League Baseball', *Personality and Social Psychology Review*, 14: 402–416.

Swiss Institute of Comparative Law (2006). *Study of Gambling Services in the Internal Market of the European Union*, Swiss Institute of Comparative Law, Lausanne.

Viscusi, W. (1990). Do smokers underestimate risks? *Journal of Political Economy* 98: 1253–1269.

Wolfers, J. (2005), 'Point shaving: corruption in NCAA basketball', *American Economic Review*, 96:279–283.

Compliance Mechanism as a Tool of Prevention?

Karen L. Jones

Abstract Many initiatives have been engaged by sports organizations as a means of providing governance in the area of preventing sports corruption. However, these initiatives, which resemble and are in fact taken from, comparable initiatives in corporations, are compliance initiatives that are usually part of a more comprehensive governance scheme that includes these internal initiatives and external oversight. While it is clear that *governance* measures alone cannot prevent match-fixing (criminal laws, penalties, disciplinary measures, etc. – must also play a role), it should also be understood that the ad hoc compliance initiatives alone without a comprehensive governance scheme will only have limited effect in aiding the prevention of match-fixing. This chapter considers these compliance initiatives by exploring limitations, and exposing what is lacking. An examination of sport as an organization as well as the core principles of organizational governance, good governance and sports organization governance, will also be discussed. In an effort to establish some form of critical oversight and accountability, this chapter goes further to explore the use of accreditation (and certification) and licensing, as tools to reinforce existing compliance initiatives and form part of a more comprehensive governance strategy in efforts to help prevent match-fixing.

Introduction: The Problem of Match-Fixing

Over the past several years, with the prevalence of sports corruption being so high, it is not surprising that in its Communication of 18 January 2011, The European Commission states: "Match-fixing violates the ethics and integrity of sport."[1]

---

[1] European Commission, 18 January 2011, Communication, *Ibid.* at p. 12.

K.L. Jones, JD, MA (✉)
T.M.C. Asser Instituut, Asser International Sports Law Centre,
30461, Hague 2500 GL, The Netherlands
e-mail: K.Jones@Asser.nl; KLYNN1234@aol.com

M.R. Haberfeld and D. Sheehan (eds.), *Match-Fixing in International Sports:*
Existing Processes, Law Enforcement, and Prevention Strategies,
DOI 10.1007/978-3-319-02582-7_11, © Springer International Publishing Switzerland 2013

More recently, The European Commissioner provided a statement reconfirming the European Commission's support of efforts to combat sports corruption by stating: "Match-Fixing and corruption pose the greatest threats to European sport today, and the European Commission is determined to do all it can to help the sports authorities tackle them."[2] Despite these very strong statements by the European Commission and others, the problem of match-fixing persists.

The definition for match-fixing, used by the Australian Sports Minister is:

Match-fixing involves the manipulation of the outcome or contingency by competitors, teams, sports agencies, support staff, referees, and officials, and venue staff. Such conduct includes:

a. The deliberate fixing of the results of a contest, or of an occurrence within the contest, or of a points spread;
b. Deliberate underperformance;
c. Withdrawal (tanking);
d. An official's deliberate misapplication of the rules of a contest;
e. Interference of the play or playing surfaces by venue staff; and
f. Abuse of insider information to support a bet placed by any of the above or placed by a gambler who has recruited such people to manipulate an outcome or contingency.[3]

A recent European Commission report on match-fixing, included the following working definition of match-fixing:

The manipulation of sports results covers the arrangement on an irregular alteration of the course or the result of a sporting competition or any of its particular events (e.g. matches, races…) in order to obtain financial advantage, for oneself or for other, and remove all or part of the uncertainty normally associated with the results of a competition.[4]

Although there still is no single authoritative definition of match-fixing, in its most basic form, match-fixing can be defined as, the act of losing, or playing to a pre-determined result, in sports matches by illegally manipulating the results in your favor.

When we are watching a match or sporting event there is an automatic trust and belief that is inherent in the idea of sport, that those engaging in the activities are doing so using their own physical, mental and strategic (non-enhanced) abilities to perform, leading to either their victory or defeat. When fraud or corruption enters into sport and the outcome is somehow pre-determined or an athlete's abilities are artificially enhanced, that tends to remove the event from the sanctity of sport and into the realm of entertainment at best. *Would people be willing to pay to see their favorite sports team in a competition that everyone knows is pre-determined or even if there is a high likelihood that the integrity of the sport event has been somehow*

---

[2] European Commission, Commission will do all it can to help tackle match-fixing and corruption in sports, says Vassiliou, 14 March 2013; http://ec.europa.eu/commission_2010-2014/vassiliou/headlines/news/2013/03/20130314-match-fixing-corruption-in-sport_en.htm

[3] Sport and Recreation Ministers' Council Communiqué 2011.

[4] European Commission Study, Match-Fixing in Sports: A Mapping of Criminal Law Provisions in EU 27 (March 2012), p. 9.

compromised? There is no doubt that sports corruption[5] puts a dark cloud over the entire industry of sports. Perhaps more specifically, it is a direct attack on the integrity of the game. If the sport is determined not by skill, strategies and physical abilities of the players but instead on who was able to "pay-off" the referee, official, team or player to "buy" the win, then it is questionable whether or not it is really sport at all. The whole concept of sports competition and the basis for our Olympic Games today began with the early games in Olympia, Greece in 776 BC. Public competition and individual achievement reflected the ancient Greek idea of *arête*, representing the Greek ideal of excellence. Even in ancient times there were those who were caught cheating.[6] Anyone caught cheating was fined and the money raised was used for a statue erected in the name of Zeus.[7] The statue would include inscriptions of the offenses committed and warning others not to cheat by skill or money and reinforcing the importance of piety, the Olympic Spirit, and fair competition.[8]

Although there is a degree of public shame associated with being charged with (or found guilty of) sports corruption, thus far the possibility of public shame has done little to deter those would be cheaters. It is likely that the solution to sports corruption will require more than charging a fine or keeping a public account of the wrongdoings.

Recent Studies: Match-Fixing

Several studies have begun to help quantify the problem of match-fixing. The Black Book on Sports Corruption was perhaps the first comprehensive empirical legal study in recent years to clearly articulate the impact to the various stakeholders, and the issues involved in this very complex problem.[9] The Black Book identified several challenges in the area of match-fixing, including the role that finances, crime, education, intimidation and violence play on incidences of match-fixing being reported, investigated and charged.[10] The European Commission report on Match-Fixing in Sports: A mapping of the EU 27 criminal law provisions[11] looks across the then 27 European Union member states to review the criminal law provisions

---

[5] Throughout this paper, sports corruption and match-fixing are used interchangeably and synonymously. At times, sports corruption may be used as a broader term to encompass other forms of illegal or inappropriate measures used to manipulate or cheat in sports (ex. doping, bribery, illegal betting, etc.) but always including match-fixing as a form of corruption.

[6] Some of the earliest sports corruptions included Eupolus of Thessaly who bribed boxers in the 98th Olympiad; Callippus of Athens bought off his competitors to secure a win in the pentathlon during the 112th Olympic festival; during the 226th Olympics two Egyptian boxers, Didas and Sarrapammon, were fined for fixing the match. *See,* Pausanius' 2nd Century A.D. Guidebook to Greece.

[7] *Id.*

[8] *Id.*

[9] FIFPro Black Book Eastern Europe, The problems professional footballers encounter: research, FIFPro Services (2012).

[10] *Id.* at pages 12–19.

[11] Match-Fixing in Sports: A mapping of the EU 27 criminal law provisions, European Commission, March 2012; http://ec.europa.eu/sport/news/documents/study-sports-fraud-final-version_en.pdf.

of each nation and the ability to bring charges against would be match-fixers under the respective provisions. The research shows that many national laws are insufficient to truly address the crime of match-fixing.[12] The report further reveals that many of the criminal law provisions that are (or could be) used to charge match-fixers do not contain specific reference to match-fixing, and there is a lack of uniformity and consistency across nations.[13] Either national laws do not identify match-fixing specifically as an offense, or even worse the existing laws around corruption, fraud, or money laundering were so limited in some countries that there was little or no basis to support the charge, should the investigation show that match-fixing had in fact occurred.[14] Similar studies continue to be conducted at the national, European and International levels.[15]

With increasing frequency, it seems the reports on incidences of suspected match-fixing or new investigations into match-fixing continue to rise. This can be attributed to new cases of match-fixing, new investigations being kicked-off, or the fact that investigations into match-fixing are often lengthy and prolonged. Much of this was summarized in the announcement earlier this year (February 2013) when the head of Europol,[16] Rob Wainright, announced the results of their 18 month covert joint investigation into international football (soccer) match-fixing activities which led them to trace much of the activities to organized crime, in particular, a single criminal syndicate out of Singapore.[17] The cases of match-fixing highlighted by the investigation, for example the cases in Germany, fixing of lower-league games, as well as qualifying games for the World Cup and Champions League, were already known or suspected.[18]

---

[12] *Id.*

[13] *Id.;* See, European Parliament News, Fighting sports match-fixing and illegal betting: call for common penalties, Plenary Session Justice and home affairs, Sport −14-03-2013 − 12:38. "EU member states should step up their joint efforts to combat corruption in sports by introducing common penalties for match-fixing, says a resolution voted on Thursday." *Id.*

[14] *Id.*

[15] For example, See VU Amsterdam starts research on match-fixing in the Netherlands, Vrije Universiteit Amsterdam (VU Amsterdam), 05 February 2013, http://www.vu.nl/en/news-agenda/news/2013/jan-mrt/VU-University-starts-research-on-match-fixing-in-the-Netherlands.asp; See also, Call for joint efforts to fight match-fixing, 20 February 2013, Asian Football Confederation (AFC), http://www.the-afc.com/en/events/events-others/fifa-interpol-conference/25193-joint-effort-needed-to-fight-corruption.html, AFC Acting President, Zhang Jilong: "We need to admit that match-fixing is a real danger to football's ethical values and needs to be eliminated to preserve the sanctity of the sport. I can assure this conference that AFC will not rest until this plague is completely stamped out in Asia...AFC will educate the players, officials and all stakeholders on raising awareness about this serious issue. We need to understand how match-fixing works in order to prevent it. We need more information on how crime syndicates operate." Id.

[16] European Union law enforcement agency. See, https://www.europol.europa.eu/content/page/about-us.

[17] See, https://www.europol.europa.eu/content/results-largest-football-match-fixing-investigation-europe; More than 425 suspected, from more than 15 countries, of attempting to fix more than 380 professional football matches. *Id; Singapore Police Arrest 14 in Match-Fixing Raids, http://www.bbc.co.uk/news/world-asia-24149076.*

[18] *See,* Buschmann, R., Match-Fixing Scandal: How international Football Has Failed, Spiegel Online, February 5, 2013.

There is little doubt that match-fixing is a wide-spread problem, and affects all levels of sport (all stakeholders). The laws that are in place at the national, European and international levels are not sufficiently addressing the problem. Many national laws are being revised or new laws established to address this problem. Criminal sanctions are being looked at to ensure that the penalties for those involved in match-fixing are increased so that the criminals do not attempt to set up shop in places where the laws, sanctions or enforcement is lax.

Sports organizations, though often looked at as having the responsibility for *governing* the arena of sport – attributed to their regulatory authority over a particular area of sport, and ability to sanction – has not been very effective in preventing match-fixing.[19] With the recent announcements about this widespread problem and ongoing investigations (amongst other things), there seems to be a loss of confidence (if it ever truly existed) that sports organizations alone can effectively contribute to its resolution.

Joint Efforts

To find other alternatives for addressing the problem of match-fixing, or to incorporate a multi-alternative approach, attention has shifted away from strictly legal enforcement to issues of sports organization responsibilities and governance activities. Sports organizations are generally vested with the responsibility of governing the particular area of sport that they represent, either at the national, European or international level.[20] As such, and perhaps at least in part due to public pressure, these organizations have begun to engage measures in an effort to counter the problem of match-fixing. These measures have the characteristics of *governance-like activities* in that they are promulgated through the sports organization, a non-governmental governance body, with the requirement that all of its members adhere to them.

A lot of recent activities have focused on training and awareness. Several initiatives have been employed to bring awareness about match-fixing and even training to sports players, coaches, and others. Most sport organization websites contain some information or reference to the problem of match-fixing or more broadly, sports integrity. Several organizations have now joined forces to address the issue of sports corruption. The Fédération Internationale de Football Association (FIFA) joined forces with INTERPOL[21] by donating 20 million dollars over ten (10) years

---

[19] *Id.*; See also, Football: UEFA unhappy over slow reforms at FIFA, Agence-France-Presse – Friday, May 31, 2013, InterAKTV.

[20] Some examples of these sports organizations include: FIFA (international), UEFA (European), United Kingdom Premier League (National). There are also sports organizations that cover a particular area of competition (ex. International Olympic Committee – IOC (International), National Olympic Committee) or a specific area of sport governance (ex. World Anti-Doping Agency – WADA (International), United States Anti-Doping Agency – USADA (National). For purposes of this chapter the focus is primarily on the former.

[21] International Policing Organization, http://www.interpol.int/Crime-areas/Corruption/Integrity-in-Sport.

to address training, education and prevention in relation to match-fixing.[22] INTERPOL has established an Integrity in Sports unit to create global programs aimed at raising awareness about match-fixing.[23] Recently, several European sports organizations joined efforts to draft a joint action plan supporting their commitment to fight sports corruption (match-fixing) and reiterate their commitment to sports integrity.[24] Transparency International has joined with German Football League (DFL) and the Association of European Football Leagues (EPFL)[25] to pilot an education and match-fixing prevention program called *Staying on Side*.[26] Another pairing with a similar goal, is the partnering of SportsAccord with the Institut de Relations Et Strategiques (IRIS).[27] In addition to these initiatives, there are many others at the national, European and international level supporting efforts to fight match-fixing, educate the community, and preserve integrity in sport.

Because of the very close connection between match-fixing and gambling, over the past few years, there has been a lot of initiatives in the area of sports betting that are also aimed at controlling sports corruption and maintaining sports integrity, including the development of the Sports Betting Intelligence Unit (SBIU)[28] established in 2010 by the Gambling Commission, and the Joint Assessment Unit (JAU)[29] put in place by the Gambling Commission to address potential sports

---

[22] IMPROVING AWARENESS AND UNDERSTANDING OF CORRUPTION IN FOOTBALL, INTERPOL, Integrity in Sport.

[23] *Id.* at page 3.

[24] European Football United for the Integrity of the Game, ECA, EPFL, FIFPro, UEFA (2013).

[25] This is one of several projects receiving funding by the European Commission in an effort to raise awareness about the problem of match-fixing amongst the public and sports communities. See, Tackling Football Match-Fixing: Prevention As Cure, 27 March 2013, http://www.transparency.org/news/feature/tackling_football_match_fixing_prevention_as_cure.

[26] A similar project was kicked-off in 2010 with Transparency International, German Football League (DFL), German Football Association, German Health Agency and Professional Football Players Union, that program called *Together Against Match-Fixing* is now being piloted in several German football clubs. *Id.*

[27] This is a transnational project with a focus on future initiatives on good governance in sports around Europe. This project includes the dissemination of the SportsAccord Integrity Package. See, SportAccord partners with IRIS to raise awareness on match-fixing in European Countries – See more at: http://www.sportaccord.com/en/news/sportaccord-partners-with-iris-to-raise-awareness-on-match-fixing-in-european-countries-0-16844#sthash.IQUWPCfE.dpuf.

[28] Sports Betting Intelligence Unit (SBIU) is a special unit established in 2010 under the United Kingdom Gambling Commission that addresses criminal activities associated with match-fixing or sports corruption related gambling. The SBIU works with sports organizations to collect information, investigate allegations and develop intelligence on sports corruption related betting activities that have ties to the Great Britain. See, http://www.gamblingcommission.gov.uk/licensing_compliance__enfo/intelligence/sbiu.aspx.

[29] The Joint Assessment Unit (JAU) was tasked with the responsibility of collecting and assessing information in an effort to fight corruption during the 2012 London Olympic games. See, UK Gambling Commission, *Working together to protect the Integrity of Sport – The role of the Joint Assessment Unit at the London 2012 Olympic Games*, March 2013. http://www.gamblingcommission.gov.uk/pdf/JAU%20report%20-%20March%202013.pdf?utm_source = EB%2B110313&utm_medium = email&utm_campaign = EB%2B110313%2Bjau.

corruption issues that may arise during the 2012 London Olympic Games. These efforts from the sports betting organizations tend to take on a more information gathering and investigative role that aids in the criminal investigation and intelligence gathering operations.

Despite all of these efforts, match-fixing continues to be a major problem. These efforts by various sports organizations, universities, think-tanks and others, has for the most part done an impressive job to quantify the problem of match-fixing, bring awareness about the relevant issues of match-fixing to the broader community, train stakeholders on the dangers of match-fixing and in some cases provide valuable information not only to sports organizations in an effort to investigate and discipline suspected offenders, but also bringing valuable information and insights to law enforcement in relation to criminal charges and penalties to those engaging in this criminal behavior.

Aside from the efforts of betting organizations and gambling authorities, these joint efforts within the sports community tend to take on similar characteristics. There is a lot of activity around codes of ethics and conduct; training and awareness; sports integrity; governing bodies and boards; transparency and sharing of investigative information or suspected cases of match-fixing; handbooks on the "do's and don'ts"; commissions, committees and integrity review boards, surveys; studies; whistleblower protections; etc. These joint efforts can have a very positive affect of building necessary collaborations and a concerted effort to tackle a common problem, which can lead to better solutions. However, these joint efforts can also have the negative effect of showing a lot of activity, but very limited results. In other words, a lot of smoke but no fire!

Why Compliance Initiatives Are Not Enough

Much of the thought around *compliance initiatives* and the concept of governance in general, are derived from the world of business, in particular corporate or organizational governance.[30] This is appropriate since sports organizations in many ways have characteristics of multi-national corporations.[31] Therefore, approaching the issue of corruption in sports and governance similar to how these issues have been approached in corporations at minimum seems logical, if not practical. However, corporations (like sports organizations) are very complex organizations and as such do not simply rely on a single or monolithic approach. For example, governance in corporations is not just a random series of activities, instead governance is embodied within the operational systems of a corporation and contains multiple parts that make operational systems work efficiently and most importantly, effectively.

Recent activities in an effort to prevent sports corruption have focused on what can be characterized as *compliance initiatives*. Compliance initiatives are usually

---

[30] Corporate governance is defined in the next section.

[31] For purposes of this paper, the terms "corporation" and "organization" are used interchangeably and synonymously.

part of an overall compliance program. A compliance program is defined as: Systematic procedures instituted by an organization to ensure that the provisions of the regulations imposed by a government agency are being met.[32] By definition the use of compliance initiatives suggest that such activities are in *compliance* with or in adherence to something. More specifically, they indicate the need to ensure internal operations are meeting some objective or satisfying the requirements established by some regulatory body to which the organization is *accountable*.[33]

Not only are compliance initiatives generally part of a much broader compliance program or governance scheme, they are often determined based on the governing organization's requirements. The activities that have been engaged by sports organizations to assist in the effort to prevent match-fixing have been determined by each sports organization; not necessarily part of a broader compliance program or governance scheme, and even more, those activities have not been determined by a governing body (ex. sports organization) nor part of a structured or broad-based governance initiative.

What this has created can be described as a *hodge-podge* or ad hoc type of pseudo-governance program, that essentially consists of a lot of individual compliance initiatives, but no comprehensive structure or consistent program across the sports organizations. Since these activities are not tied to or connected with a more comprehensive program or scheme, effectiveness can only be limited.

At present, sports organization initiatives in support of match-fixing prevention, primarily at the international and European levels consist of training, codes of ethics, disciplinary procedures, integrity boards, etc., as represented in the following model (Fig. 1).

The model (Fig. 1) captures several types of compliance initiatives (and by no means is exhaustive), most of which have been engaged by various sports organizations in an effort to prevent match-fixing. In organizations, these types of compliance initiatives are usually at the foundation of the governance model. In other words, compliance initiatives alone can only have some limited effect, because they are only one part of an overall governance scheme. Although compliance initiatives are important, alone they cannot establish the necessary oversight achieved by the other areas of a solid governance scheme (see Fig. 2) as discussed in section "Good Governance Characteristics" below. These initiatives, though important, are most effective when they are part of a much broader strategy.

The types of compliance initiatives and measures, such as operational policies, procedures, ethics codes, disciplinary process, etc., while alone they can provide some benefits such as clarity around responsibilities of some of the key actors within

---

[32] http://www.businessdictionary.com/definition/compliance-program.html

[33] The topic of accountability will not be exhaustively covered in this chapter, however, it is a very important component to the topic of effective governance, and is an important element in the author's PhD research on *Using New Institutionalism to Define Accountability of International Sports Organizations and as a Mechanism to Prevent Corruption* (working document).

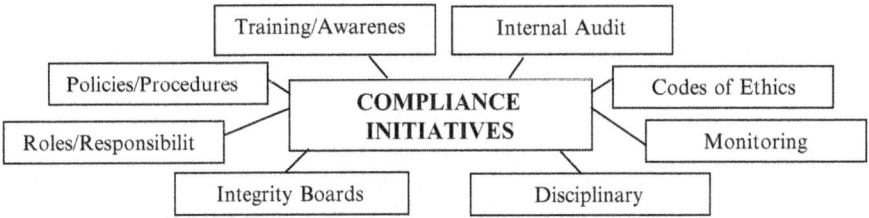

Fig. 1 Common components of a compliance initiative scheme (This model was created by the author, Karen L. Jones, JD, MA, with all rights reserved)

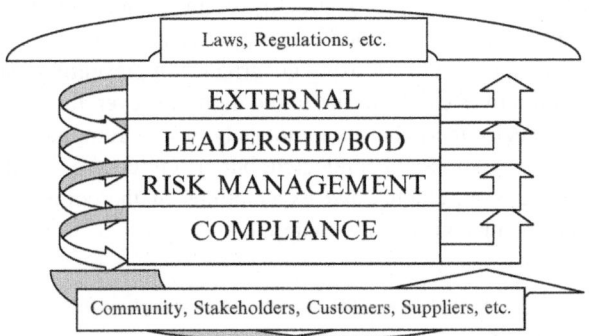

Fig. 2 High-level governance scheme (This model was created by the author, Karen L. Jones, JD, MA, with all rights reserved)

an organization, the appearance of providing useful information on a topic to the broader community or proactive announcement on the organization's position on a given topic, compliance initiatives alone do not establish a governance structure. To be part of a comprehensive governance structure, compliance initiatives are often associated with some sort of regulatory scheme requiring reporting. The reporting often feeds into a system of accountability, which is somewhat lacking in some sports organization governance schemes. Sports Organizations are not required to report to any type of regulatory body.[34] The compliance initiatives to date have primarily centered on training and aware, codes of ethics, some work with review boards and integrity boards. These are all important and necessary aspects to a complete compliance program; however, there are critical elements that are missing.

---

[34] Surrounding the concept of financial fair play, the idea of having some sort of financial reporting of sports organizations to governing bodies to bolster financial accountability of sports clubs has emerged. See, UEFA Club Licensing and Financial Fair Play CL/FFP IT Solution Toolkit, Edition 2013, APPENDIX III: Guidance for CI Package – The Reporting Perimeter, page 35.

These common compliance initiatives alone, do not address coordination of efforts amongst the various sports organizations. True transparency,[35] which would allow some sort of formalized process of review based on specified standards, is also missing. Consistency, although in some ways may seem to be an attack to organizational and even national autonomy, is none-the-less an important element for ensuring a system of effectiveness and efficiency; yet amongst the governing sports organizations this is limited. Independent initiatives by definition lack the appropriate coordination which is necessary to create a comprehensive scheme and make the programs work to achieve a broader goal of preventing match-fixing.

There are many types of governance models[36] most of which can provide some insights in the area of sports organization governance and contribute to an effective process for assisting with operational structure of an organization. Without focusing on a single model, instead the key elements of governance is most important and can provide insights to approaches for using governance in preventing match-fixing.

Compliance initiatives can form the foundation, however, there must be an adequate system of checks and balances to not only ensure compliance initiatives are being properly administered and conducted, but also to ensure that the compliance initiatives meet the requirements and expectations of the community, governing bodies, as well as being compliant with applicable laws.[37]

Importance of a Governance Approach

Before discussing the concept of a governance approach it is important to understand the application of such an approach to sports organizations. Therefore, in this section will discuss the idea of sport as an organization and the application of governance, then address the importance of a governance approach.

---

[35] Most concepts of transparency around match-fixing have dealt with issues relative to access to information on investigations and disciplinary proceedings, sharing amongst nations and stakeholders. However, here the term transparency is being used to identify a formalized process of review of internal operations. Transparency in business is defined as: "...2. Lack of hidden agendas and conditions accompanied by the availability of full information required for collaboration, cooperation, and collective decision making. 3. Minimum degree of disclosure to which agreements, dealings, practices, and transactions are open to all for verification. 4. Essential condition for a free and open exchange whereby the rules and reasons behind regulatory measures are fair and clear to all participants." See, http://www.businessdictionary.com/definition/transparency.html#ixzz2atT3zKs2.

[36] Two examples of governance models include: Benevolent Dictator Governance Model – Often depicted by a single leader; and Meritocratic Governance Model – Generally a "flat structure" that gives control away to the "community" members.

[37] These may include laws at the national, European and/or international levels, as well as sports organization rules, regulations and requirements.

The Organization of Sport

This discussion of sport as an organization should not be confused with the European Union attempts to identify the organization of sports in the European Union. These two are distinct in that the European Commission sets out what they have determined to be the organization of sports in the European Union in the White Paper on Sports.[38] In this important document that sets out the way sports are organized in the European Union, the importance of promoting certain traditions and values associated with sports is stressed.[39] However, even within the document itself limitations are confessed. They decline to identify a specific "European Sport Model" stating that at present such a determination is unrealistic given the emergence of "new challenges[40]" that are impacting the member states and thus any realistic attempt at defining a discernible sports model for Europe. Interestingly, the report further states:

> The emergence of new stakeholders (participants outside the organized disciplines, professional sports clubs, etc.) is posing new questions as regards governance, democracy and representation of interests within the sport movement.[41]

Despite the fact that the European Commission felt unable to define a European Sports Model in the original White Paper on Sport, it does not negate the fact that in some ways *sports* has characteristics that might be compared with those of a multinational organization; sporting events being the product that is produced and sports (as an entity) being the organization which governs them. Therefore, an understanding of sports corruption and identification of effective governance goes beyond simply defining the terms. Analysis of the structure of sport, or understanding the organization of sport and how sports are governed, is also important to add clarity to the terms. An organization can be defined as:

> A social unit of people, systematically structured and managed to meet a need or to pursue collective goals on a continuing basis. All organizations have a management structure that determines relationships between functions and positions, and subdivides and delegates roles, responsibilities, and authority to carry out defined tasks. Organizations are open systems in that they affect and are affected by the environment beyond their boundaries.[42]

Sport can be described as a "social unit of people" comprised of players, owners, referees and fans. The rules of the game and more importantly the way sports are organized at the local, national and international levels with its guideline requirements and rules and regulations all "...systematically structured and managed to meet a need or to pursue collective goals..."[43] The "need" or "goal" of this collective pur-

---

[38] European Commission, White Paper on Sports, COM (2007) 391 Final, Brussels 11.07.2007; http://ec.europa.eu/sport/documents/wp_on_sport_en.pdf.

[39] Id at Section 4. The Organization of Sport, p. 12.

[40] Id at Section 4, The Organization of Sport, the document points out that there are "...economic and social developments that are common to the majority of the Member States (increasing commercialization, challenges to public spending, increasing numbers of participants and stagnation in the number of voluntary workers) have resulted in new challenges for the organization of sport in Europe." p. 12.

[41] Id at Section 4, The Organization of Sport, p. 12.

[42] *See,* http://www.businessdictionary.com/definition/organization.html#ixzz1lt5JYlLi.

[43] *Ibid.*

suit can be winning a game or match, pursuit of excellence, satisfying fans, or being paid for skills and abilities. Professional sports, and to a large degree amateur sports, are organized in such a way that there is an intrinsic structure of management that not only oversees the games, but also dictates the roles and responsibilities of those who participate in the operation of a sports team, club or league. They also make decisions that impact the way the sport is played, and activities and relationships impacting sports, in a manner that carries with it a great degree of responsibility and authority. "All organizations have a management structure that determines relationships between functions and positions, and subdivides and delegates roles, responsibilities, and authority to carry out defined tasks."[44] Finally, although the White Paper on Sport talks about the autonomy of sporting organizations and representative structures",[45] sports are not autonomous in that they are impacted by and they impact the world around them making them "open systems"; autonomous structures perhaps, but open systems nonetheless.

Even if the whole of sport is not conceived in terms of an organization, certainly the entities that comprise the arena of sports such as sports federations, associations, clubs, etc., can be looked at independently as organisms that are part of a larger complex body of related entities. Another way to view sports as an organization is to look at the larger international entities that perform some degree of governance or oversight (FIFA, FIFPro, UEFA, etc.) as multi-national organizations or multi-national entities. These are non-governmental organizations that often perform almost a pseudo governmental role. Because they are non-governmental, they do not adhere to any particular *governmental* structure or requirements.

Organizational Governance

Organizational governance is also referred to as corporate governance. The terms *corporate* or *organization* are used to represent any type of *entity* whether it is given legal identity or not.

Corporate (or organizational) governance has been defined in many ways. Some of those definitions include the following:

- A generic term which describes the ways in which rights and responsibilities are shared between the various corporate participants, especially the management and shareholders.[46]
- Corporate governance is the system by which business corporations are directed and controlled. The corporate governance structure specifies the distribution of rights and responsibilities among different participants in the corporation, such as, the board, managers, shareholders and other stakeholders, and spells out the rules and procedures for making decisions on corporate affairs. By doing this, it also provides the structure

---

[44] *Ibid.*

[45] European Commission, White Paper on Sport, Section 4. The Organization of Sport, p. 13.

[46] Investorwords.Com. Search term used, Corporate Governance.

through which the company objectives are set, and the means of attaining those objectives and monitoring performance.[47]

- Corporate governance is about promoting corporate fairness, transparency and accountability.[48]
- In its barest form, corporate governance is the *system* by which companies are directed and controlled principally by a board of directors.[49]

Despite which definition of corporate (or organizational) governance is used, common themes and characteristics of, such as responsibility and accountability, begin to emerge.

Therefore, a very basic definition of organizational governance is:

The framework of rules and practices by which a board of directors ensures accountability, fairness, and transparency in a company's relationship with its stakeholders....[50]

Within the context of the idea of organizational governance is a framework that can be described as follows:

The corporate governance framework consists of (1) explicit and implicit contracts between the company and the stakeholders for distribution of responsibilities, rights, and rewards, (2) procedures for reconciling the sometimes conflicting interests of stakeholders in accordance with their duties, privileges, and roles, and (3) procedures for proper supervision, control, and information-flows to serve as a system of checks-and-balances.[51]

So a framework of corporate or organizational governance would include important elements as identified in the definition above. As relative to sports organizations, the elements of a governance framework should include:

- Explicit and implicit contracts between the sports organizations and stakeholders, which clearly identifies a distribution of responsibilities, rights and rewards;
- A dispute resolution process to help reconcile conflicting interests that might arise; and
- Procedures for proper supervision, control, and flows of information – serving as a checks-and-balances system.

The formula for a governance framework as stated above seems clear. However, part of the challenge in the current *organization* of sports is that although some contracts exist between sports organizations and certain stakeholders, there are other stakeholders where contracts, either explicit or implicit do not exist. Some contracts might exist in the European Union Social Dialogue

---

[47] OECD April 1999. OECD's definition is consistent with the one presented by Cadbury [1992, page 15].

[48] J. Wolfensohn, president of the Word bank, as quoted by an article in *Financial Times*, June 21, 1999.

[49] (Cadbury Report). It relates to the internal means by which corporations are operated and controlled (OECD Principles). In an expanded version, it is the process and structure used to direct and manage the affairs of the company towards enhancing business prosperity and corporate accountability with the ultimate objective of realizing long-term shareholder value whilst taking into account the interests of other stakeholders, (Finance Committee on Corporate Governance, Malaysia).

[50] www.BusinessDictionary.com/definition/corporate-governance.html

[51] *Id.*

on sports,[52] however, the benefactor of the outcome of these measures may leave out some key stakeholders such as some specific community interests.[53] A lack of certain contracts that impact the environment in which sports corruption exists may contribute to the proliferation of this problem.[54]

Several sports organizations have established internal means of addressing disputes, either by establishing informal or a more formalized dispute resolution process. For example, the FIFA Dispute Resolution Chamber (DRC).[55] The effectiveness of the DRC and similar dispute processes are still being determined especially in the case of sports corruption as many cases require lengthy investigation periods.

Finally, the third point in the governance framework requires procedures for proper supervision and a system of checks-and-balances. This perhaps is an area where there are significant limitations in the current system. Each sports organization is highly autonomous and therefore have limited checks-and-balances.

Arthur Levitt, the former SEC Chairman described corporate governance as "... processes indispensable to effective market discipline."[56] When we consider all of the stakeholders within the larger organization of sports, including the market participants and influences, especially those that influence or impact sports corruption and match-fixing, there are a lot of opportunities for creating a more effective system of checks-and-balances. For instance stronger controls around sports betting, which are currently being considered,[57] but also stronger limitations or controls on the type of involvement sports managers, officials, players and others directly involved in the game can have in the sports marketplace.[58]

Governance can be defined in many ways depending on the authority. However regardless of the definition, there are common consistent elements to each definition.

The definition of corporate *governance* used by the *OECD*[59] is as follows: "Procedures and processes according to which an organisation is directed and controlled. The corporate governance structure specifies the distribution of rights and responsibilities among the different participants in the organisation – such as the

---

[52] *See,* European Commission, White Paper on Sport, 5.3 Social dialogue, COM (2007) 391 Final, Brussels, 11.7.2007.

[53] *Id.*

[54] For example, stakeholders such as betting affiliates and other market participants should be contractually obligated, explicitly or implicitly, as part of the larger organization of sport, to safeguard against the influence and activities of sports corruption and match-fixing.

[55] FIFA Dispute Resolution Chamber, Official Documents, FIFA.Com; Rules Governing the Procedures of the Players' Status Committee and the Dispute Resolution Chamber (DRC) (2005)/ (2008); Regulations Status and Transfer (2012), http://www.fifa.com/aboutfifa/officialdocuments/doclists/disputeresolutionchamber.html.

[56] Levitt, A., An Essential Next Step in the Evolution of Corporate Governance. Speech to the Audit Committee Symposium, June 29, 1999.

[57] *See,* Sports betting and corruption: How to preserve the integrity of sport, IRIS, University of Salford (Manchester), Cabinet Praxes-Avocats, CCLS (Universite de Pekin) (2011).

[58] One consideration might be to restrict all those involved in sports from betting on any sports game, not just the ones in which they are involved. Severity of the limitation will require a balancing of individual rights.

[59] The Organization for Economic Co-Operations and Development (OECD).

board, managers, shareholders and other stakeholders – and lays down the rules and procedures for decision-making."[60]

The OECD definition is more process oriented in that it focuses on the components of governance – the *what* – which is similar to the approach that has been taken recently in applying compliance initiatives to the area of preventing sports corruption.

Another definition and perhaps one that is even more telling is derived from the world of business:

> The framework of rules and practices by which a board of directors ensures accountability, fairness, and transparency in a company's relationship with its stakeholders (financiers, customers, management, employees, government, and the community). The corporate governance framework consists of (1) explicit and implicit contracts between the company and the stakeholders for the distribution of responsibilities, rights, and rewards, (2) procedures for reconciling the sometimes conflicting interests of stakeholders in accordance with their duties, privileges, and roles, and (3) procedures for proper supervision, control, and information-flows to serve as a system of checks and balances.[61]

This definition is more comprehensive and focuses on how to achieve a more comprehensive governance framework.

Governance not only identifies initiatives, it also provides the necessary oversight to ensure that the initiatives are appropriately carried out. These initiatives include coordination and transparency. To help ensure impartiality, having an independent objective organization providing this oversight can often add to credibility. Having the necessary governance structure in place to ensure the proper oversight leads to credibility, helps to build a framework of accountability, and facilitates a system that can address problems that arise quickly and severely.

Therefore, a more general model for corporate or also known as "organizational" governance might appear as follows:

The model above shows the relationship of governance not only to the internal workings of an organization, but also its relation to the external community and stakeholders. The external community, which also includes stakeholders, customers, suppliers, fans, related industry actors, etc., and all those who observe or are impacted by the activities of that organization, in this case sports organizations, form the bottom of this model which fuels the need within the organization to take some sort of action. This action, which is often in response to the external community, feeds into the actions taken by the organization which can take the form of compliance initiatives. These compliance initiatives (see Fig. 1, above) should then feed into a Risk Management program. The Risk Management program looks at ways to avoid,[62] manage,[63] or mitigate[64] the risks associated with the focus of the initiatives. The activities of Risk Management, in particular a determination of the ability to avoid, manage or mitigate risks then feeds into leadership decisions and

---

[60] OECD Glossary of Statistical Terms, http://stats.oecd.org/glossary/detail.asp?ID=6778; see also, European Central Bank, 2004, Annual Report: 2004, ECB, Frankfurt, Glossary.

[61] http://www.businessdictionary.com/definition/corporate-governance.html

[62] Avoiding the risk means completely eliminating the possibility of it.

[63] Managing the risk means the risk is still there but other means are utilized to lessen the effects of it.

[64] Mitigating the risk means taking measures to make the risk itself less impactful.

actions taken at the leadership level. This then impacts a broader cross-organizational (or external oversight) scheme and the development of industry practices and standards, which likewise impacts changes to laws and regulations in a particular industry. At each of these levels of oversight (Risk Management, Leadership, External Oversight, etc.) detailed reporting is a requirement. A more detailed process flow would show the specific actors involved, exchange of information and data, etc.

On the reverse side, which is a more typical top-down model, laws and regulations help to guide external oversight (agencies, etc.). Leadership within an organization must comply with those laws and regulations. They do this by developing risk management programs that incorporate legal and regulatory requirements, and as a way to ensure internal adherence, internal auditing practices are often incorporated into the organizational scheme. The results of the risk management activities (ex. international audit) often feed into new or revised compliance initiatives by identifying best practices, new industry standards, practices and procedures, or related efficiencies that might not be otherwise discovered but for this ongoing internal review.

This cyclical process helps to encourage and even require ongoing review, responsiveness, oversight, transparency and consistency amongst the stakeholders.

Good Governance Characteristics

Corruption destroys opportunities and creates rampant inequalities. It undermines human rights and good governance, stifles economic growth and distorts markets. UN Secretary-General Ban Ki-moon, The Kooza, December 7, 2012

The idea of governance is a basic principle for any type of organization. What constitutes "good governance" is a bit more subjective. There are many opinions with regard to what good governance actually looks like and how to appropriately measure it. One model of good governance that seems to capture most (if not all) of the elements commonly associated with the ideal of good governance is the United Nations eight Characteristics of Good Governance. These eight characteristics are considered to be core for establishing a foundation of good governance for any organization. The fact that these characteristics have been developed within an international multi-national entity like the United Nations further suggests that at minimum these characteristics should be looked at and perhaps even considered when trying to create an environment of good governance within an international, multi-national or complex organization. The United Nations eight characteristics are: (1) Accountable; (2) Transparent; (3) Responsive; (4) Equitable and Inclusive; (5) Consensus Oriented; (6) Participatory; (7) Rule of Law; and (8) Effective and Efficient (see also, Fig. 3, below).

These characteristics are not necessarily surprising. Over the past year or so, much of the activity relative to preventing sports corruption and match-fixing specifically, has focused on governance-type programs and initiatives.

Governance is very complex especially applied to non-governmental organizations and often involving self-governance. However, in its broadest sense, governance can be looked at as a system of oversight and the approach used to achieve

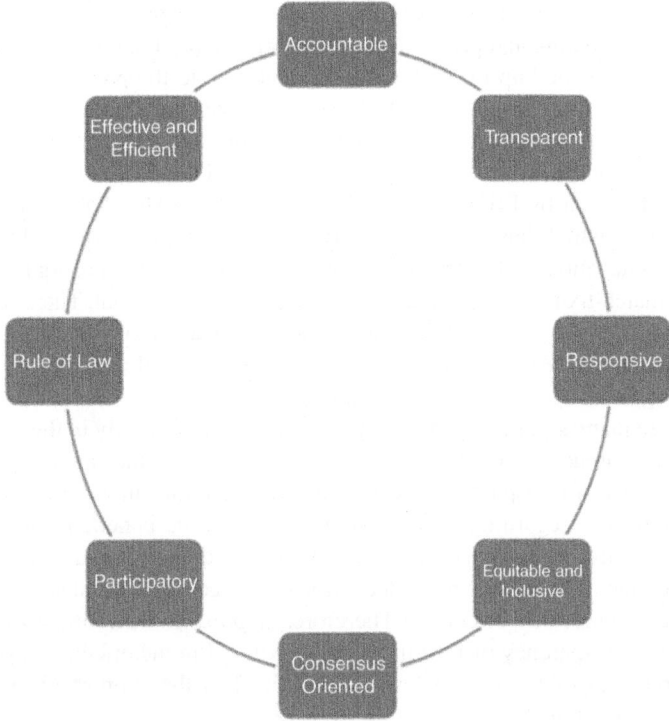

Fig. 3 United Nations eight characteristics of good governance (These characteristics are part of the United Nations model of Good Governance. The depiction of this information in the Figure was created by the author, Karen L. Jones, JD, MA, with all rights reserved)

specified goals. Because governance can occur in various contexts, it is important to identify the circumstances around the application of governance to better understand the specific requirements and components.

Good governance operates in such a way as to realize the goals of the organization and society. If sport is considered the "organization" and the goal is to prevent sports corruption, then there should be a process of governance of sport to achieve the goal that would then be applied across the organization of sport. The idea of sport as an organization is important to the application of governance. To apply governance to sport there must be a structure in place that can support the governance initiatives. What is meant by this is that in order to effectuate governance, especially good governance, there must be an identifiable organization associated with it. When that specific organization is identified and the governance goals applied, then there can also be an expectation of accountability.

Good governance in sport is a condition for the autonomy and self-regulation of sport organizations.[65]

---

[65] European Union, European dimension of sport (January 18, 2011, 4.1 Promotion of good governance in sport).

As discussed previously, several organizations have engaged in efforts to address the issue of combating and preventing sports corruption. In many cases sports organizations have teamed up to work towards a solution to the problem or at least to raise awareness amongst stakeholders. For example, the Deutsche Fusaballiga[66] joined forces with Transparency International to offer education and awareness to players and coaches in an effort to prevent match-fixing. It is worth mentioning again, the donation by FIFA of 20 million dollars to INTERPOL to help prevent match-fixing[67] which has resulted in initiatives around the world by INTERPOL to provide education and awareness as well as link institutional organizations to engage in match-fixing efforts.[68] Such approaches can be beneficial. There seems to be an effort to increase the accountability of sports organizations by these *pairings*. However, effectiveness of a true governance framework will require accountability within the governing sports organization itself.

There are many significant efforts that are occurring primarily in the area of education and awareness initiatives around match-fixing. Another area gaining some attention is that of transparency and how the organizations might more effectively share information regarding match-fixing that would be beneficial in supporting investigative efforts of law enforcement officials and sports organizations. These types of collaborations and concerted efforts are necessary to make any type of governance framework effective. Therefore, a *pairing* with organizations that increase the transparency of information that will aid in the effective investigation and enforcement of corruption laws is beneficial in the support of an effective governance structure.

Through various initiatives many of the characteristics of good governance as outlined by the United Nations are addressed within the governance efforts of sports organizations and others in the fight against sports corruption. As discussed previously with reference to joint efforts, part of the goal of these initiatives is to be participatory and responsive to the urgent need to address this issue. Recent studies and research, several sponsored by the European Commission, have addressed the limitations in the rule of law. Several sports governance organizations, such as FIFA, have established integrity boards and disciplinary chambers to assist in expediting the review and even investigation of match-fixing charges, allowing – at least to some degree – an opportunity to manage these issues effectively and efficiently.

Perhaps only suggested in the eight characteristics, but of critical importance to a pure concept of governance, is the issue of oversight. Accountability suggests that there might be a hierarchy, where at some point in the process (or perhaps at many points) someone must be responsible for the outcome or result, good or bad, and are therefore, theoretically always operating to ensure a good result throughout the process.

---

[66] German professional football leagues I and II.

[67] FIFA's historic contribution to INTERPOL in the fight against match-fixing, FIFA.com, Monday 9 May 2011.

[68] Id.

Two (2) Strategies: Options and Approaches

There are several potential strategies that can aid in supporting the compliance initiatives and governance activities engaged by various sports governing organizations.
However, two strategies that are sometimes used to encourage consistency, oversight
an accountability are: (1) Accreditation (or Certification); and (2) Licensing.

Accreditation can be defined as: "Certification of competence in a specified subject or areas of expertise, and of the integrity of an agency, firm, group, or person,
awarded by a duly recognized and respected accrediting organization."[69] (Ex.
Education). An accreditation scheme will require a certain level of competence by
the organizations that are administering the governance initiatives. This is often
obtain through specific training where individuals are required to obtain a *certificate*
as acknowledgement that they completed the required training or other confirmation
of achieving a particular competence. When a governing organization accomplishes
the timely certification of its members, they receive *accreditation* for a stated period
of time. For the organization to maintain accreditation, its members must complete
accreditation requirements according to a pre-scribed schedule. Failure to do so
means a loss of accreditation. Certification is defined as: "Formal procedure by
which an accredited or authorized person or agency assesses and verifies (and attests
in writing by issuing a certificate) the attributes, characteristics, quality, qualification, or status of individuals or organizations, goods or services, procedures or processes, or events or situations, in accordance with established requirements or
standards."[70] Therefore, certification primarily occurs at the individual level.
Accreditation primarily occurs at the organizational level.

Licensing, on the other hand, can be defined as: To permit or authorize; give permission or consent to: allow. Licensing is often used in situations where there is an
intention of maintaining some sort of quality or product control. For example, in
many countries, the sale of liquor requires a license. The license is issued by the
appropriate governing body to allow for greater controls – or checks and balances –
in an effort to regulate in that particular area. Licensing also allows the governing
body to place conditions around achieving or obtaining the license to ensure certain
standards are met.

At present, accreditation, certification and licensing, are not heavily used in the
business of sports. Perhaps the area of sports that comes closest to utilizing these
measures is with sports agents. In some nations, sports agents are required to obtain
a license in order to operate as a sports agent.[71] Most sports require that agents are

---

[69] http://www.businessdictionary.com/definition/accreditation.html

[70] http://www.businessdictionary.com/definition/certification.html

[71] For example, in the United States, in many states, agents are required to be licensed in order to
operate as a sports Agent. The often receive the licensing and requirements through a governmental agency. Tennessee is one example of a state within the USA that requires sports agents to be
licensed. http://state.tn.us/sos/sportsagent.htm. Another type of licensing common in the sports
area is licensing of broadcasting rights.

also registered at the league level.[72] They must also meet certain continuing education and other requirements on a regular basis.[73] The use of such measures should be part of a broader governance scheme. Assessing the possible use of these measures will be addressed in the next section.

Assessing Possible Use of Licensing and/or Accreditation

There are a lot of opportunities for possible use of licensing and/or accreditation in efforts to help prevent sports corruption. In this section, those possibilities will be explored and considered relative to the pros and cons of engaging such an approach.

Data

Some of the data in this section was captured during a brainstorming session on Licensing and Accreditation Options/Approaches, facilitated by this author during a breakout session at the INTERPOL Experts on Sports Integrity Conference, November 2012, in Singapore[74]: Further research and analysis has been conducted to more thoroughly examine the issues and possibilities that these approaches might offer and entail.

Some of the questions that were posed during the session and further considered thereafter, include the following:

- What are some ways that we can use licensing and accreditation in the fight against match-fixing education and awareness?
- Do you think requiring certification and sign-off by players, coaches, referees, club officials, etc., will have a positive impact on raising awareness and prevent match-fixing?
- Do you think that sports organizations and anyone providing awareness and training in match-fixing should be certified?
- Do you think a condition of certification and/or licensing should require that the individual or organization will not bet on their own sport?
- If we agree that there should be certification or accreditation in sports match-fixing, what areas should be certified? What might the audit for certification look like (what should be the goals)?

---

[72] Gaines, M. and Media, D., What License Is Needed for Sports Management?, Houston Chronicle, http://work.chron.com/license-needed-sports-management-1412.html.

[73] *Id.*

[74] *INTERPOL Global Experts Meeting for Integrity in Sports, "Match-Fixing in Football: Prevention, Reduction, and the way forward Against Corruption in Sport", 28–29 November 2012, Singapore; working paper and session leader, Confessions of a Governance Guru: Why Compliance Mechanisms alone as a means to Prevent Match-Fixing, are not enough!;* See also, *Stamping out football corruption through education focus of INTERPOL experts meeting in Singapore,* 28 November 2012, INTERPOL, http://www.interpol.int/News-and-media/News-media-releases/2012/PR097.

- What might be some of the challenges to establishing a licensing or accreditation (certification) program?
- What can the academic community do to assist with this effort?

Although some good and beneficial discussion came out of the session, each of the questions above were not fully addressed. Therefore, I will use my knowledge in the area of governance, compliance and assessment to determine how licensing and accreditation might be beneficial in addressing the prevention of match-fixing, taking into consideration some of the discussion and outcomes from the brainstorming session.

Assessment

To appropriately assess you must first determine what is being assessed. The assessment method and criteria will depend on whether you are assessing an outcome or considering the possibility of engaging a process. In the present scenario the goal is to assess the possible use of engaging accreditation (or certification) and/or licensing as a means to assist in the prevention of match-fixing. Therefore, the methods and criteria for assessment should not be outcome-based since there are no outcomes. Instead the methods and criteria will be both critical of each of the methods, as well as comparative analysis across the methods to determine whether one or both might offer an appropriate, effective and/or beneficial approach.

Assumptions

This assessment begins with the following assumptions:

- A governance approach and structure is beneficial to the prevention of match-fixing;
- These measures alone will not establish a comprehensive governance scheme;
- These are the only two approaches being considered for purposes of this chapter;
- These two approaches would potentially be beneficial in the fight against match-fixing;
- There is no weighting of the results, so the approaches being assessed are treated as equally viable alternatives;
- Other aspects of program development (ex. Design, implementation, monitoring, etc.) are not being addressed – only conceptual consideration of these approaches is being addressed here (Picture 1).

General Information

In addressing this topic, it is important to identify the focus of the content and assessment. For purposes of applying the approaches of accreditation and licensing, training, education and awareness around match-fixing is the primary focus.

Picture 1 Taken during the Accreditation and Licensing Breakout Session, INTERPOL Experts Working Group, Singapore, November 2012

The first consideration for incorporating the use of these approaches, is who are the stakeholders that might be impacted by the approach, and which approach might be appropriate for a particular stakeholder?

Data Set I: Who?

	Accreditation	Certification	Licensing	Other
Players		X		N/A
Coaches			X	N/A
Management (ex. Club owners, sports orgs, etc.)		X		N/A
Medical staff				N/A
Technical staff				N/A
Board members		X		
Referees		X	X	N/A
Sports community (Fans)				N/A
Sports agents			X	N/A
External Objective Organization (ex. Independent consultant or INTERPOL?)	X			N/A
Betting operators (Brokers)		X	X	N/A

The components for Data Set I include the items to be assessed (X-Axis)[75] and to whom those attributes should be applied (Y-Axis).[76] The X-Axis is established criteria based on the information given. The Y-Axis was determined by identifying key stakeholders. Although this is not an exhaustive list for purposes of deriving key stakeholders in the area of sports, it was determined sufficient for identifying those most relevant and impacted by the issue of sports corruption and more specifically match-fixing.

Essentially what was determined by Data Set I above is that amongst the key stakeholders within the game of sport, all of those who are potentially impacted by match-fixing can potentially benefit from some form of overview or oversight scheme. Primarily, where that scheme involves training and awareness, this is relevant to all levels, perhaps to a lesser degree depending on the particular stakeholder. For example, a player may require an in-depth training on the topic of match-fixing, whereas, a fan may only need to be aware that such activities exist and that efforts are being made to prevent it. The distinctions between the degree of training or awareness amongst the various stakeholders are of particular importance and should be a key focus when considering developments in this area.

Data Set II: What?

In Data Set II we address the issue of what should be the subject or focus of the approach for each of the identified stakeholders. Here, the X-Axis is changed to reflect several options, accreditation, certification, licensing, or training. In all cases all of the actors will need to be "trained" however, the purpose of identification of training in this dataset is to identify those who might only be receivers of the training and not necessarily required participants in the other governance schemes. All of the items included in this Data Set II are relative to match-fixing prevention unless otherwise specified.

	Accreditation	Certification	Licensing	Training	Other
Players		X		X	
Coaches		X		X	
Management (ex. Club owners, sports orgs, etc.)	X			X	
Medical staff		X		X	
Technical staff		X		X	
Referees		X	X	X	Licensing might also be beneficial

(continued)

---

[75] Used here with non-mathematical date, to refer to the information that is represented horizontally in the chart.

[76] Used here with non-mathematical data, to refer to the information that is represented vertically in the chart.

(continued)

	Accreditation	Certification	Licensing	Training	Other
Sports community (Fans)	N/A	N/A	N/A	N/A	Only awareness required
Sports agents		X	X	X	Licensing might also be beneficial
External Objective Organization (ex. Independent consultant or INTERPOL?)	X	N/A	N/A	N/A	Establish the criteria
Betting operators (Brokers)		X	X	X	

From this Data Set II it is clear that most stakeholders require some level of *training,* however, what is also clear is the expectations around the various roles that the stakeholders should play in terms of facilitating the governance of the process. Management, or some external objective organization would be candidates for being responsible (and perhaps accountable) for governing the accreditation. Those directly involved in the *game* of sport, even if only in a support role (i.e. medical staff) should be required to obtain certification in their understanding around the problem of match-fixing. Only the sports community at large, primarily fans, would not require training, but instead only a lesser degree of awareness of the problem with no requirement of certification on the topic.

Data Set III: How?

This dataset deals primarily with the delivery methods for achieving the training or awareness. For purposes of differentiating, *training* refers to a more in-depth education in the area of match-fixing, or even more broadly sports corruption. *Awareness,* refers to a more limited exercise to introduce the general concept without requiring a more in-depth understanding. In the Data Set III, T or A refers to the level or nature of education, the X-Axis contains the options or delivery methods, the Y-Axis shows the targets of the content.

	Face-to-Face[a]	Computer-based[b]	Social media[c] (ex. YouTube)	Comments
Players	T			Insiders need to talk to insiders
Coaches	T			Needs to be an opportunity to ask questions
Management (ex. Club owners, sports orgs, etc.)	T			Possibility that something that is said will strike a chord
Medical staff		A		Interaction
Technical staff		A		
Referees	T			
Sports community (Fans)			A	
Sports agents		T		

(continued)

	Face-to-Face[a]	Computer-based[b]	Social media[c] (ex. YouTube)	Comments
External Objective Organization (ex. Independent consultant or INTERPOL?)		T		
Betting operators (Brokers)		T		

[a]This would take place in person, primarily to allow for greater interaction. There is some possibility that inter-active video conferencing may also be engaged, however, in-person training is the preferred method, because there is more to be gained from the ability to read body language, tension levels, and other non-verbal forms of communication that could provide "clues" to the facilitator on topics that need more in-depth coverage or greater discussion. Another aspect of Face-to-Face training to be considered and perhaps incorporated into the training model is that of Train-the-Trainer; creating certification training for trainers to perhaps gain greater access in more remote or less accessible areas
[b]A benefit for using computer-based training, is that the users can maintain anonymity. However, with this mode of delivery, ensuring that individuals are actually completing the training themselves (and not cheating) cannot be confirmed unless it is used in a controlled environment with additional safeguards. There is also no opportunity for person-to-person engagement, however, there may be some opportunities for interaction through the use of real life examples, case scenarios and even gaming, that put the user in a compromising situation. An additional limitation of computer-based delivery is that some countries and sports stakeholders may not have ready access to computers
[c]Social media can be a good tool for attracting the younger players and fans, and providing general awareness. Probably not the best source for any type of controlled certification
T Training, A Awareness

Generally, Face-to-Face training is preferred. This affords the attendees the opportunity to ask questions and potentially creates an environment of accountability; it is more difficult for fellow teammates to sit across from one another in training and agree not to engage in match-fixing, then go out and accept a bribe to throw a game. Also, Train-the-Trainer methods might also be helpful, to use the certification process to train other trainers that can then provide more onsite Face-to-Face training with greater access.[77]

For purposes of training and ultimately accreditation, the following items should be included in the curriculum:

• What is corruption? (establishing the "culture" and definition of corruption in sports – what is considered corrupt varies from country-to-country and community-to-community)
• Ethics (and integrity)
• Legal (laws as well as sports organization guidelines, regulations, etc.)
• Penalties (monetary, but also impacts on their career and future in sport, reputation, family, etc.)
• Benefits

---

[77]Id. at FN 71. Re-certification of "trainers" can be bi-annually or every five (5) years, with continuing education requirements defined, and the training itself carries with it greater requirements not only in fully understanding all aspects of the match-fixing problem, but also effective training on the topic, sensitivity to the various stakeholders, etc.

- Case studies "don't let this happen to you"
- Testimonials (ex. Whistle-blowers, those who thwarted approaches by match-fixers, etc.)

In Dataset III, the stakeholders identified to receive *awareness* are those who are indirectly associated with sport, and serve more of a support role (ex. medical staff, sports community, fans, etc.). It is also reasonable to provide this more general awareness via other means such as computer-based training in situations where certification may or may not be required, and via social media, when the goal is to reach a much larger population to simply inform.

Possible Uses

For purposes of match-fixing prevention the various approaches might be used as follows:

Accreditation

- Accreditation can provide some degree of governance and oversight for match-fixing prevention in the area of education;
- Universities might serve as accreditation agents, by offering training programs that help to certify sports organizations;
- Alternatively, some other independent organization might confirm accreditation requirements;

Certification

- Training entities might be required to receive a certificate in order to provide match-fixing training to the relevant stakeholders;
- Stakeholders may be required to obtain a certificate to show that they have engaged in the required training;
- Certification may be required at some specified interval of time – for example annually. This can also vary per stakeholder, for example annual certification for players, referees and coaches; bi-annual certification for management.
- Certification may also require the participants to sign a statement that "...they will not engage in match-fixing..." and if they are approached about match-fixing, they will "...contact the appropriate authorities...as outlined in their sports organization's code of ethics..."

Licensing

- Those who are delivering match-fixing training should be licensed to do so;
- Betting operators should be licensed to place bets, with match-fixing training as part of the licensing process;
- The licensing authority or the one issuing the license should be an independent governmental or non-governmental agency;

- Licenses should require period renewal; if an entity violates the conditions of the license it should be revoked. Certain violations should result in revocation of eligibility for receiving a license in the future;

The options and approaches using accreditation and licensing primarily in support of educational initiatives around the problem of match-fixing, is not exhaustive. This only serves to begin looking at ways that these measures might be used to support a larger governance scheme in the area of preventing match-fixing.

Summary and Conclusions

There is a general consensus that certainly in the area of training and awareness of match-fixing, accreditation and certification might offer some assistance. There is less enthusiasm in the area of adding licensing to this scheme, unless it is with specific reference to the licensing of betting operators in relation to offering a betting service to its constituents. Education in the area of match-fixing prevention is important. On-going and multi-level approach is likely to be the most beneficial.

The questions presented at the beginning of the previous section will serve as a framework to summarize and draw some basic conclusions:

What are some ways that we can use licensing and accreditation in the fight against match-fixing education and awareness?

- Licensing and accreditation (and certification) can be used as a means to establish some degree of oversight and accountability within sports organizations. Licensing can be used as a means of making certain requirements of various sports industry stakeholders. For example, a condition to receiving a license might be to engage in specified match-fixing training.

Do you think requiring certification and/or sign-off by players, coaches, referees, club officials, etc., will have a positive impact on raising awareness and preventing match-fixing?

- Yes. At minimum it is confirmation that they received the training with a certain degree of understanding, with the hope and expectation that engaging in this training with peers and signing-off via certification, creates an "agreement" that might be morally more difficult to violate.[78]

Do you think that sports organizations and anyone providing awareness and training in match-fixing should be certified?

---

[78] The certification process could incorporate signing-off on an "agreement" that might be similar to a morality clauses in contracts or similar to framework agreements that are used at the European or international level. The basis of the agreement might confirm that the individual has personally completed the required training on match-fixing, that they will not engage in match-fixing or related sports corruption activities, and if they are approached they will report to the appropriate individuals as covered in the training.

- Yes. Certification of sports organizations and anyone providing awareness training in match-fixing helps to establish important elements of good governance. It provides consistency, accountability and a degree of oversight.

Do you think a condition of certification and/or licensing should require that the individual or organization will not bet on their own sport?

- Yes. Since there is clearly a close connection between betting and match-fixing, one obvious way to assist in efforts by betting authorities to prevent match-fixing is to find a means of enforcing a universal rule in sports that restricts those directly involved in a sport from the ability to place a bet on a sports game that they are participating in or have any type of influence over.

If we agree that there should be certification or accreditation in sports match-fixing, what areas should be certified? What might the audit for certification look like (what should be the goals)?

- The areas of certification should focus on education on the dangers of match-fixing, and betting operators.

- The audit for certification might address the following:

  - Of all registered players, how many in your organization have completed the certification requirements?
  - Do you have an established process in place to manage the disputes that might arise?
  - How many match-fixing related charges have been raised within your organization?
  - Have related policies and procedures been updated within the past year?
  - Of all players who have signed-off on the training, how many have stated they have been approached about match-fixing?
  - Etc.

What might be some of the challenges to establishing a licensing or accreditation (certification) program?

Some challenges might include the following:

- Gaining a sufficient level of buy-in from all stakeholders (all key stakeholders must first be identified, see Data Set I above as a starting point);
- Identifying the appropriate agency or entity to take on the responsibility of providing oversight through this governance mechanism – some of the sub-questions for inquiry might be: Can sports organizations serve as the oversight agency for purposes of governance enforcement? Should oversight be the responsibility of an external pseudo-enforcement type agency such as Europol or INTERPOL? What other external organizations might be appropriate to serve in this oversight capacity?;
- Obtaining the necessary level of ownership from international and European sports organizations. This is an additional level of responsibility that also opens these sports organizations up to greater scrutiny and transparency –

there may be resistance from sports organizations to the idea of losing some of its coveted autonomy;

What can the academic community do to assist with this effort?

- The academic community can possibly become an accreditation authority, especially where sports and sports programs are most prevalent.
- At minimum the academic community can help develop and deliver a curriculum on the topic of match-fixing prevention, that goes beyond simply the does and don'ts;
- The academic community might also offer assistance in developing training modules that will be most effective in training each type of stakeholder – taking into consideration nationality and cultural differences;
- The academic community tends to be a well networked community. For purposes of gaining greater exposure across the sports sector, one way to do that is to engage academia.
- The academic community can be a source of on-going research and innovative approaches for effective training and education.

Final Thoughts

The information presented is this chapter is not comprehensive, nor is it intended to be an exhaustive examination of the licensing and accreditation options and approaches. At best, it presents a starting point for further examination into the use of these approaches as one part of a larger governance scheme focused on the prevention of match-fixing.

With regard to the methods of training, a modulated training program would provide some benefits since there are various stakeholders in need of varying levels of training. The creating of various modules that can be used individually or as a whole can allow for greater flexibility for meeting the needs of individual stakeholders. Perhaps only certain modules require re-certification with a particular frequency; or perhaps certain modules must be delivered Face-to-Face while others can be offered via computer-based or internet delivery. There are many options and the choice should be based on the most effective and efficient means towards achieving the ultimate goal. A complete training and awareness strategy should be explored and developed.

Amongst the many questions that are yet to be answered, a significant issue that remains is who will be the authority or governing entity to ensure the effectiveness of training and training delivery and how will they be held accountable? Answering this question will help to move closer to a governance model that incorporates a degree of oversight and accountability which has been missing from existing compliance initiatives, and establish a governance scheme that will truly be beneficial and more effective in the prevention of match-fixing.

References

Confessions of a Governance Guru: Why Compliance Mechanisms alone as a means to Prevent Match-Fixing, are not enough!; See also, Stamping out football corruption through education focus of INTERPOL experts meeting in Singapore, 28 November 2012, INTERPOL, http://www.interpol.int/News-and-media/News-media-releases/2012/PR097

European Commission, 18 January 2011, Communication, *Ibid.* at p12.

European Commission, Commission will do all it can to help tackle match-fixing and corruption in sports, says Vassiliou, 14 March 2013; http://ec.europa.eu/commission_2010-2014/vassiliou/headlines/news/2013/03/20130314-match-fixing-corruption-in-sport_en.htm

FIFPro Black Book Eastern Europe, The problems professional footballers encounter: research, FIFPro Services (2012) pp. 12–19.

Gaines, M. and Media, D., What License Is Needed for Sports Management?, Houston Chronicle, http://work.chron.com/license-needed-sports-management-1412.html, retrieved, June 2, 2013.

http://state.tn.us/sos/sportsagent.htm, retrieved June 2, 2013.

http://www.businessdictionary.com/definition/accreditation.html, retrieved June 5, 2013.

http://www.businessdictionary.com/definition/certification.html, retrieved June 5, 2013.

http://www.sportaccord.com/en/news/sportaccord-partners-with-iris-to-raise-awareness-on-match-fixing-in-european-countries-0-16844#sthash.IQUWPCfE.dpuf., retrieved June 5, 2013.

http://www.gamblingcommission.gov.uk/pdf/JAU%20report%20-%20March%202013.pdf?utm_source=EB%2B110313&utm_medium=email&utm_campaign=EB%2B110313%2Bjau, retrieved June 5, 2013.

http://www.businessdictionary.com/definition/corporate-governance.html, retrieved, June 10, 2013.

http://www.businessdictionary.com/definition/compliance-program.html, retrieved, June 15, 2013.

International Policing Organization, http://www.interpol.int/Crime-areas/Corruption/Integrity-in-Sport

Match-Fixing in Sports: A mapping of the EU 27 criminal law provisions, European Commission, March 2012; http://ec.europa.eu/sport/news/documents/study-sports-fraud-final-version_en.pdf

Sport and Recreation Ministers' Council Communiqué 2011

European Commission Study, Match-Fixing in Sports: A Mapping of Criminal Law Provisions in EU 27 (March 2012), p 9.

Topics for an Academic Agenda: The Prevention of Match Fixing in Brazil

Letícia Godinho and Cassio Barbosa

Abstract The recommendation of match fixing prevention strategies presumes a thoughtful understanding of the actors involved and the dynamics of the events and also of the specific functioning of the legal and sports institutions of each local context. In this chapter we consider the development of an academic agenda about match fixing in Brazil by discussing the Brazilian institutional architecture and its capacity to fight and prevent match fixing, including ordinary Justice System and Sports Justice institutions. To illustrate it, we explore three famous examples of match fixing events occurred in Brazilian soccer and the official reactions. The main goal of the chapter is to bring about policy recommendations at the light of the existing literature findings, in relation to Brazilian context and its institutional debilities. By doing this, we intend to identify a possible field of studies that could be carried out by Brazilian academe and deficient areas that should receive intellectual investment.

Introduction

The most accepted and simplest definition of *Match Fixing* proposes it to be a practice that *alters the natural progression of the result of a match*. In this sense, we can argue that preventing match fixing practices is of interest to clubs, to teams, to players, to supporters, once it refers to the viability of sports competitions.

L. Godinho (✉)
Joao Pinheiro Foundation,
Av Cel José Dias Bicalho, 444 – ap. 301, Belo Horizonte 31275-050, Brazil
e-mail: leticia.godinho@fjp.mg.gov.br

C. Barbosa
Federal University of Minas Gerais,
Av. Bias Fortes, 1603 – apto 1301, Belo Horizonte 30170-012, Brazil

M.R. Haberfeld and D. Sheehan (eds.), *Match-Fixing in International Sports:* 229
Existing Processes, Law Enforcement, and Prevention Strategies,
DOI 10.1007/978-3-319-02582-7_12, © Springer International Publishing Switzerland 2013

However, in terms of public security, we can also state that preventing match fixing is important once it is a practice linked to other forms of corruption and criminal behaviors, such as money laundering, drug trafficking and prostitution. Its connections to illegal arms and human trafficking markets have been also attested by investigations conducted in the recent years. These investigations, especially the ones led by international organisms as Interpol and Europol, have shown that the match fixing market represents today the largest earnings of the Asian syndicates and criminal organizations.[1]

The Interpol coordinated task forces operations in the year 2011 resulted in the apprehension of more than 1 billion dollars and more than 300 arrests. The 2011–2013s Joint Investigation Team (JIT) (Operation VETO), coordinated by European Police – Europol – and five European federal governments, organized multiple police inquiries resulting in 425 match officials, club officials, players and criminals suspected of being involved in attempts to fix more than 380 professional football matches. These activities were estimated to include over €10 millions in betting profits and corrupt payments to those implicated in very complex organized crime operations.

Although the focus of the most important current investigations is Europe, this is a worldwide spread practice in the field of sports. In Brazil, repercussions of known match fixing events occur mostly in soccer, due to the popularity of this sports modality in the country. Nonetheless, researchers also identify some indication of match fixing occurrence in all kinds of sports modalities practiced in Brazil.

The difficulties involved in match fixing investigation, reaction and prevention in Brazil face factors that are common to all other countries but also some specific ones. In what concerns the common factors, dealing with match fixing against the existence of clandestine structures and its connections to other legal and illegal markets and an international sphere of functioning which, supposedly, brings together different cultures of enforcement and faces cultural barriers, among others. When it comes to the specific factors, there are some very ambiguously oriented institutions in the field of Sports Justice, which are not adequately equipped to handle the matter and be sensitive enough to pay attention to it. In addition, there is not enough available data to engender deep investigations, whether it is in the academic or the criminal justice fields. The production of data is the first step to start curbing the problem; it can serve to catalyze academic investigations but also to create a political and legal agenda that highlights the importance of this theme for the institutions able to react and prevent.

Creating match fixing prevention strategies presumes knowing the actors involved and the dynamics of the events. The dynamic related to each specific actor involved will engender specific prevention strategies. For instance, we could think about strategies that work for players, but that will not be adequate for referees. The same is true in what concerns the bookies, gamblers, club managers and the general

---

[1] The International Police Organization – Interpol – indicates that the illegal betting market in Asia alone is worth up to 500 billion dollars.

public or sports' supporters. Thus, the development of an academic agenda about match fixing in Brazil must grasp what the general literature has already investigated so far and map out studies that are able to understand the dynamic of match fixing and its different actors in Brazil.

On the other hand, the development of an academic agenda in Brazil concerning match fixing must be able to include the specific functioning of the institutions that are present in the country and their ability to deal with this phenomena. The creation of such an agenda within the Brazilian academe certainly contributes to the betterment of the existing institutions and the development of new ones which might seem necessary. In essence, an academic research agenda has the important role of thrusting forward the debates and its own insertion within the political and judicial systems.

This chapter is divided into three sections. In the first section, we present a Brazilian panorama on match fixing and local institutional possibilities of fighting it. We briefly present the existing institutional architecture in Brazil, which could be related to fighting and prevention of match fixing. Subsequently, we explore the famous examples of match fixing events occurred in Brazilian soccer and the institutional "reactions" to them, as a way to illustrate its capacity to intervene.

In the second section, we present a review of the literature related to match fixing. The main purpose of this section is to briefly review some possibilities of research and policy oriented analysis of the still incipient academic activity in this area. Here, we also analyze the different focus of the existing studies.

We examine the policy recommendations for match fixing prevention presented in the literature at the light of Brazilian context and institutional debilities in the final section. By doing this, we intend to identify a possible field of studies that could be carried out by Brazilian academe as a way to contribute to match fixing prevention and by identifying deficient areas that should receive intellectual investment. For example, by better identifying and diagnosing its dynamics in Brazil and identifying the existing *lacunae* in institutional and legal architecture. By analyzing match fixing context in Brazil, the academic can assist the proposal of adequate means to fight it and be helpful in creating a public agenda on the theme.

Brazilian Institutions and Their Capability to Intervene

In this section, we present a brief landscape of Brazil institutional possibilities for dealing with match fixing. To show this, we shortly present the institutional architecture in Brazil that could be related to fighting and prevention of match fixing – Sports Justice and other Brazilian institutions of the criminal justice system. We also explore three known match fixing events that occurred in Brazilian soccer and the institutional "reactions" to them, as a way to illustrate its capacity to intervene.

There are two lines of interpretation when it comes the institutional-legal matters related to match fixing. The first states that specific laws or institutions are not necessary, because the ones designed to fight general corruption are sufficient. This position is held, for example, by the United Nations, more specifically, its Office on

Drugs and Crime (UNDOC). The second affirms that specific institutions or laws against match fixing give the problem visibility and make fighting the problem a central issue. Interpol defends this argument, stating that special legislation not only helps to detect and investigate this type of criminal activity but also gives some attention to the subject.

In Brazil there are no specific institutions directed at fighting and preventing match fixing, but there are institutions with more general attributes that could handle the task. In this chapter, we will discuss two sets of institutions: the first, institutions related to Sports Justice; the second, the several laws and actors related to fighting corruption in general.

The Sports Justice and Other Institutions Charged with Fighting Sports Corruption

The first reference to Sports Justice in Brazil was made during the military dictatorship, in 1975, with Law 6.251, which brought about general rules concerning sports. One of its articles stated that the control over sports and justice were the purview of the National Council for Sports, which was responsible for the regulation and organization of sports in the country. At the end of the dictatorship there was a pull to concede more autonomy to sports bodies, resulting in article 217 of the Federal Constitution of 1988. Article 217 says that it is the State's duty to advance formal and informal sport activities, as a citizen's right (*caput*). It also affirms that the Judicial Branch will only handle actions concerning sports matters and competitions after all the instances of Sports Justice, regulated in the first item of the law (§ 1°), have dealt with it. Furthermore, according to the Federal Constitution, Sports Justice has the competence for "prosecution and trial of disciplinary and sports competitions offenses" (art. 217 § 1°); other subjects, such as labor contracting disputes, are under the purview of the ordinary justice system. Sports Justice is also regulated by Federal Law, 8.672, from 1993, known as "Zico's Law", Federal Law 9.615, from 1998, known as "Pelé's Law", Federal Law 9.981/2000 and Federal Law 10.671/2003, the "Supporters Statute".

Articles 33 through 38 of Federal Law 8.672/1993, establish that the Sports Justice would be legally bound to the Confederations or Federations of each modality of sport, each with their own Sports Justice Court. The National Council for Sports, mentioned above, was closed, with the intention being to open the way for private leadership in the sports' field. The articles also create the structure of Sports Justice, with a two-level hierarchy, the Disciplinary Commissions, which rule the initial actions and the Sports Justice Courts, which rule the appeals.

Law 9.981, from 2000, ruled on the function of the Sports Justice Superior Court (STJD, in Portuguese), giving it purview over national and interstate competitions and also the appeals of disputes from the Sports Justice Courts (TJDs, in Portuguese). In 2003, the Supporte's Statute (Law 10.671/2003) brought about some changes to sports justice (articles 34 through 36) which, in essence, had the goal of giving more visibility to their actions:

> Art. 34. It is a right of the supporter that the Sports Justice bodies, when exercising their functions, attend to the principles of impersonality, morality, celerity, publicity and independence.
>
> Art. 35. The decisions made by the Sports Justice bodies must be, under all circumstances, justified and have the same transparency as the decisions of the federal courts.
> § 1º There is no secrecy when it comes to the cases before the Sports Justice.
> § 2º The decisions regarding the most prominent cases will be made available in the site mentioned in item § 1º of article 5th.
> Art. 36. Decisions that do not follow articles 34 and 35 will be null and void.

The institutional architecture of Sports Justice was finally established as follows. There is a Sports Justice Superior Court (*Superior Tribunal de Justiça Desportiva*, in Portuguese) with competence to rule on national and interstate competitions. Below it are the Sports Justice Courts (*Tribunais de Justiça Desportiva*, in Portuguese), with competence to rule on state competitions. There is one Sports Justice Court for each state sport's federation. The Disciplinary Commissions (*Comissões Disciplinares*, in Portuguese) are named by the STCs and are Regional Disciplinary Commissions and will be as many as needed for the original proceedings of the infractions.

Sports Justice is not attached to the "common" justice system and, because of that reason, there's a large dispute in the Brazilian legal academic field on its quality. One line of interpretation argues that Sports Justice is a private institution and, because of that, it is no more than an Arbitrage Court. Authors opposing to this interpretation say that the Sports Justice was constitutionally created to resolve conflicts in the sports' field and, being the object of public interest, cannot be considered "private justice" or a mere arbitrage instance. Among those who hold this argument, one line of interpretation states that it has a "semi-litigious" function, other that it has an administrative function only. The argument which states that Sports Justice has an actual judicial function has less supporters.

Be that as it may, amongst the rules that regulate the Sports Justice functioning, there is no clarity on what "disciplinary and competition offenses" mean, even though it is its sole function as determined by the Constitution. Additionally, the functioning of the Sports Justice in Brazil is poorly regulated. In practice, there is not one instance of public control over the actions of the Sports Justice.

Also a part of the set of institutions put in place to regulate sports in Brazil is the Sports Arbitrage Court, created by article 51 of the "Pelé's Law" (Federal Law 9.615/1998), established in 2005 with a mediating quality (Arbitrage Court) and kept by the Brazilian Olympic Committee (*Comitê Olímpico Brasileiro*, in Portuguese). However, the COB is not a part of the Sports Justice or bound by it. This instrument was created to fulfill the recommendations of the International Olympic Committee with the goal of impeding interventions by the Brazilian government, meaning the Sports Justice and the ordinary justice, in the National Sports Committees.

The Court has competence to judge on matters related to the Olympics, the Pan-American games, the South-American games and any other sports competitions of equal nature. It also judges conflicts between the National Bodies and affiliated Federations, club managers, athletes, and trainers with the Brazilian Olympic Committee. It can also judge on conflicts between the mentioned bodies with third parties with which they may have established contractual relationships or are bounded together by legal dispositions.

Thus, International Olympic Committee and Brazilian Olympic Committee create institutions and rules that clearly come in conflict with the nationally instituted system – regardless of the nature of the Brazilian sports justice. International Olympic Committee's stance on turning to the Arbitrage Court is in clash with Brazilian law and the notion of soccer as a public interest.

On the other hand, Brazil has already a legal framework for fighting corruption, broadly speaking. The Brazilian institutions held responsible for investigating and fighting corruption are: the Federal Police, the Ministry of Justice, the Central Bank and the Secretariat of the Federal Revenue of Brazil, as institutions from the Executive Branch; the Federal Court of Accounts of Brazil and the National Council of Justice as institutions from the Judicial Branch; and the Federal Public Ministry, as an autonomous institution.

As for the Justice System, which involves a diverse set of institutions, it leans on an important variety of laws.[2] A compilation of the main laws that fight corruption include: firstly, the Brazilian Federal Constitution, which regulates corruption in the Public Administration (mainly in its articles 37, 317 and 333, among others); secondly, Federal Law 7.492/1986, which defines and establishes procedures regarding crimes against the National Financial System; thirdly, the Federal Law 9.612/1998, which deals with what is known as "money laundering". Also, the Federal Law 9.034/1995 is cast to establish the operational resources to prevent and fight actions held by criminal organizations – which sets the basic procedures and rules for accessing data, documents and tax information, banking, financial and electoral; environmental interception of electromagnetic signals, optical or acoustic, its recording and analysis – under judicial authorization, as well as infiltration by police or intelligence in research tasks, under judicial authorization. Finally, the International Conventions Brazil has signed, from which should be mentioned the United Nations Convention Against Corruption (signature ratified in 2005) and the Inter-American Convention Against Corruption (signature ratified in 2002).

It is out of the scope of this chapter to debate the adequacy of this legislation to cope with corruption in a broader sense. Nonetheless, in the following section, we will attempt to considerate its capacity to intervene over match fixing by showing how the above related institutions worked on actual cases of football match fixing, which were held as standpoints in its history.

---

[2] Brazilian law broadly define corruption as a kind of fraud – a malpractice in the criminal, civil or procedural field, by deception or bad faith, with the goal of prejudicing the state or third parties or to flee the performance of an obligation.

Three Cases: The "whiter" the Collar the More Ineffective the Justice Institutions?

The cases briefly summarized in this section are to serve as an example of three important occurrences or alleged occurrences of match fixing in Brazilian soccer, which is considered the most important or popular sport in the country. Because of that, those are the main cases, amongst a few, that have found publicity in the media and, probably for that sole reason, were investigated in the least. The institutional reactions were, however, very different in each case. The explanatory hypothesis we would like to present, at the end of the section, looks to relate these institutional reactions to the different political and economic interests involved in each case.

– The Ivens Mendes Case (1997)

The so called Ivens Mendes Case occurred in year 1997, and involved an official from the Brazilian Soccer Confederation (Confederação Brasileira de Futebol – CBF) and two team managers. In that year, a major Brazilian television network broadcasted a recording of a telephone conversation of an alleged negotiation of results of matches from the Brazilian Nation League. Ivens Mendes, the President of the National Arbitrage Commission, the agency in charge of appointing the referees for soccer competitions organized by CBF, had promised to favor some of the teams in the competition, in exchange for money to finance his campaign for the Brazilian National Congress.

The Commission for Education, Culture and Sports of the Federal Chamber of Deputies created a Special Sub-commission to investigate the complaint. There were eight public hearings, but the Sub-commission never heard from Ivens Mendes, who refused to appear. The hearings were never officially concluded and there was no final report, only a very generic protocol that was never voted upon by the congress people.

In the Ordinary Justice system the claim did not go forward, since the only evidence of a crime were clandestine recordings, which were considered inadmissible. In the Sports Justice, the case appeared before the Supreme Court of Sports Justice, which banned Ivens Mendes from football for life. The two other team managers involved, Mário Celso Petraglia (Atlético/PR) and Alberto Dualib (Corinthians) were barred from representing their teams before the Brazilian Soccer Confederation, but the decision did not affect their participations on the boards. Atlético/PR started the Brazilian Championship of 1997 with five negative points as punishment for Mr. Petraglia actions. The demotion of the teams Fluminense and Bragantino to Series B was revoked.

– The *CPI* (Parliamentary Commission of Investigation) on CBF-Nike Contract (2000)

A Parliamentary Commission of Investigation (CPI, in Portuguese) created to investigate the regularity of the contract between Brazilian Soccer Confederation (*CBF*, in Portuguese) and Nike was requested to convene in March 11th of 1999. A CPI is an investigation conducted by the Brazilian Parliament, with its own powers of investigation separate from the judicial authorities, with the goal to assess the claim and, if it is necessary, direct it to the Public Ministry to charge civilly or criminally the parties involved.

The aforementioned CPI was created in October of 2000, 19 months after it was requested to convene. There was indeed a great resistance to its creation, including during its proceedings, and it was faced with several difficulties and obstacles of various types that impeded the smoothness of the investigation, including threats of being shut-down.

The object of the CPI investigation was the signing, in mid-1996, of a contract between CBF and the multinational company Nike. The contract regarded a sponsorship and support agreement, between Nike Europe B.V. and the Brazilian Football Confederation, negotiated by Traffic Communications Advisor. According to the contract, Nike became cosponsor with CBF, having use of the image of the Brazilian football team, as well as endorser and sole provider of sport gear for CBF. The suspicions regarding the contract came about mainly when it was alleged that this contract gave Nike ample powers over the national team and its performance during the World Cup of 1998, in France.

The reach of the company went as far as drafting, line-up, scheduling of events that cancelled training, choice of opponents, determining dates and places of the matches. The contract also made available to Nike not only the main Brazilian soccer team, but also the sub-17 and sub-20 teams, as well as the women's team. Thus, suspicions were raised that CBF had ceded control over the Brazilian team to Nike, including the agreement upon clauses that were deemed excessive concerning the predominance of Nike's interests over CBF's, with damaging results to Brazilian soccer. CBF's and Nike's contract was signed in 1996, with a 10-year span, amounting to 160 million U.S. dollars and 150 million U.S. dollars' worth of "sports marketing" to be done by Nike. It also included 10 million U.S. dollars in payment to Umbro, a fine for rescission of the contract, 5 million U.S. dollars of sports gear to be handed over to CBF and 1 million U.S. dollars for the provision of transport vehicles for CBF delegations anywhere in the world during the contract, amounting to 326 U.S. dollars. There was also a provision that established payment of 43 million U.S. dollars in the case of an extension of the contract for another 4 years, amounting to 369 U.S. dollars total, for a 14-year contract (Azevedo and Rebelo 2002).

An example of the excessiveness of the contract is the clause that made CBF draft eight players under an undefined criterion which could be defined by Nike. In another clause, CBF gave Nike the preference of choosing the opponents and the places for 50 amicable matches over 10 years. Also, CBF was not allowed to schedule any matches in the United States, Japan, Korea or any other European country if Nike had already scheduled matches in the same places in the same year.

The CPI report concluded that, in the light of Brazilian sports legislation, the contract was in conflict with the principles of the importance of educational sports results and principles of citizenship and physical and moral development; it also conflicted with the principle of sports jurisdiction and management (Pelé's Law). In other words, it was questioned "if and how the CBF-Nike contract subjugated sports outcome (in its broader sense) to capital interests and marketing principles" (Comissão Parlamentar de Inquérito 2001). From a formal and legal standpoint, the contract had many other fundamental irregularities, such as being signed by a private entity of a foreign country in a location undisclosed by the signing parties. That would have resulted in an image of the Brazilian football team being associated with a foreign sports equipment company "implicating the commercial exploitation of the sentiment of a population" (Comissão Parlamentar de Inquérito 2001), as well as matters related to tax evasion. Finally, the third party involved, Traffic, more than just a middleman, became "holder of certain registered brands and other Property Rights belonging to CBF, which were of interest to Nike to obtain. (…) Traffic holds CBF's legal rights. So (…) we cannot sign a contract with CBF, once we are interested in acquiring rights that belong to Traffic. Thus, it has to be a part of the contract", admitted a Nike representative in a testimony given to the CPI (Comissão Parlamentar de Inquérito 2001).

When it comes to the claim of match fixing, it was about investigating if there was an alteration of the "natural outcome" of the sports results. That means, as stated previously, if and how the CBF-Nike contract subjugated the sports results to the interests of the company. That suspicion was raised specifically towards the final World Cup match of 1998 between Brazil and France. According to the CPI investigation, the star player, Ronaldo, had a seizure 7 h before the match, an event which involved millions of dollars. The medical crisis would have occurred exactly after lunchtime, when the team's doctors had come in. Oddly, no tests were done, no medication prescribed. Three hours after feeling ill, the player was finally taken to a private French neurological clinic. The trainer decided to put Ronaldo in the line-up based on the exam results from the clinic's doctors that did not veto the player's participation in the match. According to the CPI report, the decision to have Ronaldo playing was made based on Nike's interests – amongst them, the release of a new football boot during the match. The Technical Commission endangered the player's health in order to adhere to the business needs involved (Comissão Parlamentar de Inquérito 2001).

The CPI lasted for 8 months and reached no practical conclusions at all – there was no inquiry by the Public Ministry to investigate the responsibilities of the parties involved. There was only one case opened by the Federal Police and the tax authorities to investigate contractual irregularities which are not resolved whatsoever.

– Referee Edílson Pereira de Carvalho Case (2005):

The case that had soccer referee Edílson Pereira de Carvalho brought up on charges in the criminal justice system was also know in Brazil as the "Whistle Mafia". The scheme for manipulation soccer results was discovered by the attorneys from the Nucleus of Organized Crime Fighting of the Judicial System, along with the Federal Police Department. The investigation became public through a news article in the Brazilian weekly magazine "Veja", in October 2005. A group of investigators "dealt" with referee Edílson Pereira de Carvalho, part of the FIFA roster, to ensure results that were betted on through websites. Another referee was discovered as a participant in the scheme, Paulo José Danelon.

According to the investigation done by the Public Ministry, all matches refereed by both men were corrupted. The long and detailed report from the main person being accused, Edílson Pereira de Carvalho, was the principal piece of evidence obtained.

Wiretaps were placed by the police, but only after he had already refereed 20 out of 26 matches from that year and Banelon, 14 out of 15 matches. The telephones that were tapped belonged to the bettors Nagib Fayad, leader of the Mafia, and one of his partners, Daniel Gimenes, as well as the two referees. The wiretaps pointed to frauds in the results of two matches and attempted fraud of another – the criminals had discussed previous matches. The recording also showed that Pereira de Carvalho offered to defraud three matches, but the Aebet website, which was used to place the higher bets of the Mafia, did not cash them, because they suspected a scheme. However, the leader of the Whistle Mafia kept his own betting establishments and said in a deposition that, if Aebet closed betting on Edílson's matches, it was always possible to find another website to take them. Fayad also said that Edílson himself placed bets, which means he sold the victory of a team to Fayad and then betted on the victory of the opposing team (Placar 2005).

In the Sports Justice the case resulted in the annulment of 11 matches referreed by Edílson Pereira de Carvalho; however, none of Paulo José Danelon's matches, in Series B, were annulled. Both were expelled from soccer and accused by the Public Ministry of larceny, conspiracy to commit a crime and fraudulent misrepresentation. Nonetheless, the penal action was suspended in 2007 by the São Paulo Justice Court which understood that the evidence did not show a crime of larceny. This decision closed the investigation of the conspiracy charge.

The three cases discussed about alleged occurrences of match fixing in Brazilian football show different institutional reactions, which seem to depend upon the political and economic interests involved. In the first case, which involved two team managers and the president of the National Arbitrage Commission resulted, simply, in the banishment of the parties from football, at least as team representatives before the CBF – however they were able to still hold administrative functions. There was no case and, therefore, no consequences in ordinary justice. Beyond that, this case underscores two important points. The practice of match fixing with the objective to finance a political campaign to the National Congress shines a light on a common occurrence in Brazil: the existence of political representatives who are, at the same time, team directors. Although this is not illegal or morally condemnable, it is indicative of a typical characteristic of corruption crimes: the attempt by the involved parties to engrain themselves in the political system, so that their "political commodities" can be traded in illegal and legal markets that surround their network.

The second case, the Nike-CBF contract, developed into a CPI that faced an ample amount of limitations and obstacles in order to move forward. Even having the media's publicity about a case that shook up Brazilian soccer, the results of the investigation led by the CPI did not lead to the opening of a judicial process, whether in the ordinary or in the Sports justice.

Finally, the case of selling results of Brazilian Championship matches by FIFA referee Edílson Pereira de Carvalho resulted in his expulsion from soccer and in the annulment of the matches he refereed by the Sports Justice. However, that decision was inconsistent given that the matches refereed by the other referee involved, also banned from soccer, were not annulled. It is important to note that, as in the other cases, ordinary Brazilian justice was no able to bring criminal charges, which shows, possibly, a significant level of institutional debility.

Thus, for the next section we have selected some academic studies on match fixing. Our goal is to shed some light on the possibilities for action by the academy in order to improve effectiveness of the institutions that exist to fight and prevent match fixing. The specifities of this action in the Brazilian context will be the subject of the final section of this chapter.

Academic Studies on Match Fixing

In this section, we identify some analytical possibilities presented by the still incipient academic studies in the field of match fixing. The section is not meant to comprise an extensive revision of the literature, but to draw attention to the diversity of potentials in this academic field. In the last section of the chapter, we come back to this literature to stress the possible policy contributions of the studies, after contextualizing the institutional situation of Brazil.

We should start this review by stating that there are not any empirical studies in Brazil on this theme; the existing literature is concentrated on legal exegetic issues. Thus, the literature is cast to interpret the legal norms related to sports' rights and Sports Justice, not having a critical stance when it comes to the institutions and legal norms about the subject. In the international literature, we can find studies with different focuses, be that the methodological tools used to analyze the match fixing events (statistics, documental, theoretical or qualitative approaches), the object of the study – studies have been conducted on the various agents of match fixing agents (players, referees, officials, bookies) or the dynamics concerned (the bribing dynamics, the betting, the booksmarket, etc.).

One particular kind of study in the academic field attempted to analyze match fixing from an economic perspective, using rational choice theory and public choice theory arguments. When analyzed in this way, match fixing is seen as a "market", with the supposition that its intent and the choice of actions are based on the incentive structure that is offered, the risks and rewards that are presented. In this sense, Preston and Szinmanski (2003: 617) identify three main motivations to fix a match:

- First, when one side wants to win and for this it is inclined to make side payments to persuade the other not to make an effort to win, or to persuade the referee to take favorable biased decisions;
- Second, the agent – being either players, referee or officials – are eager to gain financially from the result of the match;
- Third, a competitor needs to produce a particular kind of result in a match other than winning, because of the convenience of the result in the wider context of tournament.

From this perspective, Hosmer-Henner condemns match fixing, arguing that it

... reduces the interest of fans who cease believing that the games reflect actual, fair competition and instead believe that the games are staged contests like professional wrestling matches. Whether players throw games to ensure the other team wins or merely reduce effort to affect the game's final margin (point shaving), the viability of professional and amateur sports is jeopardized when the uncertainty of the game's outcome is completely or partially eliminated (Hosmer-Henner 2010: 33).

Preston and Szimanski, in a theoretical paper that looked to establish a "cheating in contests" theory by turning it into a mathematical model, posited three types of agents involved in match fixing, which are the bookmaker, the punters and the sports player, in this way defined:

> The bookmaker is a local monopolist setting odds for a number of small punters. The bookmaker sets odds on the event that a certain sporting outcome occurs. Punters form beliefs about whether the game has been corrupted and choose whether to bet (Preston and Szimanski 2003: 621).

Also interested in developing a theoretical model of the criminal dynamics involved in match fixing, Hosmer-Henner recommends that to reduce game fixing, policymakers can affect four dimensions. The first, to be reduced, is the availability of betting opportunities; the other three, to be increased, are: the attached civil and criminal penalties; the probability of detection, the fines or salary forfeited (Hosmer-Henner 2010: 32). In the model considered, the threat of civil and criminal penalties and the fines and loss of salary, would act as deterrents to potential game-fixers (Hosmer-Henner 2010: 34). Hence, the author recommends a combination of public and private strategies: the public regulatory framework determines the level of civil and criminal penalties for offenders while the sports leagues determine the private penalties that apply to the athletes, coaches and referees (*idem*).

Preston and Szimanski (2003: 618) note that "design issues" can affect the structure of opportunities to fix the matches. Each sport has a way to define its competitions but some of them are structured in a way that can create incentives to match fixing. Subsequently, these eventual costs need to be scrutinized when thinking about the systems and set of rules of a league's tournament.

When it comes to betting opportunities, there are authors who are against prohibiting them. Rebeggiani (2009) and Hosmer-Henner (2010) develop a theoretical argument using an economic perspective. Although gambling is usually held responsible for a great part of the occurrence of match fixing, Hosmer-Henner argues that prohibiting sports betting is both ineffective and counterproductive. The argument is developed taking into consideration the case of the state of Nevada, US:

> Gambling does create the incentives to fix games, but less than one percent of sports bets placed by Americans are wagered legally in Nevada. The remainder of bets are placed outside the regulated system, thus, potential game-fixers would not be prevented from betting upon the contests they rig. Worse, prohibiting sports betting in Nevada would eliminate the most effective method of detecting game fixing. Nevada sports books have been instrumental in uncovering game-fixing scandals when irregular betting patterns raised suspicions. Nevada sports books share a mutual interest with law enforcement and the sports leagues in combating game fixing because they are the financial victims of game-fixers. Yet despite the alignment of interest, Congress and the sports leagues have called for the abolition of Nevada's sports books rather than formalizing mutually beneficial relationships with them (Hosmer-Henner 2010: 31).

Preventing match fixing would then also be important for the betting market, given that match fixing represents a threat to the financial viability of sports books. A fixed match "allows bettors with knowledge of the fix to wager without risk; every dollar these bettors win is a loss for the sports book" (Hosmer-Henner 2010: 32).

Moreover, the author maintains that the demand for sports wagering depends upon the perception among bettors that the contest is fair. It is hoped that bettors "migrate" from sport types or places to ones that offer uncorrupt games to bet upon. Thus, he concludes that both sport leagues and sport books have equal incentives to prevent match fixing.

> Sports betting itself does not threaten the integrity of sports, it can exist as an independent activity that is completely separate from the games. Harm arises only when sports and gambling become entangled. Maintaining independence between sports and gambling is positive for both sides and can be accomplished through cooperation to eliminate game fixing (Hosmer-Henner 2010: 38).

The author recommends then to improve the understanding of how each other's industry operates and to share information that is relevant to the integrity of sports betting: "Sports books can help prevent game fixing if they are viewed as allies to work with, not enemies to work against" (Hosmer-Henner 2010: 38). He exemplifies strategies that follow this idea: one of the commissioners of the NFL had a special telephone line by which informed gamblers and handicappers could call to report fixed games; the International Olympic Committee signed agreements with major betting companies to monitor irregular gambling and established a special unit to check for suspicious betting patterns in preparation for the 2008 Beijing Games (*idem*). The last also occurred in the preparation of 2012 London Olympic Games.

The empirical work of Scoppa (2008) dedicates itself to analyze one special agent of match fixing dynamics, the referee and its behavior in the Italian soccer league ("Series A"). The author used data for the 2003–2004 and 2004–2005 seasons of the Italian soccer league "Series A" and data on extra time assigned by the referee at the end of the match and controlling for factors which may influence it (players substitutions, yellow and red cards, penalty kicks, etc.). The existence of favoritism could be strongly detected in the study: the author concluded that football referees were not impartial between home and visiting teams and also between "big" teams and smaller teams.

The study showed that when home teams were losing in "close games", referees tended to add significantly more extra time (around half a minute), giving the home team more chances of equalizing. The refereeing bias increased greatly when there was no running track in the stadium and the crowd was close to the pitch.

Also following the 2006 "Series A" Italian soccer scandal, the study also tested whether favoritism emerged towards teams suspected of connections with referees, finding that these teams obtained favorable decisions – although when considered jointly the effects of favoritism towards home teams and towards suspected teams, he deduced that favoritism towards "big" teams was less pronounced than favoritism towards home teams. Nonetheless, the expected number of matches altered were 10.2. Attributing to the referee bias the goals scored after 3.62 min, the study was able to identify seven matches in the sample which could be considered as being altered because of refereeing bias: four games in 2003–2004 season and six games in the 2004–2005 season, leading to the conclusion that some teams were effectively helped and others were penalized.

Other works can be cast to exploring how the low wages of players can serve as factors that incentivize corruption. In the case of players, it is also worth noticing that, although a great amount of the focus is put on the referee or the athlete, these should be seen as the "weak" parts: beyond the monetary gains, to fix the match is frequently a condition practically imposed to evolve in the career.

The work of Boeri and Severgnini (2011) follows this direction. The article assumes that referees play a crucial role in match rigging because they provide a relatively high probability of successful fix as they retain considerable leverage in deciding over penalty and disciplinary tools, including adding extra time, and their co-operation in match fixing can be obtained at a lower cost than the co-operation of soccer players. So the study analyzes the assignment of the referees to the most important matches, as an important step in their career, and relates this choice to the performance of referees in previous matches and the evaluations they received in this context. The article finds that referees involved in match rigging were promoted to top games and that their evaluation was not negatively affected by their involvement in documented episodes of match fixing (Boeri and Severgnini 2011: 349–50).[3]

Theoretically, the decisions taken by the referees in each match are based on several factors related to both their ability and the experience and the characteristics of the match. The results of the studies indicate that intermediate referees (in comparison with "less degreed" and "top" referees) are in a crucial phase of their career; also that a higher grade for the referee increases the probability of being involved in Series A versus Series B, but has no effect on the selection for Griglia A games. However, the regressions' results indicated that past involvement in fixed matches implied a higher probability of being chosen for Griglia A matches for referees at intermediate career levels, that is, precisely those who are waiting for promotion to an international standing (Boeri and Severgnini 2011: 352–357).

The involvement of referees and linesmen in match fixing could be penalized by official evaluations of their performance. Receiving a lower grade in these evaluations could imply a lower probability of being selected for First Division games. But further tests indicated that, on the contrary, involvement in fixed episodes did increase the likelihood of being selected in Grid A games and did not yield a negative official evaluation (Boeri and Severgnini 2011: 358). The author concludes that the results of the study indicated that career concerns may function as incentives to fix a match (such as financial bribes), which reduces substantially the monetary outlays involved in it (Boeri and Severgnini 2011: 358).

---

[3] The collected data included information on referees' and linesmen's personal characteristics and career paths; their decisions during each match was obtained from the websites and printed editions of Italian daily newspapers; referees' and linesmen's grades were collected from the official evaluations provided by the Italian Referee Association; the Team Performance Index, IVS, obtained by the Panini group; the list of the matches being rigged drawn from official judicial records (Boeri and Severgnini 2011: 350).

The recommendations of the study suggest the monitoring of the behavior of agents who are in a crucial phase of their career (Boeri and Severgnini 2011: 358), which could refer to referees as much as to athletes. In the case of soccer, the authors advise to create more transparency regarding the decisions on the allocation of referees to games, their promotion to an international standing and their official evaluations as means to reduce sports corruption (Boeri and Severgnini 2011: 358).

The Role of Academe in Formation of More Effective Policies in Brazil

In this final section, we try to draft some recommendations for match fixing prevention within the Brazilian context and institutional weaknesses. In the second section, we overviewed some empirical studies that could be replicated by Brazilian academe and that offer distinct possibilities of investment in this field.

The contributions of academic investigation to match fixing fighting and prevention are larger than can be imagined. One of the main reasons for the soaring difficulty of detection of this kind of offense is tied to the fact that analyzing the game replay for search of evidence is an infertile strategy. Due to the "subjectivity" of the performance of decisions and the virtual impossibility of determining if an athlete misacted on purpose, statistical expertise has been showing itself as the most successful detection technique currently involved in law enforcement cases (Hosmer-Henner 2010: 36). As an example, we can point to the sports books of Nevada, as indicated by Homer-Henner (*idem*) or the Sports Radar recent initiative,[4] amongst others.

The empirical studies can expose the agents or dynamics involved in fixing matches in different kinds of sports. Based on the assumption that each dynamic has different aspects involved, they will demand the creation of specific prevention strategies, including identifying more vulnerable parts, usually players and referees. A survey conducted in 2000 showed an impoverishment of the Brazilian national football player; also that only 3.7 % of professionals players (765 of the 20,496) registered in CBF received more than US$1400 per month (Folha de Sao Paulo 2000 in Azevedo and Rebelo 2002). A 2011 FifPro survey indicated that 12 % of the professional football athletes had already received proposals to fix the match and 23.6 % knew cases of match fixing inside his club, showing a high correlation with bad payments – 55 % of them were not paid or had their payment delayed (Van Meegen 2012).

That is a reason why it is important also to render support to qualitative research. This kind of studies can also identify deficient institutions or fragile dimensions that should receive more invested attention. By analyzing match fixing context in Brazil the academe can, more specifically, assist with the proposals of policy recommendations and adequate means to fight it but also be fundamental in creating a public

---

[4] http://www.sportradar.com

agenda on the theme. It is a consensus that other important constraints to the existence of adequate reactions to match fixing events are the still low priority of this theme in the justice system – law enforcement institutions in Brazil have no history of intervention in this area – and, consequently, there is an absence of economic and political resources specially directed for this task.

These limitations have to deal with low levels or even no levels at all of transparency in the matter of sports, a dimension that gets deeper as more sports become an attractive economic market. The high commoditization of sports in the last years has increased the risks of match fixing and other forms of corruption. Transparency in the criteria of choosing match referees is only one aspect, as pointed out by Boeri and Severgnini (2011). However, for the Brazilian context we should also discuss the question of budgets of sports leagues and the public betting system, keeping in mind that they deal with public interest matters.

The entities that organize and control sports in Brazil – notably Brazilian Football Confederation (CBF) – have had several diagnoses by sports experts and academics of being non-transparent, non-responsive and not accountable. Added to it there is the fact that the performance of sports organizations are used for governmental or/ and public institutions promotion, for example, state enterprises that sponsor sports leagues in Brazil. There is also, the already mentioned involvement, by sports managers in elected public offices, and the intervention of lobbyists and of interests groups that taint the law enforcement. Further, it is important to develop mechanisms to ensure that law enforcement is armed against the lobbies, as well as against the self-interested politicians who are also sports managers. Also that federal government incentives to the sports activities (including financial ones) occur in accordance with Brazilian sports legislation. These processes have to occur with transparency, which is not the general rule. Legal mechanisms could be created to constrain such organizations for the full disclosure of the information concerning the way they operate.

Other existing difficulties to ensure transparency in the Brazilian setting are: the increasing incidence of non-transparent sponsoring contracts between public agencies and sports associations or clubs and the increasing incidence of non-transparent transferences of athletes to European clubs, mainly Eastern ones. In this instance there is a need to implement mechanisms to ensure transparency and publicity of the contracts involving public entities is crucial. This could also be applied to the contracts of broadcasting rights of sports competitions played in Brazil. The creation of mechanisms for more equitable distribution of the image-rights of the clubs within the competition should be instituted, so that the access to such resources could provide greater competitiveness to championships and, at the same time, reduce the probability of occurrence of corruption in these negotiations.

With regard to the difficulties of controlling the public betting system in Brazil, it is worth noting the increase in receiving of the prizes and destination of its profits, given that there are several indications of malfunctioning and suspicions of results fixing and other irregularities associated with the procedures of public gambling system. This should cause the implementation of mechanisms to ensure an adequate functioning of public betting systems and tools for the clubs to publish their financial statements so they can be able to enroll themselves in the Lottery system.

The current version of the sport, its links to the market and different moral values, introduced new features such as heterogeneous and exacerbated marketing practices. It also developed a new sphere of gentrification of practices, based on rules of marketing and buying power (Marques et al. 2009).

Ensuring sports integrity depends on the fact that sport competitions must not be determined by economic interests; individual actors, including sponsors and investors must not have too much influence on the associations, clubs and sport federations (Mineps V – Commission III Recommendations 2012). However, it also depends on building a sports integrity culture. In this sense, academe has a fundamental role in actively promoting the transmission of moral values related to the integrity-building dimension of sport itself. Not only tools directed at the education of the public against match fixing can be developed, but other educational strategies, such as those that construct "role models" for minors, can be designed by academe to build integrity in a broader sense.

References

Boeri and Severgnini (2011). Match rigging and the career concerns of referees. *Labour Economics*, 18, pp. 349–359.

Comissão Parlamentar de Inquérito (2001). *Relatório Final da CPI "destinada a investigar fatos envolvendo as associações brasileiras de futebol"*. Vols. I, II, III, IV and Anexes. Brasília, Senado Federal (in Portuguese).

Carlos Azevedo e Aldo Rebelo (2002). A Corrupção no futebol brasileiro. *Motrivivência*, N. 17, pp. 1–18 (in Portuguese).

Folha de S. Paulo (2000). *Dados da CBF revelam empobrecimento jogador nacional*. Edition of 02/29/2000. (in Portuguese).

Hosmer-Henner, Adam (2010). Preventing Game Fixing : Sports Books as Information Markets. *Gaming Law Review and Economics*. Vol. 14, N. 1, pp. 31–38.

Marques, Gutierrez, Montagner (2009). Novas configurações socioeconômicas do esporte contemporâneo. *Revista da Educação Física da UEM*. v. 20, n. 4, pp. 637–648 (in Portuguese).

Mineps (2012). 5th International Conference of Ministers and Senior Officials Responsible for Physical Education and Sports. Comission III Recommendations on 'Preserving the integrity of sport'.

Placar (2005). *Dossiê do Apito: tudo sobre a máfia que anulou jogos do Brasileirão-2005*. Edition of 3/3/2011 (in Portuguese).

Preston and Szinmanski (2003). Cheating in Contests. *Oxford Review of Economic Policy*, vol. 19. N. 4, pp. 612–624.

Rebeggiani, Luca (2009). The Liga Portuguesa decision of the European Court of Justice – An Economist View. *Rivista di Diritto ed Economia dello Sporte*, vol.5, 3, pp. 111–122.

Scoppa, Vincenzo (2008). Are subjective evaluations biased by social factors or connections? An econometric analysis of soccer referee decisions. *Empirical Economy* N. 35, pp. 123–140.

Van Meegen (2012). Preventing Match Fixing: Contemporary Approach. *Global Academic Experts – Meeting for Integrity in Sports*.

Sports-Related Crime: A Game Theory Approach

Farrukh B. Hakeem

Abstract Sports-related crime is a variant of white-collar crime, one of the modern day versions of this can be seen in the phenomenon of match-fixing. This chapter uses the Game Theory approach to analyze the problem of sports-related crime. Game theory is applied to gain insight regarding the conflict between thoughtful and deceitful adversaries and is employed to analyze the interactions between law enforcement and defendants who commit sports-related crimes. The Prisoner's Dilemma will be employed to gain further insight into the dynamics that ensue amongst the various players – law enforcement, prosecutor, and players. After examining the levels of sports-related crime, formulating a cognitive valence map along with its approximations, and estimating its legal parameters and implications, the author suggests some preventive legal strategies. It concludes by highlighting the crucial need for more data at a global level that could assist researchers, law enforcement, and academics to get a better insight into this problem. It further calls for the creation of a Global Database on Sports-Related Crime.

Introduction

This chapter seeks to examine the problem of sports-related crime as a variant of white collar crime by employing the Game Theory approach. In 1907, Ross alluded to this problem of white-collar crime by referring to the criminaloid – a business leader who, while enjoying immunity from the law, victimized an unsuspecting public (Ross 1907). Later, in 1939, criminologist Edwin Sutherland defined white collar crime as one that is committed by a person of respectability and high social status, during the course of their occupation (Sutherland 1940, 1985).

F.B. Hakeem (✉)
Department of Social Sciences, Shaw University, Raleigh, NC, USA
e-mail: fbzhus@yahoo.com

M.R. Haberfeld and D. Sheehan (eds.), *Match-Fixing in International Sports: Existing Processes, Law Enforcement, and Prevention Strategies,* DOI 10.1007/978-3-319-02582-7_13, © Springer International Publishing Switzerland 2013

Though white collar crimes do as much damage to the moral and economic fabric of society, white collar criminals are not as rigorously pursued and prosecuted. Due to the fact that most white collar crimes are committed by persons from the upper and upper middle class of society, their inherent power in society does not render them open to punishment as is the case with respect to lower class criminality. It is due to this immunity or the low probability of being caught and prosecuted that most white collar criminals thrive and benefit from their criminal acts. This paper will use the insights of game theory in order to analyze, interpret and suggest preventive measures for sports-related crime. It will first examine the nexus between white collar crime and game theory.

Basics of Game Theory

Game theory was originally developed by John von Neumann, a Hungarian-born American mathematician, along with his Princeton University colleague, Oskar Morgenstern, a German-born American economist, in order to solve problems in economics. In their book – The Theory of Games and Economic Behavior (Von Neumann and Morgenstern 1944), they argued that the mathematics developed for the physical sciences, describing the workings of a disinterested nature, was a poor model for economics. They observed that economics was very similar to a game, where players anticipate each other's moves, and therefore calls for a new type of mathematics, that they referred to as Game theory (Dixit and Nalebuff 1991; Dixit and Skeath 1999; Straffin 1993).

A branch of applied mathematics, Game theory looks at tools for the analysis of situations where parties, called players, make decisions that are interdependent. The interdependence leads each player to consider the other player's possible decisions, or strategies, while formulating the individual's own strategy. The solutions to a game delineates the optimal choices of the players, who may have similar, opposed or mixed interests, as also the outcomes that could result from these choices.

Though initially used to analyze parlor games, its applications are much broader. Presently, Game Theory is applied to a wide variety of situations where the choices of players interact in order to affect the outcome. While emphasizing the strategic aspects of decision-making, or aspects controlled by the players rather than by pure chance, the theory both supplements and goes beyond the classical theory of probability. Some of the applications of this theory have been used to determine: (1) What political coalitions or business conglomerates are likely to form; (2) The optimal price at which to sell products or services in the face of competition; (3) The power exercised by a voter or block of voters; (4) Whom to select for a jury; (5) The best site for a manufacturing plant; and (6) The behavior of certain animals and plants in their struggle for survival.

It would be preposterous if any one theory could address such an enormous range of 'games,' as such, there is no single game theory. Various theories have been proposed, with each applying to different situations along with its own concepts of what constitutes a solution.

Games may be classified according to certain unique features, the most obvious of which is the number of players. A game may be designated as being a one-person, two-person, or n-person (n greater than two) game. Games in each of these categories have their own distinctive features. Further, a player need not be an individual – this could be a corporation, a nation, or a team having many individuals with shared interests.

Types of Games: The types of games could be based on the following criteria:

(a) Information, which could be either perfect or imperfect;
(b) Goals, that either coincide or lead to conflict. These could be constant-sum games or variable-sum games that are cooperative or non-cooperative.
(c) Quantum, which could either be finite or infinite.

Games could also be classified in one of three ways and these forms could also be combined and be referred to as the theory of moves:

(a) Extensive: parlor games are an example of the extensive form of games using game trees.
(b) Normal: two-person games are normal form games. These games use the strategic payoff matrix.
(c) Characteristic Function: these games have more than two players.

Game theory is a study of conflict between thoughtful and deceitful adversaries. According to this theory, a game is any situation where two or more parties find themselves competing over interests that they cannot share amongst themselves. For our purposes, the interests are the sentences of white-collar criminals (Poundstone 1993). The prosecution seeks higher sentences, whereas defendants are desirous of lower ones.

Game theory can be employed as a means to analyze the interactions between law enforcement and defendants who commit sports-related crimes. This theory is useful for the purpose of analyzing myriad situations, though many of these may not initially resemble a game (Dresher et al. 1964; Axelrod 1984, 1997; Moulin 1986; Chess 1988).

White-Collar Crime and Game Theory

The recent spate of highly publicized corporate fraud schemes has led to a dramatic shift in white-collar crime prosecutions. These incidents have also resulted in the demise of the image of victimless crime with respect to corporate crime and white-collar crime. They have also revealed the amount of physical and financial damage that can be perpetrated by corporations that tolerated, engage in, or encourage illegal acts (Katz 1988). The perception that white-collar crimes are victimless or an

Table 1 Prisoner's dilemma

	B refuses deal	B turns state approver
A refuses deal	1 year, 1 year	3 years, 0 years
A turns state approver	0 years, 3 years	2 years, 2 years

exception to the rule is now history. As such, penalties for white-collar criminals are gradually increasing and appellate courts have been reversing light sentences with greater frequency (Calvita and Pontell 1990). Many commentators have demanded stricter sentences because the economic character and the rational, cool, and calculated intent of white-collar criminals make them ideal candidates for general deterrence. They argue that by raising the expected cost of white-collar crime it would become unprofitable and therefore cease (Bibas 2005; Posner 1986).

Game theory defines games in many different ways. A simple introductory game of cake-cutting may be taken as an example. Two children vying for the same piece of cake, need to split it between themselves. According to game theory this interaction is referred to as a zero sum game. As there is only one slice of cake, whether it is cut at the 50 % mark or the 99 % mark by one child, the other child will get the remainder. In essence, the children split the sum between them. The solution to this problem is to apply the traditional Solomonic parental method: one child is tasked with cutting the cake and the other chooses the slice. If only one child cuts the cake and chooses a slice unilaterally then, there is good reason to believe that the largest slice will be carved up. When the cutting and choosing responsibilities are divided, it does not permit either of the two to act in a unilateral manner. It forces the parties to cooperate, not based on altruistic motives, but in their own self-interest. The one who cuts the cake will endeavor to divide as equally as possible so as to prevent the other from getting a larger slice. The rules of the game give each party an incentive to act in a mutually beneficial manner. The interests of the parties are at equilibrium, since having exactly half a slice of cake is an outcome that neither party regards as their personal maximum result, but it is the best outcome that can be accomplished in the given situation. According to game theory, the point at which two players' interests balance is referred to as a "Nash Equilibrium," (Nash 1950) or a "saddle point."

However, not all games have saddle points and one can invent a game with any number of rules. Non-zero sum games, for example, do not have saddle points (Rapoport 1970). While players in zero sum games compete for a set amount of interests, there is not a set amount of interests in non-zero sum games. As there is no set sum to divide, both players can simultaneously make gains or incur losses. In zero sum games, every choice always benefits one player at the expense of the other. However, in non-zero sum games a particular strategy could, by itself, be better for both players. Though this initially simplifies the analysis, on closer scrutiny it reveals exactly how complicated non-zero sum games could be.

The Prisoner's Dilemma is a good example of the complications that ensue from non-zero sum games, Table 1 above illustrates, this game. According to the scenario, two men, charged with a joint violation of the law, are held in separate locations by the police. Each of them is informed that:

(a) If one confesses and the other refrains, then the former will be rewarded and the latter will be punished.
(b) If both confess, then they will both be fined/punished.
(c) Both of them, simultaneously, have good reason to believe that if neither of them confesses, both will be cleared.

One can appreciate the implications that games of this kind have on the issue of white-collar crime. According to this game, punishments or rewards are approximately equal to the outcomes available for modern day criminal defendants. Though criminal defendants do not face exactly the same scenario laid out in the Prisoner's Dilemma, they face a similar choice between alternatives that are less than desirable. Consequently, in this situation, they are competing not only with the other defendant, but also with the prosecutor, an entity that has two main interests – in the amount of the defendant's information, and the length of the defendant's sentence. This game was developed by Merrill Flood who called it the "Non-Cooperative Pair." Later on, his colleague, Albert W. Tucker formulated this hypothetical scenario in order to illustrate this game, giving it the name "Prisoner's Dilemma" (Isenhour 2007).

The problem of the scenario formulated in the Prisoner's Dilemma is that it is a real dilemma – a predicament that defies a satisfactory solution. The best mutual outcome is the upper left cell in Table 1 where both refuse to deal with the prosecutor. The best individual outcome is that of the lone cheater. The worst outcome is when one is suckered into sticking with the bargain (not to cooperate with the prosecutor) while the other person cheats. The best overall strategy is to cooperate with each other (not to be a rat) by being silent. This gives optimal results for both the parties. In this situation what course need a rational person follow, or alternatively, does every situation have a rational course of action?

In order to drill rationality into game theory, John Nash (1950) formulated a theory of 'equilibrium' in order to judge the outcome of the game. This can be evaluated by adopting the *Monday Morning Quarterback* analysis (Poundstone 1993). The post-game analysis survey is conducted by hypothetically asking both players regarding their satisfaction with the result. When the outcome satisfies both parties, it results in what is referred to as the Nash Equilibrium (Moulin 1986).

The Prisoner's Dilemma presents an interesting application of the Nash Equilibrium. Should both players have cooperated, then they both would have wished to have been the lone defector. If one party defected while the other cooperated, then the cooperator would wish to also have defected. However, if they both defect, then they will have achieved the Nash Equilibrium (Nash 1953). In the short term one-iteration game, the Nash theory proves that neither player can do better than to defect. However, the failure to acknowledge the mutually beneficial outcome that cooperation offers, leaves one with the feeling that something is amiss in the state of game theory.

Dissatisfied with the odd prediction of the Nash Equilibrium, researchers decided to further study this hypothetical game. They hoped that games with many iterations, would offer solutions to the dilemma if the players were allowed to develop behavioral patterns. According to Axelrod (1997) the Prisoner's Dilemma offers an interesting insight into the intricate dynamics of human behavior. What it encapsulates so well is the tension between the advantages of selfishness in the short run compared to the need to elicit cooperation from the other player in the long run. The pure simplicity of the Prisoner's Dilemma is very valuable in helping discover and appreciate the deep consequences of the fundamental processes while dealing with this tension.

Through the medium of computer simulations, academics from various fields studied the behavior of players of the Prisoner's Dilemma. The most interesting results were obtained by Robert Axelrod (1997) and his colleagues from computer simulations and tournaments. A computer simulation was set up with a limited set of rules. Each outcome was assigned a point value instead of a number of years of imprisonment. The researchers further solicited contributions of strategies (rules) from academics and professionals. The rules were then matched against one another to decipher what rules would garner the highest scores. The researchers found that the most successful strategies were those that elicited cooperation from the other player. Those strategies that leaned towards defection did not elicit as many points.

The lessons drawn from these tournaments were that players who are allowed to develop patterns of behavior tend to cooperate more often. The short term benefits of defection decrease as players realize that they stand to gain more from setting up mutually beneficial relationships of cooperation.

Axelrod (1997) and his colleagues further examined these tournaments by examining the rules from an evolutionary perspective. Axelrod found that cooperation was necessary for survival and that mutual cooperation fared much better than mutual defection. This study proved that initially, poor programs and good programs are represented in equal proportion. However, with the passage of time, the poorer ones atrophy and the good ones thrive. Though defection is near universal in the short term, long term strategies emerge when players react to each other through repeated iterations.

Though these computer simulations were very helpful to researchers in evaluating strategies between perfectly rational players, when these simulations were conducted on humans they did not fare that well. Computers tend to be logical opponents, having a perfect memory of past moves, with a perfect understanding of the rules, and any possible ramifications of actions. People, on the other hand, tend not be any of the preceding. People tend to act randomly, competitively, altruistically, collusively, and according to notions of chivalry. They also tend to act according to their superstitions, premonitions, prejudices, and all other ways that cannot be imagined by a rational computer. This element of non-rationality adds a completely new dimension to the real life Prisoner's Dilemma. If a game is played between two completely rational players, then they will always come to the same result. However, when played against a person, there is no guarantee that the other party will act in a rational manner. Even if one acts rationally, they cannot be assured of any particular result. According to Axelrod (1997), this randomness and uncertainty in action was referred to as 'noise.' Comprehension of the effects of iterations on the rationality of cooperation, coupled with the non-rationality of noise is crucial to understanding the application of game theory in concrete situations.

Game Theory and Law Enforcement

Game theory can become useful to law enforcement when Game theorists realize that what they can get from the Prisoner's Dilemma is one of the main functions of the government – to ensure that when individuals do not have private incentives to cooperate, they will opt for the socially useful thing anyway. The government can then step in and change the effective payoffs. As such, game theory becomes relevant to the law from a public policy perspective. Through its knowledge of the rules that are likely to promote beneficial choices in different situations, the government is facilitated in structuring the laws. Game theory enables the government to predict which laws will encourage cooperation among parties, and also the laws that will disincentivize cooperation. If the payouts and the structure of the game lead to an incentive to perform the governments' desired action, then the policy can be considered sound. However, if the game deters the desired conduct, then the government policy is faulty. Ascertaining whether a stated policy encourages the desired result is difficult.

The decisional matrix of the average criminal defendant can be quite complex (Richman 1995). For the participants, the problem is that the prosecutor tends to be the one who determines the payoff for the game. Standen (1993) narrates how a prosecutor can manipulate the overlap of sentences under the guidelines to expand or reduce the sentence at will. According to the sentencing guidelines, any amount of charges could cover a defendant's criminal actions, and the prosecutor can then charge bargain with the defendant. The current trend of disallowing downward departures for white-collar sentencing gives the prosecutor even more leverage now that the defendants know that 'what *they* charge is what *you* get.'

According to this scheme, prosecutors have been defined as 'monopsonists,' those who are the sole buyers of information that is offered by criminal defendants (Standen 1993). Within this monopsonistic market, the prosecutor (the sole buyer), is the one who sets the price and is at liberty to discriminate based on factors that are totally unrelated to the desire and ability to sell, and the relative value of the information. Standen (1993) argues that the legislative rules structuring sales of convictions do not appear to protect against this monopoly, but instead tend to encourage prosecutors to monopolize their superior bargaining position. This leaves the defendant in a quandary. The only prospect for the defendant to get leniency is by selling information, however, the price that is going to be paid for this information is dependent on the prosecutor.

In response to this unbalanced situation there is a countervailing factor that assists in stabilizing the monopsonist market. Within the arena of a criminal trial, every prosecution constitutes an independent game that is played between two individual adversaries. According to Weinstein (1999), in these parlays, Game theory predicts that in these exchanges, the government will always win, because by offering such low prices, both the players are more than likely to defect. The defendants cannot shift the risk back to the government, because as an individual supplier, the defendant is a one shot player, who cannot engage in collective bargaining, and is therefore compelled to sell a commodity to the prosecutor who enjoys a superior negotiating position (Weinstein 1999).

However, within this dynamic there is another game that is in motion – this is a macro game taking place between the defense bar and the government. With respect to white-collar crime, defense attorneys play a role that is disproportionate to their roles when dealing in the trials of common criminals (Weisburd et al. 1991). According to Stuntz (1989) the disproportionate presence of private defense counsel transforms the game from being a one shot bargain, into one that is an iterated Prisoner's Dilemma. The defense attorneys, being part of the courtroom workgroup, are repeat players with whom the government has to deal with on an ongoing basis. In this situation, Game theory predicts that the disproportionate presence of defense counsel tends to turn the game in favor of the defense bar. As a consequence, among well-represented white-collar criminals, defection (turning state's evidence) is much lower than in cases of common criminals who do not have the benefit of privately retained counsel. These defense attorneys have good reason to push for cooperation as defection (turning state's evidence) damages the interest of their client base at the macro level. In the uphill battle against the arbiter/player of the game, the defense attorney represents a formidable adversary to the prosecutor (by itself, this counterbalancing factor could stabilize prices, but is not sufficient to tip the scales in favor of cooperation among defendants).

Levels of Operation for Sports-Related Crime

This table seeks to analyze the problem of match-fixing using a Game theory perspective. As a very simple example it will analyze the problem using five different dimensions for a game that has two teams. The first dimension could be that of the two teams which are to some degree cooperators as well as competitors when it relates to the game at hand. On the next level would be the judge/referee, who determines the outcome of the game. At this level there could be corruption of the game when the judge/referee is bribed by external factors to force a result. The third dimension would examine the spectators and the role that they play regarding the ongoing games. The fourth dimension focuses on the role the gambler/bettor plays in this dynamic. Finally, the fifth dimension examines the media and how it interprets the ongoing game and its reporting about it (Table 2).

Table 2 Dimensions of match fixing

Dimensions	Part	Part
I	Team A	Team B
II	Referee	Financier
III	Spectator	Spectator
IV	Bettor/Gambler	Bettor/Gambler
V	Media	Media

Cognitive Valence Map for Sports Related Crime

Table 3 draws upon a cognitive valence map to explain the logistics of match-fixing. This table analyzes match-fixing on three different variables.

(a) Action taken by law enforcement;
(b) The level of interest by the participants; and
(c) The reasons for game participation.

At the law enforcement level it will be hypothesized that players would be more likely to act appropriately by following the law when law enforcement adopts a proactive policy. If law enforcement takes on a reactive policy, players will be more likely to indulge in cheating. With respect to the other two variables, level of interest and reason for playing – at the interest level we examine the various parties such as the players, referees, bookies, gamblers, spectators, and the media. So far as the third variable is concerned, we examine the reason why various parties take an interest in the game. These could be either for profit, entertainment, or satisfaction in playing the game. A questionnaire/survey could be formulated to estimate this empirically. The survey/questionnaire could be formulated so as to address all the cells of this $2 \times 6 \times 3$ table.

Cognitive Value Approximations

In Table 4 this researcher seeks to formulate an approximation of values for each of the 36 cells in this $2 \times 6 \times 3$ table. A further analysis of each of these cells needs to be conducted and empirically tested in order to determine the values for each cell. Upon empirical validation for each of these cells, law enforcement resources could be appropriately marshaled to deter the crime of match-fixing.

Legal Aspects of Sports-Related Crime

Match-fixing can be regarded as a variant of sports-related crime, it violates the ethics and integrity of sport. Whether related to influencing betting or to sporting objectives, it is a form of corruption and as such prohibited by national criminal law.

Table 3 Cognitive valence map

Action	Level	Profit	Entertain	Satisfaction
Reactive	Player (H)	3	2	1
	Referee	3	2	1
	Bookie (M)	3	0	0
	Gambler	3	2	1
	Spectator (L)	0	3	2
	Media	3	2	0
Proactive	Player (H)	1	2	3
	Referee	1	2	3
	Bookie (M)	3	1	2
	Gambler	3	2	1
	Spectator (L)	1	3	2
	Media	3	1	2

Table 4 Cognitive value approximations

Action	Level	Profit	Entertain	Satisfaction
Reactive	Player (H)	.6 (r1c1)	.3 (r1c2)	.1 (r1c3)
	Referee	.6 (r2c1)	.3 (r2c2)	.1 (r2c3)
	Bookie (M)	.8 (r3c1)	.1 (r3c2)	.1 (r3c3)
	Gambler	.8 (r4c1)	,1 (r4c2)	.1 (r4c3)
	Spectator (L)	.1 (r5c1)	.8 (r5c2)	.1 (r5c3)
	Media	.7 (r6c1)	.2 (r6c2)	.1 (r6c3)
Proactive	Player (H)	.1 (r7c1)	.2 (r7c2)	.7 (r7c3)
	Referee	.1 (r8c1)	.2 (r8c2)	.7 (r8c3)
	Bookie (M)	.7 (r9c1)	.1 (r9c2)	.2 (r9c3)
	Gambler	.7 (r10c1)	.2 (r10c2)	.1 (r10c3)
	Spectator (L)	.1 (r11c1)	.8 (r11c2)	.1 (r11c3)
	Media	.8 (r12c1)	.1 (r12c2)	.1 (r12c3)

International criminal networks play a nefarious role in match-fixing associated with illegal betting. Due to the worldwide popularity of sport and the trans-frontier nature of betting activities, the problem often goes beyond the territorial jurisdiction of national authorities. Sport stakeholders have been working with public and private betting companies to establish early warning systems and educational programs, with mixed results. The European commission has been cooperating with the council of Europe in analyzing the factors that could contribute to more effectively addressing the issue of match-fixing at the national, European and international level. Integrity in sport is also one of the issues that is addressed by the Commission with consultation on the provision of online gambling services in the EU.

At the European level, match-fixing is determined by examining the expression "manipulation of sports results" which covers the arrangement of an irregular alteration of the course or the result of a sporting competition or any of its particular events (e.g. Matches, races) in order to obtain an advantage for oneself or for others and to remove all or part of the uncertainty normally associated with the result of a competition.

Sports-Related Crime Pertaining to India

So far as sports-related crime in India is concerned a majority of the crimes pertain to football (soccer), cricket and field hockey since these tend to be the most popular games for the Indian masses. With respect to football (soccer), most of the teams that play football are in the north-eastern part of the county. The major venues that host the football teams are the Nehru cup, Mohan Bagan and Mohammedan sporting in Bengal. In 2012, the Gauhati Town Club (GTC) opted to disband its senior team and not participate in any football tournaments for 3 years due to allegations of match-fixing by its players. According to the GTC general secretary, the abominable element of match-fixing had found its way into Indian football and had ruined the sport. Even the star footballer, Bhaichung Bhutia, was accused of being involved in match-fixing. In yet another case, a complaint had been lodged with the All India Football Federation alleging that United Sikkim had bribed its key players to lose a match. With respect to the Cuttack leg of the tournament, there were serious allegations of match-fixing. The Football Federation found out that two of the matches against leading Calcutta teams had been fixed. An investigation revealed that players had been bribed to throw the matches (Ahmed 2012).

So far as cricket is concerned, there have been many serious complaints about issues of match-fixing, spot-fixing and throwing of matches by players in the Indian Premier League (IPL) and the One Day Internationals (ODI). Cricket players from countries such as South Africa, India, Pakistan, and Australia have all been involved in sports-related crime (see note 1 regarding some of the major scandals in cricket).

Recently, the chairman of the Board of Control for Cricket in India (BCCI) was forced to step aside pending an investigation, due to allegations of spot-fixing scandal that negatively affected the game in India. It led to the arrest of his son-in-law. In May 2013, three cricketers were arrested due to allegations that they had taken money to concede a pre-determined number of runs in the IPL matches (ABC news 2013).

The next sport, field hockey, one of the most popular national sports in India has also been hit by scandal by allegations of match-fixing. A former coach of the Indian Hockey team, Harendra Singh, accused players of match-fixing (Sports Betting 2013).

Most of the problems regarding sports-related crime began in the 1990s due to the advent of sports-betting sites on the Internet (see note 2). The influx of unregulated money into sports has led to a corruption of the game. Though gambling is highly restricted in India, this is not the case with online gambling. In spite of prohibitive legislation (Gambling Act 1867), the Indian gambling market is worth $60 billion per year. Half of this amount is spent on illegal betting (Thompson 2009).

Some Indian officials are in favor of legalizing sports betting because of the belief that profits generated by the underground bookies are used to fund drugs and terrorism. In May 2011, India passed the Information Technology Act, which is supposed to control Internet gambling. This act covers gambling sites and tasks the Internet Service Providers with blocking offshore betting sites (Lakshmi 2013).

Preventive Strategies for Sports-Related Crime

Some of the preventive strategies that could be instituted in order to control the problem of sports-related crime are:

- Increase the salaries of the players;
- Increase the salaries of the referees/umpires;
- Have a proactive law enforcement approach to look out for irregularities by bookies and financiers;
- Adopt an ongoing, compulsory, ethics education course that should be taken by all persons involved with the game.
- Publicize lists of persons who have committed irregularities with respect to sports-related crime.
- Determine whether there are any irregularities with respect to the betting process when it relates to a game;
- Institute a time delay in the broadcast signals when a popular game is being broadcast live.
- Institute stringent and quick prosecutions against any actor who commits a sports-related crime.

Conclusions Recommendations

There should be a Global Database on Sports-Related Crime (GDSRC) that needs to be set up at the international level. An International law enforcement agency such as Interpol should be tasked with setting up this project. This GDSRC should be set up as a one stop clearing house for all matters pertaining to sports-related crimes. The data set should be easily available to scholars, academics, and law enforcement officials at the international level.

At the initial compilation stage, care should be taken to compile and code all the various games along with the appropriate coding for these games. A penal law format that aggregates all the national codes and their violations should be aggregated into the database. Individual country, region, and international factors should also be taken into account when constructing this dataset. Once the data has been compiled and populated it should be assembled into a machine-readable format so as to be accessible to scholars using standard statistical packages such as SAS or SPSS. When this dataset has been completed it can be used for analysis, validation, prediction, learning and prevention purposes. This dataset, once it is populated with sufficient data points, could also be used to run simulations with various Game theory scenarios in order to evaluate and improve law enforcement processes and policies. The new data and further research would offer interesting new insights into this new area of white-collar crime.

Notes

1. There were six famous match-fixing scandals in India with respect to cricket.

    (i) Hansie Cronje of South Africa was charged by Delhi Police with fixing the One Day International (ODI) on April 4, 2000. He was also charged with taking money from bookmakers.
    (ii) Azharuddin was found guilty of match-fixing on 11/27/2000 and Kapil Dev was charged with under performing in the game of cricket on 5/24/2000.
    (iii) Salim Malik of Pakistan was charged with match-fixing in cricket during a match between Pakistan and Australia. In 1994, he asked the Aussie players to bowl badly and lose the Karachi test. On 5/24/200 he was found guilty of match-fixing.
    (iv) Wasim Akram of Pakistan was charged with match-fixing in a game between Pakistan and New Zealand. In 1998 he asked the Kiwis (New Zealand) to bowl badly. On 5/24/2000 he was found guilty.
    (v) On 11/3/2011, the following players were charged with the no ball scandal: Salman Butt, Mohd. Asif, Mohd. Aamer.
    (vi) In 1998 Warne and Waugh passed on weather and pitch information to Indian bookies. Both of them were fined.

2. Some of these Indian betting sites are:

    (i) Bet365
    (ii) Bodog
    (iii) William Hill
    (iv) Ladbrokes

References

Ahmed, Imtiaz (2012) GTC Disbands Senior Football Team Amid Match-Fix Slur. The Telegraph, Calcutta, India. URL: at www.telegraphindia.com/1120306/jsp/frontpage/story_15218103.jsp#.UmKabBaVIXO accessed on 8/13/2012.

Axelrod, Robert (1984) The Evolution of Cooperation. New York: Basic Books.

Axelrod, Robert (1997) The Complexity of Cooperation: Agent Based Models of Competition and Collaboration. Princeton, NJ: Princeton University Press.

Bibas, Stephanos (2005) White-Collar Plea Bargaining and Sentencing after Booker. 47 William and Mary Law Review, pp 721

Calvita, K. and Henry N. Pontell (1990) Heads I win, Tails You Lose: Deregulation, Crime and Crisis in the Savings and Loan Industry. 36 Crime and Delinquency 321 (1990).

Chess, David M. (1988) Simulating the Evolution of Behavior: The Iterated Prisoner's Dilemma Problem. 2 Complex Systems.

Dixit, Avinash K. and Barry J. Nalebuff (1991) Thinking Strategically: The Competitive Edge in Business, Politics, and Everyday Life. New York: W.W. Norton.

Dixit, Avinash K. and Susan Skeath (1999) Games of Strategy. New York: W.W. Norton.

Dresher, M. L.S. Shapely, and A.W. Tucker (1964) Advances in Game Theory. Annals of Mathematical Studies. No. 52. Princeton, NJ: Princeton University Press.

Isenhour, F.E. (2007) Note: United States v. Martin: Game Theory and Cooperation in White-Collar Criminal Sentencing. Liberty University Law Review. Vol. 2: pp 271–303.

Katz, Jack (1988) The Seduction of Crime: Moral and Sensual Attractions in Doing Evil. New York: Basic Books.

Lakshmi, Rama (2013) India Considers Legalizing Sports Gambling as Way to Curb Match Fixing. The Washington Post. URL:// www.washingtonpost.com/blogs/worldviews/wp/2013/06/25/india-considers-legalizing-sports-gambling-as-way-to-curb-match-fixing/ accessed 7-27-2013.

Moulin, Herve (1986) Game Theory for the Social Sciences. New York: NYU Press.

Nash, John F. (1950) Equilibrium Points in N-Person Games. 36 Proc. Nat. Acad. Sci. U.S.A. 48 (1950).

Nash, John F. (1953) Two-Person Cooperative Games. Econometrica. Vol. 21, no. 1, pp. 128–140.

Posner, Richard A. (1986) Economic Analysis of Law. New York: Little, Brown and Company.

Poundstone, William (1993) Prisoner's Dilemma. New York: First Anchor Books.

Rapoport, Anatol (1970) N-Person Game Theory: Concepts and Applications. Ann Arbor: University of Michigan Press.

Richman, Daniel C. (1995) Cooperating Clients. 56 OHIO ST. L. J. 69, 89 (1995).

Ross, Edward Allsworth (1907) Sin and Society: An Analysis of Latter-Day Iniquity. Boston: Houghton Mifflin.

Standen, Jeffrey (1993) Plea Bargaining in the Shadow of the Guidelines. 81 CAL. L. REV. 1471 (1993).

Sutherland, Edwin (1940) White Collar Criminality. American Sociological Review, vol. 5. No. 1 (Feb., 1940) pp. 1–12.

Sutherland, Edwin (1985) White Collar Crime: The Uncut Version. New Haven, CT: Yale University Press.

Straffin, Philip D. (1993) Game Theory and Strategy. Washington, DC: Mathematical Association of America.

Stuntz, William J. (1989) Waiving Rights in Criminal Procedure. 75 VA. L. REV. 761 (1989).

Thompson, James (2009) Betfair and William Hill Target India. The Independent. URL: www.independent.co.uk/news/business/news/betfair-and-william-hill-target-india-1810025.html retrieved 10-28-2009.

Von Neumann, John and Oskar Morgenstern (1944) Theory of Games and Economic Behavior. Princeton, NJ: Princeton University Press.

Weinstein, Ian (1999) Regulating the Markets for Snitches. 47 BUFF. LAW REV. (563)

Weisburd, David, Stanton Wheeler, Elin Waring and Nancy Bode (1991) Crimes of the Middle Classes. White-Collar Offenders in Federal Courts. New Haven, CT: Yale University Press.

Part III
Future: Where Do We Go from Here?

The INTERPOL Approach to Tackling Match Fixing in Football

John Abbott and Dale Sheehan

Abstract Increasingly, professional criminals are operating internationally to exploit football and make money through match fixing and irregular betting. Investigations, whether undertaken by law enforcement or the football authorities, are complex, lengthy, costly and uncertain in their outcome. The major criminals pulling the strings of the criminal networks of match fixers are rarely caught. A more effective approach is to enhance the prevention of match fixing. This chapter provides an overview of the implementation of the INTERPOL – FIFA Initiative which seeks to promote training, education and prevention as an effective response to match fixing in football.

Introduction

The manipulation of sporting contests is not new but the level of reported match fixing in football, particularly for financial gain through the betting markets, has rocketed in recent years.[1] There is no doubt that this criminal activity – corrupting participants in a sport and defrauding the betting market (and other punters who believe the game is being honestly played) – is attractive to professional criminals and organised crime networks. These criminals are not in the slightest bit concerned about the integrity of any sport, nor of the positive economic and social contribution sport makes to the development of society generally and human beings individually.

---

[1] Match fixing has reared its head in a number of sports in recent years. In addition to football, badminton, cricket, cycling, handball, horse racing, snooker, sumo wrestling, volleyball and tennis come to mind.

J. Abbott • D. Sheehan (✉)
INTERPOL, Lyon, France
e-mail: d.sheehan@interpol.int

M.R. Haberfeld and D. Sheehan (eds.), *Match-Fixing in International Sports:
Existing Processes, Law Enforcement, and Prevention Strategies*,
DOI 10.1007/978-3-319-02582-7_14, © Springer International Publishing Switzerland 2013

Criminals engaged in match fixing have been assisted by a number of developments in society in recent times, many of which are interconnected. These include globalisation (the shrinking of the world in terms of mobility and communication); the spread of the internet as a global market place for doing business (both legal and illegal); significant expansion in the betting markets in the sporting world (both in terms of the number of legal and illegal organisations offering betting facilities and the range of bets available to the punter, not least 'in play' betting); and the naivety and under preparedness of sport participants (not only players and referees, also administrators, coaches and managers).

INTERPOL has been engaged in tackling corruption in sport for a number of years, coordinating operations in several countries to crack down on illegal gambling dens, supporting the security and safety of major sporting events and bringing together law enforcement investigators engaged in tackling match fixing to share information and good practice, and assist each other in their investigations. But in May 2011, INTERPOL embarked on a new venture with the Federation Internationale De Football Association (FIFA) under the headline 'the INTERPOL – FIFA Anti Corruption Initiative'. In this 20 million Euro agreement over 10 years, INTERPOL will provide football related anti-corruption training, education and prevention programmes in order to better tackle the problem of corruption in football, especially corruption linked to match fixing and irregular and illegal betting.[2]

This chapter will seek to explain, from INTERPOL's perspective:

- The nature of the problem of match fixing in football;
- The key elements to tackle match fixing more effectively, both nationally and internationally; and
- The approach of the INTERPOL – FIFA training programme designed to tackle corruption in football.

What's the Problem?

According to open source reporting, more than 70 countries have encountered match fixing in football in some form or other between June 2012 and May 2013. A common assumption is that this is just a European problem, fuelled by the betting syndicates in South East Asia. However, it is clear that no part of the globe is exempt – every continent has reported allegations of match fixing in football in recent times, every continent has rich pickings in terms of players (or referees or administrators) who can be 'persuaded' to take part in a fix, and every continent has criminals.[3]

---

[2] Details of the INTERPOL – FIFA Initiative are contained within a Press release issued by INTERPOL on 09 May 2011 (www.interpol.int).

[3] This conclusion is reached based upon analysis of open source reports of allegations of match fixing in football collated by INTERPOL's Integrity in Sport Unit and circulated in their 'Weekly Media report'.

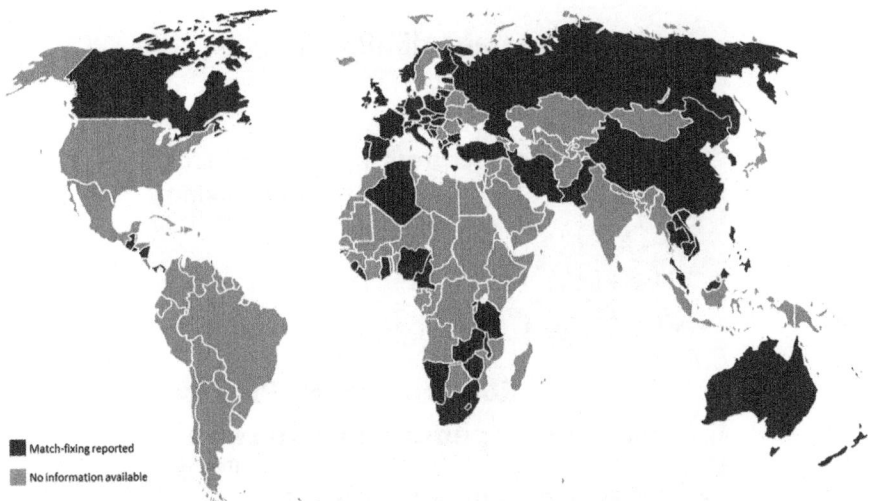

The global scale of match-fixing: this map represents countries that have allegations, investigations or imposed penalties for match-fixing in football between June 2012 and May 2013 and is drawn from open source media reporting collated by INTERPOL's Integrity in Sport Unit

There should be no doubt that every country is at risk. It is not just economically wealthy countries or poor countries; and the size of the country has little relevance either. In football, international matches at the highest level have been fixed; matches in international club competitions have been fixed; and nationally, in many leagues from the highest level down to the fourth or fifth level games have been fixed.

Match fixing is generally defined as manipulating the result or course of the game for advantage.[4] It may be for so called 'sporting advantage' (to avoid relegation, to achieve promotion etc) or it may be for direct financial gain. Most commentators recognise that manipulation for 'sporting advantage' has existed for a long time, persists now and will very probably continue to do so in the future.

Match fixing to make money through irregular or illegal betting appears to be the real growth industry in recent times, fuelled by the range of betting options available through both the legal and illegal markets, the relatively poorly developed and inconsistently applied rules and regulations around betting, and an underprepared football industry. It is also fair to say that in many countries, the investigation of allegations of match fixing is not a priority for law enforcement agencies in comparison with more pressing demands – such as tackling terrorism, murder, violence and gangs. It is also frequently desperately difficult – but not impossible – to investigate, given the international and fast moving nature of the criminality.[5]

---

[4] Part of the problem is that there is no universally accepted definition of the term although the Council of Europe is seeking to come up with a definition of 'manipulation of sports competitions' in its draft Convention.

[5] Many countries have reported the lack of relevant and suitable legislation including offences, penalties and powers to investigate.

3rd Lebanese football official gets 6 months jail
-Channel News Asia

Bari prosecutors investigate 20 for alleged match-fixing
-Gazetta del Sud

FIFA EXTENDS LIFETIME BAN OF NICARAGUAN PLAYER -FIFA.COM

Romania coach Piturca handed suspended prison term"
-Reuters

Black mark of match-fixing leaves Canadian soccer dealing with fallout
-Ottawa Citizen

Probe into match-fixing -Fiji Times

Singapore nabs 74 as part of Asia-wide illegal soccer betting arrests
-Channel News Asia

Created by the Integrity in Sport Unit, INTERPOL from open source media reporting

Not surprisingly, professional criminals have noted these opportunities and concluded that the rewards outweigh the risks. There are high profits to be made and at relatively low risk, in comparison with other criminal activities. Those arranging match fixing have resources – both financial and human – to do the job; they are very well organised and do their research meticulously – to ensure they approach the best targets and to minimise the chances of being caught; they identify the 'weak' links in the football family – those who are the best, and easiest, to exploit; they identify those countries with little or no legislation to tackle match fixing, or to investigate it; they have global links and contacts around the world to enable them to activate match fixing and to place their bets; and their greatest advantage, as with most criminal activity, is that they choose when to activate the fix, where to activate it and how to activate it.

However, there are some risks for the match fixer – things that law enforcement and the football community can exploit to prevent and investigate match fixing. Firstly, criminals (including match fixers) have a lack of trust and a fear of betrayal – they are worried about players who decline their offers to fix matches and may report it to the authorities, they are also worried about each other (there is 'no honour amongst thieves'!); secondly, they do get a little concerned when more effective legislation, rules, regulations and codes of practice are established, as this makes the risks higher for them.

The activities of match fixers are, of course, covert but understanding the modus operandi (tactics) used by the match fixers is essential to being able to investigate allegations and, more importantly, to design plans to prevent match fixing ruining the most popular sport in the world. Here are four short case studies drawn from public open source reporting which demonstrate the international and global nature of match fixing in football[6]:

Case Study #1: Bochum

In May 2011 in Bochum, north-western Germany, Ante Sapina was being sent to prison – again – on football corruption charges. In 2005 the Croatian was jailed for 3 years, along with his brother Milan, for masterminding the scandal that engulfed Robert Hoyzer, the disgraced referee who was banned for life in Germany. On his release from prison Sapina, restarted his criminal network with links to illegal gambling rings in Asia. But whereas the Hoyzer scandal centred on lower leagues in Germany, Sapina's new network was far more ambitious. Sapina was jailed after confessing to a role in fixing around 20 matches between 2008 and 2009. He targeted leagues outside Germany where players were modestly paid and where large bets from Asia would go unnoticed. Sapina revealed in court that they used a rating system to analyse matches, with five stars ensuring that the result was almost certain thanks to payments to players and officials. Crucially, they did not try to fix the final result of matches. Instead, they concentrated on the "in-play" betting market, where internet bets can be placed in real time on events such as the number of goals scored in injury time.

Sapina admitted to manipulating more than 20 games, including the 2010 World Cup qualifier between Liechtenstein and Finland in September 2009. Sapina testified that he had met a Bosnian referee in a Sarajevo car park. He agreed to pay him €40,000 Euros to fix the result of the otherwise meaningless World Cup qualifier by ensuring that two goals would be scored in the second half. The match ended in a 1–1 draw with both goals indeed coming in the second half – one the result of a questionable penalty decision.[7]

---

[6] These case studies were researched by the INTERPOL Integrity in Sport Unit and included in the Training Needs Assessment 2012/13.

[7] "Match-fixing: a threat to the integrity of the game," World Soccer Today, 4 July 2011. http://www.worldsoccer.com/news/match-fixing-a-threat-to-the-integrity-of-the-game#1ToG2 BoSDjUGbsPl.99.

Sapina was a member of a sophisticated network of transnational crime groups who were running a substantial match-fixing operation.[8] Wire-tapping was employed by the police during the investigation and gave investigators insight into modus operandi and illegal betting patterns. The modus operandi was found to be highly methodical and greatly varied, involving the purchasing of individual participants or entire clubs, the financing by criminal betting syndicates in Asia, and sometimes the organisation of ghost friendly matches. Millions of Euro were bet, with profits for criminal syndicates estimated to be €8.5 million.[9]

Case Study #2: Wilson Raj Perumal

In January 2010, authorities in Zimbabwe opened an investigation into a series of international friendly matches that the national football team played in Asia between 2007 and 2009.[10] The matches, in which Zimbabwe players were given money to lose, were organized by a Singaporean named Wilson Raj Perumal working with officials of the Zimbabwe Football Association. As a result of the investigation, 93 players and officials received suspensions ranging from 6 months to lifetime bans.[11]

In September 2010, a friendly match was played between Togo and Bahrain. The Bahrain team, which won the match 3-0, questioned the quality of the Togo squad, with the coach even remarking that "They were not fit enough to play 90 minutes".[12] When the Togo Football Federation confirmed that the national team had not travelled to Bahrain, it was discovered that imposters were used in the match. The former coach of the Togo national team admitted that he was involved in setting up the match and a similar one in Egypt – although Perumal was the actual match agent – allegedly spending $60,000 USD on flights, hotels and other expenses.[13]

---

[8] "Sports betting and corruption: How to preserve the integrity of sport," Institute of International and Strategic Relations (IRIS), February 2012.

[9] "Match-fixing Joint Investigation Team JIT Veto," Europol, Presentation delivered at The Hague, 4 February 2013.

[10] Smith, David, "Zimbabwe suspends 80 footballers as part of 'Asiagate' match-fixing probe." The Guardian 1 February 2012. http://www.guardian.co.uk/world/2012/feb/01/zimbabwe-footballers-suspended-asiagate-match-fixing.

[11] "93 players and officials in Zimbabwe face bans after year-long probe into soccer match-fixing," Associated Press, 16 October 2012. http://www.foxnews.com/sports/2012/10/16/3-players-and-officials-in-zimbabwe- face-bans-after-year-long-probe-into-soccer/.

[12] "'Fake' Togo football team at Bahrain match being investigated," BBC, 14 September 2010. http://www.bbc.co.uk/news/world-middle-east-11304208.

[13] Gauthier Villars, David, "When Togo Played Bahrain, the Whole Match Was a Fake," The Wall Street Journal, 3 October 2010. http://online.wsj.com/article/SB10001424052748703384204575509830139498188.html.

In interviews given after his eventual arrest, Perumal claims to have worked for a Singaporean crime syndicate. The syndicate used front companies with names like Football4U and FootyMedia to sign agreements with football federations in need of money, to organize international friendly matches on their behalf. Perumal would often select the match officials and also bribe members of the team.[14]

In October 2010 for example, the Bolivian Football Federation signed an agreement with FootyMedia – which they believed to be a legitimate company – that gave the company sponsorship rights to arrange international friendly competitions. In February 2011, an associate of Perumal arranged two international friendly matches in Antalya, Turkey: Bolivia versus Latvia and Estonia versus Bulgaria. FootyMedia supplied all match officials, from Bulgaria and Hungary.[15]

The friendly matches raised the suspicion of FIFA and UEFA even before they took place as the games were not televised and there was no promotion of the event. In fact, there were only about 100 spectators at the games. After the matches were played, an investigation was launched as all seven goals scored in the two matches were as the result of penalties. Reports indicate that one of the spot-kicks was even re-taken after the initial penalty had been missed. Irregular betting patterns were also detected by monitoring agencies. FIFA banned all six match officials for life for manipulating the results.[16]

The syndicate has also been implicated in a match-fixing scandal in South Africa, where the 'Football4U' company signed an agreement with the South African Football Association (SAFA) to organize four international matches for the South African squad in the lead-up to the 2010 World Cup. Perumal arranged the referees for all four matches – against Thailand, Bulgaria, Colombia and Guatemala, with the outcomes benefitting the Singaporean syndicate. A number of SAFA officials have been implicated in the scandal which, as of 2013, is under judicial review.

Perumal was eventually arrested in Finland for fixing matches in the Finnish League where he confessed to his crimes. After serving a 2 year sentence in Finland, he was extradited to Hungary where he was also wanted in connection to match-fixing.[17]

---

[14] Forrest, Brett, "All the world is staged," ESPN The Magazine, 15 August 2012. http://espn.go.com/sports/soccer/story/_/id/7927946/soccer-wilson-raj-perumal-world-most-prolific-criminal-match-fixer-espn-magazine.

[15] Kelso, Paul and Rory Smith, "Match fixing: how Bolivia was dragged into scandal," The Telegraph, 10 May 2011. http://www.telegraph.co.uk/sport/football/international/8504061/Match-fixing-how-Bolivia-was-dragged-into-scandal.html.

[16] "FIFA ban six Eastern European match officials over match-fixing in internationals," The Daily Mail, 10 August 2011. http://www.dailymail.co.uk/sport/football/article-2024572/FIFA-ban-Eastern-European-match-officials-match-fixing.html#ixzz2Un0LEOhG.

[17] Forrest, Brett, "All the world is staged," ESPN The Magazine, 15 August 2012. http://espn.go.com/sports/soccer/story/_/id/7927946/soccer-wilson-raj-perumal-world-most-prolific-criminal-match-fixer-espn-magazine.

Case Study #3: Turkey

In July 2011 police arrested 61 people including the President of Turkey's top team Fenerbahce, as part of an investigation into allegations of match-fixing in 19 matches in Turkey's top league. Some of the speculation offered in the media at the time as to how the matches were fixed included bribing players not to score or deliberately not saving a goal, and referee selection. Suspicions were raised when Fenerbahce, far back in the league standings, had managed to climb its way to an 18th consecutive league title by winning 16 out of its last 17 matches played, and also allowed them to stay in the Champions League.[18] The financial benefit for Fenerbahce to remain in the UEFA Champions League was estimated at 58.5 million US dollars a year.[19]

At trial in 2012, wire taps revealed that officials of Fenerbahce employed an elaborate code to discuss their match-fixing activities: 'buildings under construction' referred to games in the process of being fixed; 'goats in the field' referred to players; 'crops being watered' were match-fixing payments, and 'ploughing, planting and sowing' were efforts to fix games. The agricultural terms used by the city-dwelling soccer officials often did not correspond with the actual farming seasons, prosecutors noted. Fenerbahce were also alleged to have made large transfer payments to players that were actually bribes to fix matches.[20]

Case Study #4: Republic of Korea

In May 2011 arrest warrants were issued for current and former players and brokers operating in Korea's K League, the top league in the country. The investigation centered on 15 matches in which it was discovered that players were bribed to manipulate matches by brokers making illegal gains through both legal and illegal betting channels. One goalkeeper received over $100,000 USD for fixing four matches in a domestic cup competition where he intentionally allowed 11 goals to be scored against him.[21]

By February 2012, over 80 current and former football players were charged with or convicted of match-fixing with about 50 players receiving lifetime bans. One coach was also charged with blackmailing a player to share his match-fixing

---

[18] "Turkey: Fenerbahce boss remanded on match-fix charge," BBC News, 10 July 2011. http://www.bbc.co.uk/news/world-europe-14100659.

[19] "In Turkey, trial of Fenerbach owner Aziz Yildirim shows that soccer's match-fixing scandal goes all the way to the top." Associated Press, 13 February 2013. http://www.nydailynews.com/sports/more-sports/fenerbach-scandal-shows-match-fixing-straight-top-article-1.1263144.

[20] Ibid.

[21] 30Lee Hyo-sik, "Over 10 footballers under probe for match-rigging scam," The Korea Times, 26 May 2011. http://www.koreatimes.co.kr/www/news/nation/2012/12/117_87763.html.

profit with him.[22] As a result of the investigation, a wide-spread match-fixing epidemic was uncovered affecting not only football, but volleyball, motorboat racing, and allegedly baseball, Korea's most popular sport. The government responded by issuing stiff penalties: from heavy fines to long-term prison sentences of up to 7 years in prison. Tragically, three players and one coach involved in the scandal died by suicide.[23]

These examples demonstrate that the way in which criminals operate varies. There is no end to the ingenuity of match fixers in finding new ways to achieve the results they are aiming for – namely to create the circumstances where they can influence the outcome, or part of, the sporting event.

MATCH FIXING – The match fixer's view[i]

"Hello, I'm a match fixer.

I think football is a beautiful game. A really beautiful game! I make buckets of money out of football. It's a beautiful game for me.

I am a very successful businessman. Some people call me a professional criminal. OK, I agree, I do make money for myself and my network by helping to organise the results of a few football matches. Well, quite a lot actually. It's a growing part of my business. I also fix a few other sports too, but the real money-maker is football.

I am just helping a few mates make a bit of money at the bookies. We all like to beat the bookies, and the betting companies, don't we? After all, they're not short of money.

But honestly, it's just so easy. All I want is high profit and low risk for my business ventures. And if one of my mates or I do get caught, we want to make sure we don't go to prison. But that's easy too! I'll tell you later.

You see, match fixing is so much easier than all my other criminal activities: trafficking drugs or smuggling people is pretty dodgy nowadays – the police do a lot of work trying to catch us; they see it as a priority apparently. The laws are strong, the police have got lots of clever equipment to detect us – they call them 'special investigative techniques'; and the penalties are quite frightening – they execute you in some countries.

Fraud is easier, especially over the internet, but it is not without risk as we leave a footprint showing where we broke into the system.

But match fixing is dead easy. Especially in football. You wouldn't believe how easy it is.

---

[i] This is a fictional example presented at the INTERPOL – FIFA Regional Conference 'Match Fixing – the ugly side of the beautiful game' in Kuala Lumpur on 20 February 2013.

(continued)

---

[22] Choe Sang-Hun, "South Korea Cracks Down on Match-Fixing Epidemic," The New York Times, 21 February 2012. http://www.nytimes.com/2012/02/22/sports/22iht-fixing22.html?_r=0.

[23] Dan Orlowitz, "Former K-League player Lee Kyung-Hwan commits suicide after match-fixing involvement," Goal.com, 16 April 2012. http://www.goal.com/en/news/3800/korea/2012/04/16/3039296/former-k-league- player-lee-kyung-hwan-commits-suicide-after.

First of all, there are lots of what we call 'targets'. We can target the players; we like getting them young, possibly through their family and friends. Give them a little present – we call it a 'sweetener' in my business; say 'you're the best player I've seen for years; you can be the next Pele' – anything like that. ALL people love being told how good they are. They always fall for it!

Or buy a few drinks and a meal; provide some sexual favours – we can do anything. Then they can be encouraged to let a goal in – we like to get a goalkeeper. But it doesn't really matter where they play – the central defenders can be useful – anyone who can miss a tackle. If they don't play ball, we can always threaten them. End their career if necessary. But usually they are so naive – most of them don't know what they've got into, until it's too late. Lovely!

What many people don't realise is that most footballers are very ambitious to progress in their sport. They think everyone wants to help them. And most don't get paid much at all. In some places in the world, the controls on players' wages are lousy; some go weeks, or even months, without being paid. That makes our job easy too.

Then there are referees and their assistants. The referees are a good catch because they control the game; they can help the score along with a few goals – we like them - goals; or a couple of penalties; or a red card. Easy! Often, referees don't get paid much either, and they are ambitious too – easy again!

It doesn't end there. We target former players, players' agents, coaches, managers. I know them all. I've got a couple of mates who have actually bought football clubs. That makes it pretty easy too.

I suppose I've got five things that I do well in my business. Of course, I am proactive. I initiate things and see they get done. I have ideas, and put them into action through my network.

I've got good partners. I've got links all round the world. I need an effective and efficient network, with reliable people who know their job, to help my business along. We are in partnership, each doing our bit for the common good - making money.

We have a lot of football on the TV nowadays and the development of the internet and mobile telecommunications has really helped me keep in contact with them, pass on last minute requests. I've got some great partnerships – they work really well and help my business. I can rely on my contacts to do what I ask them – they know the consequences if they don't.

I do need reliable information that I can use. It's quite a complex business and it operates 24/7. There are games being played at all times of the day and night, everywhere. And here's the clever thing – we don't only target the big matches, we reach down into the lower leagues sometimes too – less TV coverage, more ambitious young players and referees.

Then there is the betting. That's easy. Sometimes I bet with so called illegal bookmakers because in some countries betting is illegal. In other countries the sports betting is run by state owned companies and in others there is a private sector betting market – loads of betting companies and their number is growing day by day. I can access a whole range of betting companies over the internet. Me and my partners have got accounts all over the place. Sports betting is a growing business, especially betting on football. The profit on the bets is different depending on which route you take. I don't really mind getting a low profit for my bets – that way it stays below the radar. Little and often, that's what I say.

So I need information to help me do my job. I get it from a variety of sources. Inside information is really useful. Helps us to prioritise what we are going to do,

(continued)

when we are going to do it, where and how. It also helps to identify our potential targets.

Information is also important to us so we can keep one – or several – steps ahead of the police and the national football authorities. Not that they are too interested in most countries. They have other priorities. That's great for my business.

And we can access the betting markets easily for information about the best betting options. The internet has been a great help, so too the 'in-game' betting arrangements which show the odds moving all the time. That's really useful information to help us put money on, or ease off because the odds are shortening. So, all in all, we are pretty well co-ordinated and able to use information quickly.

What's really helpful to my business is that most people don't understand what I do or how I do it. In addition to that, it is really helpful that most countries don't have laws in place to stop my activities. Some do, and there has been a worrying increase in attention to match fixing in the last couple of years. I keep a close eye on legislation in countries to pick up any developments that might get in my way. Don't want to slip up. Thankfully, most countries are pretty disorganised or disinterested. They don't have up to date laws on match fixing, often having to apply existing legislation for bribery or corruption. That's difficult for them.

The police do not usually have the necessary powers to collect information, and they don't share information very well, especially between countries. That's very helpful to me. In many countries, the police don't see tackling these issues as a priority or they don't have the tools to do an investigation. Most of them are not familiar with the latest betting arrangements we exploit, either.

Fortunately, the national football associations are not well organised in many countries. Often, they don't give training to players or referees, or others – they call them administrators I think; and, of course, they don't really know how to investigate. They don't seem to talk with the police either. That's helpful to me.

Of course, I have to be a bit cautious. And I do worry about some recent developments. I always keep my eye on them as they are a threat to my business. I don't know what you think, but there seem to be more and more match fixers around. They are competition to me. Normally I deal with them effectively. Some are getting caught; and worse, talking to the police about how we do our business. That's not helpful to me.

Most of all, I worry about the increasing visibility of football match fixing. Lots of people seem to be talking about it now in comparison with a few years ago. In some countries, players and referees are rejecting my offers. There has been a lot of publicity about some recent investigations in several parts of the world.

It is beginning to look like national football associations, the police, governments and the betting companies, are coordinating better in some places. In some countries they are talking more and more about integrity in sport. I hear they are introducing training and awareness for players, referees and administrators. And whistle blowing hotlines for the reporting of suspicious activities.

There seems to be betting monitoring systems popping up everywhere. Some national football associations have appointed 'national integrity officers' to tackle match fixing better. There is even talk about some sort of international convention on manipulating sport.

I am beginning to get a little concerned about some of these developments. Perhaps the match fixing business is going to get too risky. But I'm an entrepreneurial type of guy – I'll stay in this while it's good and move on if it gets too risky. We'll see".

It is vitally important that stakeholders in football, including those who run the game (football associations), club administrators, referees and players all understand how the 'bad guys' operate. They need to know how to say no to an offer that may be very hard to refuse. It is only then that effective anti corruption measures can be identified, implemented and monitored to protect the sport.

The Key Elements of a Strategy to Tackle Match Fixing in Football

At the start of the INTERPOL – FIFA Initiative we undertook a range of research to help us better understand the scale and scope of the problem of match fixing in football. This included a documentary review, questionnaires to all 209 football member associations of FIFA, discussions with global, confederation and national representatives of all the stakeholders, the completion of an initial 'training needs analysis' and the holding of formal 'expert' meetings with selected representatives.

As a result of this research and these consultations, as well as a number of 'pilot' workshops at the national and regional level, it is clear that there are some commonly agreed strategic themes that are crucial to developing a more effective response to the threats posed to football by corrupt activities.[24] These themes provide a broad framework which we believe is helpful for those involved in protecting football; and they all need to be in place as they link together, supporting each other. They form the basis of the approach adopted by INTERPOL in the implementation of the INTERPOL – FIFA Initiative and are explained in greater detail below.[25]

Partnerships	• All Stakeholders - Government, Football Associations, Clubs, Representative Bodies (of all key actors and targets), Agents, sports related targets of match - fixers, Betting Industry & Regulators, Law Enforcement
Information	• Good practice, research, current developments in modus operandi and sports betting, statistics • Codes of conduct, rules, laws, regulations • Collection, storage, analysis and application/use of information
Coordination	• National, regional and international procedures, information sharing, enforcement strategies • Nominated points of contact, clear roles and responsibilies
Prevention	• Awareness Raising, Training and Education • Alignment and improvement of governance, rules, laws, codes, enforcement, reporting mechanisms
Proactivity	• Recognise individual responsibility, address barriers and resistance, motivate key actors • Ethical Leadership

Prepared by the INTERPOL Integrity in Sport team following the 'Outcome Statements' of two Regional Conferences in Europe and Asia in January and February 2013

---

[24] Indeed, this approach may be applicable to all sports.

[25] From the INTERPOL Programme Management Plan in Explanatory note to Year 3 of the first 3-Year Action Plan (29 April 2013).

Partnerships

There is broad agreement that given the global nature of football, match fixing cannot be effectively tackled by any single organisation. There are many 'stakeholders' involved.

Obviously, there are a number of different partners within football itself, including the players and referees who are so often the primary targets of the match fixers, their representative bodies, to coaches and managers, club officials, directors and owners of football clubs, and the various governing bodies in football at the national and regional level, and globally.

In addition, there are other interested parties who may have a role to play in the prevention and investigation of match fixing and the protection of sport. These include relevant national government bodies and institutions such as the ministry responsible for sport, for social development and education.

If there is legal betting in a country, there may be an organisation responsible for the regulation and oversight of the betting market – the betting (or gambling) regulator. There may also be representative bodies of legal betting companies, national lotteries and betting monitoring organisations where a free market for betting has been developed.

Law enforcement agencies also have a role to play in protecting football. While disciplinary investigations should be undertaken by sports governing bodies, should a criminal investigation be necessary it is going to be conducted by a relevant law enforcement agency such as the police, or a specific anti-corruption body should it have such a responsibility, together with the prosecution authority. Given the nature of match fixing in football, where it has become clear that it is frequently international in nature, often involving international organised crime networks and professional criminals, this will also require international cooperation and the support of relevant international organisations.

There are also a number of national and international organisations directly or indirectly promoting the protection of sport, good governance and anti corruption initiatives (for example the United Nations, regional bodies such as the Council of Europe, Sportaccord, Transparency International, academic experts) who may be appropriate partners that can be involved in and support the development and implementation of strategies to counter match fixing in football.

All the evidence received from the panels of experts we have consulted have emphasised how important a holistic approach, involving the widest possible range of partners, is to preventing and tackling match fixing. Similarly, our own experience has demonstrated that in most countries such partnerships are not well developed. There are exceptions, but most frequently there are not even 'single points of contact' existing in the various organisations to discuss matters relating to match fixing in football, let alone a coherent structure bringing together relevant parties to identify and agree what needs to be done and who should do it.

Of course, it is necessary to recognise that different partners may have different priorities and responsibilities. Not everyone will see the same picture and always agree on the way forward. But it is surely better to try and bring together the interested parties to understand those differences, and the similarities; to identify who can do what, and know what each of the parties can and cannot do. If the various partners pool their information about a common threat, and jointly agree a way forward, identifying who will do what, this must be better than ignoring the problem, crossing our fingers and hoping it will go away. All the evidence relating to match fixing and football suggests it will not go away without better partnerships between all the stakeholders.[26]

Information

We all need information to help us make better decisions. It is a fact of life that many regard information as their own property and they are reluctant to share it (information is often perceived as power). Successful organisations are usually those who have thought about what information they need and how they are going to get it. They have also thought about how they are going to keep it and analyse it and ultimately, who they are going to share the information with and how best to use it.

Each of the partners involved in tackling match fixing needs information. Some of this information will be unique to their own requirements but some will be common. All partners need to understand how match fixers operate – their modus operandi – so that coherent plans can be developed to stop them successfully exploiting the 'beautiful game'. All the evidence we have collected in the early stages of the initiative to protect football from match fixing indicates, with a few exceptions, that little thought has been given to the information requirement and even less thought has been given to sharing and using that information. In many countries, knowledge of the nature and extent of match fixing, both globally and nationally, is sparse. A shared understanding of the challenges posed by match fixing has to be beneficial for all involved.

While much information can be gleaned from 'open source' material, many of the partners identified in the previous section also have extremely useful information about match fixing – whether it be about the latest modus operandi of the match fixers, how betting operates and is exploited by criminals[27] or the latest 'good practice' in preventing and investigating match fixing. So there is a great need for a common understanding of the threat and potential solutions – measures that will protect football from match fixers.

It is important to be systematic about collecting information, keeping information, analysing information, sharing information and using information. There are different types of information – some is general information about the nature of the problem

---

[26] As concluded by the INTERPOL Experts meeting on Integrity in Sports held on 18/19 October 2011.

[27] Betting monitoring organisations, such as the FIFA-EWS (Early Warning System) can provide 'live' information.

that all the partners need to understand. Then there is more specific information that will directly assist partners with specific responsibilities. For example, what are the rules and regulations relevant to corruption in sport and match fixing; what information do players, referees and others need to help them in recognising, resisting and reporting suspicious approaches; what information can betting monitoring agencies provide; what information is needed to carry out an investigation, whether it is for a disciplinary enquiry or a criminal investigation; what prevention initiatives and training programmes are being undertaken?

Identifying the information requirement and how to use information, is a crucial aspect of the strategic framework to tackle match fixing more effectively. Not surprisingly, it is not without some difficulties. Some organisations and partners will have constraints – real or imagined – about sharing information, not least in relation to personal data (which may fall within a data protection regime). There may also be a lack of willingness to share, engendered by a lack of trust between partner agencies. There will not always be easy solutions to these and other challenges but by working together in a partnership framework it will enable these issues to be raised, discussed and solutions to be identified.[28]

Coordination

Given the number of partners involved, it is imperative that all the stakeholders seek to operate in a coordinated manner to ensure a comprehensive approach to both the prevention of match fixing and the response to any allegation of match fixing.

Our research indicates that, with some notable exceptions,[29] few attempts have been made to bring together the various stakeholders involved in preventing match fixing. Most commonly, individual sports in individual countries appear under-prepared, adopting an ostrich-like approach to the subject, hoping it just won't happen. While the threat that match fixing poses to football and other sports is real and growing, there are few, if any, human resources directly devoted to protecting football from match fixing By contrast, it appears that professional criminals are extremely well coordinated and able to exploit the under-preparedness of the stakeholders and public authorities at national level.

There are a number of ways in which coordination can be enhanced. The bringing together of all stakeholders or partners at national level is a starting point. In some countries, an 'all-sport' approach has been adopted in which representatives from the governing bodies of major sports are involved as 'partners' with the

---

[28] As illustrated and advocated in the AUSTRALIA: SPORT AND RECREATION MINISTERS' COUNCIL COMMUNIQUE (2011). National Policy on Match Fixing in Sport as agreed by Australian Governments on 10 June 2011 and the United Kingdom Report of the Sports Betting Integrity Panel (chairman Rick PARRY) (February 2010).

[29] For example in countries such as Australia, Italy, the Republic of Korea and the United Kingdom a coordinated approach has been adopted (this list is not exhaustive).

other stakeholders from public authorities, the betting companies and law enforcement. In others, it may be only the football authorities (or any other sport[30]) who are engaged in such partnerships. This is a matter of national choice.

Regardless of the approach adopted identifying single points of contact (SPOCs) for each organisation can further enhance coordination. This increases the opportunity to share information and seek solutions to problems. Equally, it enables the various stakeholders to build mutual trust and is an essential requirement nationally and internationally. The identification of 'Integrity Officers' within each UEFA member country is seen as a positive step on the part of member associations in the football community by creating a focal point for all matters relating to match fixing and corruption.

The general purpose of developing a coordination mechanism, in particular at the national level, is to coordinate activities to protect integrity in sport. There are several specific objectives for such a body: to provide better general information upon which to make decisions; and, when incidences of match fixing or related activities are suspected, better investigation; finally, such a coordination body can ensure better implementation of prevention activities.

Firstly, better information enables a better understanding of the challenges posed by match fixing, whether it is general information about the nature and extent of match fixing or specific information about a particular suspicious activity (irregular betting or match fixing) to be gathered. Obtaining information from, and the perspectives of, a range of stakeholders including the sport governing body (or bodies), national government representatives, the betting organisations and law enforcement enables a more complete picture of the threat to be drawn. The better you understand a problem, the better chance there is to identify the best solution to tackle it.

Secondly, when an allegation of match fixing does arise, coordination between the parties involved is crucial to put in place the enforcement or regulatory strategy. Who will investigate the allegation? Is it a disciplinary matter to be investigated and adjudicated by the sport governing body or a criminal matter to be investigated by law enforcement and adjudicated before a court of law? In some cases it may be both. In any case, the investigator will want access to the best available information, intelligence and evidence – which may be held by different organisations. Not surprisingly, it is most helpful if these issues have been thought through beforehand and there is a system in place, perhaps a 'standard operating procedure', protocols and an investigators' guide, rather than waiting for it to happen and then making up the process as you go along. At the very least, it would be helpful for the investigator to know there is an organisation and points of contact who can be used and assist.

Thirdly, there is a real need to coordinate prevention activities. The issue of prevention is covered in more detail in the next section. But there is a need for national level coordination for prevention activities generally. In particular, agreeing the need for a reporting system (sometimes called a 'whistleblower' system or 'hotline'), for the collection and collation of information and intelligence, for the

---

[30] For example horse racing.

production of threat or risk assessments, the preparation and use of education programmes and training materials, the delivery of training to acceptable standards and licensing procedures will all benefit from a more coordinated approach.[31]

Prevention

In all of our meetings with experts and stakeholders they emphasised the importance and value of preventing match fixing. We agree. This is the most important factor in tackling match fixing and corruption in football.

There are a number of aspects to prevention and some, such as education, awareness and training, are obviously and directly related to match fixing. But it is also argued that other broader issues, such as those related to integrity and good governance in the way the sport is managed must also be addressed. The whole area of prevention, and the development of a coherent prevention strategy, should be a core activity of the coordinating body (such as a national or football 'integrity in sport unit').

One of the broader issues relating to the prevention of match fixing is having relevant *legislation* in place nationally, both to act as a deterrent and also to enable proper investigation. It is necessary to have evidence gathering and prosecution when incidences of match fixing requiring a criminal justice remedy occur, as well as an effective sport controlled disciplinary approach. At present, many countries seek to use associated criminal law legislation which has been put in place for other reasons, such as fraud, bribery, cheating, corruption or deception. This is not always a good fit and recent research has demonstrated that few countries are satisfied with their legislative arrangements to protect the integrity of sport. Several experts with experience of investigating criminal law allegations of match fixing have expressed concern about the suitability of the criminal offences and investigatory powers available. It is also important to recognise that professional criminals' behaviour is often affected by their assessment of the risk and if there is inadequate legislation in place, this may encourage them to consider certain countries as 'low risk' opportunities.

Identifying the specific content of legislation will be a matter for discussion within a country but some of the essential elements will include the need for clarity on the identification of the actual offences relating to match fixing, the provision of realistic sanctions which will have a deterrent effect, clarity of investigatory powers and breadth of jurisdiction (they need to allow for the 'international' nature of match fixing) and the identification of resources (who will do what).[32]

---

[31] Enhanced coordination between all stakeholders to prevent and investigate match fixing is emphasised by all observers and participants in INTERPOL – FIFA regional and national workshops as a key outcome required to be developed. It is also urged in the Preliminary Draft Convention Against manipulation of Sports Results, Article 5 by EPAS dated 4 September 2012, and many other national and international sports bodies.

[32] At the international level the Council of Europe (EPAS) is working with a host of organisations to develop an international convention to combat the manipulation of sports competitions.

Another of the broader prevention priorities relates to the need for sports governing bodies – in the case of football the national football association or federation,
and football clubs – to demonstrate that they adhere to the latest *good governance
rules and practice* to promote integrity and prevent corruption. Good governance in
business (and football is a business) emphasises the importance of transparency,
responsibility and accountability, the articulation of ethics and values, open policies
and processes (especially in relation to selection, remuneration and elections), and
explicit zero tolerance for corruption. More detailed guidance in this respect can be
obtained from a variety of sources (including the IMF and 'Transparency
International').

It is helpful, in terms of prevention, if the rules of the national football federation
refer explicitly to the issue of match fixing (and other integrity in sport issues such
as racism and doping), prohibit betting on football by all its participants, forbid the
passing of inside information to outsiders, require reporting to the authorities of any
suspicious activities and provide investigations and sanctions procedures. In addition, the rules of the federation should require an up to date and relevant code of
conduct for all participants,[33] the provision of a reporting line – so that suspicious
activities can be notified to the authorities, contracts (or licences) for players and
referees that are explicit about adhering to integrity in sport issues, and a requirement for all participants in the 'football family' to undertake regular anti match
fixing awareness training.

Awareness raising, education and training are central to effective prevention,
regardless of the issue being 'prevented'. A recent survey by INTERPOL with the
209 national football association members of FIFA revealed that the extent and
nature of training on anti match fixing and integrity in sport issues remains very
limited.[34] Despite a number of initiatives by several organisations in recent years,[35]
there are only a few countries where there are ongoing, coordinated procedures
providing regular, systematic training to players, referees and other relevant 'actors'
in football (such as coaches, managers, players agents, administrators, directors and
club owners).

At the national level it is important to identify who should receive training. It is
well known that players and match officials – as they are on the field of play – are
primary targets for match fixers. Young players, particularly those selected for
national and club academies, also need to be a priority in terms of prevention. But
the other 'actors' referred to in the preceding paragraph should also be considered.

Equally, there is an identified need for training for those involved in investigating
allegations of match fixing. This refers to two types of 'investigator': law

---

[33] The FIFA Code of Conduct, updated in 2012 is a useful guide.

[34] Undertaken by the INTERPOL Integrity in Sport Unit as part of the research for the Training
Needs Analysis 2012/13.

[35] For example, training by FIFPro, Transparency International and INTERPOL in relation to football match fixing. The European Elite Athletes Association and Sportaccord provide training for a
range of sports. There are also training programmes about resisting match fixing in cricket, tennis
and rugby.

enforcement officials responsible for collecting evidence and preparing prosecution cases, and 'fact-finders' used by football associations to investigate and collect evidence in relation to a sport-led 'disciplinary' inquiry. Both groups need training about what to look for, essential points to prove, how to collect information and evidence, how to record it and how to present it.

Integrity in Sport, or specific anti match fixing training needs to be tailored to the needs of the audience and different training methods can be used such as 'e-learning' or 'face-to-face'. The content of the training usually focuses on explaining the problem of match fixing and how match fixing happens – in other words the modus operandi of match fixers; the importance of not getting involved in any match fixing and the consequences of doing so (including an honest recognition of the difficulty of resisting because of the size of the benefit or the fear of the threat), and the need to report any suspicious activity the individual may become aware of. In short, it should be designed to enable the audience to **recognise** match fixing, **resist** it and **report** it.

Thought should also be given as to who delivers the training (someone who is respected by the audience), its frequency and the means by which attendance at such training is recorded. In some countries, the fact that the individual has been the subject of training and knows the requirements expected of them is referred to in contracts or participants are required to sign a specific 'integrity agreement'.

Increasing the awareness of those involved in football of the dangers of match fixing can be supplemented by a variety of methods – for example through the use of posters, the internet, mobile telecommunications and briefing notes.

Pro-activity

This is easy to explain, perhaps more difficult to do. Put simply, it means effectively implementing the four headings identified above – better partnerships, information, coordination and prevention – to tackle match fixing in football.

Do we sit and wait, carry on as normal in the hope that match fixing won't happen? Or do we need to prepare, to put measures and mechanisms in place to protect football from the real threat of criminal exploitation? All the evidence now available indicates that criminals are pro-active, global, innovative, nimble on their feet and ruthless in their pursuit of their desired outcome – to make money out of football regardless of the impact on the sport.

Those engaged in developing football honestly need to recognise that the game needs to be better protected. This requires active leadership, champions and role models who promote integrity and ethics in football. It includes those in positions of responsibility within the 'football family' – in football clubs, national football associations and governing bodies – as well as those in public authorities (such as government and law enforcement) and the betting industry to work together to develop and implement a coherent approach to make football less attractive to those criminals seeking to exploit it.

The 'leaders' of the various stakeholder groups (football authorities, the betting organisations, law enforcement and other public authorities) have a crucial role to play in the identification of the overall strategy and its implementation, and this includes finding ways to enable the building of trust between agencies and the identification and ongoing support for single points of contact (SPOCs).

The INTERPOL – FIFA Training Initiative

INTERPOL has been providing services relating to the prevention of corruption generally, the security of international major sporting events and specific support to, and coordination of, international policing operations and investigations for many years.[36] Notable examples of the latter have been coordinated enforcement activities against illegal soccer gambling in Asia over the last decade and the associated anti match fixing task force.

The INTERPOL – FIFA Anti-Corruption Training Initiative started in May 2011 with 'the overall objective of tackling sports corruption in football, with a principal focus on illegal and irregular betting and match fixing, through providing various training programmes to improve key individuals' awareness and understanding of corruption in football, of the tactics used by its perpetrators and of methods to detect and counteract them'. The Initiative provides support for the development of an 'anti-corruption training wing' at the forthcoming INTERPOL Global Complex for Innovation and a focus on football related anti-corruption training, education and prevention programmes.[37]

In practical terms the INTERPOL – FIFA Initiative is delivered by an 'Integrity in Sport' team which works closely with remainder of INTERPOL's assets at its General Secretariat, in its Regional Bureaux, and with law enforcement agencies and other partners through the National Central Bureau of INTERPOL located in each of its 190 member countries. In addition, close working relationships have been (or in some cases are being) developed with the FIFA Security Director and his team, with the six football Confederations and 209 national member associations of FIFA. Other partners include players and referees representative organisations, various international sporting bodies, regional and national government departments responsible for the promotion of sport, anti corruption agencies and betting regulatory and representative organisations.

Following consultation with a number of experts and the completion of a training needs analysis, an action plan was developed and agreed with FIFA which focuses on the three key elements of training, education and prevention. These three elements

---

[36] This is the practical implementation of the INTERPOL – FIFA Agreement signed in 2011 outlining the 'General Conditions governing FIFA's contribution to the benefit of the ICPO INTERPOL within the framework of the INTERPOL – FIFA Anti-Corruption Initiative' (9 May 2011).
[37] Ibid.

are fully interdependent – in other words, they all support and assist each other. Emphasis is placed on the importance of developing the strategic themes referred to above, namely identifying partnerships and engaging with all the key stakeholders, the need to establish what information is required, how it is to be collected and used, developing appropriate coordination mechanisms necessary to anticipate and deal with issues, the identification of a full range of prevention measures and the adoption of a pro-active approach to protecting the integrity of football.

In the 'training' pillar the activities concentrate upon the delivery of 'face to face' training and the development of 'e-learning' programmes.

The 'face to face' training takes a variety of forms including two day regional workshops for six to eight countries, two day national workshops for individual countries and training for specific 'events' whether identified by FIFA Security Division or other stakeholders. In the preparation phase, the INTERPOL Integrity in Sport team works with the regional and national football authorities and law enforcement agencies to assess the current arrangements to tackle match fixing, to identify who should be invited to attend (a wide range of stakeholders is encouraged) and to agree the detailed agenda for the training session.

The workshops focus upon three objectives: to better understand the problem of match fixing; to recognise good practice in tackling match fixing (both from within the audience and from elsewhere in the world); and to encourage participants to identify the next steps that need to be taken to further develop their approach to tackling match fixing in football.

A bespoke workshop agenda is developed to seek to address the issues relevant to the delegates and delivered using a range of training techniques (presentations, participative exercises and focused discussions). These are delivered by experienced trainers, facilitators and speakers including representatives from FIFA, from INTERPOL, legal experts on sports law, international experts in the field of promoting integrity in sport and from within the region/country involved in the workshop.

A number of other 'awareness' training sessions have also been delivered, for example to the FIFA Referees and Assistant Referees shortlisted for the FIFA World Cup in Brazil in 2014, to FIFA technical Directors and Development Officers, to representatives of qualifying teams for the U17 and U20 Women's World Cups, and to a number of other stakeholders – either nationally based or organisation based. These sessions tend to be of 1 or 2 h duration and form part of a broader agenda of a pre-arranged meeting. They emphasise the nature of match fixing, the modus operandi of the match fixers and those behind them, the consequences of becoming involved and what to do if approached by a match fixer or if concerned about a suspicious event. These issues are encapsulated in the headline '**recognise, resist and report**'.

An area currently being developed is a programme for 'train the trainers' – to enable anti match fixing training to be delivered by 'local' or 'organisation' based trainers. Workshops focusing upon improving understanding and investigation techniques for law enforcement officials and football association 'fact finders' are also being developed.

To date, the training workshops have been extremely well received by delegates who have evaluated them as relevant, constructive and valuable. The INTERPOL team follows up the workshops some 12 months after the event to ask whether progress in developing the response to match fixing has been continued, to seek good practice and areas of difficulty.

'E-learning' programmes are a valuable tool to be used within the overall 'training approach'. While they may not be suitable for all environments, they can be extremely useful for raising awareness and sometimes can be used as a requirement for the relevant audience to complete. In conjunction with a range of stakeholders, INTERPOL have developed a generic anti match fixing e-learning module for all players and other, more specific, modules for referees, young players and coaches/ managers will be available in 2013.

The 'education' pillar of activity includes the regular updating of the 'training needs assessment (TNA)' to ensure that the activities of the programme remain relevant and focused on addressing current and future developments in match fixing. The design of all of the training curricula referred to above is based upon the TNA and also on the advice, guidance and good practice received from regular 'experts meetings' held on specific subject matters.

Another aspect of the 'education' activity undertaken by INTERPOL is the sharing of information about match fixing with all national football associations, law enforcement agencies and other stakeholders. A newsletter is published three to four times per year and each week a 'weekly media recap' is circulated containing the latest open source reporting of match fixing investigations and associated occurrences, sanctions and good practice. The 'weekly media recap' has proved to be a very popular source of information. In addition, the INTERPOL website contains both general and specific information about match fixing, the 'e-learning' programme and a number of presentations which can be accessed through the Integrity in Sport Unit. The social media is also used with videos highlighting match fixing and integrity in sport issues posted on INTERPOL's official Youtube channel and a regularly updated twitter account.[38]

In the future, a number of 'guidance' documents to prevent and tackle match fixing will be produced in consultation with FIFA, national football associations and other stakeholders.

'Prevention' activity (of course, the whole INTERPOL – FIFA Initiative is about prevention) includes Confederation-wide 'kick-off' conferences focusing upon raising general awareness about match fixing and what can be done to prevent it. Two significant events have been held for Europe and Asia already and more are planned in the near future. The 'outcome' statement from the two conferences already held have endorsed the importance of the partnership, information, coordination, prevention and pro-activity approach to tackle match fixing.

The team at INTERPOL is also working with FIFPro[39] to develop a short video to heighten player awareness and seeking, in conjunction with all stakeholders, to identify more 'programme ambassadors' to promote the prevention message.

Within the 'prevention' pillar is included 'outreach and partnership' activity where INTERPOL staff attend and contribute to relevant meetings, seminars and conferences within the sports world and law enforcement community to maintain ongoing research activities relating to corruption in football and to market, promote and further the INTERPOL – FIFA initiative.

Conclusion

Match fixing in football, particularly the manipulation by criminals often operating at a global level seeking to exploit the betting markets, is an increasing challenge which threatens the integrity of the game. Many football organisations and other stakeholders remain underprepared to tackle this challenge.

The INTERPOL – FIFA Initiative seeks to increase awareness among all stakeholders with a responsibility to protect football of the dangers of match fixing and to urge them to put in place a series of measures designed to minimise criminal opportunities. They include the identification of a number of 'strategic themes' – partnerships, information, coordination, prevention and pro-activity – which, if implemented properly, will provide greater protection for the 'beautiful game' and the billions of people who enjoy it. An encouraging start has been made.

However, significant challenges remain to be addressed but the INTERPOL – FIFA Initiative will continue to work with all stakeholders to better protect integrity in football.

---

[38] '@INTERPOL_SPORT for the twitter account'.

[39] The International Federation of Professional Footballers.

Bibliography

Australian Governments on 10 June 2011; Department of Regional Australia, Local Government, Arts and Sport. (2011). *National policy on match-fixing in sport (as agreed 10 June 2011)*. Canberra.

Berninger, A. (2013). Establishing good governance. Presentation to INTERPOL-FIFA National Workshop in Turkey on 4/5 February 2013.

Bower, T. (2007). *Broken dreams: Vanity, greed and the souring of British football*. London: Simon & Schuster.

Enlarged Partial Agreement on Sport. (2012). *Preliminary draft Convention against manipulation of sports results*. Strasbourg: Council of Europe.

Council meeting in Brussels on 28/29 November 2011; Council of the European Union. (2011). *Council conclusions on combating match-fixing*. Brussels.

England and Wales Cricket Board. (2011). *Anti-corruption code for players and player support personnel*. London.

EUROPOL (2013). Match Fixing: Joint Investigation Team 'VETO'; press conference slides 4 February 2013;

FIFA (2013). Circular 1336 entitled 'Integrity Declaration for the international referees, assistant referees (etc) on the 2013 FIFA Lists (22 January 2013);

FIFA regulations and guidelines (2012). Including updated Code of Conduct, Disciplinary Code, Code of Ethics, Match agents regulations, Players' Agent regulations, Guidelines for FIFA match officials;

FIFA WORLD. (2012). Fighting Talk: An interview with Chris EATON (January/February 2012 edition);

FIFA World. (2012, January/February). Fighting talk: An interview with Chris Eaton. *FIFA World*, pp. 20–23.

FIFPro Black Book Eastern Europe: The problems professional footballers encounter: research (07 February 2012);

FIFPro. (2012). *FIFPro black book Eastern Europe*. Netherlands: Author.

Hill, D. (2010). *The fix: Soccer and organized crime*. Toronto: McClelland & Stewart.

Independent Governance Committee to the Executive Committee of FIFA. (2012). *FIFA governance reform project: First report by the independent governance committee to the executive committee of FIFA*. Basel, Switzerland: Author.

International Olympic Committee. (2011). *Founding working group on the fight against irregular and illegal sports betting* (experts meeting 2 November). Lausanne, Switzerland: Author.

International Olympic Committee. (2012, February 2). IOC's fight against irregular and illegal betting in sport moves into implementation phase. *International Olympic Committee*. Retrieved from http://www.olympic.org/news/ioc-s-fight-against-irregular-and-illegal-betting-in-sport-moves-to-implementation-phase/151887.

INTERPOL (2011). Notes of the Experts meeting on Integrity in Sports held on 18/19 October 2011 (25 November 2011);

INTERPOL (2013). Annual Activity Report for the INTERPOL – FIFA Initiative 2012/13 (3 July 2013);

INTERPOL(2013). Explanatory note to Year 3 of the first 3-Year Action Plan (29 April 2013);

INTERPOL (2013). 'Outcome Statements' from International Conferences in Rome (18 January 2013) and Kuala Lumpur (21 February 2013). 'Match Fixing: The Ugly side of the beautiful game';

INTERPOL (2013). Programme Management Plan, INTERPOL – FIFA Initiative;

INTERPOL (2011 and 2013). Training Needs Assessment Reports (December 2011 and 12 June 2013);

INTERPOL (2012, 2013). Extracts from Weekly media reports;

INTERPOL – FIFA Agreement (2011). General Conditions governing FIFA's contribution to the benefit of the ICPO INTERPOL within the framework of the INTERPOL – FIFA Anti-Corruption Initiative (9 May 2011);

IRIS (Institut de relations Internationales et strategiques) (2012). Sports Betting and Corruption: How to preserve the integrity of sport;

L'Institut de relations internationales et stratégiques. (2012). *Sports betting and corruption : How to preserve the integrity of sport.* Paris.

Jennings, A. (2007). *Foul! The secret world of FIFA: Bribes, vote rigging and ticket scandals.* HarperSport.

SportAccord. (2011). *Model rules on sports integrity in relation on sports betting* (version 2). Lausanne, Switzerland.

Schenk, S. (2011). *Safe hands: Building integrity and transparency at FIFA.* Berlin: Transparency International.

UNESCO (United Nations Educational, Scientific and Cultural Organization) (2013). Declaration of Berlin (from MINEPS V – the 5th International Conference of Ministers and Senior Officials responsible for Physical Education and Sport);UNITED KINGDOM (Department of Culture, Media and Sport) (2010). Report of the Sports Betting Integrity Panel (chairman Rick PARRY) (February 2010);

Sports Betting Integrity Panel. (2010). *Report of the Sports Betting Integrity Panel.* XXXX: United Kingdom Department of Culture, Media and Sport.

The Role of the Academe in Sports Integrity: The Objectives and Shape of a Sports Integrity Training Course

Lydia Segal

Abstract Reformers are issuing multiple proposals to boost integrity in sports. So far, the potential contributions of the academe to this effort have been largely glossed over. Yet the academe is a unique source of expertise in teaching ethics and can reach many more stakeholders than athletes, which is all most existing sports integrity training programs do. This chapter outlines the ways in which the academe can enhance sports integrity. It offers ideas on the possible goals and shapes of a sports integrity course and discusses ways in which to increase the ethical awareness of those involved in sports, elevate their level of moral reasoning, and give them the skills to navigate the situational pressures encountered in the world of sports.

The Importance of Targeting the Individual Decision-Maker

A growing chorus of experts around the world is proposing strategies to combat match-fixing and corruption in sport. Many of the proposals focus on fixing the larger context of sport, such as strengthening law enforcement, standardizing the regulatory environment across countries, and legalizing and regulating gambling, which spurs much corruption (*see* e.g. McLaren 2012). While these factors are critical to combating corruption in sport, unethical decisions are ultimately made by individuals. Individuals always have the choice to reject unethical choices, even if it means going against the tide.

Recent history shows that in a multitude of industries plagued by corruption, it was brave individuals who stood up and ultimately helped topple or expose these systems – whether Sharon Watkins at Enron in the financial industry or Colman Genn in New York City in the public education system. To combat corruption in sport, it is

L. Segal (✉)
Business School, Suffolk University, 73 Tremont Street, Boston, MA, USA
e-mail: lydiasegal@yahoo.com

M.R. Haberfeld and D. Sheehan (eds.), *Match-Fixing in International Sports: Existing Processes, Law Enforcement, and Prevention Strategies,*
DOI 10.1007/978-3-319-02582-7_15, © Springer International Publishing Switzerland 2013

therefore critical that reforms target and bolster the integrity of the individuals involved. Ethics and moral courage can and must be taught to individuals in order to fulfill the meaning of reform proposals underway. As Shadnam and Thomas (2011) note, integrity flows "from moral communities of individuals through organizations and from individuals through organizations to moral communities of individuals."

Until a few years ago, little was done to train individuals in sports integrity. Recently, however, SportAccord has launched an e-learning Program for athletes and officials called "How to Prevent Match-Fixing from Destroying your Career." The ICC created of an education and awareness program for players. Its integrity unit, TIU, developed an e-learning education program, the Uniform Tennis Anti-Corruption Program that, as of 2012, was mandatory for all Grand Slam tournament players. They must pass a test to prove that they learned. In 2011, UEFA established training seminars at U-17 and U-19 events. The US National Football League (NFL), US National Basketball Association (NBA), and the National Collegiate Athletic Association (NCAA) launched education programs for their players. The NBA does not allow athletes to play in their league unless they complete a course that includes corruption.

While these integrity initiatives are commendable, to make full use of the latest proven strategies to enhance ethics learning, the academe should be involved. The academe, especially business schools, – which since 1979 have been required by accreditation bodies like the AACSB to teach ethics, – have professors who special-ize in the field. These experts know how to maximize ethics learning in the class-room and generally have experience delivering a variety of ethics programs – in person, online, and hybrid, – to different audiences – graduate, undergraduate and different majors.

At the same time, the academe can reach a much wider range of people than only athletes, which is all sports organizations target. The academe reaches many of the people who are or will become spectators, fans, managers, gamblers,[1] and business sponsors and executives in the world of sports – all of whom can make individual decisions that collectively help determine the future status of sports integrity.

The Challenges of Cultivating Integrity in Sports Require the Most Effective Integrity Training Available

The reason state-of-the arts ethics training is needed in sport is that the pressures to engage in wrongdoing are powerful and widespread – indeed virtually inescapable. Countering these pressures requires more than lecturing at students. Consider the challenges educators face:

- *Fans may not care about or believe charges of match-fixing.* Consider the furious reaction of Juventus fans to charges that their team was engaged in corruption in

---

[1] As an NCAA study found, undergraduates can participate significantly in sports betting (NCAA 1999).

the Calciopoli saga. They refused to believe it. If the prime consumers of sports do not care about and do not want to hear about corruption – it is that much easier for those involved to get away with wrongdoing.

- *Moral ambiguity.* Moreover, match-fixing could seem more like largely innocuous meddling than throwing a match to the minds of those involved. While the rules and laws proscribe most forms of match-fixing, it may not "feel" wrong to win by a little bit more or less if winning or to throw a foul ball here or there if that does not change who the victor is. Usually, we "feel" something is wrong when we can see the harm we inflict. When a situation is perceived as morally ambiguous, it is easy to use techniques of neutralization – to tell oneself that the laws are senseless and that one is not doing anything wrong (Sykes and Matza 1957).
- *The media promotes a culture of betting.* Brash adverts on television, such as Ray Winstone's disembodied head spouting odds for Bet365.com, promote the gambling industry and feed the globalization of sports gambling, facilitated by the Internet. Sports betting, especially illegal sports betting, then opens the door to the influence of organized crime (*see* Sports Accord April 2012).

Ethics Can Be Taught

The pressures above may seem insurmountable. However, research shows that ethics can be taught (*see* e.g. Jones 2009; Dellaportas 2006). Teaching ethics can improve ethics attitudes (Conroy and Emerson 2008). James Rest and Lawrence Kohlberg, luminaries in the study of moral development, found that moral growth and ethical decision making skills develop sequentially over time (Kohlberg 1984a; Trevino 1992). Ethics training can speed up the development of moral reasoning. When people are sensitized to the importance of ethical behavior, they advance in their ethnical decision-making (Cano and Sams). Ethics training can also reduce a person's intention of doing something wrong that they otherwise would have wanted to do. (*see* e.g. Shaw et al. 2007).

Integrity training results a higher order of moral reasoning. Without training, undergraduates in one study relied mostly on thinking about avoidance of punishment – pre-conventional thinking – in deciding to cheat. The key question was whether they thought they could get away with it. In contrast, a significant number of undergraduates who had had ethics training thought in terms of abiding by the system's rules and wanting to be a good person – conventional thinking. This group of students focused on their own responsibility rather than blaming the system, the professor, or the opportunity to cheat (Cano and Sams).

Athletes and Others Involved in Sport Are Likely to Be Receptive to Ethics Training

Research suggests that students in different majors are receptive to ethics training at different rates (Segal et al. 2011). Students' personality traits and values, including ethical values, influence the area to which they are drawn and want to specialize in. Interestingly, research shows that students who are more ethical before receiving ethics training, are not necessarily more inclined to absorb ethics training than students who were less ethical before training. So, for example, Segal, Gideon, and Haberfeld (2011) found that, although entering business students tended to be less ethical than entering criminal justice students, business students were more open to ethics inculcation than criminal justice students. After receiving ethics training, their moral reasoning improved significantly more dramatically than did criminal justice students. The study hypothesized that, rather than being immoral, entering business students are amoral – i.e. they see business as a game and do "not cognitively attend to moral issues." The finding of malleability to training is consistent with the view of business as amoral: once students are made aware of ethics through an ethics course, their ethical attitudes improve. If they were immoral, they'd be cynical and not improve.

Little is known about the comparative receptivity of athletes and others involved in sport to ethics training. However, there seems to be much similarity between the world of sports and of business.

First, business insiders often view business as a game in which the ethics of the rest of the world do not apply. Sport is similarly often perceived as a "'world within a world' where the typical concerns and moral constraints of everyday life are temporarily set aside" (Bredemeir and Shields 1986, p. 7). Turiel (1978) notes that reasoning in sports is separate from moral reasoning. Upton (2011) goes so far as to argue that athletes may have moral obligation to cheat. Gambling is similarly viewed as its own world divorced from the moral concerns of the rest of the world. It is thus plausible that, like business students, athletes and others involved in sport may regard their activities as a game, an area where ethics, at least temporarily, do not quite apply and where winning is everything. Just as shareholders can reinforce this outlook in business by caring mostly about the growth of their stock's value, spectators and fans may reinforce this outlook in sport by caring mostly about watching a great game. So, the players in both the business and sports world may be "amoral" – not immoral – and therefore open to ethics training, as Segal, Gideon, and Haberfeld (2011) found.

Second, those involved in the management, marketing and sponsoring side of sport are generally business people, so they will be susceptible to training.

Third, athletes, team captains and college gamblers (we are not talking here about professional gamblers or gamblers with addiction issues) share values and personality traits with business students that may translate into their having a similar openness to ethical training. They all put a premium on winning. They all value competition, excitement, challenges, and risk-taking. Athletes, like business people, tend to be outgoing, extroverted, and socially aggressive. College football players, for instance, are more outgoing and socially aggressive than non-football players in college (Fletcher 1971). College gamblers are in it mostly for the excitement and challenge. In one federal study, the reason most frequently mentioned for betting with bookies was the "challenge" (US CRNPTG 1976). "Excitement" was given as a reason more often for friendly betting, while "to make money" was given as a reason for bookie betting (US CRNPTG 1976). Another study suggested that what makes sports gamblers tick is the challenge to their "intellectual and judgment capacities," as well as "the pleasure they derive out of beating the system, wanting to make money, and sharing a feeling of camaraderie" (Smith 1991). All this suggests that college gamblers view their world as a game with its own rules – making it more likely that they are amoral, rather than immoral, and thus susceptible to ethical training. Indeed, supporting this characterization, Layden (1995, p. 76) says that college sports gamblers are generally "bright, if often naïve" and "often clueless about the realm they have entered." These are precisely the kinds of people who are likely to benefit from ethics training.

The Objectives of a Sports Integrity Course

The literature posits a number of possible objectives of ethics courses (see e.g. Williams and Dewett 2005; Alam 1998; Brinkmann and Sims 2001). Drawing on these, we propose three objectives for a sports integrity course: (1) enhancing moral awareness, (2) promoting moral development, and (3) teaching skills to handle situational pressures. The objectives, especially the first two, overlap. However, it is helpful to distinguish them for the purpose of analysis.

1. Enhancing moral awareness
   Moral awareness is foundational to integrity. Most scholars on the subject agree that ethics courses should enhance students' awareness of and sensitivity to the moral consequences of their decisions (e.g. Williams and Dewett 2005; Alam 1998; Brinkmann and Sims 2001). Linda Trevino's (1986) interactionist model of ethical decision-making underscores the importance of being ethically aware. Enhancing ethical awareness involves helping students engage in perspective-taking and use their imagination to see the range of possible outcomes that might result in the short and long term for as many stakeholders (potential victims) as possible, from those closest to the situation (in sport that would be, for instance, oneself, one's family, one's team) to those who seem farthest from it (e.g. sponsors, the future of the particular sport, spectators, the global sports community, etc). (*See* e.g. Ciulla 1991).
      The idea behind enhancing moral awareness goes back to Aristotle's (1985) notion that human beings are inherently good or virtuous in their potential, and that they feel better (*eudaimonia*) when they achieve their virtuous potential

(*See* Nussbaum 1990; Hartman 2006). So the assumption is that, when students are asked to imagine and think about all the people and all the ways in which their decisions can be harmful, this will naturally awaken or sensitize them to their innate ethical potential. Thus, as their ethical awareness is heightened and they begin to see their responsibility in potentially hurting others, their sense of moral obligation and personal responsibility should also be elevated (Brinkmann and Sims 2001, p. 176; Ciulla 1991). As Rest and Narváez (1994, p. 23) note, enhancing moral awareness entails "developing empathy." Part of enhancing moral awareness also entails studying scandals, and the laws and rules that pertain to sport.

2. Promoting moral development

The goal of enhancing moral awareness overlaps with what might be considered a second goal of a sports integrity course – elevating students' moral reasoning. "Moral reasoning, or moral judgment, refers to the ways in which individuals define whether a course of action is morally right, such as by their evaluating different courses of action and their taking into account ethical principles when determining their stance about an ethical issue" (Jones 2009, pp. 367–68). The higher a person's level of moral reasoning, the less vulnerable they are to situational pressures to behave unethically (Trevino 1986). One's stage of moral development affects behaviors ranging from cheating and whistleblowing (Trevino 1992) to stealing (Greenberg 2002).

Kohlberg (1969) posited a sequence of increasingly refined stages of moral development. He posited three broad stages, each of which is comprised of two stages. People climb up the stages essentially by learning to think in a way that is based increasingly on higher, larger principles and decreasingly on individual selfish wants. In the two lowest stages (called pre-conventional), the person defines right and wrong on the basis of whether they think they will be punished or rewarded – i.e. their immediate interests. In stages three and four (called conventional), they define right and wrong on the basis of what the group that they belong to expects. In stage three, the motivation is to fulfill the expectations of others in one's relatively small group. In stage four it is to fulfill society's expectations. In stages five and six (called post-conventional), the person's definition of right and wrong goes beyond norms and laws and is based on the broad principles that uphold the welfare of all.

Research shows that the higher the level of one's moral reasoning, the more moral one's behavior (Greenberg 2002; Trevino 1992). So many researchers advocate elevating moral reasoning as a goal of ethics training (e.g. Desplaces et al. 2007; Brinkmann and Sims 2001).

3. Teaching the skills to handle situational pressures

The third goal is to give students the tools to negotiate the pressures and situations that could lead to match-fixing and others forms of corruption in sport. They need to be taught what to expect, how to respond, whom to call, etc.

Proven Ways to Achieve the Objectives of a Sports Integrity Course

There are a number of proven ways to achieve the three objectives outlined above.

- Simulation and role-play.

  Two highly effective teaching techniques – that are almost completely absent from current sports integrity courses – are role-play and simulation. Role-play has been found to deepen students' appreciation for moral behavior by shifting their focus away from simply wanting to know the rules and game the system to caring about principles and doing the right thing (Seiler et al. 2011; *see also* Loui 2009; Rest and Narvaez 1994).

  Simulation exercises bridge the gap between the classroom and the real world through experiential learning experiences (Hertel and Millis 2002; Xu and Yang 2010). Students are guided to imagine themselves with a rich background of varied data (e.g. married with kids, in debt, etc.) and prompted to react to multiple pressured social scenarios. Their reactions to these simulated pressures then form the basis for analysis and reflection – much as their physical reactions on the field are examined for them to improve in their sport. In sophisticated simulations, students may also be involved in designing the kinds of pressured scenarios they might face, and be involved in developing strategies to handle them, deepening their learning.

  Simulation and role-play also give students tools and skills to deal with the pressures that invariably arise in sport, as students simulate the experience of the multiple ways in which they can be approached. They see how seemingly unimportant decisions can erode their integrity and trigger a chain of events with a tragic conclusion.

- Case-based discussion

  There is also too little systemic use of case-based discussion in current sports integrity training. Research shows that using cases is highly effective for elevating ethical decision making and promoting self-awareness (Pettifor et al. 2000). Discussing actual sports scandals is likely to positively affect athletes' ethical decision-making, just as studying actual business scandals did for business students (Cagle and Baucus 2006). Kohlberg (1976) noted that group discussion helped students evolve to higher levels of moral judgment. (*See also* Schlaefli et al. 1985). Case-based discussions are far superior to lectures to promote critical thinking about ethics (Kim et al. 2006), engage and hold students' interest (Richards et al. 1995), and promote higher order thinking (Dori et al. 2003). People remember stories and cases better than they remember dry warnings or rules (see e.g. Menkel-Meadow 2000–2001). Jones (2009), for instance, used class discussion of cases to significantly make students more principled in their moral reasoning.

- Inspiring students with role models and charismatic leaders
  As students climb to higher levels of moral reasoning, they are essentially adopting or refining moral values and becoming less selfish and more principled. However, the dilemma in terms of how to teach this is that many scholars argue that it is not the place for ethics courses to instill values or indoctrinate students. Instead, they argue, ethics courses should only enhance students' moral awareness and encourage them to critically examine their pre-existing attitudes and values (e.g. Brinkmann and Sims 2001) – so that students can work out their own values and moral thresholds. As Oddo (1997, p. 296) put it, the objective should be "to get students … to apply their own personal values to resolve the issues… not to change values" (Oddo 1997, p. 296). The thinking is that this process will lead students to become self-critical and thus to naturally progress to a higher level of moral reasoning (Brinkmann and Sims 2001).

  If this were so, there would be nothing specific to do to teach moral reasoning. However, the literature on role models and charismatic and transformational leaders suggests that inviting such people to speak to students can elevate their values by inspiring them to generate courage to stand up to match fixing (*see* e.g. Bass 1985). Transformational, charismatic leaders make people want to identify with and emulate their aspirations and behaviors (Shamir et al. 1993; Bass and Steidlmeier 1999). They motivate followers to have the confidence and desire to transform themselves as they adopt the leader's vision (Kanungo and Mendonca 1996; Fairholm 1998; Bass and Steidlmeier 1999). The process often has a transcendent, spiritual dimension (ibid.). Moreover, when students realize "that the typical hero can be a regular person, they begin to acknowledge that their own behavior can set an example for others." (Apostolou and Apostolou 1997).

  The role of inspiration in instilling ethical values is often overlooked in the research on teaching ethics with some exceptions (e.g. Apostolou and Apostolou 1997). However, Interpol and FIFA are beginning to use this by inviting speakers such as Simone Farina, the Italian soccer player who famously stood up to match-fixing pressures.

The Possible Shapes of a Course on Sports Integrity

Stand-Alone Class Versus Integrating Sports Integrity Training into the Curriculum

It is known by now that stand-alone ethics courses can have a positive impact on students' moral reasoning abilities (Eynon et al. 1997; Gautschi III and Jones 1998). However, it is also effective to integrate ethics teaching into a larger curriculum, where instruction is repeated in various courses so that students are exposed to ethics throughout their degree program, usually with a capstone course for seniors to assess the level of learning achieved (Bishop 1992; Cox et al. 2009).

Sports integrity could be integrated into the syllabi of a number of undergraduate classes, particularly in management and marketing. Suffolk University's Sawyer Business School, for instance, offers a concentration in sports marketing. Sports ethics could easily be integrated into existing classes such as "Sports Marketing," "Relationship Marketing in Sports Business," "The Business of Sports and the Media," and internships with 17-time world champion Boston Celtics, with whom the school has a partnership.

In terms of whether it is enough to have a stand-alone class and whether it is necessary to repeat ethics instruction in various other classes in a degree program, no one knows exactly how long the effects of training last. Some studies show that people rarely fall back to lower levels of moral development (Colby et al. 1983; Jones 2009). On the other hand, other studies suggest that repeatedly reinforcing ethics training is important to ensuring that students will use their skills when they encounter real-life scenarios (e.g. Oddo 1997).

So, to be safe, sports ethics could be offered as both a stand-alone course as well as be integrated in a larger curriculum. If athletes are not in school, discussion about ethics should be incorporated into as many aspects of athletic life as possible, ranging from coaching to discussions with sponsors, marketing companies, and managers.

How Long Should a Stand-Alone Sports Integrity Course Last?

Most research shows that integrity training tends to be non-significant when the program is shorter than 3 weeks (Schlaefli et al. 1985). However, in one study, a shorter time – just five 75 min ethics classes offered over several weeks – yielded a significant improvement in students' moral judgment (Jones 2009).

How Early Should Sport Integrity Training Start?

It may be best to train students in ethics as early as possible to try to counteract all of the competing messages about cheating and self-interested pursuits in sport and society in general. Research demonstrates that people naturally mature in their moral reasoning as they progress through life, according to Lawrence Kohlberg (1984b, 1969), whose pioneering research on moral development, as modified by more recent research by Rest and others, hypothesized a graduated series of increasingly refined stages of moral growth (*see also* Colby et al. 1983). However, it is possible to speed the process up with ethics or integrity training. As Jones (2009) notes, the effects of training are generally strongest among individuals aged 24 and up. However, it is possible to start teaching values to children as early as primary-school-age. At the primary school age, the child's moral development is generally limited in understanding right and wrong in terms of whether they will be punished and what their school, family, or religious experiences say is right and wrong. There is no deeper understanding of why right is right and wrong is wrong at this age. Kohlberg categorizes this as the "preconventional" or "premoral" level.

By the time young people reach high-school-age, however, they are able to internalize the norms of the group with which they affiliate and define right and wrong on the basis of that group's beliefs (DeHaan and Hanford 1997; Rest et al. 1999; Williams et al. 2003). At this stage, the understanding of right and wrong prompts them to maximize the quality of relationships and win the approval of their group. This is sometimes referred to as "conventional morality." (Kohlberg). Many people remain at this level all their lives.

However, by the time they reach college, young people (aged 18–23) are more ripe for significantly advancing in moral reasoning (King and Mayhew 2002). They can progress to the stage where they are able to understand that they have a duty to obey the law in order to uphold the larger social order. Although still categorized as conventional morality, the understanding of morality in terms of the good of the larger social order is a critical advance over the more selfish personal perspective of caring about right and wrong because it results in personal acceptance within one's group. Although few people reach this stage, with the right training and experiences, college-aged students may even advance to a "post-conventional" morality where their understanding of right and wrong becomes increasingly more principled and concerned with others' needs.

At the same time, it is in college – and not before – that some studies show a significant difference between the moral reasoning of athletes and non-althletes, with non-athletes displaying less maturity in moral reasoning and greater selfishness. Bredemeier and Shields 1986.

Although age correlates with the stage of moral reasoning, schooling correlates even more powerfully. Studies show that even just a couple of years of college significantly contributes to moral development – far more than comparable young people with no college (Foster and LaForce 1999; Rest 1979; Rest and Thoma 1985). Indeed, one of the most powerful effects of college is on moral reasoning (McNeel 1994).

The practical upshot is that, although integrity training can begin early in life, it is around the time young people reach college-age when sports integrity training would probably be most effective and critical. Some of the biggest obstacles to integrity in sports are peer pressure, self-centeredness, and a refusal to take personal responsibility for one's own actions. It is between ages 18–23 when young people can most easily break away from caring so much about their peer group's views and think more independently in terms of the impact of their conduct on the larger social order. It is when they are college-aged that individuals are most likely to learn to stand up to the pressure of having other players and officers take bribes; to care about the good of the greater whole as opposed to only one's own personal interests; and to take personal responsibility instead of only blaming external situations.

References

Alam, K. F. (1998). Ethics and accounting education. Teaching Business Ethics, 2(3): 261–272.
Apostolou, Barbara; Apostolou Nicholas 1997. "Heroes as a Context for Teaching Ethics" Journal of Education for Business 73(2):121–25.Aristotle. 1985. Nicomachean ethics. T. H. Irwin (Trans.) Indianapolis, IN: Hackett Publishing Company.
Bass, B. M. (1985). Leadership and performance beyond expectations. New York: Free Press.
Bass, B. & Steidlmeier, P. (1999). Ethics, Character, and Authentic Transformational leadership behavior. The Leadership Quarterly 10(2):181–217.
Bishop, T. (1992). Integrating Business Ethics into an Undergraduate Curriculum Journal of Business Ethics 11:291–299.
Bredemeir and Shields Bredemeier, Brenda Jo and David L. Shields, (1986). The Journal of Genetic Psychology: Research and Theory on Human Development 147(1): 7–18.
Brinkmann, J. & Sims, R. R. (2001). Stakeholder sensitive business ethics teaching. Teaching Business Ethics, 5(2): 171–193.
Cagle, J. and Baucus, M. 2006. "Case Studies of Ethics Scandals: Effects on Ethical Perceptions of Finance Students" Journal of Business Ethics 64(3): 213–229.
Cano, C. and Sams, D. Advancing cognitive moral development: a field observation of college students, Journal of Academic and Business Ethics
Ciulla, J. B.: 1991, 'Business Ethics as Moral Imagination', in R. E. Freeman (ed.), Business Ethics, the State of the Art, Oxford University Press, New York, 212–220
Colby, A., Gibbs, J., Lieberman, M. and Kohlberg, L.: 1983. A Longitudinal Study of Moral Judgment: A Monograph for the Society of Research in Child Development (University of Chicago Press).
Conroy, S. & Emerson, T. (2008). Ethical Cycles and Trends: Evidence and Implications. Journal of Business Ethics, 81(4):905–911.
Cox, P. L.; Friedman, B. A.; Edwards, A. 2009. "Enron: The Smartest Guys in the Room—Using the Enron Film to Examine Student Attitudes towards Business Ethics" Journal of Behavioral & Applied Management 10(2): 263–290.
DeHaan, R. & Hanford, R. (1997). Promoting ethical reasoning, affect and behavior among high school students: An evaluation of three teaching strategies Journal of Moral Education 26(1): 5–20.
Dellaportas, S. (2006). Making a difference with a discrete course on accounting ethics. Journal of Business Ethics, 65(4):391–404.
Desplaces, D.; Melchar, D.; Beauvais, L; Bosco, S. 2007. "The Impact of Business Education on Moral Judgment Competence: An Empirical Study" Journal of Business Ethics. 74(1):73–87.
Dori, Yehudit J.; Tal· Revital; and Tsaushu, Masha 2003. "Teaching biotechnology through case studies—can we improve higher order thinking skills of nonscience majors?" Science Education 87(6): 767–793.
Eynon, Gail; Hill, Nancy Thorley; Stevens, Kevin T. 1997. "Factors that influence the Moral reasoning abilities of accountants: implications for universities and the profession" Journal of Business Ethics 16(12/13): 1297–1309.
Fairholm, G. W. 1998. Perspectives on leadership: From the science of management to its spiritual heart. Westport, CT: Quorum Books.
Fletcher 1971. "Selected Personality Characteristics of High School Athletes and Nonathletes." The Journal of Psychology: Interdisciplinary and Applied 77(1): 39–41.
Foster, J. D. & LaForce, B. (1999) A longitudinal study of moral, religious, and identity development in a Christian liberal arts environment. Journal of Psychology and Theology, 27: 52–68.
Gautschi III, F. H. and Jones, T. M. 1998. "Enhancing the Ability of Business Students to Recognize Ethical Issues: An Empirical Assessment of the Effectiveness of a Course in Business Ethics." Journal of Business Ethics. 17(2): 205–216.
Greenberg, J.: 2002, 'Who Stole the Money and When? Individual and Situational Determinants of Employee Theft', Organizational Behavior and Human Decision Processes 89: 985–1003.

Hartman, Edwin M.. 2006. "Can We Teach Character? An Aristotelian Answer" Academy of Management Learning and Education 5(1): 68–81.

Hertel, J. P. and Millis, B. J (2002) "Using simulations to promote learning in higher education: an introduction." Sterling, VA: Stylus Publishing.

Jones, D. 2009. "A Novel Approach to Business Ethics Training: Improving Moral Reasoning in Just a Few Weeks" Journal of Business Ethics 88(2): 367–379.

Kanungo, R. N., & Mendonca, M. 1996. Ethical dimensions in leadership. Beverly Hills, CA: Sage Publications

Kim, Sara; Phillips, William R; Pinsky; Linda; Brock, Doug; Phillips, Kathryn; and Keary Jane 2006. "A conceptual framework for developing teaching cases: A review and synthesis of the literature across disciplines" Medical Education 40(9): 867–876.

King, P.M. & Mayhew, M.J. 2002. "Moral judgement development in higher education: Insights from the Defining Issues Test." Journal of Moral Education, 31(3): 247–270.

Kohlberg, Lawrence. 1976. "Moral stages and moralization: The cognitive-developmental approach" in T. Lickona, ed. Moral Development and Behavior: Theory, Research and Social Issues. NY, Holt, Rinehart, Winston.

Kohlberg, L. 1969. Stage and sequence: The cognitive developmental approach to socialization. In D. A. Goslin (Ed.), Handbook of socialization theory and research (pp. 347–480). Chicago: Rand McNally.

Kohlberg, L. 1984(a). Essays on moral development: Volume 2, The psychology of moral development. New York, NY: Harper & Row.

Kohlberg, L. 1984(b). The psychology of moral development: The nature and validity of moral stages. Harper & Row: San Francisco.

Layden, T. 1995. "Campus Gambling – Better Education – First of Three Parts." Sports Illustrated April 3.

Loui, Michael 2009. "What can students learn from an extended role-play simulation on technology and society?" Bulletin of Science, Technology & Society 29(1) 37–47.

McLaren, R. 2012. "Is Sport Losing its Integrity?" Marquette Sports Law Review, 21(2)).

McNeel, S. P. 1994. College teaching and student moral development. In J.R. Rest & D. Narvarez, Moral development in the professions: Psychology and applied ethics (pp. 27–49). Hillsdale, NJ: Erlbaum.

Menkel-Meadow, Carrie. 2000–2001. "Telling Stories in School: Using Case Studies and Stories to Teach Legal Ethics" 69 Fordham L. Rev. 787.

Nussbaum, M. C. 1990. Finely aware and richly responsible: Literature and the moral imagination. In Love's knowledge: Essays on philosophy and literature, 148–167. New York: Oxford University Press.

Oddo, Alfonso. 1997. "A Framework for Teaching Business Ethics," Journal of Business Ethics 16(3):293–297.

Pettifor, J. L., I. Estay and S. Paquet: 2000, 'Preferred Strategies for Learning Ethics in the Practice of a Discipline', Canadian Psychology 43 (4), 260–269.

Richards, Larry G.; Gorman, Michael; Scherer, William T.; Landel· Robert D. 1995. "Promoting Active Learning with Cases and Instructional Modules" Journal of Engineering Education 84(4): 375–381.

Rest, J. R. 1979. The impact of higher education on moral judgment development (Technical report no. 5) Minneapolis, MN, Moral Research Projects.

Rest, J. R. and Thoma, S.. 1985. Relationship of moral judgment development to formal education. Developmental Psychology, 21: 709–714.

Rossouw, G. J. (2002). Three approaches to teaching business ethics. Teaching Business Ethics, 6(4): 411–433.

Rest, J. and D. Narvaez (eds.). 1994, Moral Development in the Professions, Erlbaum, Hillsdale NJ.

Rest, J. R., Narvaez, D., Thoma, S. J., Bebeau, M. J.. 1999. DIT2: Devising and Testing a Revised Instrument of Moral Judgment Journal of Educational Psychology 91(4): 644–659.

Schlaefli, A., J. R. Rest and S. J. Thoma: 1985, 'Does Moral Education Improve Moral Judgment? A Meta-Analysis of Intervention Studies Using the Defining Issues Test', Review of Educational Research 55 (3), 319–352.

Segal, L.; Gideon, L., Haberfeld, M. 2011. "Comparing the Ethical Attitudes of Business and Criminal Justice Students" *Social Science Quarterly* 92(4): 1021–1043.

Seiler, S. N., Brummel, B. J., Anderson, K. L., Kim, K. J., Wee, S., Gunsalus, C. K. and Loui, M. C. 2011. "Outcomes assessment of role-play scenarios for teaching responsible conduct of research" *Accountability in Research* 18(4) 217–246.

Shadnam, Masoud; Lawrence, Thomas. 2011 Business Ethics Quarterly 21(3):379–407.

Shamir, B., House, R. J., and Arthur, M. B. (1993). "The motivational effects of charismatic leaders: A self-concept based theory." Organization Science, 4, 577–594.

Shaw, D., Shiu, E., Hassan, L, Bekin, C. and Hogg, G. (2007) *Intending to be Ethical: An Examination of Consumer Choice in Sweatshop Avoidance*. Advances in Consumer Research, Orlando, FL.

Smith, Garry. 1991. "The *'To Do' over What To Do about Sports Gambling*," in William. R. Eadington and Judy A. Cornelius, Eds., *Gambling and Public Policy* (Reno, NV: Institute for the Study of Gambling & Commercial Gaming, University of Nevada).

Sykes, G.M., and Matza, D. 1957. "Techniques of neutralization: A theory of Delinquency", *American Sociological Review* 22: 664–670.

Trevino, Linda. 1986. "Ethical Decision Making in Organizations: A Person-Situation Interactionist Model." Academy of Management Review 11(3): 601–617.

Trevino, L. K. 1992. Moral reasoning and business ethics: Implications for research, education, and management, Journal of Business Ethics, 11: 445–459.

Turiel, E. (1978). The develop of concepts of social structure: Social convention. In J. Glick and K. A. Clarke-Stewart (Eds.) *The development of social understanding*. NY: Gardner Press.

Upton, Hugh. 2011. "Can there be a Moral Duty to Cheat in Sport?" *Sport, Ethics and Philosophy* 161–174.

US CRNPTG, 1976. "Gambling in America: final report of the Commission on the Review of the National Policy Toward Gambling." USA, Washington, D.C.

Williams, D. D., Yanchar, S. C., Jensen, L. C., & Lewis, C. (2003). Character education in a public high school: A multi-year inquiry into Unified Studies. *Journal of Moral Education* 32(1): 3–33.

Williams, Scott David; Dewett, Todd. 2005. "Yes, You Can Teach Business Ethics: A Review and Research Agenda" *Journal of Leadership & Organizational Studies* 12(2): 109–120.

Xu, Yang; and Yang, Yi. 2010. "Student Learning in Business Simulation: An Empirical Investigation" *Journal of Education for Business* 85(4): 223–228.

The Role of the Academe in Match-Fixing

Robert F. Vodde

Abstract The academe, otherwise referred to as the University, has a long and rich history which is renowned for its contributions in the areas of research, education, and public service. Today, the academe continues to serve as a resource to an ever-increasing and expansive number of disciplines and constituencies, not the least of which includes the transnational study of crime within the greater criminal justice system. Given the pervasive and systemic problem of match-fixing which breeds corruption and undermines the integrity in sport, the academe has been identified as a valuable resource in addressing the problem of match-fixing. Specifically, it can assist in: (1) identifying the scope and breath of the problem, (2) identifying and collaborating with the key stakeholders in developing tactics and strategies to address the problem, and (3) develop comprehensive curricula, training, and educational programs for the various stakeholders, the greater sports community, and the public at-large.

Robert F. Vodde serves as professor and director of the School of Criminal Justice and Legal Studies at Fairleigh Dickinson University. He holds a PhD from the University of Leicester, an MA from John Jay College of Criminal Justice, an MPA from Fairleigh Dickinson University, and a BS from William Paterson University. Before entering academia, Dr. Vodde enjoyed a 25 year career in law enforcement; his last 10 years as Chief of Police. A graduate of the FBI National Academy, Prof. Vodde continues to instruct, consult, and conduct research in the area of police training and education, specifically as it relates to learning theory and practice.

Dr. Vodde can be reached at Fairleigh Dickinson – University College – School of Criminal Justice and Legal Studies: http://www.fdu.edu.

R.F. Vodde, Ph.D. (✉)
Fairleigh Dickinson University, Teaneck, NJ 07666, USA

1000 River Road, Teaneck, NJ 07666, USA
e-mail: rvodde@fdu.edu

M.R. Haberfeld and D. Sheehan (eds.), *Match-Fixing in International Sports:*
Existing Processes, Law Enforcement, and Prevention Strategies,
DOI 10.1007/978-3-319-02582-7_16, © Springer International Publishing Switzerland 2013

Introduction

The history and role of the academe,[1] more commonly referred to as the University, has a rich history that has evolved to its present day status and recognition within modern society. Coming from the Latin *universitas magistraorum et scholarium*, the origin of the University dates back to the early monasteries of the sixth century whose mission was ostensibly to educate monks and priests, although according to Rudy (1984), the concept of higher learning "had flourished for at least three millennia before the first European universities were established." Originating in the European Middle Ages, the academe became "the primary vehicle in all parts of the world for the preservation and transmission of the highest learning, the advancement of scholarship, the training of specialists in fields of endeavor vital to society, and the improvement of national life" (Rudy 1984, p. 11; 14). During this time, from approximately the sixth through to the fifteenth centuries, the academe evolved into an acclaimed institution for higher learning, research, enrichment, and scholarship that emphasized the study of the liberal arts, namely, arithmetic, geometry, astronomy, music, grammar, logic, and rhetoric, as in the art of discourse and persuasion. Rudy addressing the first universities explained that "the increasingly complex society of the Middle Ages had a great need for trained administrators, lawyers, notaries, physicians, and ecclesiastics;" a testament to the role and responsibility of the academe then as within today's society (1984, pp. 14–16).

Duryea and Williams (2000), addressing the evolution of the academe, notes that the influence of the medieval university still resonates in our present day society to include a course of study and curriculum that leads to the baccalaureate, master's, and doctorial degrees. He explains that "contemporary Western culture itself originated in the centuries followed by the "dark ages," in which the university served as one of the major institutions by which this culture has been transmitted over the years," and that it is within this context, that certain aspects of the university continue to have important medieval precedents (p. 4).

The rise of such institutions as the Universities of Bologna (1088), Paris (1150), Oxford (1167), Palencia (1208), Cambridge (1209), Salerno (1231), and in later years Harvard (1636) and Princeton (1746), underscores society's emphasis on scholasticism and the value of learning. Building upon its original mission to advance the study of the classics and the liberal arts, its role over time evolved and expanded to include the study and research of new disciplines. In the United States as an example, the study of agriculture and mechanical arts ushered in by the Morrill Land-Grant Act of 1862, later gave way to the introduction of even newer disciplines in the areas of education, computer science, nursing, and more recently, criminology and criminal justice; the latter an outgrowth of sociology and anthropology.

---

[1] Also referred to as the gymnasium during 1920s, the words *academe, college, higher education,* and *university* within the context of this chapter may be used interchangeably. Earlier references to higher learning have also been described as *lyceums*.

In keeping with its historical development and maturation, the modern academe through research and education, serves to develop the whole person, foster knowledge, understanding, critical thinking, cultivate creativity, encourage social and cultural sensitivities, increase passion for life and learning, and to engage in civic and public service. Today, the academe serves as a resource to an ever-increasing and expansive number of disciplines that serve multiple constituencies to include government, the private sector, non-governmental organizations, and society at-large. The study of social order and control, crime, criminology, and the greater criminal justice system on the international stage has once again called on the academe to provide a critical role in the study and research of new and evolving issues in the social sciences. Disciplines that were once unheard of, now represent not only new areas of study and curricula, but within some universities have meta-morphosed into singular departments and schools. Strongly influenced by the exponential growth and development of technology, such new disciplines now include cyber-crime, terrorism, homeland security, and a wide array of transnational crime, not the least of which includes match-fixing – a growing and systemic problem on the international stage that not only undermines the integrity of the sport, but breeds crime and corruption on multi-dimensional levels.

Speaking to the state of the modern university during the 1930s, Flexner writes that the university "like all other human institutions – like the church, like governments, like philanthropic organizations – is not outside, but inside the general social fabric of a given era" (1930, p. 3). Given its role within greater society, he points out that "universities must at times give society not what society wants, but what it needs" (p. 5). In this regard, the role and responsibility of the academe encompasses many disciplines and venues, and consequently, can potentially serve a host of constituencies, not the least of which includes the sporting community.

History of Sports Betting

To understand the current problem of match-fixing, it is important to acknowledge that betting on the outcome of sporting events date back to the origin of sport which is popularly chronicled with the introduction of the original Olympian games of ancient Greece. While legend holds that the ancient Olympics were founded by Hercules, recorded history indicates that they date back to Greece in 776 B.C. Held every 4 years, the ancient Olympics originally consisted of two major competitions that involved equestrian events such as chariot racing and riding, and pentathlon, which later evolved to include field and track, wrestling, javelin and discus throwing. Although they experienced numerous interruptions, the spirit of the Olympics, as with sports in general, speaks to the human spirit associated with healthy competition, athleticism, and sportsmanship.

As passionate as society's interest has been with the competition of sporting events, so too has its interest been on waging on its outcome. Notwithstanding its entertainment value, wagering has also prompted cheating. Addressing the long history of betting on sports and corruption, Hill (2008), who wrote the acclaimed *The Fix: Soccer and Organized Crime*, explains that wagering bets on sporting events has prompted all forms of illicit activities and corruption that dates back for nearly 2,800 years Hill (2010). Given human nature, Hill argues that some form of corruption will unfortunately continue to overshadow the integrity traditionally associated with competitive sports.

Addressing the nature of the sporting industry and sports betting, a report on the *Fédération Internationale de Football Association's* (FIFA) website explains that while the sports industry generates approximately $300 billion a year, sports betting by contrast yields an estimated annual $350–$400 billion, of which an estimated 50 % comprises bets placed on what it describes as the grey and black markets. Arguing its inevitability, one commentator noted that betting on sporting events is part of human nature and reflects a passion for gambling inherent to the thrill associated with the prospect of realizing a financial gain (*"Sports betting under the microscope* – FIFA.com" 2012). While many positive attributes are associated with professional sports, not the least of which includes an appreciation for exceptional talent and athleticism, the exhilaration of competition, instilling regional and national pride, encouraging camaraderie among athletes and fans, and the mere entertainment associated with sporting events – man's less redeeming qualities, namely greed and selfishness, has not only undermined the integrity of sports, but has resulted in systemic corruption and crime.

Sports-Betting and Match-Fixing

In a *Fédération Internationale de Football Association* brochure entitled *Integrity in Sport*, which highlights its *Early Warning System GmbH* (a system designed to mitigate match-fixing), it states that "sport is often said to be the most beautiful pastime in the world, and betting on events adds an even greater thrill to the "sporting" experience," emphasizing that "the majority of those who place bets do so out of enjoyment of sport and simply wish to chance their luck." However, because there is a small minority who misappropriate and exploit sport for their selfish interests, the *Early Warning System* was developed to safeguard the integrity of sport ("Early Warning System" – FIFA 2010). More on this system is discussed in the section *Professional Sports Organizations*.

While sports-betting involves placing a wager on the predicted outcome of a sporting event – a predominately legitimate activity throughout most parts of the world – despite its entertainment value, it can lead to any number of social problems and criminal activities, not the least of which includes a pervasive degradation of societal values. Corruption in sports, which FIFA's President, Joseph S. Blatter denounced, shakes the very foundations of sports. He explained that corruption in sports is associated with numerous illicit activities, the most prominent being highlighted with recent scandals associated with the use of drugs to enhance athletic performance (doping) and match-fixing, or otherwise described as sports manipulation, sporting fraud, or spot-fixing – all of which ostensibly involves the intentional and deliberate manipulation of a game toward a pre-determined out-come. While various definitions abound to describe match-fixing, the recent report commissioned *European Commission Directorate-General for Education and Culture,* emphasized the importance for developing a standardized definition in the criminal law in its report entitled *Match-fixing in Sport* (2012). It states that its defi-nition "echoes the essential elements of the one provided by the recent *Recommendation of the Council of Europe,*" which states that:

> The manipulation of sports results covers the arrangement on an irregular alteration of the course or the result of a sporting competition or any of its particular events (e.g. matches, races…) in order to obtain financial advantage for oneself or for other, and remove all or part of the uncertainty normally associated with the results of a competition (2012, p. 9).

While the systemic problem of match-fixing is examined in greater detail within this book, it is important to acknowledge that given the many unscrupulous indi-viduals that are involved in such corruptive behavior, similarly, it require an equal, if not greater number of individuals and organizations to address the ever-growing, elusive, and clandestine problem of match-fixing, not the least of which can include the academe. Underscoring the extent of the problem, a news article in *Slate Magazine* reports that in a typical day, there are more deals made within Asian sports betting markets alone than on the New York Stock Exchange ("Soccer match-fixing scandal: How do you rig a soccer game? – Slate Magazine" 2011).

Given its rich history and long-standing mission, the academe is well-positioned to: (1) to coordinate and undertake substantive and qualified research in identifying the scope and breadth of the problem, (2) collaborate in identifying and develop-ing viable tactics and strategies to comprehensively address the cancerous problem of match-fixing, (3) serve as a venue, conduit, and catalyst in bringing together the various stakeholders and constituencies needed to address the problem, and (4) provide the requisite training and education to the various stakeholders identi-fied hereinafter.

Integrity and Social Values

While to avoid any presumptuous portent of self-righteousness on the part of the sporting community, it is nevertheless necessary to recognize the importance that soci-ety places on ethical values and principles. Despite what may appear to be the degra-dation thereof within modern society, the significance of personal and professional integrity still resonates as the bedrock of man's value system. Coming from the Latin *integer*, meaning whole or complete, integrity speaks to the consistency of one's val-ues, principles, methods, and expectations. It deals with honesty and truthfulness; an unimpaired state, soundness, whole, completeness, or a steadfast adherence to a strict moral or ethical code. Synonyms for the word integrity include character, decency, goodness, honesty, morality, probity, rectitude, uprightness, and virtuousness.

Stanford's Encyclopedia of Philosophy (2013), explains that ordinary discourse about integrity involves two fundamental intuitions: first, that integrity is primarily a formal relation one has to oneself, or between parts or aspects of one's self; and second, that integrity is connected in an important way to acting morally; that is, there are some substantive or normative constraints on what it is to act with integrity ("Integrity (Stanford Encyclopedia of Philosophy)" 2013). Williams and Arrigo (2008), addressing *Ethics, Crime, and Criminal Justice*, explain that when dealing with issues of crime, law, and justice, they inherently deal with matters of morality. They argue that matters related to crime and criminal justice is predicated on "matters of personal and social responsibility, free will and choice-making, reasoned judgment, and moral responsibility" (p. 4). Notwithstanding differentiations between ethics (socially prescribed behavior) and integrity (personal valued behavior), the principles upon which they predicated are diametrically opposed to the corrupt behaviors associated with match-fixing.

It is for this reason that the *International Criminal Police Organization* (INTERPOL), in partnership with *Fédération Internationale de Football Association* (FIFA), entitled its 2012 Singapore conference, *Integrity in Sport*, which also appears as a prominent feature on their respective websites. Not only did that conference, along with so many others, underscore the importance placed on maintaining the integrity of sports, but reflects the contempt for those that undermine society's trust and confidence. Such concern is echoed in the European Union's 2012 study that addresses the importance for unifying criminal laws that relate to *Match-fixing in Sport*, where in its executive summary it states that "the development of the European dimension in sport by promoting fairness in sporting competitions, as well as the physical and moral integrity of sportsmen and sportswomen, is one of the of the objectives of the European Union in the field of sport" (Husting et al. 2012, p. 2). Underscoring the seriousness of the problem, the report further explains that the European Union and many other European organizations such as legitimate betting organizations and sport organizations, "have clearly shown their commitment to fight against match-fixing," calling "attention to the problem of match-fixing and call on national governments to ensure legislation sanctions match-fixing in accordance with the seriousness of the conduct and to make illegal activities affecting the integrity of sport a criminal offense" (Council of Europe Recommendation 2012, p. 2). Recognizing the seriousness of the practice and the extent to which it undermines and frays the social fabric of society, "France amended the Criminal Code to include betting related match-fixing as a modality of the offence of corruption; Sweden introduced a bill referring to betting corruption; and Greece presented a proposal to modify the Sports Law to ensure that betting related match-fixing is punished with 10 years of imprisonment" (2012, p. 2).

Hanson and Savage (2013), addressing the importance of ethics and slow degradation of the long held value of integrity within sports, make a point of differentiating between sportsmanship and gamesmanship. Gamesmanship, they ardently argue, is solely predicated on winning to the exclusion of any consideration for sportsmanship. They write that in gamesmanship "athletes and coaches are encouraged to bend the rules wherever possible in order to gain a competitive advantage over an opponent, and to pay less attention to the safety and welfare of the competition." They describe the key tenants of gamesmanship as "it's only cheating if you get caught," "it is the referee's job to catch wrongdoing, and the athletes and coaches have no inherent responsibility to follow the rules," "winning is everything," and "the ends always justify the means." Such misguided attitudes, and lack of values and respect, unscrupulously undermines the integrity of sports and breeds a culture that is ripe for match-fixing and corrupt behavior.

By contrast, sportsmanship represents a collegiate and ethical approach to athletics. "Under a sportsmanship model," they contend, "healthy competition is seen as a means of cultivating personal honor, virtue, and character. It contributes to a community of respect and trust between competitors and in society. The goal in sportsmanship is not simply to win, but to pursue victory with honor by giving one's best effort." They advocate "that ethics in sport requires four key virtues: fairness, integrity, responsibility, and respect." Recognizing that competitive sports requires tough and sustaining play to win, doing so does not compromise sportsmanship, which Hansen and Savage contend is built on the notion that "sport both demonstrates and encourages character development, which then influences the moral character of the broader community" (*What Role Does Ethics Play in Sports? 2013*).

While the role of the academe appropriately focuses on research, education, and service, given the importance of integrity and how it plays into the greater equation of match-fixing, points to the important contributions that the academe can make in raising the level of awareness among the various stakeholders and the society at-large about the moral and ethical values inherently associated with maintaining the integrity of sports.

The Role and Influence of the Academe

Notwithstanding the longstanding debate among some academicians about whether the primary mission of the academe is in research, education, or serving the greater community, there appears a general refrain that such a trinity is indeed part and parcel of all universities. Brubacher (1977) addressing the philosophy of the academe acknowledges that higher education "is characterized by greater sophistication than other levels of the educational ladder," and yet has "inescapable implications" obligations to serving the greater community (p. 8–9). Nevertheless, given its long history and influence within society, its potential for serving the greater good, including that of the sporting community, is evident by the growing number of graduate and undergraduate programs that are now dedicated to sports education, sports management and administration, and sport psychology.

Given their growing popularity, many such programs recognize and collaborate with the growing number of professional associations, most whom underscore the critical importance for maintaining integrity in sport. As an example, *SportAccord*, an umbrella organization for both Olympic and non-Olympic international sports federations, declares in their mission statement that they advocate for an "ethical and socially responsible sports movement that adheres to principles of good governance and sustainability" ("Mission and values – *SportAccord* International Sports Federations" 2013). Similarly, other professional sport organizations also advance professionalism and integrity of sport such as the *International Academy of Sports Science and Technology* headquartered in Switzerland (*Académie Internationale des Sciences et Techniques du Sport*[2] – *AISTS*), the *North American Society for Sport Management*[3] (NASSM), the *Professional Footballers' Association*, the *Sports Management Association*, and already mentioned, the renowned *Fédération Internationale de Football Association* (International Federation Association of Football – FIFA), which comprises 209 national associations.

Given that these organizations, such as the *North American Society for Sport Management* "promote, stimulate, and encourage study, research, scholarly writing, and professional development in the area of sport management – both theoretical and applied aspects," their collaborative participation with the academe and the greater sporting community, can serve as one of many examples where the various stakeholders who hold a vested interest within sports can be commissioned to address the growing problem of match-fixing and the systemic problems that undermine the spirit and principles upon which sport is based.

Veysey (1965) addressing the influence of the academe in research and teaching, points to the historical leadership role it has played within the greater community. Hackman and Johnson (2013) addressing the power and influence of public leadership note that it "is one of the most visible and dynamic forms of social influence." They note that many entities such as religious organizations, political authorities, social activists, educators, and universities, have a significant influence on "the attitudes and behaviors of mass audiences" (2013, p. 272). Effective public leaders, they note, can "shape public opinion through public relations activities, public speaking, and persuasive campaigns," adding that effective public relations initiatives can influence "important audiences (publics) through a cluster of coordinated activities," thus pointing to the influence of the academe.

Altbach, Reisberg, and Rumbley (2009), addressing the role of the university within modern society, acknowledge the debate about its primary role, yet nevertheless concede that its mission is threefold: to teach, conduct research, and provide public service. Although they argue that these three activities can potentially "live in constant tension with each other," within the organizational setting of a university and its mission, the academe can nevertheless serve a valuable resource to the sports community and the challenges it faces relative to match-fixing. Addressing the significance of research within the academe, the authors note that "research has

---

[2] The *Académie Internationale des Sciences et Techniques du Sport* mission "is to bring a positive contribution to the management of sport through post-graduate and executive education, as well as applied research, by developing, integrating and delivering knowledge from human sciences, life sciences and engineering sciences" (http://aists.org).

[3] The purpose of the *North American Society for Sport Management* is to promote, stimulate, and encourage study, research, scholarly writing, and professional development in the area of sport management – both theoretical and applied aspects (http://www.nassm.com/).

been and continues to be an extremely important contribution of the university to the larger society" (p. 131). While it is apparent that significant time and energy has already been undertaken to study the problem of match-fixing, surely, given the academe's passion and experience for research, it can serve as a valuable resource to the greater sports community.

The Resources of the Academe, Globalization, and Technology

As evident, match-fixing has become a global problem, in great part due to the access, speed, anonymity, and sophistication of today's ever-expanding technologies and the Internet. Hill (2008) explains that globalization has totally transformed match-fixing to a new level, not unlike what globalization has done to the music, book, and travel industry. Traditional social, cultural, and political boundaries, modes of communication, laws and regulations, and other conventional obstacles and impediments to illicit gambling activities have ostensibly become superfluous within today's technologically advanced society. Placing wagers on nearly any sporting event worldwide is instantaneously facilitated. Technology has provided the means, power, speed, convenience, and anonymity to place bets and fix events. In kind, however, globalization and those same technological advances and resources can serve as one of many tools toward developing innovative and creative strategies, tactics, and solutions to detect and counter the challenges associated with corruption in sports and match-fixing; FIFA's *Early Warning System* being one of many.

In addition to utilizing technologies in equal and greater sophistication than those employed by crime syndicates to facilitate match-fixing, their use can also assist the academe in a wide-range of diverse training and education initiatives. The use of technology within higher education is widely used for research and education in areas such as online learning, interaction television (ITV), developing community partnerships, curriculum development, discussion forums, program management and evaluation, and assessment. Additionally, emerging technologies such as synchronous discussion boards and chat rooms, tablet computing, *Massive Open Online Courses* (MOOCs), learning analytics, games/gamification (game thinking and mechanics), 3D printing, and wearable technologies (ubiquitous computing, e.g., *Google Glass*), hold promise as means to enhance and facilitate training and education to a wide-range of audiences.

Notwithstanding the advantages and influence of employing state-of-the-art technologies, conducting traditional meetings, conferences, and workshops, such as the one convened in Singapore in late 2012, by the *Fédération Internationale de Football Association* and the *International Criminal Police Organization*, which involved leading academics from universities worldwide provide important opportunities for face-to-face dialogue and networking.

Research

Altback, Reisberg, and Rumbley (2009) addressing research and trends in global higher education, explain that "research has been and continues to be an extremely important contribution of the university to the larger society" (p. 131). Indeed, one of the principle activities within the academe is to conduct research, which Hagen (2006) explains can be labeled as pure or applied research. While "pure research" is concerned "with the acquisition of new knowledge for the sake of science or the development of the field," "practical or applied research" is concerned with solving immediate policy questions" (p. 10). To this point, Altback et al. contend that "in recent decades...basic and applied research have prospered in universities laboratories as well as industry," thus pointing to the complimentary benefits that can be realized when government and private organizations such as the *International Criminal Police Organization International* and the *Fédération Internationale de Football Association* (FIFA) collaborate with universities in researching areas of common interest and concern. Given the challenges associated with match-fixing, both forms of research can prove fruitful, which Hagen points out is not mutually exclusive. He explains "being on the front lines of the criminal justice system, practitioners are most interested in applied research, studies, and findings that speak directly to policy issues," while academics, "are more concerned with pure research, which may have no immediate applicability but contributes to the knowledge base and scientific development of the discipline" (p. 12). The two methods of research, therefore, can serve to compliment their common cause in addressing the nature, scope and breadth, and options in dealing with match-fixing.

Notwithstanding the foregoing distinctions between the types of research, social science research – which is most applicable to match-fixing – serves to explain associations, explore specific problems, describe the nature and scope of problems, provide explanations, and ideally, can provide practical applications and solutions to public policy issues such as match-fixing. In this pursuit, numerous methodologies toward achieving these ends are available to a researcher. These include, but are not limited to idiographic and nomothetic explanations, inductive and deductive reasoning, and collecting, assessing, and analyzing quantitative and qualitative data (Maxfield and Babbie 2012). It is the latter of these methodologies that can serve the interest of addressing match-fixing; specifically, in conducting observations and interviews, administering survey questionnaires, and conducting data analysis.

Observations. Observations involve a strategy of data collection in which the investigator attempts to examine the activity of subjects while keeping one's presence hidden or unobtrusive (Hagen 2006). Maxfield and Babbi (2012), explain that the defining characteristic of direct observation is obtaining measurements by observing the behavior of others. The observation of sporting events and those potentially associated with match-fixing, to include but not limited to observing players, coaches, referees, owners, fans and spectators, legitimate and illegitimate betting organizations, Internet betting operations, etcetera, by researchers and other investigators,[4] can serve as one of many avenues toward indentifying the nature and scope of the problem. Addressing observations as a form of qualitative measurement, Schutt (2001), explains that "observations can be used to measure characteristics of individuals, events, and places" (p. 80). While in some studies and forms of social research observations may serve as a primary form of measurement, given the scope and breadth of match-fixing, it can serve as one of multiple measurements, thus providing for triangulation.[5]

Interviews. Interviews serve as another effective means of collecting data and information. Orlich (1978) explains that a key advantage of conducting interviews is the personal contact that is made with a respondent, along with the ability to immediately clarify any question or response. Interviews have notable advantages as they allow for discerning a respondent's feelings and opinions, allows for open-ended discussion, affords respondents the opportunity to freely express themselves, provides the interviewer the opportunity to observe and tabulate nonverbal behaviors, and solicit a respondent's personal information, attitudes, beliefs, and perceptions that might not be gained on a written instrument. Interviews also often provide the interviewer an opportunity to follow-up or probe for leads.

Survey Research. Hagen (2006) addressing survey research, notes that it continues to serve as an emerging strength in crime analysis, criminal justice research, and an excellent tool for gathering primary data. Schutt (2001) explains that "survey research involves the collection of information from a sample of individuals through responses to questions" and "owes its popularity to three features: versatility, efficiency, and generalizability." (p. 209). One of the most popular and useful methods of conducting survey research is through the use of survey questionnaires, which Maxfield and Babbi (2012) explains is an instrument designed to elicit information for analysis. Notwithstanding the logistics associated with conducting survey research and issues pertaining to survey construction, sampling, response rates, anonymity, informed consent, and data quality, it nevertheless serves as an excellent tool for obtaining data and information. Moreover, the use of electronic survey instruments facilitated via the Internet such as *SurveyMonkey* (www.surveymonkey. com), *Zoomerang* (www.zoomerang.com), and *SurveyGizmo* (www.surveygizmo. com), serve as useful tools in data collection, particularly considering the effect of globalization on match-fixing.

Data Analysis. Given the various research practices and techniques common to researchers, determining the reliability and validity of collected data is essential to discerning the scope and breadth of the problem of match-fixing. Data analysis is

---

[4] While the role of the academe is to remain neutral and objective in securing valid and reliable data, information and intelligence developed by law enforcement and its operatives can contribute to identifying the nature and scope of the problem.

[5] Triangulation, also referred to as convergent-discriminate validation, represents multiple methods to measure multiple traits to determine the validity of data using purposive sampling.

the process of systematically ordering and organizing raw data, often using statistical or logical techniques, so that useful information and conclusions can be drawn to assist in decision making. Analysis from data can take the form of qualitative and quantitative analysis. While qualitative analysis involves the non-numerical examination and interpretation of observations, with the objective of discovering underlying meaning and patterns of relationships, quantitative analysis involves the process and techniques employed by researchers to covert data to a numerical form and subject it to statistical analyses (Maxfield & Babbie, 2012).

Analysis of Crime Statistics. Crime statistics and analysis, which entails the systematic study of crime and disorder, to include socio-demographic, spatial, and temporal factors, can provide valuable data in identifying the scope and breadth of match-fixing. Schmalleger (2013) addressing the significance of crime statistics explains that "if used properly, a statistical picture of crime can serve as a powerful tool for creating social policy" (p. 30). Policymakers and decisions makers on all levels, Schmalleger adds, "rely on crime data to analyze and evaluate existing programs, to fashion and design new crime-control initiatives, to develop funding requests, and to plan new laws and crime control legislation (p. 30). Working in concert with, or utilizing the resources of professional organizations such as the *International Criminal Police Organization* (INTERPOL), the *European Police Office* (EUROPOL), the *United Nations*, the *U.S. Bureau of Justice Statistics* (BJS), the *Police Executive Research Forum* (PERF), and other similar organizations worldwide, the academe can serve a useful resource in collaborating with such organizations in the collection, collation, and analysis of crime data, especially considering the extent to which match-fixing taxes the resources of such organizations, and the vast and pervasive revenues that it generates to support the ability of organized crime syndicates to engage in a host of other transnational criminal activities.

Identifying and Engaging Stakeholders

There are countless numbers of individuals, organizations, and sovereignties that need to be involved and brought together to address match-fixing. Otherwise referred to as stakeholders, these entities comprise individuals, groups, and organizations that not only have an interest in the actions of an organization and its cause, but who are affected by it in a positive or negative manner, and who have the ability to influence it. While it would appear that the various stakeholders would be coalesced toward the common goal of addressing match-fixing, it is important to recognize that their interests for doing so, and the means toward achieving those ends, may conflict.

To this point, Robbins (2000) addressing the role and influence of stakeholders, notes that their respective interest and demands should not be overlooked. Moreover, stakeholders need to be carefully and systematically identified, assessed on their relative power, and have a clear understanding of their expectations. As an example, if players, coaches, and referees possess the requisite integrity, the involvement of the many other stakeholders would be mute, as would the matter of identifying the necessary resources, strategies, and tactics to address the problem. However, putting aside naivety and considering human nature's proclivity toward what is often deemed as the seven deadly sins – not the least of which include greed (the desire for material wealth or gain) – the reality is that the problem exists and has wide implications socially, culturally, politically, legally, financially, geographically, and technologically. Similarly, identifying the financial resources to combat match-fixing can potentially place the various stakeholders at odds; that is, should the costs associated with combating match-fixing come from the players, coaches, referees, team owners, professional associations, legitimate betting organizations, sponsors, fans and spectators, government (which ostensibly is financed by taxpayers), or a combination of all these stakeholders.

Albanese (1988), addressing the significance of stakeholders, explains that among many things, they provide "a foundation for thinking about social responsibility," which given the deleterious effect that match-fixing has on society at-large, underscores the importance of their input and cooperation (p. 659). To effectively address integrity in sport, match-fixing, and the resonant corruptive effects it has on sports and society at-large, will require the involvement and commitment of stakeholders on multiple levels. Recognizing the many individuals within the respective groups of stakeholders, their individual and collective contributions are essential to identifying the problem, its scope and breadth, and viable strategies and tactics to mitigate its corrosive effects.

While it is important that the academe does actively engage in politics, it nevertheless needs to be sensitive to the reality of its existence and its dynamics, and as such, its role and neutrality can provide an appropriate venue in objectively addressing the issue of match-fixing, while at the same time respecting the concerns and perspectives of all stakeholders. While many stakeholders should be considered into the greater equation, principal stakeholders (as noted) should include the players, coaches, referees, team owners, professional sport organizations, sponsors, legislators, police and law enforcement agencies, legitimate betting organizations, fans and spectators, the media, and the general public. Summarily, in addition to conducting the requisite research to identify the nature, scope, and breadth of the problem of match-fixing, the academe can serve as a neutral, respected, and recognized venue comprised of academics that can help to facilitate the coordination, cooperation, and collaboration of the various stakeholders and constituencies, as well as provide important training and education on numerous levels addressed later in this chapter. Stakeholders who are essential to the process of addressing match-fixing, include, but are not necessarily limited to the following groups.

Players. While many individuals are culpable in the corrupt and detestable act of match-fixing, perhaps the key principals are the athletes (players) themselves. Despite that match-fixing within soccer has taken center stage, reports resonate within nearly all professional sporting events. As an example, a June 13, 2013, news report by the *Mail Newspaper* covering the prestigious Wimbledon tennis match writes that:

> With the world's most prestigious tennis tournament due to start at Wimbledon a fortnight tomorrow, match-fixing experts have voiced fears that up to a dozen top-50 players who have been involved in 'suspicious' matches could be in action at the All England Club... adding that ... one senior official with a long track record of tackling sports corruption has told *The Mail* on Sunday that the Tennis Integrity Unit (TIU), who have the task of eradicating match-fixing in the sport, is not equipped to deal with the problem ...
>
> The TIU have a policy of never discussing cases in public, or even revealing details of their verdicts. But this means the unit's operations and subsequent disciplinary proceedings are carried out in almost total secrecy and this lack of transparency has alarmed critics...

The official who spoke to *The Mail on Sunday* said: 'The "tennis family" were aware that there was no smoke without fire. They'd had years of accusations of fixing and plenty of hard betting data indicative of fixing. They knew there were people who were corrupt, and corruptible, and there still are. Almost 4 years after the TIU were set up, I can only conclude that they're not as effective as they might have been... there are a lot of cheats out there ("Match-fixing experts fear corrupt tennis players will be playing at Wimbledon Championships – Mail Online" 2013).

A similar news headline by Fox News July 10, 2013, reports that:

> "The Italian soccer federation says Lazio, Genoa and Lecce and eight players, including Lazio captain Stefan Mauri, face charges related to match-fixing," in which the federation claims "include rigging games and failing to report fixing for two Serie A matches – Lazio-Genoa and Lecce-Lazio in May 2011 ("Italian soccer federation says Lazio, Genoa, Lecce plus 8 players face match-fixing trial | Fox News", July 10, 2013)."

And another report in early 2013 by *the European Times* reported that "organised gambling rings and criminal groups have corrupted football, threatening the integrity of the world's most popular sport," adding that:

> European football is facing its biggest challenge as a massive corruption and match-fixing scandal threatens the integrity of the sport. Europol revealed early this month some 680 matches, including World Cup and European Championship qualifiers and two Champions League games, had been fixed. The investigation found 380 suspicious matches in Europe and another 300 questionable games outside the continent, mainly in Africa, Asia, South and Central America. Investigators said 425 match officials, club officials, players and criminals from at least 15 countries were involved in fixing football games dating back to 2008 ("Massive match-fixing scandal blasts Europe's football (SETimes.com)").

While similar stories abound about rouge players in all sports, society is hopeful that the majority of athletes possess the requisite integrity and positive character traits that has been traditionally associated with sports, although not until the problem is thoroughly researched and studied, can such a presumption be made. Appealing to the majority of such players and soliciting their input and assistance in identifying the scope and breadth of the problem of match-fixing can serve as an appropriate and logical starting point. Encouraging their input in the development of rules and regulations, the legislation of laws and public policy, recruitment, vetting new players, instituting incentive programs for those who uphold society's expectations for honesty and athleticism, along with providing incentives for reporting rogue players and others engaged in match-fixing, are one of many steps that can serve to address the problem and restore the confidence and trust that the public expects of professional athletes and sports in general. Toward this end and as so noted, the academe can begin by engaging players by conducting observations, facilitating interviews, administering survey questionnaires, and participating in a wide range of educational seminars and workshops.

Referees. While match-fixing is most often attributed to players, increasing evidence points to the involvement of referees (linesmen, umpires, etc.). Not unlike players, referees have a significant influence on the outcome of a sporting event. Their ability to influence a sporting event can include the timing of calls, false calls, ignoring violations, imposing fouls and penalties, along with making any number of decisions that can influence the outcome of the game. In 2007, an investigation by the U.S. *Federal Bureau of Investigation* led to charges against Tom Donaghy, a referee with the *National Basketball Association* (NBA) that he bet on games that he officiated during which he made calls that affected the point spread.

Two other recent examples were reported by the *British Broadcasting Corporation* (BBC) and the *Washington Times* underscore the degree to which organized crime syndicates can influence referees. In August 2011, the BBC reported that the FIFA banned "six referees for life after finding them guilty of match-fixing in a tournament where all the goals scored were from penalties" (*BBC Sport – Fifa bans referees for life for match-fixing* 2011). And more recently, on June 10, 2013, the *Washington Times* reported that "three Lebanese soccer referees pleaded guilty in Singapore…to rigging a match in exchange for sex in a deal with a global company that's linked to the gambling industry" (*Lebanese soccer referees caught fixing match for sex – Washington Times* 2013).

Coaches and Team Owners. Not unlike players and referees, coaches and team owners have a significance influence on the outcome of a sporting event. Whether making decisions independently or in collusion with corrupt players, coaches and team owners can affect the outcome of a game by changing lineups, replacing key players with less talented ones, encouraging or allowing goals, forcing penalties or injuries, or by simply intimidating or coercing players. Coaches and team owners, along with players and referees, represent one of many weak links within the chain of match-fixing. Two prominent cases reported by *The Guardian* and *The Telegraph* underscore the extent to which match-fixing has infiltrated and corrupted coaches and team owners. On February 5, 2013, based on an investigation by *Europol*, *The Guardian* reported that Paul Put, coach of the Belgium soccer team *Burkina Fasoa* was charged with fixing as many as 380 matches in Europe for which he was suspended for 3 years. The newspaper reported that Put "remains adamant he was just a scapegoat and that the practice is widespread," in which he emphasized that "match-fixing has always existed in football." Put claimed that "you have to see what's going on in football. There are a lot of big international players who are involved in match-fixing." In trying to justify his actions, Put claimed:

> I was threatened by the mafia, my children were threatened, the mafia threatened me with weapons and things like that so it's not nice to talk about these things but this is the reality. I was forced into it …And remember, I was just the coach. I had to listen to people above me and the players as well ('Match-fixing is reality' says Burkina Faso coach banned in Belgium | Football | The Guardian", 2013).

In a case involving a team owner in May 2013, the Australian newspaper, *The Telegraph*, reported that "Gurunath Meiyappan, the son-in-law of *Board of Control for Cricket in India* President Narainswamy Srinivasan, was arrested by Mumbai police in match-fixing." The paper reports that "Meiyappan's arrest was met with calls for the sacking of Srinivasan, considered the most powerful man in world cricket, owing to India's financial clout in the sport," adding that "Srinivasan, who is managing director of *India Cements* – which owns the Chennai team, has often been criticised for holding offices which have a conflict of interest since he is both a top board official and runs a company that owns an IPL franchise" ("Probe fire under BCCI chair – Telegraph" 2013).

Many other news reports similarly reveal corruption on the part of team owners have resonated worldwide to include countries such as Brazil, Germany, Hungary, Portugal, Singapore, and the United States. A May 2013, news report by Alam Srinivas of Cricket Country exclaimed that the Indian Premier League (IPL) "was rocked by scandals of illegal betting, match-fixing and conflicts." Underscoring the pervasiveness and far-reaching problems, the report states that "IPL team owners, players, umpires and cricket administrators were accused of being involved with the betting syndicates" (*Playing by the bookmaker – Cricket News & Articles – CricketCountry.com*. 2013).

Professional Sport Organizations. While players, referees, coaches, and team owners are important stakeholders who can assist and benefit from the resources of the academe given their active role in sporting events, there are other important stakeholders who have a significant influence on match-fixing; not the least of which include professional sport organizations. While it is important to acknowledge that many professional sports organizations located throughout the world advocate for professional standards and integrity within sport, given the impetus for this book, it is apropos to acknowledge the role of the *Fédération Internationale de Football Association* (FIFA), whose commitment to combat match-fixing led to an unprecedented partnership that involved the *International Criminal Police Organization* and the academic community. As one of many professional sports associations that have taken the lead in advocating for integrity in sport, FIFA's core values promote authenticity, unity, performance and integrity. In May 2011, FIFA announced that "INTERPOL's longest-ever funded initiative will target illegal and irregular betting and match-fixing, the scale of which has been highlighted by recent fixing allegations and the involvement of Asian gambling syndicates in global match-fixing – with estimates by INTERPOL's global law enforcement network that illegal football gambling is worth up to hundreds of millions of US dollars in Asia alone each year." In declaring its partnership with INTERPOL, FIFA's President Joseph S. Blatter, stated that "match-fixing shakes the very foundations of sport, namely fair play, respect and discipline, the threat of which represents a major concern to the integrity of sport."

Applauding its partnership, INTERPOL's Secretary General Ronald K. Noble stated that "illicit betting and match-fixing rings have demonstrated their global reach to fundamentally undermine football from one continent to another by corrupting administrators, officials and players," adding, "as INTERPOL and FIFA look to the future, basing this anti-corruption initiative at INTERPOL's upcoming Global Complex in Singapore, while delivering training programmes from INTERPOL Regional Bureaus and offices all over the world, will help both INTERPOL and FIFA achieve their common goal of keeping the world's most popular sport free of the corrupt influences of transnational organised crime syndicates," many of which are based in Asia (*FIFA's historic contribution to INTERPOL in fight against match-fixing –FIFA.com*. 2013). Attesting to the importance of maintaining the integrity of sport and the history of match-fixing, Section 6 of FIFA's disciplinary code specifically addresses "Corruption" which states:

Anyone who offers, promises or grants an unjustified advantage to a body of FIFA, a match official, a player or an official on behalf of himself or a third party in an attempt to incite it or him to violate the regulations of FIFA will be sanctioned. Passive corruption (soliciting, being promised or accepting an unjustified advantage) will be sanctioned in the same manner. In serious cases and in the case of repetition, sanction 1b) may be pronounced for life. In any case, the body will order the confiscation of the assets involved in committing the infringement. These assets will be used for football development programmes.

Furthermore, Section 10 of FIFA's disciplinary code entitled "Unlawfully influencing match results" states that:

> Anyone who conspires to influence the result of a match in a manner contrary to sporting ethics shall be sanctioned with a match suspension or a ban on taking part in any football-related activity as well as a fine of at least CHF 15,000. In serious cases, a lifetime ban on taking part in any football related activity shall be imposed.
>
> In the case of a player or official unlawfully influencing the result of a match in accordance with par. 1, the club or association to which the player or official belongs may be fined. Serious offences may be sanctioned with expulsion from a competition, relegation to a lower division, a points deduction and the return of awards (Fédération Internationale de Football Association. 2011. FIFA Disciplinary Code. Zurich: Switzerland).

Adding to its arsenal for combating match-fixing, FIFA established an *Early Warning System GmbH* (EWS); an automated system that monitors sports betting on all FIFA tournaments. Working in collaboration with over 400 bookmakers and betting organizations worldwide, the *Early Warning System* is tasked with monitoring the worldwide sports betting market. Using its own monitoring system to detect and prevent the influence of FIFA matches with a view to obtaining unfair winnings, the system monitors the worldwide sports betting market, the system has been expanded to include "a hotline in which players, referees, officials and anyone else could leave messages if they became aware, in any way, of possible influences." Since being established, EWS has reported that "it has made a name for itself through its monitoring of the sports betting market and has progressively expanded and optimised the warning system over the last four years" (*FIFA.com – Early Warning System* 2013). In an information document, EWS explains that "sport can only win the battle to protect its integrity if it has the support of responsible sports betting providers. EWS not only carries out monitoring activities, but also aims to increase awareness of the problem of manipulation." It states that its goal is to provide specialist information and raise public awareness in its fight against match-fixing and corruption (Early Warning System, FIFA 2013).

Legitimate Betting Organizations. Throughout the world of sports, betting is a popular pastime and activity. While most popular in sports such as soccer, cricket, rugby, football, baseball, basketball, boxing, and many other professional sports, there is no limit to which individuals will wager on the various outcomes of sport, whether on individual plays, goals, points, fouls, penalties, who wins or loses, along with any number of other schemes and scenarios. Notwithstanding the countless number of wagers that are placed between private individuals, the stakes are typically higher when placed through legitimate organized betting establishments. Some such legitimate organizations comprise the *European Lotteries*, the *European Gaming and Betting Association* (EGBA), the *Remote Gambling Association* (RGA), and the *International Sports Betting Association* (ISBA) whose mission statement declares that its goal is to advocate for the need to establish favorable laws that provide sports bettors and bookmakers with a secure, safe, and regulated place to play that encourages transparency. It further states that:

> The ISBA is committed to defending the rights of sports bettors and bookmakers. On behalf of our membership, we will promote and protect sports betting through advocacy work not only with our overseas partners but also in Washington, D.C., and in each state capitol throughout the United States. The ISBA: International Sports Betting Association will work with key lawmakers to ensure a thoughtful and productive dialogue that represents everyone who enjoys and wants to protect the right to place a bet on their favorite sport without fear of prosecution.

Other organizations such as *Gaming Intelligence* advocates that it is dedicated exclusively to serving the business intelligence needs of the global interactive gaming industry, and that it provides "timely coverage and analysis of all the developments impacting industry stakeholders," and that its serves as an "invaluable daily tool amongst key decision makers within gaming operators, national regulators, the legal and financial communities and the wider media" (*Gaming Intelligence* 2013).

Legislators and Public Policy. Legislators, who are typically elected into office to represent the needs and interests of their communities and constituencies, hold significant power, authority, and responsibility. Among their many responsibilities is the legislation of laws, which in principle, contributes to maintaining social order and control. Such laws can be civil, criminal, and regulatory in nature. The process of legislating laws leads to public policy which affects citizens – whether locally, regionally, nationally, or internationally – in a variety of ways. Usually represented and embodied in legislative acts or judicial decisions, public policy represents governmental courses of actions, regulatory measures, laws, and funding priorities. Cochran, Mayer, Carr, Mckenzie and Peck et al. (2012), define public policy "as a set of actions by the government that includes, but is not limited to, making laws and is defined in terms of a common goal or purpose" (p. 1). They explain that "making policy requires choosing among goals and alternatives, and choice always involves intention," emphasizing that "public policy is not a single action, but is a set of actions coordinated to achieve a goal" (p. 2). When considering public policy, the authors suggest that there exist contextual considerations, namely, institutional, economic, demographic, ideological, and cultural.

Given these and the many other considerations that factor into enacting public policy and law, not the least of which involve the political process itself, the involvement of legislators in addressing corruption in sports, and specifically match-fixing, is of critical importance. Cochran, et al., (2012) emphasize that lawmaking alone is not enough to establish a policy; rather the process also involves consideration of the implementation, interpretation, enforcement, and impact of policies and laws. Given the social, cultural, legal, political, economic, and logistical implications of enacting public policy, especially as it relates to match-fixing, involves many individuals and dynamics; a process that can prove to be quite challenging. While enacting public policy on the local, regional, and national level can prove to be a daunting task to the best of legislators, doing so on an international level will require extraordinary measures and initiatives. Nevertheless, without the support of legislators who can enact substantive criminal law and public policy to address the systemic problem of match-fixing, the sporting community and society at-large will be plagued by the abhorrent and unscrupulous behavior of society's criminals.

Police and Law Enforcement. While identifying and engaging those stakeholders who are vulnerable to falling victim to, and who participate in match-fixing, namely players, referees, coaches, and owners, their input and contributions would be meaningless without the work of police and law enforcement agencies who are tasked with the enormous challenge of investigating and enforcing the laws associated with match-fixing. Given the nature of the problem, doing so can be an undaunting task. Investigating and enforcing such laws require an enormous amount of logistics and resources in terms of personnel, equipment, finances, and the requisite technologies to adequately investigate and enforce the laws. This need is exasperated by (1) the transnational nature of match-fixing, (2) the extent to which technologies plays such an important role, and (3) its perceived insignificance and relative unimportance when compared to the serious nature of so many other domestic and transnational crimes that pressure sovereignties worldwide such as terrorism, human trafficking, and the drug and weapons trade.

Nevertheless, given the extent to which match-fixing plays into and contributes to many other crimes such as money-laundering, prostitution, embezzlement, terrorism, human-trafficking, and drug and weapons trafficking, by comprehensively researching and studying the problem – to include identifying the many direct and indirect organized crime syndicates involved – can point to the seriousness and extent of the problem. Despite the seriousness and pervasiveness of the problem, the caliber and professionalism of personnel that represent and comprise local, regional, national, and transnational police and law enforcement agencies are exceptionally qualified to meet the challenge associated with match-fixing. Agencies such as the *International Criminal Police Organization* (INTERPOL), the *European Police Organization* (EUROPOL), the *International Association of Chiefs of Police* (IACP), the *Federal Bureau of Investigation* (FBI), the respective national police agencies of the world's free and democratic countries, and renowned city policing agencies such as the *New York City Police* and the *London Metropolitan Police* (*Scotland Yard*), are but a few of the hundreds of police and law enforcement organizations that can be solicited for their expertise, experience, and potential contributions. As has been demonstrated in the past, universities throughout the world have worked in close partnership and collaboration with police and law enforcement agencies that have yielded exceptional research that has significantly influenced public policy and practice.

Civilian Experts and Resources. Although limited, there are civilian individuals and organizations that can serve as valuable resources in studying and researching the subject of match-fixing. Organizations such as the *Bureau of Justice Statistics* (BJS), the *National Institute of Justice* (NIJ), the *Police Executive Research Forum* (PERF), and the *National Criminal Justice Reference Services* are but a few of other resources that can serve in researching the problem and challenges associated with match-fixing. Similarly, in collaboration with lead organizations such as FIFA and INTERPOL, the faculty and graduate students of colleges and universities who specialize in crime and justice studies can serve as valuable resources. Often, grants are available, such as that provided by FIFA to INTERPOL assist to support research, education, and enforcement. Others resources can include investigative reporters and journalists such as Declan Hill who authored the book *The Fix: Soccer and Organized Crime* (2008), Bret Forrest who wrote *All the World is Staged* (2012), and *Match-Fixing in Romanian Football* (2011) by Barnabas Crist Bal, who can provide unique insights into the depth of match-fixing and tentacles of organized crime syndicates.

In addition to conducting valid and reliable research, the academe can provide other valuable resources to the sporting and law enforcement communities, and society at-large. These can include, but are not limited to: (1) developing and sponsoring educational seminars and workshops on the local, regional, and international level, (2) serve as a conduit and venue for bringing together the various stakeholders who have influence in the fight against match-fixing, (3) provide objective research based data for public dissemination, (4) develop courses and certification programs for traditional classroom and web-based delivery, and (5) develop interdisciplinary courses of study within undergraduate and graduate programs that underscore the importance of maintaining integrity in sport, as well as studying the corrupt practices associated with match-fixing and the manner in which it supports other organized crime activities.

While many organizations have rallied against the threat of match-fixing, the recent introduction of the *International Centre for Sport Security* (ICSS) established in 2010, exemplifies one of many such concerns. As part of its mission, it strongly advocates for maintaining the integrity of sport, declaring that: (1) integrity is the most fundamental value to sport, (2) corruption erodes the very spirit of sport, and (3) without integrity competition is meaningless. They explain that "breaches of integrity not only damage these values, but will shape a sport's popularity and ultimately its business and sponsorship viability, and even its survival." Their website states that "while many sports have taken active steps towards safeguarding competitions, the threats to integrity today are so internationally significant – so growing and so constantly changing – that the ICSS established a specialist Sport Integrity Directorate staffed with industry-leading experts so that the ICSS can provide valued integrity support to all sports." In what they describe as the three pillars for ensuring the integrity of sport, their model is one from which the academic community can learn, and in kind, can compliment by contributing and providing reciprocal opportunities to address the problem of match-fixing.

Its first Integrity Pillar provides what they describe as *Protection of Sport through Training and Education.* This involves: (1) providing sport integrity awareness seminars to groups of professionals on the challenge of crime and corruption to sport, for global, regional and national sport bodies, police and commercial sponsors; (2) providing training programs in the *design and* implementation of integrity protection and corruption prevention tools, designed for global, regional and national sport bodies; and (3) providing training programs on investigating corruption in sport for the protection of sport for integrity professionals within sport.

Its second *Integrity Pillar* provides what they describe as *Protection of Sport through Investigation and Intelligence.* This involves establishing (1) an international database of open-source knowledge and investigative information on corruption in sport and the criminals who take advantage of sport, for use by global, regional and national sport bodies, and (2) providing investigative support for sport bodies through the deployment of a team of experienced and discrete specialists, to assist global, regional and national sport bodies.

Its third *Integrity* Pillar provides what they describe as *Protection of Sport through Enforcing Consequences in Sport.* This involves developing (1) a network and forum of specialized sport legal officers and prosecutors to share experiences, cases, and a database of discipline and integrity knowledge for use by sport legal officers and prosecutors, and (2) acquiring specialist advice on the design, implementation and maintenance of internal regulatory systems targeting prevention and consequences for internal sport corruption, and its harmonization with government regulators, police investigations and criminal prosecutions (*Sport Integrity | ICSS International Centre For Sport Security* (2013)).

Fans, Spectators, and the General Public

While sport psychologists make distinctions between sport fans and sport spectators, as a collective group of sport enthusiasts, they along with the public at-large, share a common distain for any form of corruption in sports. Such concerns are regularly reported by the news media in headlines such as those that appeared on February 12, 2013, by the *Diplomat* which declared that *Matching-Fixing and Doping Investigation Shocks Sports Fan*; a February 6, 2013, *Yahoo* blog that exclaimed *Singapore football fans dismayed over match-fixing scandal*; and a May 17, 2013, report by *The Times of India* that declared *IPL spot-fixing has cricket fans fuming*. Attesting to the popularity of sports are the dozens of magazines dedicated to sports, its daily coverage in every televised news report, and the *Entertainment and Sports Programming Network*, more commonly referred to as ESPN, which provides around the clock coverage of sports throughout the world on cable television and the Internet, which weighs in heavily on the corruption of match-fixing.

Indisputably, an integral part of all sporting events are its fans and spectators. For many, their lives revolve sports, whether as participants, or as casual or devout fans. Because of their dedication to sports and the trust and confidence they place in their teams and respective players, they provide an invaluable resource to ensuring that integrity of sport is not threatened by the unsavory practices of criminals who engage in match-fixing. Public outcry and disillusionment with any form of corrupt behavior, most notably, doping and match-fixing, can serve as an impetus for engaging fans and spectators, the media, legislators, and the general public in a common cause against corruption in sports and to advocate for ensuring its integrity. As with all of the stakeholders identified, sports fans, spectators, and the general public can serve as invaluable resources.

The Media and Public Relations. According to the *Public Relations Society of America* (PRSA), the founding member of the *Global Alliance for Public Relations and Communications Management*, which represents 160,000 practitioners and academics worldwide, public relations is a strategic communications process that builds mutually beneficial relationships between organizations and their publics. As a management function, PRSA explains that public relations encompasses (1) anticipating, analyzing, and interpreting public opinion, attitudes and issues that might impact the operations of organizations, (2) counseling management at levels of the organization with regard to policy decisions, courses of action and communication, taking into account public ramifications, and the organizations social and citizenship responsibilities, (3) researching, conducting, and evaluating programs of action, to include marketing, fund raising, community and government relations, and (4) planning and implementing the organization's efforts to influence or change public policy ("Public Relations Resources & PR Tools for Communications Professionals: Public Relations Society of America (PRSA)" 2013).

Inherent to the challenge of addressing match-fixing is the need to inform and educate the general public. Elected officials and legislators, when influenced and pressured by their constituencies can, and do, respond. The general public can influence public officials, public policy, and the legislation of laws. "Sparked by the growth of the mass media and the rising importance of public opinion," Hackman and Johnson (2013) explain that public relations encompass a wide range of activities to include marketing programs, lobbying governmental agencies, researching public attitudes, organizing persuasive campaigns, and working with media representatives.

While the role of the academe is not to directly engage in the enterprise of public relations as it relates to match-fixing, it can nevertheless serve as an important resource and conduit to professional public relations organizations. Given the number of stakeholders that need to be engaged in addressing the problem of match-fixing, it can behoove professional sports organizations such as FIFA and professional public relations firms to work in concert with, and take advantage of research provided by the academe.

Stakeholders Collective Role and Responsibility

In compliment to the many initiatives that have already been undertaken to address match-fixing, appealing to and engaging the various stakeholders that collectively possess the requisite power and influence to bear upon the problem of match-fixing can serve as one of many other initiatives in which the academe can serve as a resource. The valued input of stakeholders in identifying the scope and breath of the problem can lend itself to developing the necessary strategies and tactics to confront and mitigate match-fixing. This can include the development and enhancement of new and existing of rules and regulations, the legislation of laws and public policy, the recruitment and vetting of new players, instituting incentive programs to reward those who uphold society's expectations for honesty and athleticism, developing systems and processes to reward those that report those that engage in match-fixing, and developing educational programs, are but one of many steps that can serve to mitigate the corrosive impact of match-fixing. Toward this end, the academe can facilitate qualified research by conducting observations, interviews, survey questionnaires, focus groups, provide educational seminars and workshops, and aid in the recommendation and facilitation of annual mandatory training and education.

Conclusion

In keeping with its rich history, tradition, and mission, today's academe continues to serve society through research, education, and public service. Dedicated to its cause, the academe serves to develop the whole person, foster knowledge, understanding, critical thinking, cultivate creativity, encourage social and cultural sensitivities, increase passion for life and learning, and to contribute to civic causes and public service. Inherent to its perennial growth, development, and maturation, the academe is recognized as an altruistic resource to an ever-increasing and expansive number of disciplines and constituencies, the latter of which include, but are not limited to government, private and non-profit sectors, quasi and non-governmental organizations, philanthropic causes, and the community at-large.

To keep current with the infinite number of social, cultural, legal, political, economic, and technological changes that characterize and transform today's fast-paced society, the academe continues to advance new and innovative research and development. This has been evident with the introduction of new disciplines of study to which many undergraduate and graduate programs are now dedicated. Bachelor, Masters, and Doctor of Philosophy degrees in criminal justice and criminology, which years ago were ostensibly nonexistent, now flourish and are expanding to meet the challenges posed by terrorism, homeland security, cyber-crime, and transnational crime. In this context, the academe has once again been identified as a resource to assist in the study, research, training, and education surrounding the corruptive practice of match-fixing and other related criminal activities that undermine the integrity of sport.

Given the serious implications of match-fixing, its corrosive effects on society in fueling organized crime and corruption, and the extent to which it undermines the importance society places on maintaining the integrity of sport, addressing the problem has become a collective and multilateral concern among many organizations, to include that of the academe. While the academe recognizes the limitations of its potential contributions in addressing the corruptive practices associated with match-fixing, its experience and expertise in research, education, and public service can nevertheless prove to be a valuable resource and commodity to the various stakeholders, whom include but are not limited to players, referees, coaches, team owners, professional sport organizations, legislators, police and law enforcement, the media, fans and spectators, and the society at-large.

Given its focus on research, training and education, and providing public service to the greater community, the academe can: (1) conduct substantive research and data analyses into identifying the scope and breadth of the problem of match-fixing, (2) work in collaborative partnership with the various stakeholders in developing strategies and tactics to mitigate and marginalize match-fixing and related corruption, (3) serve as a conduit and venue for bringing together the various stakeholders who possess the power and influence to address the problem of match-fixing, and (4) provide qualified experts and subject specific training and education to players, coaches, referees, team owners, sponsors, fans and spectators, legitimate betting organizations, legislators, police and law enforcement, the media, and the general public in the following ways:

- Develop, sponsor, deliver, and/or present educational seminars, workshops, and conferences on the local, regional, national, and international level that focus on the importance of maintaining integrity in sport, and the adverse consequences that match-fixing has on crime and corruption.[6]

---

[6]Examples of topics could include Ethical and professional behavior, *gamesmanship* versus *sportsmanship*, the perils of the *slippery slope*, prostitution, loan-sharking, etcetera.

- Assist in the development of legal and ethical practices in recruiting, vetting, selecting, cultivating, and maintaining an environment that promotes integrity in sport.[7]
- Assist in the research, development, and legislation of national and transnational criminal laws that specifically address match-fixing to include severe and commensurate sanctions.[8]
- Develop a comprehensive course of study that could lead to certification of players, coaches, referees, and team owners in the area of *Sport Integrity Assurance and Professionalism.*
- Develop a curriculum and course of study for traditional classroom and web-based delivery that could lead to concentrations within undergraduate or graduate degree programs such as Criminal Justice, Criminology, Sports Management and Administration programs, in *Sports Integrity Assurance and Professionalism.*
- Develop and sponsor public service information sessions and workshops to the media and general public underscoring the importance for integrity in sport, the adverse impact of crime and corruption, and its corrosive and undermining effect it has on public trust and confidence.

Finally, traditional or web-based courses that can be offered independently as part of a compendium, certification, or concentration within a specific course of study such as criminology, criminal justice, philosophy, or sport management and administration, may include titles such as:

Integrity in Sport	Sports Management and Administration
Laws, Ethics, and Decision-making	Match-fixing and Corruption in Sports
Organized and Transnational Crime	Gaming, Sports Betting, and Gambling

References

Albanese, R. (1988). *Management.* Cincinnati, Ohio: South-Western Publishing.

Altbach, P.G., Reisberg, L, and Rumbley, L.E. (2009). *Trends in Global Higher Education: Tracking an Academic Revolution.* Boston, MA: Boston College Center for International Education.

BBC Sport – Fifa bans referees for life for match-fixing. (n.d.). Retrieved from http://www.bbc.co.uk/sport/0/football/14481355.

Brubacher, J. S. (1977). *On the philosophy of higher education.* San Francisco: Jossey-Bass Publishers.

Cochran, C. E., Mayer, L. C., Carr, T. R., Cayer, N. J., McKenzie, M., and Peck, L.R. (2012). American Public Policy: An Introduction. Boston, MA: Wadsworth-Cengage Publishing.

Council of Europe Recommendation. (2012). Match-fixing in sport: A mapping of criminal law provisions in EU 27. March 2012.

---

[7] Organizations such as *Fédération Internationale de Football Association* and the *International Centre for Sport Security* can serve as excellent references for developing mission statements, guiding principles, and rules and regulations.

[8] See *Matching-fixing in Sport: A mapping of criminal law provision in EU 27. Brussels: KEA European Affairs.*

Early Warning System (FIFA). (2010). Retrieved from http://www.jfa.or.jp/jfa/riji-kai/2010/20101111/pdf/k20101111_02_02.pdf.

European Commission Directorate-General for Education and Culture (2012). *Match-fixing in Sport: A mapping of criminal law provision in EU 27*.

Duryea, E. D., & Williams, D. T. (2000). *The academic corporation: A history of college and university governing boards*. New York: Falmer Press.

FIFA.com – Early Warning System. (n.d.). Retrieved from http://www.fifa.com/aboutfifa/organisation/footballgovernance/earlywarningsystem.html

FIFA's historic contribution to INTERPOL in fight against match-fixing – FIFA.com. (n.d.). Retrieved from http://www.fifa.com/aboutfifa/organisation/news/newsid=1431884/

Flexner, J. A. (1968). Universities: American, English, German. New York: Oxford University Press.

Gaming Intelligence. (n.d.). Retrieved from http://www.gamingintelligence.com/.

Hackman, M.Z., & Johnson, C.E. (2013). *Leadership: A Communication Perspective* (6th Ed.) Long Grove, Ill: Waveland Press, Inc.

Hagen, F.E. (2006). Research Methods in Criminal Justice and Criminology, 7th Ed. Boston, MA: Pearson Education, Inc.

Hanson, K. O., & Savage, M. (2013). What *Role Does Ethics Play in Sports?* (n.d.). Retrieved from http://www.scu.edu/ethics/publications/submitted/sports-ethics.html.

Hill, D. (2008). *The Fix: Soccer and Organized Crime*. Toronto: McClelland and Steward, Ltd.

Husting, A., Iglesias, M., Kern, P., and Buinickaite, Z. (2012). *Matching-fixing in Sport: A mapping of criminal law provision in EU 27. Brussels: KEA European Affairs*.

Integrity (Stanford Encyclopedia of Philosophy). (n.d.). In *Stanford Encyclopedia of Philosophy*. Retrieved from http://plato.stanford.edu/entries/integrity/.

Italian soccer federation says Lazio, Genoa, Lecce plus 8 players face match-fixing trial | Fox News. (July 10, 2013). Retrieved from http://www.foxnews.com/sports/2013/07/10/italian-soccer-federation-says-lazio-genoa-lecce-plus-8-players-face-match/

Lebanese soccer referees caught fixing match for sex – Washington Times. (n.d.). Retrieved from http://www.washingtontimes.com/news/2013/jun/10/lebanese-soccer-referees-caught-fixing-match-sex/

Massive match-fixing scandal blasts Europe's football (SETimes.com). (n.d.). Retrieved from http://www.setimes.com/cocoon/setimes/xhtml/en_GB/features/setimes/articles/2013/02/19/reportage-01.

Match-fixing experts fear corrupt tennis players will be playing at Wimbledon Championships | Mail Online. (n.d.). Retrieved from http://www.dailymail.co.uk/sport/tennis/article-2338054/Match-fixing-experts-fear-corrupt-tennis-players-playing-Wimbledon-Championships.html

'Match-fixing is reality' says Burkina Faso coach banned in Belgium | Football | The Guardian. (2013). Retrieved from http://www.theguardian.com/football/2013/feb/05/burkina-faso-match-fixing-paul-put

Maxfield, M. G., & Babbie, E. R. (2012). *Basics of research methods for criminal justice and criminology* (3rd ed.). Belmont, CA: Thomson/Wadsworth.

Mission and values – SportAccord International Sports Federations. (2013). Retrieved from http://www.sportaccord.com/en/who-we-are/mission-and-values/.

Orlich, D.C. (1978). *Designing Sensible Surveys*. Pleasantville, NY: Redgrave Publishing Company.

Playing by the bookmaker – Cricket News & Articles | CricketCountry.com. (n.d.). Retrieved from http://www.cricketcountry.com/cricket-articles/Playing-by-the-bookmaker/28537.

Probe fire under BCCI chair. (n.d.). Retrieved from http://www.telegraphindia.com/1130524/jsp/frontpage/story_16932619.jsp.

Public Relations Resources & PR Tools for Communications Professionals: Public Relations Society of America (PRSA). (n.d.). Retrieved from http://www.prsa.org.

Robbins, S. P. (2000). *Managing today!* Upper Saddle River, NJ: Prentice Hall.

Rudy, W. (1984). *The Universities of Europe 1100–1914: A History*. London: Associated University Presses, Inc.

Schmalleger, F. (2013). *Criminal justice today: An introductory text for the 21st century.* (12th ed.). Upper Saddle River, NJ: Pearson Prentice Hall.

Schutt, R. K. (2001). *Investigating the social world: The process and practice of research.* Thousand Oaks, California: Pine Forge Press.

Soccer match-fixing scandal: How do you rig a soccer game? – Slate Magazine. (2011). Retrieved from http://www.slate.com/articles/sports/explainer/2011/12/soccer_match_fixing_scandal_how_do_you_rig_a_soccer_game_.html.

Sports betting under the microscope – FIFA.com. (n.d.). Retrieved from http://www.fifa.com/aboutfifa/organisation/footballgovernance/news/newsid=1406983/index.html

Sport Integrity | ICSS International Centre For Sport Security. (n.d.). Retrieved from http://www.theicss.org/services/sport-integrity/.

Veysey, L. R. (1965). *The emergence of the American university.* Chicago: University of Chicago Press.

What Role Does Ethics Play in Sports?. (n.d.). Retrieved from http://www.scu.edu/ethics/publications/submitted/sports-ethics.html.

Williams, C.R, and Arrigo, A. (2008). Ethics, Crime and Criminal Justice. Upper Saddle River, NJ: Pearson Prentice Hall.

Catching Sports Cheaters: An Example of Successful Police Operations

Irfan Demir and Kutluer Karademir

Abstract Economists examining the 'rational' dimension dominate existing explanations for match fixing, yet we need to know more about how match fixing occurs. This chapter examines the actors, vehicles and processes of match fixing by applying the case of match fixing scandal in Turkey to a framework extracted from Hill's (*The Fix Soccer and Organized Crime.* Toronto: McClelland & Stewart, 2008) text on the subject. This analysis finds that the actors, vehicles and processes of a match fixing case in Turkey perfectly fit the characteristics identified by Hill.

Introduction

Soccer (interchangeably used with the word "football") has become a global phenomenon that has significant impacts on social life, politics, economy, fashion and culture (Kuper 1996; Foer 2004). In fact the exorbitant public interest in the game has been converted not only into cash but also social and political benefits. The Fascist regime in Italy, for example, recognized the great public interest in the game and tried to construct a fascist national identity via football (Martin 2004). The first

I. Demir, Ph.D. (✉)
Istanbul Emniyet Mudurlugu, Gokalp Mah. Prof. Dr. M. Aksoy Cad.,
No:1 Kat: 6 (Egitim Sube Md.), Zeytinburnu, Istanbul, Turkey
e-mail: irfandemir25@yahoo.com

K. Karademir, Ph.D.
İstanbul Emniyet Mudurlugu,
EKKM Sube Mudurlugu A blok Kat 5 Adnan Menderes Bulvarı (Vatan Cad.),
Fatih- Istanbul, Turkey
e-mail: kutluerk@hotmail.com

M.R. Haberfeld and D. Sheehan (eds.), *Match-Fixing in International Sports:*   331
Existing Processes, Law Enforcement, and Prevention Strategies,
DOI 10.1007/978-3-319-02582-7_17, © Springer International Publishing Switzerland 2013

president of Ghana, Kwame Nkumrah, aimed higher in taking advantage of the interest in football to harvest political fruits. Nkumrah struggled to unite the entire African continent by creating an "African Personality," which stands for a new African generation which can stand on their own feet and independently compete with the rest of the world, using football as the cement (Rosbrook-Thompson and Armstrong 2010). Nevertheless, neither Mussolini nor Nkumrah were able to realize their goals because football invigorates local and regional identities yielding in the long run more separation than unification (Martin 2004; Rosbrook-Thompson and Armstrong 2010).

Observing that most of effort spent by politicians to obtain political outcomes via football could not reach their target, the next question might be: is the turnover created by the 'football industry' being distributed, as it should be? The scandals of match fixing that occurred even in the most prestigious tournaments indicate that, it is not easy to answer this question. Match fixing is the purposeful under-performing by players or manipulation by coaches to affect the outcome of individual matches or tournaments in return for incentives (Preston and Szymanski 2003). Shedding some light on how match fixing is put into practice, we examine a recent case of match fixing in Turkey.

The football industry generates revenues from ticket and equipment (i.e., jerseys of popular players) sales, sponsorship agreements, TV broadcasts, gambling, player transfers and stock market speculation. Thanks to these and several other sources of income, the economics of football amount to billions of dollars. The TV broadcasting of soccer matches in popular leagues such as the Premiere League of England, Srerie A of Italy or La Liga of Spain via satellite and cable generates significant advertising revenues for the broadcasters and these soccer leagues. Additionally, the Internet offers fans both the joy of watching first quality soccer games, while also creating a global betting market which presents great advantages for the criminal syndicates to fix matches (Horrie 2000). As the volume and velocity of money, prestige and interest attached to football grows, this also paves the way for 'illegal entrepreneurs' to earn money by taking the uncertainty factor out of the games (McLaren 2008).

Match fixing in sports contests is generally explained by economists within the context of the design of the tournament, which includes the rules for regulating the volume and the distribution regimes of incentives and punishments, fixture and point systems, and the vertical and horizontal movements of teams or players within the hierarchy of leagues or ranking classifications. Economists agree that the design of a tournament is crucial in terms of shaping the perceived value attached to winning among players (Hillman and Riley 1989; Nti 2004; Preston and Szymanski 2003; Caruso 2007). According to Preston and Szymanski (2003), the probability of match fixing is proportional to the imbalance between the perceived gains of the rivals upon winning. A match fixing attempt will be more probable if winning begot great amounts of benefits to one of the contestants (team or individual player) and little or no benefits to the other. Preston and Szymanski (2003) contend that:

Match fixing occurs either because one side 'needs' to win to the extent that it is willing to make side payments to persuade the other side not to make effort or to persuade the referees to make biased decisions, or because players or officials stand to gain financially from gambling on the outcome of a match (p. 617).

Therefore, it can be argued that low-profile players or referees that are paid less are more vulnerable to match fixing (Humphreys 2011).

The theoretical models of economists were supported by empirical studies. Shepotylo (2005) found some empirical evidence that after the introduction of the "3 points for a win" rule, football matches in Ukraine became more corruptible especially in the long-run tournaments. Similarly Caruso (2007) showed the impact of tournament design on the evaluation of the stakes among contestants, using examples from two differently designed tournaments, the FIFA World Cup and the UEFA Champions League. Duggan and Levitt (2002) found indirect empirical evidence by examining more than 32,000 Sumo matches in Japan. They found that Sumo wrestling was more likely to be fixed before the match when one of the wrestlers is on the brink of promoting to a higher category, which will provide him with considerable advantages and benefits in terms of money and prestige.

Economics literature provides a solid baseline for the rational calculation process of the probable actors of the game. In sum, the probability of match fixing grows proportional to the imbalance between the amount of expected gains upon winning between the rivals based on the design of the competition, the amount and the distribution of incentives, fixtures and pointing systems, issues such as promotion and relegation, the number of matches etc. Thus recommended solutions to match fixing concentrate on either increasing the amount of punishment for the perpetrators (Preston and Szymanski 2003), which is difficult due to the popularity of sports figures, or lessening the amounts of incentives attached to winning (Caruso 2007), which is apparently unrealistic given the turnover in the football industry.

These explanations of match fixing help us understand the motivations that may yield to match fixing, but we need to know more about how the match fixing process runs, who the more probable actors are, and what types of vehicles are used. This chapter attempts to shed some light on the operationalization of the factors affecting match fixing through examining a case of match fixing in Turkey within the framework of the actors, vehicles and processes as extracted from Hill's study (2008). We begin with laying out the framework that includes actors, vehicles and processes of match fixing based on Hill's study; next, we describe the state of football in Turkey; following this we examine the details of the police operation that elicited a series of match fixing scandals in Turkey using the framework detailed earlier; and conclude with a discussion of our conclusions and recommended policy implications. The case study is built upon a content analysis from daily newspapers, data form official documents and interviews with officers who conducted surveillance and interdiction operations on Turkish match fixing case.

The Framework: Actors, Vehicles and Processes of Match Fixing

Economics literature convincingly elaborates reasons for why match fixing might occur, but more knowledge is necessary on how match fixing is actually practiced. A comprehensive examination of match fixing that answers the above questions was done by Declan Hill (2008). Hill presented striking examples of match fixing in football games in different levels of tournaments ranging from several national leagues to the FIFA World Cup. Extracting components from Hill, a framework of actors, vehicles and processes of match fixing was constructed to allow subsequent application and analysis.

The Actors of Match Fixing

There are two sub-categories of actors associated with match fixing; fixers and targets. Fixers include organized crime groups (the mafia or syndicates) that fix matches to acquire money or power, club directors, and "runners." The targets category includes referees and players. Hill also mentions "project managers" who can be accepted as a secondary hub between runners and players. Project managers are influential players inside the team who tempt teammates into participating in the match fixing scheme (Hill 2008).

Organized crime groups mostly engage in match fixing to guarantee wining a gambling wager. These are the most dangerous and pervasive actors of match fixing who maintain the ongoing corruption of the sport. These groups perceive sports as a business and are never interested in who wins or loses. The only interest of these actors is to maximize their gains through fixing matches (Hill 2008).

Alternatively, club directors have different motivations for match fixing. They fix matches to win the games and maintain their powerful status in the club. Within this context, they develop long-term relationships with other club directors to create a mutual benefit system. By so doing, especially the directors of big clubs guarantee their victories and satisfy the masses that support them and the directors of smaller clubs earn money by transferring their players to big clubs (Hill 2008).

Runners are the mediators between the fixers and the targets. These are generally ex-players who are recognized by and have direct access to clubs or teams. They maintain connections with the team and mark players in terms of their inclination to match fixing. They also detect the weak sides of players and inform their superiors in the scheme about these. The runner operates between the fixers and the team mostly through secondary hubs called project managers. Project managers are generally influential players in the team. The project manager should beguile at least 2 or 3 players including at least the goalkeeper, one defender and one striker to guarantee the success of the scheme. Referees are generally approached directly by fixers and are offered expensive presents or money in return for making biased decisions during the game. When players are fixed, in comparison to referees, the probability of a successful match fixing attempt is 4 % higher (Hill 2008).

The Vehicles of Match Fixing

The vehicles of match fixing can be categorized into positive and negative. The positive vehicles of match fixing are money, expensive gifts (i.e., watches, cars, holiday trips etc.), women and on some occasions promises to transfer to a more prestigious club. The negative vehicles are threats of violent activities such as blackmail, and threatening physical violence, up to and including threats of death. There is also a psychological dimension that accompanies these factors. That is, the fixers use rhetoric that sooths the feeling of guilt that emerges owing to the corrupt behavior of the target. Hill (2008) notes that fixers are very good at manipulating human psychology and they avoid using offensive words that might make the target feel guilty.

The Processes of Match Fixing

The processes of match fixing refer to a set of activities that are committed to arrange the scheme from beginning to end. These activities involve how the relationship between the actors are established and run; how the targets actually implement match fixing on the pitch; and when and how the positive and negative vehicles are employed.

Hill (2008) notes that the fixing processes are somewhat different in match fixing to win the game and match fixing to win a bet. The former type of match fixing is generally conducted by club directors and is simpler than the latter. The fixer determines the match to be fixed and contacts the runner. The runner connects with the project manager who then tempts selected teammates. If it is the referee to be fixed, they are generally contacted directly by club directors. The first contacts with players are mostly established through runners. The runner then conveys the match fixing offer to the project manager and if the offer is accepted the project manager arranges the process with his teammates (Hill 2008).

Match fixing to win the bet is more complex because the fixers have to control both the players and the bet market simultaneously. Here the fixers have to wait until the last minute before betting to maximize their earnings and not to trigger the FIFA's early warning system. The bet fixers generally target weak teams' players and ask them to lose because doing so raises less doubt. They control the scores of the games by telling the players exactly when to give away the goals. By so doing they are able to invest in more complex betting schemes such as the Asian Handicap and considerably increase their profit. Thus, in this type of scheme the players are given the "instructions" a few minutes before the game starts. At this point certain symbols and gestures are used between the runner and fixed players to communicate. For example, the runner wears a certain color outfit when the team should lose the game and a different color if it should perform well. In return, the players in the scheme put their hands on their chest in the ceremony to indicate that they got the message (Hill 2008).

When it comes to the implementation of the match fixing scheme on the pitch, this is generally done by deliberate negligence and simple mistakes such as wrong moves at the wrong time. Contrary to the general perception, corrupt players refrain from deliberately seeking a red card, causing penalties or scoring own goals because doing so will raise more doubts among observers. Furthermore most of the goals are scored at the earlier phases of games when matches are fixed (Hill 2008).

After the scheme is completed the money or other incentives are given to the project manager and he distributes the prize among his teammates who took part in the scheme. According to Hill, trust is the cement that holds this entire sector of match fixing together. The fixers pay extreme attention in their reputations as trustworthy actors. Therefore payments are done promptly and precisely (Hill 2008).

Turkish Football at a Glance

Turkish professional football leagues were started in 1951 and are currently run in four professional categories (Turkish Super League, League 1, League 2 A and League 2 B) with 124 teams on a promotion and relegation basis. Except for these leagues, The National Cup is also run based on a group and elimination system, which is similar to the UEFA Champions League. According to official website of the Turkish Football Association (TFA) there are 466,500 licensed football players (including amateur players) in the country ("Lisanslı Futbolcu Sayısı" 2010). In the international arena, a few Turkish teams and the Turkish National Team won noteworthy achievements. For example Galatasaray won the UEFA Cup and the UEFA Super Cup in the1999–2000 season and qualified to quarterfinals in the UEFA Champions League the next season. Fenerbahçe also qualified to quarterfinals in the UEFA Champions League in the 2007–2008 season. The Turkish National Football Team won a 3rd degree in the 2002 FIFA World Cup and another 3rd degree in the 2008 UEFA European Cup.

As in many other countries, there is great local interest in Turkish football. It starts from childhood and playing football in the street. A great majority of Turkish men have keen interest in the sport and talk about their favorite teams and players. Matches take place on the weekends and are the subject of discussion at the work place on Monday mornings, if not the entire week. It is not uncommon to witness quarrels, even fights coming out of football chats. In short, football is a social phenomenon across the entire country. According to the UEFA report (2010) Turkey is ranked sixth in Europe in total stadium attendance with a 3.4 million total attendance and with 11,000 in attendance (on average) per match. In addition, club revenue growth between 2006 and 2010 is 27.6 % in Turkey (UEFA 2010). There are three major daily sports newspapers with a total daily circulation of approximately 450,000 that accounts for almost 10 % of the total daily newspaper circulation in Turkey.

The official bet system was established in 2004 and as of 2012 there were six official betting platforms in the country. According to the official data, 3.5 million people are involved in betting on a weekly basis. About 500,000 online gamblers participate annually with an estimated turnover of around 2.5 billion dollars ("Futbol Kumar Masasında" 2012).

When it comes to the design of the football leagues, the league system is similar to many others with promotion and relegation in Europe. The distribution of broadcast revenues, which is around $500,000,000 annually, is conducted through a pool system. Before 2008, the pool system was offering more advantage to more prestigious clubs by distributing 50 % of the broadcast revenues to clubs with earlier championships. After 2008, though, this system was changed. According to the current system 35 % of the broadcast revenues are equally distributed to each team in the league, 44 % is distributed as performance bonus where each win is awarded with 740,000 Turkish Liras (TL) and each draw is awarded with 370,000 TL (approximately $400,000 and $200,000 respectively). Fourteen percent of the broadcast revenues are distributed to clubs with early championship titles; and 7 % is distributed based on the end of season achievements. Before the introduction of this system, there were only four clubs with championship titles, but in the 2009–2010 season a fifth club, Bursaspor, won its first championship title.

In sum, there is great interest in football in Turkey. Football players, club managers and directors are popular as celebrities across the country. Since the turnover of betting is considerable it is likely that organized crime groups are interested in manipulating the Turkish gambling market. Also, the amount of broadcast revenues is astronomic ($500 M per year including taxes) and football clubs have to win more to get larger shares. Within this system, smaller teams are considered successful as long as they are able to stay in the Super League and benefit from this pool. Nevertheless, for big clubs success is measured only by the championship, or to a certain extend winning the second place that will open the door for participating the Champions League, at the end of the season. This is very important for the club directors in order to stay in power because they are seriously criticized and protested against if the team lets down the fans in consecutive seasons. Therefore, from the perspective of the scholars of Economics the value attached to winning is considerably imbalanced between bigger and smaller clubs. In such a domain match fixing attempts can be expected by both organized crime groups and club directors.

Several cases of match fixing were revealed when the police conducted a comprehensive 6 month operation ending on July 3, 2011, with a myriad of arrests including club presidents, star players, player representatives, coaches and many others. Both judicial and administrative investigations were started after the operation. The judicial trial lasted for 1 year and the trial court reached a verdict on the July 2, 2011, finding nearly half those accused guilty. Elaborating on the important details of this operation allows the identification of the actors, vehicles, and processes of this match fixing event. Using content analysis from newspapers, official documents, and court testimony, as well as the reasoned verdict of the court allows the application of Hill's (2008) framework. Additionally, the following analysis incorporates interviews with officers who conducted the operation. These elements are then compared and contrasted with the framework proposed by Hill (2008) to explore the similarities and differences between theoretical constructs and actual events, shedding light on our understanding of match fixing.

The July 3rd Operation

The Background of the Operation

The July 2011 match fixing scandal in Turkey resulted from a police operation and has became the leading issue of the country for months. According to the indictment, the investigation began in 2009 when a prosecution pursued by German authorities was expanded to include several matches played in the Turkish league. Based on this earlier investigation, the Turkish Football Association (TFA) applied to the Turkish prosecutor to initiate an investigation on those who had been allegedly involved in match fixing and betting schemes.

The indictment mentions that the police focused on the mafia-football nexus and found that due to the potential financial and power benefits, organized crime groups had been increasingly engaging in the football sector since the 1980s. Within this context the president of a second division football club, Giresunspor, applied to the police and made a complaint against his predecessor, Olgun Peker, accusing him of committing several crimes including document forgery, and compelling the players to lose matches in order to force the new club president to resign. Olgun Peker had a criminal record of being the member of an organized crime group headed by Sedat Peker. Sedat Peker used to be a fan-group leader in Fenerbahçe football club, one of the prestigious football clubs of the country with an estimated 25 million fans throughout Turkey. Olgun Peker and Mecnun Odyakmaz were Sedat's closest henchmen. Sedat Peker gained more power over time and became one of the most powerful so-called mafia leaders of the country until being arrested in 2004. Sedat Peker was sentenced to more than 14 years in prison for founding and leading an organized crime group. Olgun Peker and Mecnun Odyakmaz remained engaged in football by running player representative firms. These firms enabled them to undertake the representativeness of hundreds of players at very young ages and control them throughout their careers. By so doing, they were able to earn commissions on the transfers of players and use their influence on players to affect the scores of matches (Indictment 2011).

The investigation on Olgun Peker then expanded to include several important figures of the Turkish football community, such as club presidents and directors, managers, active and retired players, player representatives, referees and federation staff including the ex-president of the TFA. Police collected evidence through technical and physical surveillance throughout the preliminary investigation. Based on this evidence the police conducted an operation on July 3, 2011, arresting more than 40 people. The primary suspects of the investigation were Olgun Peker, Aziz Yıldırım – the president of Fenerbahçe Sports Club – and three other club directors of Fenerbahçe. Although there were several other defendants, Aziz Yıldırım was at the core of the media interest throughout the entire trial process.

As of the 2010–2011 season, Aziz Yıldırım had been the club president for 12 straight years and the football team had won four championship titles under his presidency. In the indictment, Aziz Yıldırım and many of his entourage were charged with founding a crime group to manipulate the scores of several football matches. Yıldırım had promised to win the championship for the following three consecutive seasons in his 2009 reelection campaign. Interestingly, the team dramatically lost the championship in the last game that very season causing great anguish and disappointment for millions of Fenerbahçe fans in and out of Turkey. Even worse was that Fenerbahçe had a very bad start in the 2010–2011 season. At the end of the first half of the season, they were nine points behind Trabzonspor and they had been eliminated from the Turkish National Cup by a weak second division team. Interestingly enough, they won 16 of the 17 games and one game ended in a draw in the second half of the season. Both Fenerbahçe and Trabzonspor completed the season with 82 points but Fenerbahçe won its 18th title on goal average. In his victory speech, Yıldırım acknowledged the great efforts of some "secret heroes" who worked very hard to get the championship. According to the indictment, after having lost the championship twice in the last four seasons and seeing that the team was falling away from the championship, Yıldırım and his entourage decided to manipulate the scores of the games so that Fenerbahçe would either win or Trabzonspor, their primary rival, lose. Within this frame several players were contacted before matches to fix the games. Many other match fixing attempts by directors, managers and players of miscellaneous teams also took place according to the indictment (2011).

The Post-operation Process

An administrative investigation by the TFA and a judicial trial were started simultaneously after the police operation and both were completed within 1 year. Before getting into the details of these trials, it is important to examine some of the milestones of the period between July 3, 2011, and the beginning of the judicial trial on February 14, 2012, to shed light on the chaos and limbo triggered by the operation.

On July 6th the police department declared that they detected match fixing activities in 19 matches ("19 Maçta Şike" 2011). On July 7th the UEFA made a statement on zero tolerance to match fixing ("UEFA'dan Yeni Açıklama" 2011). The kick-off date of the Turkish football leagues was postponed from August the 8th to September the 14th ("Süper Lig 9 Eylül'de" 2011). On August 22nd UEFA Chief Discipline Inspector Pierre Corno visited the prosecutor and received information on the case ("UEFA El Koydu" 2011). Four days later Fenerbahçe was dismissed from the UEFA Champions League by the TFA ("Fenerbahçe Şampiyonlar Ligi'nden" 2011). Trabzonspor was declared as the Turkish representative in the Champions League instead. Fenerbahçe appealed to CASS against the UEFA demanding €45 million redress for their losses for being banned from the Champions League. They also applied to the TFA and demanded to be relegated, but this demand was rejected by the TFA ("Fenerbahçe, Bank Asya'ya" 2011). Concurrently, tens of thousands of Fenerbahçe fans held protests claiming that the whole process was a plot against their club and the club president ("Taraftarlara Biber Gazlı" 2011).

The match fixing process also occupied the top agenda of politicians. The 6222 Act sets mandatory sentences for match fixing crimes. Many politicians called these sentencing guidelines too strict and on November 22nd all of the political parties represented in Parliament agreed on an amendment to the 6222 Act that reduced the length of sentences for match fixing (" Siddet Yasasinda Beklenen" 2011). Turkey's President vetoed the bill implementing this amended law. The reason behind the veto decision was declared to be "the strong perception in the public opinion that the amendment was passed specifically to intervene in an ongoing case" ("Şike Yasasına Gulden" 2011). However, the amendment was again sent to the President by parliament without any changes. This time the President had a constitutional obligation to sign the amendment bill into law, which he did on December 14th ("Cumhurbaşkanı Gül, bedelli" 2011). After the amendment, the sentences decreed for match fixing were lowered from 5–12 years in jail to 1–3 years.

Article 58 of the Football Discipline Directive ("TFF Olağanüstü Genel" 2011), decrees *the relegation of a club if its players or directors commit or attempt to commit match fixing*. Fenerbahçe strictly objected to TFA's attempt to change this rule and declared that they can withdraw the football league if such a change is made ("Açıklama" 2012). The president of TFA asked the clubs for a one-time suspension of Article 58, yet was unanimously refused. Hence the TFA directors' board resigned ("Mehmet ali Aydınlar'dan" 2012). This resulted in the president of Beşiktaş football club, Yıldırım Demirören, being elected as the new TFA president ("TFF'nin Yeni Başkanı" 2012). Beşiktaş was one of the clubs involved in the match fixing case. The coach and a few directors of Beşiktaş had been arrested during the police operation. After the election of Demirören as the TFA president, new members were appointed to the executive and audit boards.

Highlights on the Police Investigation

The July 3rd investigation was conducted by the Organized Crime Unit of the Istanbul Police Department. Police officers stated during the interviews that, initially, investigators were not looking into match fixing issues, nor were they much interested in football in general, beyond mainstream Turkish fans interest. They were originally investigating organized crime activities within their jurisdiction and they did not expect the issue to expand into match fixing. However, during the course of the investigations, they ended up discovering some of the targets being involved in match fixing along with other criminal activities. As the scope of the investigation expanded, additional suspects were identified. Meanwhile, the police investigations team felt that it would be wise to enhance the team members' grasp of technical knowledge of football, beyond the level of ordinary football fans. They used every means available to educate themselves, to be able to interpret all activities within the scope of their investigations such as following all matches, keeping up with the media output on football, receiving technical knowledge from relevant sources and studying all the data sources in a structured manner. Some of the team members attempted to put themselves in the shoes of sports columnists, while others tried to envision themselves as if they were club managers, key players and player representatives. The strategy turned out to be an outstanding means of developing a team concept within the department. After a short while, the team was able to interpret all the activities in the league and moves of the suspects. Whenever needed, they also received some support from other units that do not directly deal with the subject matter (Interview with detectives, August 30, 2012).

Detectives were also subjected to many personal sacrifices, from physical surveillance squads to the technical staff, the entire team worked meticulously, making the effort worthwhile. At one point, a squad started tracking a suspect, who they believed would be heading back to his home, only to end up chasing him across the country as he decided to leave town and meet other associates at a far-away city. The squad had to keep tracking him without being able to notify their own families of their location or potential return date (Interview with detectives, August 30, 2012).

Several similar examples were mentioned during interviews with the investigators. Actual money transfers used to bribe relevant parties involved in match fixing were photographed and a brand new luxury car was videotaped being driven out of the auto dealership with the suspect inside, who actually registered the car under a relative's name. One important point mentioned by the investigation team related to the phone tapping that had to be supported by other supplementary evidence in this case (Interview with detectives, September 7, 2012).

The investigation team identified several significant lessons that could be applied to future investigations of match fixing. First, the need for specific laws against match fixing. The investigators used the comprehensive regulations within their jurisdiction to carry out the investigation and prepare the evidence for presentation to the prosecutor. However, more detailed legal grounds with specific details covering match fixing and other relevant issues could have expedited the process resulting in a more cost-effective effort. It was also reported by detectives that a specialized unit to deal with the specific match fixing cases has to be established. Additionally, an early warning system to signal that the potential match fixing may be occurring should be developed and utilized by the police for earlier intervention. Earlier cooperative efforts with relevant institutions such as the sports federation and prosecutorial authorities would help as well (Interview with detectives, September 7, 2012).

One final and striking point made during interviews with detectives is that football fans themselves offer investigators a valuable tool. Idle fans point out and talk about potential evidence (changes in performance, player injuries, etc.) that can be used in fight against match fixing globally. Should this weapon against match fixing be properly utilized, there could be a significant effect on reduction of cases of sports corruption. This point will be further examined in the discussion section.

The Administrative Investigation

The administrative investigation was pursued by the Professional Football Discipline Board (PFDB) of the TFA within the legal framework of the Football Discipline

Directive. Article 58 of this directive regulates match fixing and decrees relegation of relevant football clubs in the event match fixing is proved. After the police investigation, a copy of the police file was sent to the PFDB by the prosecutor. The PFDB investigated the police evidence and wrote a report on August 15, 2011. This report was never officially shared with the police or prosecutor, but somehow was leaked out to the press ("Mehmet Baransu Şike" 2012) indicating that the club president of Fenerbahçe and some of the club executives had fixed six matches, and attempted to fix another six matches. The report also pointed to article 58 of the discipline directive and suggested the relegation of Fenerbahçe since the actions of the club president and top executives should be considered the actions of the club. The former president of the TFA argued against such action, stating the institutions and individuals should be separated in the investigation. In other words, football clubs should not be punished for the wrong doings of their managers. Thus, as mentioned above, Aydınlar wanted to change article 58 of the directive on a one-time only basis which would be ad hoc to the ongoing match fixing case. After this attempt was refused by the clubs the TFA president and the members of the executive board resigned. All those who resigned were replaced. The disciplinary board examined the file for 8 months and issued a new report on April 22, 2012. In the new report Aziz Yıldırım was acquitted, nevertheless, three of his top executives were found guilty of fixing and attempting to fix a total of six matches. The ex-coach of Beşiktaş was also acquitted in the report. Moreover, the Ethics Board declared that after watching the videos of the suspicious matches despite the fact that there were attempts of match fixing based on the surveillance reports, none of these attempts was successfully implemented on the pitch. The Ethics Board declared that the difference between the reports was normal because the first report was written based solely on the indictment. In the second report the testimony of the defendants was taken into account, videos of matches were watched and new evidence and documents that had been added to the file were examined. After the report was issued Fenerbahçe withdrew the case against the UEFA which was ongoing at the CASS ("Fenerbahçe CAS'tı" 2012).

The report of the Ethics Board was advisory and the final decision would be made by the TFA executive board. After a 1 week retreat, at a hotel in Antalya, to assess the situation the TFA president declared that the report would be sent to the Disciplinary Board for assessment and award of punishment. More importantly, Demirören stated that article 58 of the disciplinary directive had been changed. In the amended form of the article, the commission and attempt to fix matches separated and a new category of action, "gross violation" was included. According to the new article those who commit match fixing are punished with permanent deprivation of rights; if these are the directors of a club, then the club is relegated. For attempting to engage in match fixing individuals can be deprived of rights for 1–3 years and the club gets point reduction punishment up to 12 points only when a gross violation is detected. Demirören declared that the Discipline Board would make their decision in 48 hours based on the amended form of the directive ("Demirören Tarihi Kararları" 2012). No definitive criteria are mentioned as to how to assess the seriousness of the violation in the event of an attempt to match fix.

The Disciplinary Board made their decision on May 7, 2012. No club was punished by the Disciplinary Board. On the other hand, three directors of Fenerbahçe, three football players and four others were punished for attempts related to match fixing ("PFDK Şike Kararlarını" 2012).

The Judicial Trial

The judicial trial process took 1 year and a total of 93 defendants were judged. The top defendant in the case was Olgun Peker who was accused for establishing and leading an armed crime group. The second defendant was Aziz Yıldırım, the president of Fenerbahçe Sports Club. Other defendants were directors, managers, coaches and officials of different clubs, player representatives, and ex-referees. As previously mentioned, interventions in the judicial trial process from the political domain occurred and resulted in the reduction of the sentences decreed for match fixing. At the end of the judicial trial process, court reached a verdict finding 44 of 92 defendants guilty. Contrary to the report of the Ethics Committee, the court found Aziz Yıldırım guilty of inciting others to fix five matches, and also leading a crime group. Yıldırım was sentenced to 6 years and 3 months in prison, but the court released him and other defendants taking into consideration the year they had been imprisoned during the trial. While this chapter was being written in 2013, the case file awaits the outcome of the Court of Appeals decision, and Aziz Yıldırım was still the president of Fenerbahçe Sports Club.

Actors Vehicles Processes

Applying the framework extracted from Hill (2008) to the case specifics as gleaned from the judicial verdict which includes case evidence, media reports, and interviews with the police investigators, it can be concluded that the actors of the match fixing case in Turkey fits the framework. It should be mentioned here that this case fits in only one type of match fixing, which is the "old-fashioned" type of match fixing by club directors, because no incident of a betting scheme was found. Therefore the following analysis pertains to this particular type of match fixing.

The fixers are organized crime groups, club presidents and directors. The targets are players. No attempts for fixing the referees was found in this case, nevertheless, Aziz Yıldırım forced one of several former presidents of the TFA to appoint certain referees to his club's matches. He then defended himself saying "I did that because those were good referees and there is no other reason beyond that" (Justified verdict 2012). Yıldırım's henchmen and associates of the club's top executives played the part of runners. One interesting point is that the fixers conduct match fixing activities with a very limited number of people whom they trust the most. Thus most of the executive board members generally were not aware of what was going on before matches. A second significant finding is that there is a very close relationship between player representatives and the mafia because the legal status of player representativeness is full of gaps allowing for an easy infiltration by organized crime groups.

Organized crime groups started player representative firms to recruit both poor and skilled players at very young age, developing control of them throughout their careers. Ex-players were also used as runners to contact and deceive target players.

The vehicles used in this case of match fixing also matched the framework gleaned from Hill (2008). Both positive and negative vehicles were used. Positive vehicles included cash, expensive gifts (including a Mini Cooper automobile), and promises of transfers to better clubs. The negative vehicles were employed mostly by mafia groups, rather than club directors. Primary negative vehicles were employed to influence the performance of opponent teams rather than threatening players. Cash is the mostly preferred vehicle in the process. Cash is generally delivered to spur the performance of the players who will play against the major rival of the fixer. This type of an action is called incentive pay and it is legally on a par with paying one's own rival to throw the match. In this case both Fenerbahçe and Trabzonspor allegedly attempted to pay incentives to the each other's rivals. The ex-coach of Beşiktaş used transfer promises in an attempt to neutralize the forward of their rival before the final match of the Turkish Cup. A more difficult case was that of Emenike – a Nigerian national playing forward for a modest Anatolian team, Karabükspor. According to the indictment, the match fixing group in Fenerbahçe contacted Emenike and asked him not to play in the upcoming league match between Karabükspor and Fenerbahçe. According to the allegations, the player was not playing for months due to a serious injury, yet had recovered and could have been played in the match. The player was transferred to Fenerbahçe immediately after the end of the season. In the judicial verdict (2012), the court stated that there definitely was an attempt to compensate this player for not playing in the match, but it is not possible to make sure whether the player did not play because of the offer or because he was really not ready for the match.

The processes of match fixing in the Turkish case also fits in Hill's (2008) framework. The fixing process was started by the club president by contacting a few close directors to take action. Directors then contacted runners and ask them to check the atmosphere in the target team for potential collusion in the scheme. When an open door was detected the target was contacted by a player representative, usually by phone, and an offer was made. After the match, the president took action to start the payment cycle. The money or other incentives were then distributed as promised. By definition, incentive payments are normally made prior to the match, however, in this case they were made after the match. Interestingly enough, most of these arrangements are made on the phone, yet the fixers use a ciphered language. For example such terms as "cultivating the farm" or "watering the farm" were used for fixed matches and the term "workers" were used for players (Interview with detectives, September 10, 2012).

Discussion

After examining the Turkish case of match fixing, it is clear that the framework derived from Declan Hill (2008) provides a valid model for analysis. In this case the president of a popular sports club formed and led a narrow circle for the purpose of manipulating both their own and their major opponent's matches. The primary motivation for match fixing was the desperate need of the president to maintain his status by winning the championship. Within this context, the conspirators offered and paid money and gave expensive gifts to the targets that were mostly key players of rival teams. Also, incentive payments were offered or paid to the rivals' of the opponents by both sides. Drawing attention to the case was the complex relationships among club directors, player representatives and the mafia.

One important policy suggestion after the review of this case is that the players need education regarding the context and dimensions of match fixing. A striking example of this is the wire tape record of a ridiculous conversation between a player and a cleric in which the player informs the cleric that he had been offered €100.000 for underperforming during the match and asked if it would be OK to accept that money (Interview with detectives, September 10, 2012).

Another suggestion for combating match fixing mentioned by police officers during the interviews is that information gathered through both wire taping and physical surveillance had been very effective in providing evidence of match fixing. The officers argued that the extension of legal limits for technical and physical surveillance, to include preventive issues, will render more concrete results.

Additionally, an important finding of this case study was the impact of football on policy-making processes. This was demonstrated by the political interference seen in both administrative and judicial trial processes. The great popularity of football in the country forced the politicians to take action in order to reduce the duration of sentences decreed in the relevant laws and regulations. This is a substantial issue to be explored through further research because the relationship between figures administrating the football sector in a country and the holders of political power might be a variable explaining some crucial aspects of match fixing in other countries as well.

A Comprehensive Approach to Raise Awareness Across Millions

When it comes to policy implications, the authors of this chapter propose reaching out to the millions of soccer fans through the entertainment/movie industry in order to raise awareness and trigger a grassroots uprising against corruption in football. Educating certain identifiable targets such as players, coaches or club managers sounds quite reasonable. Official entities such as FIFA, Interpol, or governmental authorities may well be successful in such efforts. However, educating billions of unidentified targets all over the world, such as fans and supporters, may not be feasible through the conventional means as it applies to the former group. Since we cannot disregard the importance of involving and raising awareness of such a critical mass of the football world, unconventional means of indirect education should be considered to reach out to these target populations and raise their awareness and ensure their involvement and inputs in the fight against match fixing.

Hollywood movie industry has long proven to have a strong ability to convey messages to countless people, regardless of national borders, cultures, and languages.

Football is one of the most common points of interest shared by most nations across the world. Football is also a common denominator that spans cultures and languages. A state of the art movie on football would literally reach billions of people who are fans of the sport. Once the story and other elements of such a movie are secured, any kind of messages can be incorporated into the film and conveyed to people in an effort to raise their awareness, mobilize them, and unite them against match fixing and those who corrupt the sport. Once the movie is released to the worldwide audience, it would influence countless people faster than an official government sponsored effort.

Such a movie should include at least the following concepts:

1. Behind the scene depictions of the discussions in the locker rooms
2. Details of how match fixers approach players and referees
3. Examples of threats against family members and loved ones
4. The cost associated with illegal gambling paid by the innocent fans, and
5. The involvement of politicians to protect their favored teams.

It can be anticipated that the course of future match fixing will deviate from the case examined here. However, after an appropriate movie has been seen by millions, football fans may question any suspicious move through different venues of communication such as social media. Individual gamblers may raise their voices in different ways. Mass media may take a different stance towards match fixing. Those who witness or feel suspicious about any illegal activity may be more aware and willing to report what they know to police or relevant authorities. Such initiatives may pave the way for future investigations, convictions, and legal/administrative sanctions. Fan involvement may serve as a tool for law enforcement and judicial authorities facing problems in conducting investigations and finding evidence to use during judicial processes. Such a movie will, at a minimum, inform those who take part in match fixing to have second thoughts about carrying out their efforts, and for targets to consider accepting bribes and gifts. It would be much more difficult to get away with match fixing when there are millions of eyes looking for evidence of corruption.

Equally important would be to conduct a meticulous cross-section population survey to determine the impacts of any mass media effort to influence potential match fixers, targets, and the fans. This would best be accomplished through utilization of the pretest/posttest methodology of a subsection of the total population exposed to such a mass media effort. Additionally, subsequent long-term studies should be carried out to determine the lasting influence and carry-over of intended lessons to subsequent generations of players, coaches, and fans who may not have seen the original mass media effort.

References

19 Maçta Şike ve TeşvikPrimi Var., (2011, July.06). Retrieved from: http://hurarsiv.hurriyet.com. tr/goster/haber.aspx?id=18187835&tarih=2011-07-06.

Açıklama., (2012, January.14). Retrieved from: http://www.Fenerbahçe.org/detay.asp?ContentID= 27463.

Caruso, R., (2007), The Economics of Match-Fixing, MPRA Paper, University Library of Munich, Germany, http://EconPapers.repec.org/RePEc:pra:mprapa:3085.

Cumhurbaşkanı Gül, Bedelli ve Şike Yasasını Onayladı., (2011, December.14). Retrieved from:http://www.zaman.com.tr/politika_cumhurbaskani-gul-bedelli-ve-sike-yasasini-onayladi_1214698.html.

Demirören Tarihi Kararları Açıkladı., (2012, April.30). Retrieved from:http://spor.milliyet.com.tr/ Demirören-tarihi-kararlari-acikladi/spor/spordetay/30.04.2012/1534504/default.htm.

Duggan M., Levitt S.D., (2002), Winning isn't Everything: Corruption in Sumo Wrestling, *American Economic Review*, vol. 92, n.5, pp. 1594–1605.

Fenerbahçe CAS'tı Çünkü., (2012, April.27). Retrieved from: http://www.hurriyet.com.tr/spor/ futbol/20431213.asp.

Fenerbahçe Şampiyonlar Ligi'nden Men Edildi., (2011, August.24). Retrieved from:http://www. bbc.co.uk/turkce/haberler/2011/08/110824_fb_champions.shtml.

Fenerbahçe, Bank Asya'ya Düşürülmek İçin TFF'ye Başvurdu., (2011, August.26). Retrieved from: http://www.turkspor.net/detay.asp?id=65505.

Foer, F., (2004), Football vs. Mc World, *Foreign Policy*, No. 140 pp. 32–40.

Futbol Kumar Masasinda., (2012, January.09). Retrieved from: http://www.milligazete.com.tr/ haber/Futbol_kumar_masasinda/222881#.Udu-zKx5evB.

Hill, D., (2008), *TheFix: Soccer and organized crime*. Toronto: McClelland&Stewart.

Hillman A.L., Riley J.G., (1989), Politically Contestable Rents and Transfers, *Economics and Politics*, vol. 1, no.1, pp. 17–39.

Horrie, C. (2000), Football isn't fit for TV, *New Statesman*; Jul 24, 2000; 13, 615; p. R19.

Humphreys, B. R. (2011), Online Sports Betting and International Relations, *SAIS Rewiev*, No:1, pp. 103–115.

Indictment., (2011). Retrieved From: http://www.hurriyet.com.tr/spor/futbol/19428696.asp.

Justified Verdict., (2012). Retrieved From: http://www.hurriyet.com.tr/spor/futbol/21200052.asp.

Kuper, S., (1996). Football Against the Enemy. UK: Orion.

Lisanslı Futbolcu Sayısı 466 Bine Ulaştı., (2010), Retrieved from: http://www.tff.org/default.aspx ?pageID=204&ftxtID=10581

Martin, S., (2004). Football and Fascism: The National Game Under Mussolini. New York: Berg Publishers.

McLaren, R.H. (2008) Corruption: Its Impact on Fair Play, Marquette Sports Law Review, vol 19 no 1 pp. 15-38 Available at: http://scholarship.law.marquette.edu/sportslaw/vol19/iss1/3.

Mehmet ali Aydınlar'dan açıklama., (2012, January.31). Retrieved from: http://www.tff.org/ default.aspx?pageID=285&ftxtID=14402.

Mehmet Baransu Şike RaporunuYayınladı., (2012, May.09). Retrieved from:http://www.habera. com/haber/Mehmet-Baransu-sike-raporunu-yayinladi/147050.

Nti K.O., (2004), Maximum Efforts in contests with asymmetric valuations, *European Journal of Political Economy, vol. 20, pp. 1059–1066.*

PFDK Şike Kararını Açıkladı., (2012, May. 07). Retrieved from:http://www.ntvspor.net/haber/ spor-toto-super-lig/64322/pfdk-sike-kararini-acikladi-video.

Preston I., Szymanski S. (2003), Cheating in Contests, *Oxford Review of Economic Policy*, vol. 19, no.4, pp. 612–624.

Rosbrook-Thompson, J. & Armstrong, G. (2010). Fields and Visions: The 'African Personality' and Ghanaian Soccer *Du Bois Review*, 7:2 (2010) 293–314.

Shepotylo, O, Three-Point-For-Win in Soccer: Are There Incentives for Match Fixing? (November 8, 2005). Available at SSRN: http://ssrn.com/abstract=755264 or http://dx.doi.org/10.2139/ssrn.755264.
Siddet Yasasinda Beklenen Gelisme., (2011, November.22).Retrieved from: http://spor.milliyet. com.tr/-siddet-yasasi-nda-beklenen-gelisme-/spor/spordetay/22.11.2011/1466121/default. htm.
Şike Yasasına Gulden Veto., (2011, December.02). Retrieved from: http://spor.milliyet.com.tr/ sike-yasasina-gul-den-veto/spor/spordetay/02.12.2011/1470384/default.htm.
Süper Lig 9 Eylül'de, Bank Asya ise 10 Eylül'de Başlayacak., (2011, July.07). Retrieved from:http://hurarsiv.hurriyet.com.tr/goster/haber.aspx?id=18336432&tarih=2011-07-25.
Taraftarlara Biber Gazlı Müdahale. (2011, July.11). Retrieved from: http://www.hurriyet.com.tr/ spor/futbol/18218613.asp?gid=381.
TFF Olağanüstü Genel Kurulu 26 Ocak'ta Yapılacak., (2011, December.28). Retrieved from: http://www.tff.org/default.aspx?pageID=285&ftxtID=14191.
TFF'ninYeni BaşkanıYıldırım Demirören. (2012, February.27). Retrieved from: http://www.tff. org/default.aspx?pageID=285&ftxtID=14590.
UEFA (2010), The European Club footballing Landscape, *Club Licensing benchmarking report financial year 2010.* Retrievedfrom:http://www.uefa.com/MultimediaFiles/Download/Tech/ uefaorg/General/01/74/41/25/1744125_DOWNLOAD.pdf.
UEFA El Koydu., (2011, August.22). Retrieved from: http://spor.milliyet.com.tr/uefa-el-koydu/ spor/spordetay/22.08.2011/1429717/default.htm.
UEFA'dan Yeni Açıklama: Şikeye Sıfır Tolerans., (2011, July.07). Retrieved from: http:// www.dw.de/uefadan-yeni-a%C3%A7%C4%B1klama-%C5%9Fikeye-s%C4%B1f%C4%B1r-tolerans/a-15218978-1.

Way Forward: Law Enforcement – Academic Paradigm

M.R. Haberfeld and John Abbott

Abstract In November of 2012 INTERPOL organized a Global Experts Meeting, which brought together international experts from the academe to discuss issues surrounding match-fixing and how to combat corruption in football through channels of education. The purpose was to identify to what extent and in which ways academia can play a role in developing and implementing training modules and academic courses including certification procedures to prevent match-fixing and develop lines of study at all educational levels. It was anticipated that the proposals and partnerships that may stem from this meeting will help counteract the lack of international awareness of the problems associated with match-fixing and the degree to which key agents in sport, in particular young people, are vulnerable. In addition the feasibility of incorporating modules and courses focusing specifically on integrity in sport into graduate and post-graduate level was the identified as one of the objectives.

This final chapter provides a rough framework of concepts that were identified by the participants to be introduced, further discussed, vetted and/or implemented in the future. Furthermore, some additional ideas are presented about the possibility of engaging INTERPOL in future collaboration between the academic and practitioners worlds.

M.R. Haberfeld (✉)
John Jay College of Criminal Justice, 899 Tenth Avenue, New York, NY 10019, USA
e-mail: mhaberfeld@jjay.cuny.edu

J. Abbott
INTERPOL, INTERPOL General Secretariat, c/o Integrity in Sport Unit,
200 Quai Charles De Gaulle, Lyon 69006, France
e-mail: c.m.a@tesco.net

M.R. Haberfeld and D. Sheehan (eds.), *Match-Fixing in International Sports:*   349
Existing Processes, Law Enforcement, and Prevention Strategies,
DOI 10.1007/978-3-319-02582-7_18, © Springer International Publishing Switzerland 2013

The final chapter of this book is dedicated to the academics and practitioners meeting that took place in Singapore, in November of 2012. This academic conference, sponsored by **INTERPOL**, was aimed at operationalization of the match fixing problem, as a serious criminal activity that needs to be tackled by a joint effort between law enforcement, local and international on one end, and various academic institutions on the other.

As much as the previous chapters identified various themes and ideas that could be utilized by law enforcement, the judicial branches and the academe, this chapter summarizes the concepts identified by academics and practitioners from around the world who came together during the few days of the conference and create a thought provoking template for future action.

How to Combat Corruption in Football Through Channels of Education?

A number of themes were identified by the participants with regard to the question of how to combat corruption in football through channels of education. The themes were divided into a number of categories in which academics can assist other entities in facing this problem.

The first theme identified by the participants was the **legal** one. Some laws of the country, depending on the legal system, originate in the academic world. The participants were not unanimous about which laws can and should be originated or suggested by the academic world but there was a clear consensus about the need to establish a common legal framework that would require a coordination between the different legal systems within one country and internationally in order to identify global standards of what constitutes illegal behavior. Such global standards would lead to the establishment of a Global Database on Sports-Related Crimes. This will be conducive to the establishment of "Global Penal Law Coding" format which, in turn would help create an educational template that can translate into the creation of courses on corruption in sports and other ethics courses that would tackle this problem from a global perspective, which would be more appealing to various graduate programs. Establishment of a common legal framework would require coordination between the common and legal systems, and would open up a whole new dimension on the matter.

Currently the legal responses of various countries are not consistent. Once a uniform approach is adopted some proposed solutions include using the "Tort law" against match-fixers to hurt them a little more where it hurts most, financially; use entrapment laws; and the creation of new laws – like the American RICO Statute, etc.

The second theme was the problem of **common definition**. It is hard for academics to research and educate about problems that are not clearly defined. What constitutes "match-fixing" is currently a rather vague concept. The effectiveness of any educational or training module is directly related to the clarity of the concepts discussed in classroom environments. We need international jurists to come up with a new framework so that we can have a new convention concerning match-fixing – to create a taxonomy. We need to articulate these definitions, values and repeat them to ensure that it becomes a standard and a practice, and should not be left to chance.

Recognizing the difficulties involved in consistent and standardized definitions would help to frame an approach to the matter.

Match fixing is a problem that spills outside of the boundaries of sport; it enters arenas such as the mafia and organized crime – hence the need for parameters of definitions.

The third emerging theme had to do with the **audience**. Society has to be convinced of the real threat, the impact to everyone and the priority of match-fixing among other threats. Who shall we educate and through which means and methods? Are we targeting the participants, the institutions or the general public? If we are to target the general public maybe it has to be approached from the standpoint of engaging the media. Academic institutions can play a role in the education of the media, in various journalism related degrees and also through sponsoring/calling for academic conferences that will include media participants. Identifying potential partners on these issues is another strategy, through outreach (via conferences, symposia, etc.) and collaboration with the stakeholders like various media outlets. Inclusion of integrity and corruption issues in sports-related classes at the university level, for instance in a module on sports law can contain integrity and corruption issues, as well as the delivery of such self-contained issues through seminars and workshops.

The academia has a major role to play in research. There is a need to look at it from the learner's standpoint. Identify the schools with some strong sports management programs and look at their curricula. Research can spawn on its own.

The participants were in agreement that education should start at the earliest possible level thus, the students at the university level are already exposed to the dangers of match fixing and its impact on society. Maybe a collaboration with highschools and input into their curricula could produce some base line for this concept. However, a decision must be reached: does it pay to educate the fans about matchfixing? Again, here the role of the academe is emphasized one more time in helping to **operationalize (define)** the problem of match-fixing and change the public perception that this is, at most, a "victimless crime".

The fourth theme was the role of the academe in gaining **community support**. There has to be a perception of zero tolerance among the public about corruption in sports. Education has to focus on the consequences of match-fixing on the larger society. Society must be conscious of what they deserve and the price they are willing to pay. We need a multi-disciplinary framework to understand the problem as academics before we move into its prevention through education and ask for community support. In addition, for mobilization of community support and for prevention to work we need to identify the mechanisms that we can use in order to fight against match-fixing. One of the proposed measures or mechanisms was to lobby for a comprehensive education from a very early age but, it has to be specifically adapted to the local culture.

The fifth theme identified was **international collaboration**. The "broken windows" theory can be applied to football; when you are able to put a stop to the little signs, the little actions or activities that might not technically be considered criminal in nature, you might end up solving the bigger problem. A global map with specific countries and the issues at hand should be created, with research, to establish what is happening in different countries. One implementation of legislation to all countries might be a disproportionate response for some countries, and insufficient measures in others.

Another area where academics can make a valuable contribution is in bringing about a collaboration of what different countries are currently doing to combat this issue. Academics can engage in collaborative research in the area of match fixing, research that is helpful and introduces new information, evaluates the situation, provides some new perspectives and new angles, and so on. Academics might not be suitable to be the actual people conducting the training, but they can certainly manage the information aspects of the situation and build collaborative networks. It is quite plausible that **INTERPOL** can play a significant role in assisting and enabling such international collaboration through information sharing, data access and the creation of training modules based on the knowledge and awareness of the scope of the problem in different countries. In order for academics to be successful in their research they need access to data and this is something that can be facilitated by **INTERPOL**.

Finally, the last theme of where the academic world should start involving itself is in **lobbying public officials**. An example was made of the situation in Africa, where it was stated that if the government, football organizations, educational institutions and law enforcement started to work in a collaborative manner then it would have been perceived as an interference and would disrupt the sport. Thus the opportunity for the academe to change this perception within the cultural context. Academia can play a role currently in creating courses that deal with overlapping issues with other topics like intellectual cultural or sub-cultural influences that affect the perception of match-fixing and the severity of the consequences. The perception that cheating is part of a professional ethic in sports needs to be targeted by involving public officials to make statements about the severity of this crime. A well informed public official is one who can support their rhetoric with empirical research and the role of the academe is to provide the findings that support the rhetoric. For example, it was noted that in Romania in once case it was argued that the bribe was a reward to the players who won the game, not a bribe to win the game. If such cases are studied and result in clear legal definitions it will be much easier for public officials to support their rhetoric against match-fixing, otherwise hard to draw the line.

When we talk about building integrity, we are really talking about accepted moral norms, ethical standards and practices of the group, which in this case is the football club – players, referees, fans, etc. If the academe is to change and influence the accepted moral norms, ethical standards and practices of the groups it needs a clear legal, definitional baseline prior to being able to influence larger audiences and public officials.

To What Extent and in Which Ways Academia Can Play a Role in Developing and Implementing Training Modules and Academic Courses to Prevent Match-Fixing and Develop Lines of Study at All Educational Levels?

In principle the concept of developing and implementing academic courses at different educational levels has a lot to do with the awareness of academics that certain topics are worthy of studying and are not, currently, part of a given academic institution curricula. Training modules are primarily offered by academic institutions that have Schools of Professional Education and those are governed by different principles, more closely related to the "demand and supply model". Thus the answers to the questions posed above were divided into a number of concepts related to awareness, acceptance and academic rigor.

The **awareness** theme emerged around the concept that criminologists must be convinced that match-fixing is a real problem rather than a passing "fear-mania" or they will not understand or try to analyze how match-fixing works, thus there will be no pull towards development of courses or academic programs or certificates. Furthermore, since the practitioners in the field are currently not knowledgeable enough of how much of the situation referred to as "match-fixing" really includes or spills over into the organized crime phenomenon and what is the real damage to society, the academic might be under the impression that the problem is just another dimension of organized crime and therefore doesn't need to be approached separately by creating new programs or courses.

Law enforcement agencies and personnel should be on the same page as academics regarding the importance of this matter; it would not be conducive to any progress if academics were scrutinizing this in all seriousness, and law enforcement people were downplaying the problem, or viewing all this as matters of low priority. This is where **INTERPOL** can play a major role by raising awareness of academic institutions and individual researchers by disseminating information about the magnitude of the problem, either through various academic/practitioner attended workshops and/or through a direct reach out to individual institutions. Multidisciplinary effort to curb match-fixing must be undertaken with many stakeholders involved. Information must be evidence-based rather than speculation, which is what currently exists in the academic field. **FIFA and INTERPOL** put a lot of emphasis on Sports Integrity and Ethics and there needs to be an amplification of this awareness.

Once the awareness is created within the academic community – **acceptance** will follow. However, this does not mean that various academic institutions have the skills, the knowledge and the desire to be involved in targeting the match-fixing problem. Distinction needs to be made between the acceptance of the problem by an individual or a group of academics and the desire of the organization to be involved in the creation of a new major/course/or program. Such decisions are not always and more frequently than not related not just to the problem itself but to a host of external and internal variables. Match- fixing as a 'module' has not quite made it to ethics and anti-corruption education/training. Is there a place for it, or any university interested in a train the trainer program? Is there room for **INTERPOL** to collaborate here with academe? The answers will vary by the rigor with which this new initiative will be introduced and whether or not FIFA is going to be involved in creating rules and making sure that there are compliance mechanisms in place, that national sports governing bodies and clubs will follow, as education itself is not going to work without compliance mechanisms.

Academic rigor refers not just to the manner in which research is being conducted but also to the concept of implementation of a new field of study/new course/new program. For one, economic analysis can be pretty useful in devising changes in incentives and in compensation schemes that could prevent match rigging and such an approach can be incorporated into the teaching of integrity.

If **FIFA and/or INTERPOL** are willing to contribute in various shapes or forms to the resource development of the courses and an attractive packaging of such, as well as the funding of visiting scholarships to institutions to study the various facets of this phenomenon, it will be more attractive to academe. **INTERPOL** can definitely assist in the delivery of the content for the creation of the new classes/programs.

Referees are being trained through FIFA initiated training courses and other training modules around the world. There is a need to identify the appropriate schools within universities (Business Schools, Schools of Professional Education, Schools of Continuing Education, etc.) that may be interested in getting involved to help identify and deliver modules/classes in this topic.

To What Extent and in Which Ways Academia Can Play a Role in Developing and Implementing Certification Procedures to Prevent Match-Fixing and Develop Lines of Study at All Educational Levels?

The extent to which the academe can play a role in developing and implementing certification procedures to prevent match-fixing and develop lines of study at all educational levels will be defined be a number of variables: the evidence based information, cooperation between the soccer association and institutions of higher education and criteria for licensing.

Currently, it appears as there is not enough **evidence based information** on match fixing, and not enough public awareness on the issue. (For example: in America, curbing these illegal actions was only effective when match-fixing was thought to be tied to the Mafia, therefore police had a higher priority to solve it).

In order to further academic knowledge the first hurdle, which appears to be the reluctance amongst law enforcement agencies and football associations to share personal data with each other needs to be tackled, maybe by **INTERPOL**. If academics are provided with enough data, then a theoretical model can be created with regard to the development and implementation of the certificate procedures.

This would include reaching out to the unions that represent the players and getting their endorsement for the educational approach to match fixing that will be based on the unions' endorsement.

The **academe should invest in better cooperation with soccer associations** and offer education through/with their cooperation based on the following concepts:

(a) The training of players on sports ethics and the legal consequences of match-fixing is important, and it is suggested that players sign [an] ethics contract when they are given the licence

(b) All the stake holders should be licensed:

- Trainers (need Accreditation first to train others and subsequently obtain licenses)
- Coaches (need licensing – to educate players)
- Referees (licensing can be beneficial, after the referees are mandated to attend a relevant course)
- Medical staff
- Technical staff
- Sports community
- Players
- Club Managers/Owners/betting companies/brokers/Sports Agents

A set of **criteria for licensing** and accreditation needs to be set up, so when certain corrupted actions taken by a club would result in the club owners losing their license and accreditation. FIFA is reviewing the licensing of sports agents, which they used to do themselves, but it was discovered the system was not working ideally, and they are now considering outsourcing this role instead of continuing to do it themselves – maybe it can be the role for the academe in cooperation with **INTERPOL**?

Responsibilities for holding a license have to be set. If there is a breach, the license is revoked and suspended for a period of time. The criteria of integrity must be defined and these "integrity criteria" can be defined by the academic world. It was felt that the majority of players do not have a high level of education. They need to be educated, so that they don't have any excuse to commit the crime and here, yet again, the academe can step in and identify the baseline of knowledge that needs to be included in a certificate/license to be issued to the players.

A curriculum that can be devised to deal with ethics, to demonstrate a clear idea of the consequences involved – consequences such as fines, going to jail, being banned from games, and losing your career. Criteria to license must be set, and should pertain to areas of security, prevention and education.

No license should be issued for life; it should carry a limited term, subject to renewal after a scrutiny is conducted. The license can be suspended during the term if there is non-compliance. Every sporting contract carries some rules and these rules can be outlined with help from the academe.

The license should apply to the individual. Training should emphasis the process, the "Do's and Don'ts" and the causes for the license to be revoked.

Finally, many academic institutions today are engaged in 'on-line' course delivery. The training can be some form of online test. When a club is accredited, those who own the club could set the guidelines, just as many clubs have their own rules. These rules and guidelines can be clarified with cooperation between academic institutions, club owners and practitioners.

How Can Academe Assist in Creating Partnerships and Help Counteract the Lack of International Awareness of the Problems Associated with Match-Fixing and the Degree to Which Key Agents in Sport, in Particular, Young People Are Vulnerable?

The dissemination of **research findings** in the academic world have traditionally taken the form of publishing in **peer review journals** or other peer review outlets and through participation in **national and international conferences**.

An **international, academic convention/conference** could be a major step forward with an objective to help create an agreement/consensus on how national federations operate their football domestically. That would be a very helpful starting point for all the concerned. Such an academic conference, similar to the one held in Singapore, could be a great addition to the ones that are already in place, like the Sportaccord events, ICSS and MINEPS. Developing **Networks** – these conferences are very important for building up networks. These are not just formal networks, these are also the informal networks that will facilitate the dissemination of the threat and how to tackle it.

Another objective would be to redefine the concept of "sports ethics" – rather a narrow focus on just the issue of match-fixing – may be best inculcated where sport is actually being played, where youngsters are playing, e.g., in amateur clubs and involving a wide gamut of other players such as community groups, coaches, mentors and officials. The steps and processes how to best reach out to these other groups can be discussed and analyzed. A contrarian approach to the above was also introduced by the academics who felt that the focus of research should be on the players, referees and administrators, and not on their public. Players, referees and administrators are the ones that need to be educated. Educating the public that 'football is corrupt' is in fact the wrong message and won't work, as it just simply ruins the image of the sport. Fans do not want to hear about these issues – how do you change this through education/awareness?

Ongoing education of the players, referees, administrators and owners of the nature of the consequence of the money laundering in sports is needed as seen in the Pakistani cricket case when the family of the player was surprised when their son went to jail.

It was felt that currently, sports related topics, in most academic institutions, are not considered a very serious subject – how can we change it? Academics can change this attitude and create a curriculum that makes sports courses compulsory and not necessarily electives with a strong focus placed on prevention before it becomes an addiction as then it is much harder to eliminate. Again, in order to further this approach academics need to be exposed to more data, international conferences and research opportunities. One such example can be seen in England where in Physical Education or Sports Science the curriculum includes anti-doping, anti-drugs but not match-fixing. There is a need to look at providing train-the-trainer courses for countries to enable coaches and people who run football club academies, where the youngsters are. If the program can reach out to the young, it would be ideal and then replicated by other countries.

There were few examples of successful ethics training for professional athletes, but there are many successful examples from the business world and the consensus was that training is important at every level of sports. Youth academies of Germany Football Associations have a new (2 years old) project which targets on 15–16 year-olds aspiring athletes.

There is a need to identify "**best practices**" for academics to embrace and subject to further analysis, especially in countries that lag behind in addressing the problem with the younger generations. An example of such best practices can be to identify the differences between the markets more susceptible to fixing, versus the ones less so; identify how could the conditions in the markets currently less susceptible to fixing be replicated in other markets and push for dissemination of such research findings internationally.

A **4 point plan was identified that INTERPOL could lead** based on an appeal to governments, not just on the issue of match fixing but a much broader concept that corruption in sport:

1. Is a conduit for transnational, organized crime;
2. Needs to be emphasized that when it comes to sports bodies, it is a corrosive, corruptive threat;
3. Requires concentrated national/international initiatives including the academic world;
4. Emphasizes the importance of education in prevention of the threat.

It is very hard for academics to push a specific agenda ahead in terms of federal/state research funding without "hard core" proof or crime figures that can be supplied by **INTERPOL**.

What Is the Feasibility of Incorporating Modules and Courses Focusing Specifically on Integrity in Sport into Graduate and Post-graduate Level Studies?

As previously stated a collaborative approach between **INTERPOL** and various academic institutions should pave a way to incorporation of courses dealing with integrity in sports into graduate and post-graduate level studies.

INTERPOL could take the lead and find a way of offering different systems of e-learning, which can then be propagated through a network of national satellites to regional scholars and students. The personnel involved should be "culturally competent" to translate certain ideas to cultures not already familiar with them.

The curriculum that needs to be developed has to appeal to the audience in a manner that they can appreciate and it is probably the more mature students' population at the graduate and post-graduate level that can appreciate it more than the undergraduates. However, it is not only the universities who can impart that knowledge. **INTERPOL can deliver the material**. It could be adding material to university programs that exist. The reasons the university would want to use **INTERPOL** developed curriculum would be to support scholarship, research and funding.

Another suggestion involved two different models. The first model is for **INTERPOL** to set a criterion to all colleges that are interested so that everybody is teaching the same thing. Then research is a completely different phenomenon that can spawn on its own from a central platform. The second model is to facilitate the integration of anti-corruption teaching into the curriculum at universities, make it as easy as possible for teachers to include it (an example based on the UNODC model – 60 universities).

The approach to the graduate and post-graduate academic institutions should be based on a **3-steps plan: Cooperation, research, and action.**

Some final thoughts and additional points worth consideration due to their impact on the role academe can serve within the larger collaborative framework with **INTERPOL**, were identified, and they include:

1. **INTERPOL** can use media to its advantage by spreading awareness campaigns on investigations and come up with a report on the cases to be disseminated by the media;
2. A branch of **INTERPOL** dealing with sports integrity can be a monitoring agency and bring the media on board;
3. The line between education and deterrence is interesting and complex. Making a player take the lie test does not guarantee that the player will get caught, but it may have a deterrent effect;
4. There are three groups of match fixers who are able to directly influence the match events: players, coaches and officials related to the team, and referees – each group has to be approached from a different angle in terms of prevention and education;
5. Referees are by far the most influential, and therefore the most important and efforts should be directed at them;
6. Reluctance amongst law enforcement agencies and football associations to share personal data with each other. If the different stakeholders are not able to improve the quality of communications, it will be very hard to move forward on the matter. Currently, the various parties are not engaging and communicating sufficiently – **maybe INTERPOL can facilitate this exchange?**

It is these authors hope that the templates for action identified throughout this book, and summarized in this chapter, will serve as a guidebook for current and future researchers, practitioners and legislators in a united way to eradicate the newly operationalized global threat of Sports Related Crime (SRC) or Sports Corruption (SC) that corrodes the fabric of ethical and moral views of our societies.

Authors' Note This chapter was written based on the summary of the proceedings from the conference that took place in Singapore, on November 26 through 27th, hence the ideas presented here are a product of brainstorming of the participants who were engaged in original presentations and workshops prepared exclusively for this conference.

References

INTERPOL's Integrity in Sport Global Academic Experts Meeting in Singapore, November 28-29, 2012.

Index

M.R. Haberfeld and D. Sheehan (eds.), *Match-Fixing in International Sports:*
Existing Processes, Law Enforcement, and Prevention Strategies,
DOI 10.1007/978-3-319-02582-7, © Springer International Publishing Switzerland 2013

Printed by Printforce, the Netherlands